1

Annotated Teacher's E...

Grammar Connection

STRUCTURE

THROUGH

CONTENT

SERIES EDITORS

Marianne Celce-Murcia

M. E. Sokolik

Staci Sabbagh Johnson

THOMSON

HEINLE

Australia • Canada • Mexico • Singapore • United Kingdom • United States

THOMSON
—★—
HEINLE

Grammar Connection 1: Structure Through Content
Annotated Teacher's Edition
Series Editors: Marianne Celce-Murcia, M.E. Sokolik
Staci Sabbagh Johnson

Publisher: *Sherrise Roehr*
Consulting Editor: *James W. Brown*
Acquisitions Editor: *Tom Jefferies*
Director of Content Development:
  Anita Raducanu
Director of Product Marketing: *Amy Mabley*
Executive Marketing Manager:
  Jim McDonough
Senior Field Marketing Manager:
  Donna Lee Kennedy
Product Marketing Manager: *Katie Kelley*

Assistant Development Editor: *Sarah Spader*
Editoral Assistant: *Katherine Reilly*
Associate Production Editor: *Erika Hokanson*
Manufacturing Buyer: *Betsy Donaghey*
Production Project Manager: *Chrystie Hopkins*
Composition: *Parkwood Composition Services*
Copyediting and Proofreading: *Argosy Publishing*
Interior Design: *InContext Publishing Partners*
Cover Design: *Linda Beaupre*
Printer: *Edwards Brothers*

Cover Image: © Larry Brownstein/Photodisc Red/Getty/RF

Printed in the United States of America.
1 2 3 4 5 6 7 8 9 10 — 10 09 08 07 06

For more information contact Thomson Heinle,
25 Thomson Place, Boston, Massachusetts
02210 USA, or you can visit our Internet site at
http://elt.thomson.com

For permission to use material from this text or product,
submit a request online at http://www.thomsonrights.com

Any additional questions about permissions can be
submitted by email to thomsonrights@thomson.com

ISBN 10: 1-4240-0214-1
ISBN 13: 978-1-4240-0214-6

Contents

Using language grammatically and being able to communicate authentically are important goals for students. My grammar research suggests that students' mastery of grammar improves when they interpret and produce grammar in meaningful contexts at the discourse level. *Grammar Connection* connects learners to academic success, allowing them to reach their goals and master the grammar.

— Marianne Celce-Murcia

"Connections" is probably the most useful concept in any instructor's vocabulary. To help students connect what they are learning to the rest of their lives is the most important task I fulfill as an instructor. *Grammar Connection* lets instructors and students find those connections. The series connects grammar to reading, writing, and speaking. It also connects students with the ability to function academically, to use the Internet for interesting research, and to collaborate with others on projects and presentations.   — M. E. Sokolik

Dear Instructor,

With experience in language teaching, teacher training, and research, we created *Grammar Connection* to be uniquely relevant for academically and professionally oriented courses and students. Every lesson in the series deals with academic content to help students become familiar with the language of college and the university and to feel more comfortable in all of their courses, not just English.

While academic content provides the context for this series, our goal is for the learner to go well beyond sentence-level exercises in order to use grammar as a resource for comprehending and producing academic discourse. Students move from shorter, more controlled exercises to longer, more self-directed, authentic ones. Taking a multi-skills approach, *Grammar Connection* includes essential grammar that students need to know at each level. Concise lessons allow instructors to use the material easily in any classroom situation.

We hope that you and your students find our approach to the teaching and learning of grammar for academic and professional purposes in *Grammar Connection* effective and innovative.

Marianne Celce-Murcia
Series Editor

M. E. Sokolik
Series Editor

Welcome to *Grammar Connection*

■ **What is *Grammar Connection*?**

Grammar Connection is a five-level grammar series that integrates content with grammar instruction in an engaging format to prepare students for future academic and professional success.

■ **What is the content?**

The content in *Grammar Connection* is drawn from various academic disciplines: sociology, psychology, medical sciences, computer science, communications, biology, engineering, business, and the social sciences.

■ **Why does *Grammar Connection* incorporate content into the lessons?**

The content is used to provide high-interest contexts for exploring the grammar. The charts and exercises are contextualized with the content in each lesson. Learning content is not the focus of *Grammar Connection*—it sets the scene for learning grammar.

■ **Is *Grammar Connection* "discourse-based"?**

Yes. With *Grammar Connection*, learners go beyond sentence-level exercises in order to use grammar as a resource for comprehending and producing academic discourse. These discourses include conversations, narratives, and exposition.

■ **Does *Grammar Connection* include communicative practice?**

Yes. *Grammar Connection* takes a multi-skills approach. The series includes listening activities as well as texts for reading, and the production tasks elicit both spoken and written output via pair or group work tasks.

■ **Why are the lessons shorter than in other books?**

Concise lessons allow instructors to use the material easily in any classroom situation. For example, one part of a lesson could be covered in a 50-minute period, allowing instructors with shorter class times to feel a sense of completion. Alternatively, a single lesson could fit into a longer, multi-skills class period. For longer, grammar-focused classes, more than one lesson could be covered.

■ **Does *Grammar Connection* include opportunities for students to review the grammar?**

Yes. A Review section is included after every five lessons. These tests can also be used by instructors to measure student understanding of the grammar taught. In addition, there are practice exercises in the Workbook and on the website (elt.thomson.com/grammarconnection).

■ **Does *Grammar Connection* assist students in learning new vocabulary?**

Yes. The Content Vocabulary section in each lesson of *Grammar Connection* incorporates academic vocabulary building and journaling. In Book 1 this takes a picture dictionary approach. In later books words from the Academic Word List are used. This, along with the content focus, ensures that students expand their vocabulary along with their grammatical capability.

Grammar Connection is organized into thirty concise lessons, each containing two or three parts of connected grammar points. Every lesson follows a unique pedagogical approach.

A **picture-based vocabulary** section in lower levels familiarizes students with the content-based academic vocabulary that is used in the lesson. At higher levels, students are introduced to words from the **Academic Word List.**

The grammar in each lesson is **contextualized** with topics from different **academic disciplines.**

Thought-provoking **discussion questions** activate students' knowledge of the content area. The questions can also be used as **diagnostic tests** to assess students' mastery of the grammar before it is taught.

An integrated **audio program** allows students to listen to the content readings and dialogues.

Content readings and dialogues present the grammar in a meaningful and interesting way.

Contextualized **grammar charts** provide **easy-to-understand** clear explanations of grammar form as well as notes on usage.

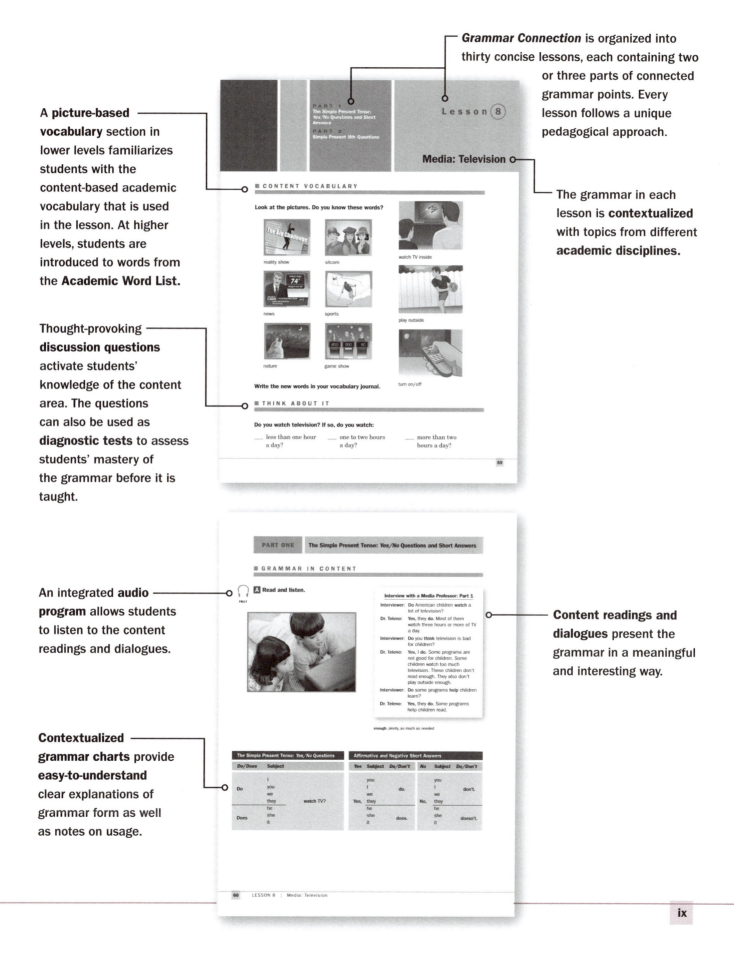

PART 1
The Simple Present Tense: Yes/No Questions and Short Answers
PART 2
Simple Present Wh- Questions

Lesson 8

Media: Television

■ CONTENT VOCABULARY

Look at the pictures. Do you know these words?

reality show

sitcom

watch TV inside

news

sports

play outside

nature

game show

turn on/off

Write the new words in your vocabulary journal.

■ THINK ABOUT IT

Do you watch television? If so, do you watch:

____ less than one hour a day?   ____ one to two hours a day?   ____ more than two hours a day?

59

PART ONE   The Simple Present Tense: Yes/No Questions and Short Answers

■ GRAMMAR IN CONTENT

A Read and listen.

Interview with a Media Professor: Part 1

Interviewer: Do American children **watch** a lot of television?

Dr. Teleno: Yes, they do. Most of them watch three hours or more of TV a day.

Interviewer: Do you **think** television is bad for children?

Dr. Teleno: Yes, I do. Some programs are not good for children. Some children watch too much television. These children don't read enough. They also don't play outside enough.

Interviewer: Do some programs **help** children learn?

Dr. Teleno: Yes, they do. Some programs help children read.

enough: plenty, as much as needed

The Simple Present Tense: Yes/No Questions		
Do/Does	Subject	
Do	I you we they	watch TV?
Does	he she it	

Affirmative and Negative Short Answers					
Yes	Subject	Do/Don't	No	Subject	Do/Don't
Yes,	you I we they	do.	No,	you I we they	don't.
	he she it	does.		he she it	doesn't.

Students move from a variety of controlled exercises to more self-directed ones enabling students to become comfortable using the grammar.

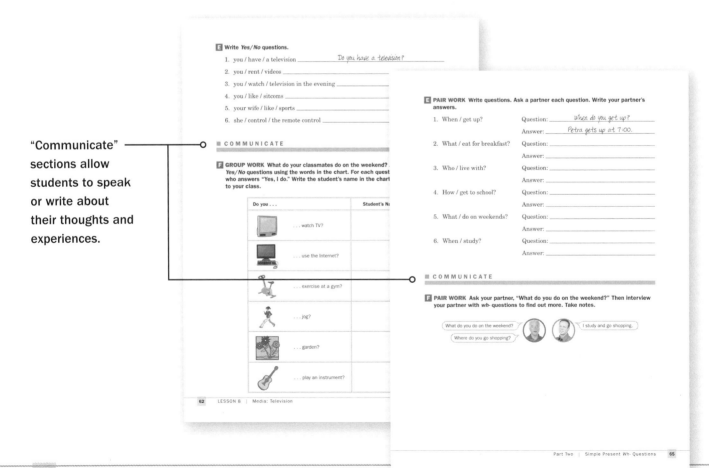

B Look at the dialogue "Interview with a Media Professor: Part 1." Answer the questions with short answers.

1. Do American children watch a lot of television? _____
2. Do they watch one hour of TV a day? _____
3. Do they watch three hours of TV a day? _____
4. Does Dr. Teleno think television is bad for children
5. Do some programs help children learn? _____

C **PAIR WORK** Answer the questions about yourself. Use your partner the questions. Complete the chart with s

	Me
1. Do you like television?	
2. Do you watch the news?	
3. Do you watch sitcoms?	
4. Do you watch reality shows?	
5. Do you eat dinner with the television on?	
6. Do you study with the television on?	
7. Do you watch too much television?	

D Put the words in the correct order.

1. at night / you / do / watch television ___Do you w___
2. no / don't / I _____
3. send e-mails / you / do / at night _____
4. don't / no / I _____,
5. study / do / at night / you _____
6. I / do / yes _____, _____

Part One | The Simple Present Tense: Yes/

---

4. What _____ her son like? _____
5. Where _____ the children watch TV? _____

C Complete the questions. Write *wh-* words.

1. **Q:** _Who_ do you live with? **A:** I live with my husband and son.
2. **Q:** _____ do you study? **A:** I study computer science.
3. **Q:** _____ do you study computer science? **A:** Because I love computers.
4. **Q:** _____ do you relax? **A:** I watch television.
5. **Q:** _____ do you watch? **A:** I watch reality TV programs.
6. **Q:** _____ does your husband work? **A:** He works in an office.
7. **Q:** _____ does he relax? **A:** He reads the newspaper and watches the news.
8. **Q:** _____ does your son watch on TV? **A:** He watches cartoons.

D Complete the dialogue. Write *wh-* questions.

A: There's an interesting program on TV. It's about kangaroos.
B: Really? ___Where do kangaroos live___? (1)
A: Kangaroos live in Australia, Tasmania, and New Guinea.
B: _____? (2)
A: They eat grass and leaves.
B: _____? (3)
A: They eat in the late afternoon and early evening.
B: _____ during the day? (4)
A: During the day they rest in the shade.
B: _____ get from one place to another? (5)
A: They hop!
B: _____ communicate? (6)
A: They thump their feet.

E Write *Yes/No* questions.

1. you / have / a television ___Do you have a television?___
2. you / rent / videos _____
3. you / watch / television in the evening _____
4. you / like / sitcoms _____
5. your wife / like / sports _____
6. she / control / the remote control _____

■ COMMUNICATE

F **GROUP WORK** What do your classmates do on the weekend? *Yes/No* questions using the words in the chart. For each quest who answers "Yes, I do." Write the student's name in the chart to your class.

Do you . . .	Student's N
. . . watch TV?	
. . . use the Internet?	
. . . exercise at a gym?	
. . . jog?	
. . . garden?	
. . . play an instrument?	

"Communicate" sections allow students to speak or write about their thoughts and experiences.

E **PAIR WORK** Write questions. Ask a partner each question. Write your partner's answers.

1. When / get up? Question: ___When do you get up?___
   Answer: ___Petra gets up at 7:00.___
2. What / eat for breakfast? Question: _____
   Answer: _____
3. Who / live with? Question: _____
   Answer: _____
4. How / get to school? Question: _____
   Answer: _____
5. What / do on weekends? Question: _____
   Answer: _____
6. When / study? Question: _____
   Answer: _____

■ COMMUNICATE

F **PAIR WORK** Ask your partner, "What do you do on the weekend?" Then interview your partner with *wh-* questions to find out more. Take notes.

What do you do on the weekend?
Where do you go shopping?

I study and go shopping.

At the end of each lesson, students are encouraged to put together the **grammar and vocabulary** from the lesson in a productive way.

Interesting projects allow students to put newly learned grammatical forms and vocabulary to use in ways that encourage additional independent reading, **research,** and/or communication. Many of these activities are group activities, further requiring students to put their language skills to work.

Internet activities encourage students to connect the grammar with online resources.

Connection | Putting It Together

GRAMMAR AND VOCABULARY Work with a partner. Ask your partner questions about his or her television habits. Use the grammar and vocabulary from this lesson.

Do you like television?   Yes, I do.
When do you watch television?

PROJECT Create a bar graph about favorite TV shows.

1. With your class, discuss the following kinds of programs: reality shows, sitcoms, news, sports, nature shows, and game shows.
2. For each kind of show, take a vote: Who likes this kind of show best? Count the number of students who say it is their favorite.
3. Make a bar graph to show the results of your vote.

Our Favorite Show

INTERNET Go online. Find out what is on television tonight. Use the keywords "television schedule." Imagine you will watch television tonight. Choose the programs you will watch.

VOCABULARY JOURNAL Write sentences for new vocabulary you learned in this lesson.

Example: *I think sitcoms are funny.*

66   LESSON 8 | Media: Television

Review | Lessons 6–10

A Review section after every five lessons helps assess and reinforce language learning.

A Circle the correct answers.

Alba is pregnant. She (play / plays) classical music for her baby every day.
                              (1)
She (sing / sings) to her baby. Why does she do this? She (know / knows) about
          (2)   (3)
a theory called *The Mozart Effect*. Some researchers say music (help / helps)
                                                                        (4)
babies' brains develop. Other researchers (do not / does not) believe in *The*
                                                  (5)
Mozart Effect. However, Alba (do not / does not) car...
                                      (6)
(listen / listens) to music every day. It (help / helps
      (7)   (8)

B Circle the correct answers.

Aiko is a nursing student in her sophomore year.
(in / on) Monday, Wednesday, and Friday. She (do / d...
    (3)   (4)
a hospital (on / at) Tuesday and Thursday. She stud...
                  (4)
(in / on) the weekend. She (have / has) a busy wee...
    (6)   (7)
friends (at / on) Sunday evenings. She meets these
              (8)
(on / at) 6:00 for dinner and a movie.
      (9)

C Circle the correct answers.

Q: (When / What) do you do on the weekend?
          (1)
Q: (What / Where) do you relax?
          (2)
Q: (How / Where) do you relax?
          (3)
Q: (Do / Does) you watch educational programs?
          (4)
Q: (Do / Does) you watch soap operas?
          (6)
Q: (Who / How) do you watch TV with?
          (8)

D Complete the sentences. Use *do, does, am, is, are,* or the correct form of the missing verb.

Question: Where _____ dolphins live?
                        (1)
Answer: Dolphins _____ in most oceans and seas.
                          (2)
Question: _____ dolphins intelligent?
                    (3)
Answer: Yes, they _____.
                          (4)
Question: _____ they like humans?
                    (5)
Answer: Yes, they _____. They _____ very friendly with humans.
                          (6)   (7)

E Look at Fatima's class schedule. Complete the sentences. Use each word or phrase in the box once.

How often   twice a week   every day   always   rarely   never

	Monday	Tuesday	Wednesday	Thursday	Friday
Intro to Teaching	X		X		X
Child Development		X		X	
Technology in Education	X		X		X

1. Fatima goes to school _____.
2. She takes "Child Development" _____.
3. She _____ goes to "Child Development" on Tuesday and Thursday.
4. She _____ takes "Intro to Teaching" on Thursday.
5. _____ does she take "Child Development"?
6. She _____ has free time during the week!

A learner log encourages students to reflect on what they have learned and enhances learner independence.

LEARNER LOG Check (✓) *Yes* or *I Need More Practice.*

Lesson	I Can Use . . .	Yes	I Need More Practice
6	The Present Tense: Affirmative and Negative Statements		
7	Irregular Verbs: *Have, Go, Do;* Prepositions of Time: *On, In, At*		
8	Simple Present *Yes/No* Questions; Short Answers and *Wh-* Questions		
9	Present Tense of *Be* vs. Simple Present Tense: Statements		
10	Adverbs of Frequency; Questions with *How Often;* Frequency Expressions		

84   REVIEW | Lessons 6–10

Supplements

■ Audio Program

Audio CDs and Audio Tapes allow students to listen to every reading in the book to build listening skills and fluency.

■ Workbook

The workbooks review and practice all the grammar points in the Student Book. In addition each workbook includes six Writing Tutorials and vocabulary expansion exercises.

■ Website

Features additional grammar practice activities, vocabulary test items, and other resources: elt.thomson.com/grammarconnection.

■ Annotated Teacher's Edition with Presentation Tool CD-ROM

Offers comprehensive lesson planning advice and teaching tips, as well as a full answer key. The Presentation Tool CD-ROM includes a PowerPoint presentation for selected lessons and includes all the grammar charts from the book.

■ Assessment CD-ROM with ExamView® Pro Test Generator

The customizable generator features lesson, review, mid-term, and term-end assessment items to monitor student progress.

Grammar Connection is based on scientific research on the most effective means of teaching grammar to adult learners of English.

■ Discourse-based Grammar

Research by Celce-Murcia and Olshtain (2000) suggests that learners should go beyond sentence-level exercises in order to use grammar as a resource for comprehending and producing academic discourse. *Grammar Connection* lets students move from controlled exercises to more self-expressive and self-directed ones.

■ Communicative Grammar

Research shows that communicative exercises should complement traditional exercises (Comeau, 1987; Herschensohn, 1988). *Grammar Connection* balances effective controlled activities, such as fill-in-the blanks, with meaningful interactive exercises.

■ Learner-centered Content

Van Duzer (1999) emphasizes that research on adult English language learners shows that "learners should read texts that meet their needs and are interesting." In *Grammar Connection* the content readings are carefully selected and adapted to be both high-interest and relevant to the needs of learners.

■ Vocabulary Development

A number of recent studies have shown the effectiveness of helping English language learners develop independent skills in vocabulary development (Nation, 1990, 2001; Nist & Simpson, 2001; Schmitt, 2000). In *Grammar Connection*, care has been taken to introduce useful academic vocabulary, based in part on Coxhead's (2000) work.

■ Using Background Knowledge

Because research shows that background knowledge facilitates comprehension (Eskey, 1997), each lesson of *Grammar Connection* opens with a "Think About It" section related to the lesson theme.

■ Student Interaction

Learning is enhanced when students work with each other to co-construct knowledge (Grennon-Brooks & Brooks, 1993; Sutherland & Bonwell, 1996). *Grammar Connection* includes many pair and group work exercises as well as interactive projects.

■ References

Celce-Murcia, M., & Olshtain, E. (2000). *Discourse and Context in Language Teaching.* New York: Cambridge University Press.

Comeau, R. Interactive Oral Grammar Exercises. In W. M. Rivers (Ed.), *Interactive Language Teaching* (57–69). Cambridge: Cambridge University Press, 1987.

Coxhead, A. (2000). "A New Academic Word List." *TESOL Quarterly,* 34 (2), 213–238.

Eskey, D. (1997). "Models of Reading and the ESOL Student." *Focus on Basics 1 (B),* 9–11.

Grennon Brooks, J., & Brooks, M. G. (1993). *In Search of Understanding: The Case for Constructivist Classrooms.* Alexandria, VA: Association for Supervision and Curriculum Development.

Herschensohn, J. (1988). "Linguistic Accuracy of Textbook Grammar." *Modern Language Journal 72(4),* 409–414.

Nation, I. S. P. (2001). *Learning Vocabulary in Another Language.* New York: Cambridge University Press.

Nation, I. S. P. (1990). *Teaching and Learning Vocabulary.* Boston: Thomson Heinle.

Nist, S. L., & Simpson, M. L. (2001). *Developing Vocabulary for College Thinking.* Boston: Allyn & Bacon.

Schmitt, N. (2000). *Vocabulary in Language Teaching.* New York: Cambridge University Press.

Sutherland, T. E., & Bonwell, C. C. (Eds.). (1996). "Using Active Learning in College Classes: A Range of Options for Faculty." *New Directions for Teaching and Learning, Number 67,* Fall 1996. San Francisco, CA: Jossey-Bass Publishers.

VanDuzer, C. (1999). "Reading and the Adult Language Learner." *ERIC Digest.* Washington, D.C.: National Center for ESL Literacy Education.

Acknowledgments

Many thanks to the Thomson ELT team, especially Tom Jefferies and Jim Brown, for their guidance, insight, hard work, and good humor.

This book is dedicated to Mike and Anna—for their love and support, and for keeping me sane and laughing through it all.

— *Jill Korey O'Sullivan*

The author, series editors, and publisher wish to thank the following people for their contributions:

Susan Alexandre
Trimble Technical High School
Fort Worth, TX

Joan Amore
Triton College
River Grove, IL

Cally Andriotis-Williams
Newcomers High School
Long Island City, NY

Ana Maria Cepero
Miami Dade College
Miami, FL

Jacqueline Cunningham
Harold Washington College
Chicago, IL

Kathleen Flynn
Glendale Community College
Glendale, CA

Sally Gearhart
Santa Rosa Junior College
Santa Rosa, CA

Janet Harclerode
Santa Monica College
Santa Monica, CA

Carolyn Ho
North Harris College
Houston, TX

Eugenia Krimmel
Lititz, PA

Dana Liebowitz
Palm Beach Central High
   School
Wellington, FL

Shirley Lundblade
Mt. San Antonio College
Walnut, CA

Craig Machado
Norwalk Community College
Norwalk, CT

Myo Myint
Mission College
Santa Clara, CA

Myra Redman
Miami Dade College
Miami, FL

Eric Rosenbaum
BEGIN Managed Programs
New York, NY

Marilyn Santos
Valencia Community College
Valencia, FL

Laura Sicola
University of Pennsylvania
Philadelphia, PA

Barbara Smith-Palinkas
University of South Florida
Tampa, FL

Kathy Sucher
Santa Monica College
Santa Monica, CA

Patricia Turner
San Diego City College
San Diego, CA

America Vasquez
Miami Dade College, Inter-
   American Campus
Miami, FL

Tracy von Mulaski
El Paso Community College
El Paso, TX

Jane Wang
Mt. San Antonio College
Walnut, CA

Lucy Watel
City College of Chicago - Harry
   S. Truman College
Chicago, IL

Donald Weasenforth
Collin County Community
   College
Plano, TX

Teacher's Notes

Each lesson is organized around different content; courses that students might study at a college or university. No specific knowledge of this content is required to teach the lesson. In the *Content Notes* section of this Teacher's Edition, you will find more information and some suggestions on how to focus on the theme.

The following sections are in each lesson:

CONTENT VOCABULARY

This section introduces the context and new vocabulary, using a labeled picture that will focus the students' attention on the topic of the lesson.

THINK ABOUT IT

This section gives students discussion questions or checklists to get them thinking about the topic of the lesson.

GRAMMAR IN CONTENT

This section exposes students to a theme-based listening and reading that includes examples of the target structure. Following each reading are grammar charts that students can use to help them complete the exercises.

COMMUNICATE

This section allows students to practice the grammar points in more communicative, less-controlled ways through speaking and writing activities.

CONNECTION: PUTTING IT TOGETHER

The purpose of this section of the lesson is to connect and extend students' understanding of the grammar, vocabulary, and content from the lesson. This section contains pair and group tasks as well as a project and Internet activity.

PAIR WORK

There are many activities suggested in this teacher's manual that ask students to work with a partner.

1. Decide if you want students to work with any student sitting around them or if you want to specifically pair up students. Some possible ways to pair students are:
   - ❑ same language background
   - ❑ different language background
   - ❑ same English level
   - ❑ different English level
   - ❑ same gender
   - ❑ different gender
2. Make sure students understand what they are supposed to do before they begin working on the task.
3. As students are working together, walk around and listen and ask questions when appropriate.

GROUP WORK

In the Connection section of each lesson, students will work with a group to accomplish a task. When forming groups, decide whether you want students to choose their own groups or whether you want to decide who should work together. (Possible ways to group students are listed above in the Pair Work suggestions.)

1. A group should have 3–5 students.
2. It is a good idea for each group member to have a specific responsibility. That way, everyone in the group will feel important. You can help students come up with positions for each group activity or have them decide among themselves what the different team members will do. Some possible titles are: leader, secretary, timekeeper, artist, etc.
3. While groups are working, walk around and talk to each group. Find out what they are doing and what each member individually is contributing to the group.
4. For groups that finish their work quickly, have some extra activities for them to do or encourage them to expand on what they've already done.

PROJECTS

In the Connection section of each lesson, students will work with a group on a project. The project is designed to help students practice everything they learned in the lesson. (See Group Work suggestions for ideas on managing groups.) Specifically for projects:

1. Make sure students understand what they are supposed to do before they begin working on the project.
2. Ask students to identify what role they will play in the group.
3. Keep students on track by focusing their efforts on one task at a time. Have the groups periodically report to the class what they have come up with.
4. Encourage students to present their final projects to the class and, if appropriate, post their projects in the classroom for everyone to see.

INTERNET ACTIVITIES

If you have access to computers in the classroom, this part of each lesson offers research tasks that will help students learn more information about the topic of the lesson. If not, students can do the research at home or at a library and bring what they learn back to class the next day. Suggestions for doing Internet activities in the classroom:

1. Pair students with little or no experience with those who have experience. Explain to the experienced computer user that he or she will be the "teacher." It is important that the less experienced user not just watch what his or her partner is doing but also learn how to do it himself or herself.
2. Give students possible search engines to use to find the information.
3. Encourage students to show you the information they've found.

WRITING

Although the focus of this student book is grammar, the students will be asked to write paragraphs using the new vocabulary and grammar they have learned. Decide how formal you would like the students' writing to be. Some suggestions:

1. Make sure students know what you are expecting of them.
2. Give students a model. Often times, there will be a model in the book. It is a good idea to write an additional model on the board.
3. Encourage students to share their work with a partner, have partners offer suggestions.
4. If you collect the students' work, let them know what content and grammar you will be focusing on. Encourage the students to correct their own mistakes and write a final draft.

PART 1
Parts of Speech

PART 2
Classroom Instructions

PART 3
Vocabulary Journal

Pre-Lesson

Orientation

PART ONE	Parts of Speech

NOUNS

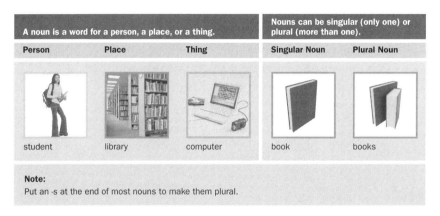

A noun is a word for a person, a place, or a thing.			Nouns can be singular (only one) or plural (more than one).	
Person	Place	Thing	Singular Noun	Plural Noun
student	library	computer	book	books

Note:
Put an -s at the end of most nouns to make them plural.

A Write the singular or plural noun.

	Singular	Plural		Singular	Plural
1.	book	*books*	4.	**door**	doors
2.	**window**	windows	5.	computer	**computers**
3.	student	**students**	6.	**chair**	chairs

B (Circle) the noun.

1.	(a teacher)	happy	sit	4.	fast	on	(a desk)
2.	read	(a book)	big	5.	work	(a mother)	up
3.	study	green	(a school)	6.	small	(a house)	eat

1

PART ONE: PARTS OF SPEECH

NOUNS

1. Elicit students' prior knowledge. Write *noun* on the board and see if students can help you define it.
2. See if students can give you some examples of nouns.

GRAMMAR CHART: NOUNS

Go over the chart with the students. Go over the Notes. As you go through both of these, refer to other nouns in the classroom to give students more examples.

EXERCISE A

1. Go over the example with students and make sure they understand what they are supposed to do.
2. When students are finished, ask for volunteers to write the words on the board.

EXERCISE B

1. Go over the example with students and make sure they understand what they are supposed to do.
2. Go over the answers as a class.

CONTENT NOTES

The purpose of this lesson is to review basic grammatical concepts that students should already know. It is a good chance for you to see what your students have already mastered and what they might need more practice with. Throughout this manual, there will be notes that will have you refer students back to this lesson if they need more information about basic grammatical terms.

EXPANSION IDEA

Exercise B

1. Have students work in groups to come up with more nouns.
2. Have them make a list of the singular and plural forms of these nouns. (Give students a time limit to do this.)
3. Ask for a volunteers from each group to read their list aloud. As they read each noun, ask the other groups if they had that same noun. Have groups cross out any nouns that are duplicates. The group with the most original nouns wins.

■ SUBJECT PRONOUNS

1. Elicit students' prior knowledge. Write *subject pronouns* on the board and see if students can help you define it.

2. See if students can give you some examples of subject pronouns.

■ GRAMMAR CHART: SUBJECT PRONOUNS

Go over the chart with the students. Go over the Notes. As you go through both of these, refer to students in the classroom to give students concrete examples.

■ EXERCISE C

1. Go over the example with students and make sure they understand what they are supposed to do.

2. When students are finished, ask for volunteers to write the correct subject pronouns on the board.

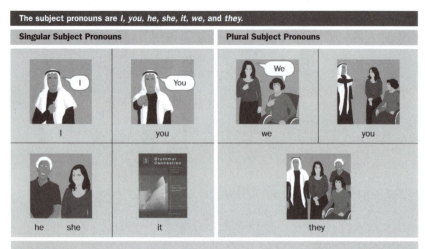

The subject pronouns are *I, you, he, she, it, we,* and *they.*

Singular Subject Pronouns	Plural Subject Pronouns

Notes:
• Subject pronouns take the place of nouns. For example:
   Mother is at home. = ***She*** is at home.
   John and Susan are in class. = ***They*** are in class.
• We use *it* to talk about singular objects. We use *they* to talk about plural things.
   The book is on the desk. = ***It*** is on the desk.
   The books are on the desk. = ***They*** are on the desk.

C Write a pronoun for the person or thing(s) in the pictures.

1. *he*   2. **it**   3. **they**

4. **she**   5. **they**   6. **it**

■ EXPANSION IDEAS

Exercise C

1. Have students work in pairs to come up with subject pronoun examples in the classroom. For example, have them point to an object and say *it.* Have them point to a girl and say *she.*

D Write a pronoun for the nouns.

1. The pen _it_
2. The man _he_
3. Mary _she_
4. David _he_
5. David and Mary _they_
6. David and I _we_
7. The dictionary _it_
8. The chairs _they_
9. The chair _it_
10. My mother _she_
11. My parents _they_
12. The school _it_

■ **VERBS**

Verbs are "action" words.	

talk	write

Verbs also tell about feelings, states, or conditions.	

love	think

E (Circle) the verb in each group.

1. a home	(walk)	she	4. (talk)	a telephone	on
2. (study)	good	a student	5. a book	(read)	big
3. a pen	blue	(write)	6. chocolate	I	(love)

F **PAIR WORK** Choose a verb. Perform the verb for your partner. Your partner will guess the verb. Take turns.

■ **EXERCISE D**

1. Go over the example with students and make sure they understand what they are supposed to do.
2. When students are finished, ask for volunteers to write the correct subject pronouns on the board.

■ **VERBS**

1. Elicit students' prior knowledge. Write *verb* on the board and see if students can help you define it.
2. ee if students can give you some examples of verbs.

■ **GRAMMAR CHART: VERBS**

Go over the chart with the students. Go over the Notes. As you go through both of these, see if students can give you some more examples of verbs.

■ **EXERCISE E**

1. Go over the example with students and make sure they understand what they are supposed to do.
2. When students are finished, go over the correct answers as a class.

■ **EXERCISE F**

1. Model this activity for students by acting out the following verbs and having the class guess: dance, walk, jump, call.
2. Have students do the same activity with a partner for 5 minutes.

■ **EXPANSION IDEA**

Exercise F

1. Divide the class in half and have each team choose an "actor". The actor will act out verbs for the other teams.
2. Have each team work as a group to come up with a list of verbs the "actor" will act out for the other team.
3. When teams are ready have them take turns acting out and guessing. The team who guesses the most correct verbs wins.

■ ADJECTIVES

1. Elicit students' prior knowledge. Write *adjective* on the board and see if students can help you define it.
2. See if students can give you some examples of adjectives.

■ GRAMMAR CHART: ADJECTIVES

Go over the chart with the students. Go over the Notes. As you go through both of these, see if students can give you some more examples of adjectives. You can prompt them by asking them to describe things in the classroom.

■ EXERCISE G

1. Go over the example with students and make sure they understand the meaning of *opposite*.
2. When students are finished, go over the correct answers as a class.

■ EXERCISE H

1. Model this activity for students by reading each sentence aloud and filling in your own answers.
2. Have students complete the sentences, filling in their own answers.
3. Ask for volunteers to read their sentences aloud.

■ EXERCISE I

Students should complete with their own ideas.

Adjectives describe nouns.

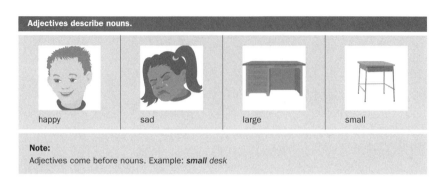

| happy | sad | large | small |

Note:
Adjectives come before nouns. Example: *small desk*

G (Circle) the adjective in each group.

1. on   (blue)   a backpack
2. sit   a chair   large
3. new   buy   shoes
4. a book   carry   heavy
5. nice   a friend   she
6. a teacher   difficult   homework

H Match the opposites.

1. _c_ new   a. cheap
2. _a_ expensive b. closed
3. _d_ black   c. old
4. _b_ open   d. white
5. _e_ fast   e. slow

I Complete the sentences. **Answers will vary.**

1. I have a new _____.
2. I have an old _____.
3. I have an expensive _____.
4. I have a cheap _____.
5. I have a white _____.
6. I have a black _____.

■ EXPANSION IDEA

Exercise H

1. Write the following conversation on the board:
   A: *I have a **new** _____.*
   B: *Really? I have a **new** _____.*
   A: *How interesting!*
2. Model the conversation for students, showing them how to fill in the answers they wrote.
3. Model the conversation again, this time using the different adjectives from exercise H.
4. Have students walk around the classroom and talk to different students, using the conversation on the board with all the different adjectives from exercise H.

read

listen

What's your name?   My name is Kaito.   I think that . . .
ask   answer

I think . . .
discuss

Instruction	Example
Underline the adjective.	I have a <u>new</u> dictionary.
Circle the verb.	You (work) in a school.
Fill in the blank.	She __is__ a teacher.
Complete the sentence.	I speak _Spanish and English._
Match the items.	1. _b_ noun a. new 2. _a_ adjective b. book
Correct the sentence.	I is a student. 　　am
Choose the correct answer.	They (is / (are)) my friends.
Check (✔) the correct answer.	English is a country. ____ English is a language. ✔
Put the words in order.	from are We China. _We are from China._
Write a sentence.	_I am a student._
Write a paragraph.	_I am a student. I study history._ _One day I want to be a history_ _professor at a university._

A **Match the items.**

1. _b_ listen   a. noun
2. _a_ instructor   b. verb
3. _d_ small   c. pronoun
4. _c_ she   d. adjective

■ PART TWO: CLASSROOM INSTRUCTIONS

1. Have students look at the pictures and ask them what is happening in each picture.
2. Ask them what all of these pictures have in common (*things you do in a classroom*).

■ CHART

Go over the chart with the students. Go over each example and discuss with students if you think more explanation is necessary.

■ EXERCISES A–E

1. Have students complete exercises A through E without giving them any help or instructions. Since the purpose of this section is for students to learn about classroom instructions, this is your opportunity to see if they can follow directions without your help.
2. Go over the answers of each activity as a class.

■ EXPANSION IDEA

Grammar Chart

1. Go through each exercise in the Pre-Lesson that students have already completed. Ask them which classroom instructions would apply to each exercise.

■ PART THREE: VOCABULARY JOURNAL

1. As a class, talk about the importance of vocabulary journals. To make this journal, each student will need his or her own notebook.
2. Go over the directions of how to create a vocabulary journal.
3. Do a few examples on the board.

B Underline the nouns.

<u>a clock</u>   listen   white   <u>a teacher</u>   happy   run   <u>a backpack</u>

C (Circle) the verbs.

(read)   a book   a house   (eat)   old   (talk)   expensive

D Check (✔) the correct answers.

1. "a cat" is: ✔ a noun   ___ a verb
2. "eat" is: ___ a noun   ✔ a verb
3. "happy" is: ___ a verb   ✔ an adjective
4. "they" is: ___ an adjective   ✔ a pronoun

E Correct the sentences.

1. "An instructor" is a verb.   3. "It" is <s>an adjective</s>. ^a pronoun^

2. "Eat" is a <s>noun</s>. ^verb^   *noun*   4. "Happy" is <s>a pronoun</s>. ^an adjective^

<table>
<tr><td>PART THREE</td><td>Vocabulary Journal</td></tr>
</table>

In this textbook you will learn a lot of new vocabulary. Use a vocabulary journal to help you learn these new words. To create a vocabulary journal you should:

1. Write a letter of the alphabet at the top of each page.
2. Write new words in your vocabulary journal under the correct letter.
3. Draw a picture or write a definition and a sentence using each word.
4. Study the words every evening.

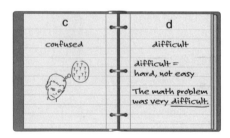

■ EXPANSION IDEA

Vocabulary Journal

1. Have students work in pairs to create a vocabulary journal entry.
2. Have students go through the Pre-Lesson and choose one word to create an entry for.
3. When each pair is finished, ask them to come to the board and write their entries.

PART 1
The Present Tense of *Be*:
Affirmative Statements; *Be* +
Adjective

PART 2
The Present Tense of *Be*:
Negative Statements

Lesson (1)

College Success:
First Day

Lesson (1)

Overview

1. Elicit students' prior knowledge. Ask: *What do you think we will learn about in this lesson?*

2. Have students share their knowledge and personal experiences about studying in large college classrooms or lecture halls. Possible questions you might ask include: *Did you study in college or university in your country? Were you nervous or excited when you went to class for the first time?*

■ CONTENT VOCABULARY

Look at the picture. Do you know these words?

class

Write the new words in your vocabulary journal.

■ THINK ABOUT IT

Check (✔) the statements you agree with. Answers will vary.

1. On the first day of class, students are often:

   excited ___   nervous ___   happy ___   confused ___

2. My school is big. ___   My school is old. ___

   The instructors are good. ___   The classes are interesting. ___

7

■ CONTENT VOCABULARY

1. Direct students' attention to the pictures and the labeled vocabulary words. Ask: *What do you see in the picture?* Ask students if they know what the word *Sociology* means. Explain that this is a required college class and that the number *101* is the lowest level of a college course.

2. Focus on the feeling words: *excited*, *nervous*, and *confused*. Have students share with a partner how they feel (or felt) on the first day of this class.

■ THINK ABOUT IT

1. Have students do this activity by themselves and then share their answers with a partner.

2. Ask each pair to add two adjectives to question 1 and two statements to question 2.

■ CONTENT NOTES

College Success

The topic for this lesson is College Success: First Day. The first day is a chance for students to meet their instructor and classmates and learn what to expect from the class.

Building a community in your classroom in which all students know each other will create a rich learning environment. Students will feel comfortable practicing their English and will not be afraid to make mistakes.

Community Building Idea

Have students form a big circle. Start by introducing yourself and giving one piece of personal information. Then encourage the student sitting next to you to do the same. To help students learn everyone's name, have the student next to you repeat your name and information also. Go around the circle until all students have introduced themselves and repeated the information about the people who spoke before them. The last student will say the names of everyone in the class!

PART ONE

The Present Tense of *Be*: Affirmative Statements; *Be* + Adjective

Part 1 introduces students to affirmative statements and contractions with *be*. If necessary, refer students to the Pre-lesson (page 3) for an explanation of verbs.

■ GRAMMAR IN CONTENT

This section exposes students to a theme-based reading that includes examples of the target structure. Students can refer to the grammar chart(s) to complete the controlled practice activities.

■ EXERCISE A *Track 1*

1. Ask students to look at the picture. Ask the following questions: *Where do you think this woman is from? How old do you think she is? How do you think she feels?*
2. Play the audio and have students follow along.
3. Compare students' predictions with the information about Bella in the reading.

■ GRAMMAR CHART

The Present Tense of Be: *Affirmative Statements*

Go over the chart with the students. Say the sentence with the full form of *be* and have students repeat. Then say the sentence with the contraction and have students repeat. Go over the Notes. As you go through these, refer to the examples from the reading to reinforce the rules.

■ GRAMMAR IN CONTENT

A Read and listen.

TR1

First Day of College

My name is Bella. I am from Mexico. Today is my first day at college. I'm excited. I'm also nervous. It is 1:30 now. I am in Chemistry 105. The students are nice. They are from different countries. Mr. Frank is the instructor. He's nice, too.

countries: for example: Mexico, Japan, Australia

The Present Tense of *Be*: Affirmative Statements					
Subject	***Be***		**Contraction**		
I	am	a student.	I'm		a student.
He She It	is	from China.	He's She's It's		from China.
You We They	are	in class.	You're We're They're		in class.

Be + Adjective		
Subject	***Be***	**Adjective**
I	am	happy.
He She It	is	tall.
You We They	are	Brazilian.

Notes:
- Use *be*:
  1. to say what someone or something is. Example: *I am a student.*
  2. to describe someone or something. Example: *I am nervous.*
  3. to talk about where someone or something is. Example: *I am in class.*
  4. to talk about where someone is from. Example: *I am from Mexico.*
  5. to talk about age. Example: *I am 25.*
  6. with *it* to talk about weather or time. Example: *It is 2:45.*
- Contractions are used in informal speech and writing.
- *You* is both singular and plural.

8   LESSON 1 | College Success: First Day

■ EXPANSION IDEA

Grammar Chart
1. Have each student write one of the following words on a note card or piece of paper: *happy, excited, nervous.*
2. Put students in groups of four or five and have them practice using the *be* verb with their words.

For example:
Student 1: *I am nervous.*
Student 2: *I am excited.*
Student 3: *I am nervous.*
Student 4: *I am happy.*
Student 5: *I am happy.*

Student 1: (points at Student 2) *You are excited.*
Student 2: (points at Student 3) *You are nervous.*
Student 3: (points at himself and Student 1) *We are nervous.*

This can continue as long as you think students need practice.

3. Do this same activity with other information from the Notes (nationality and age).

B Look at the reading "First Day of College." Circle the correct form of *be*.

1. Bella (am / (is)) a student.
2. She says, "I ((am) / is) excited."
3. It ((is) / are) the first day of college.
4. The students (is / (are)) nice.
5. They (am / (are)) from many different countries.
6. Mr. Frank (am / (is)) her instructor.

C Complete the paragraph. Use *am*, *is*, or *are*.

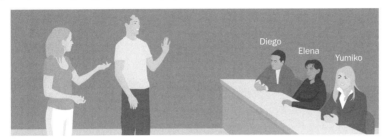

Welcome to English 103! I __am__ Julia Marks. I __am__ the instructor. Class,
                          (1)   (2)
this is Ivan. He __is__ from Russia. We __are__ happy to meet you, Ivan. Please
                 (3)   (4)
sit with Yumiko, Diego, and Elena. They __are__ excellent students. Yumiko
                                         (5)
__is__ a computer science student. She __is__ from Japan. Diego and Elena
(6)   (7)
__are__ from South America. Diego __is__ from Columbia. He __is__ a biology
(8)   (9)   (10)
student. Elena __is__ from Brazil. She __is__ a nursing student. You __are__
               (11)   (12)   (13)
lucky. You __are__ in a great class. The students __are__ nice. And the teacher
           (14)   (15)
__is__ excellent.
(16)

D Rewrite the sentences. Use contractions.

1. She is a biology student. ___*She's a biology student.*___
2. I am 23. ___**I'm 23.**___
3. They are from China. ___**They're from China.**___
4. He is nervous. ___**He's nervous.**___
5. We are in room 208. ___**We're in room 208.**___
6. It is 4:15. ___**It's 4:15.**___

EXERCISE B

As you go over the answers, have students tell you why they selected the form of the verb *be* that they did. (Example: Bella *is* . . . because Bella is like "she." We use *is* with "he," "she," or "it.")

EXERCISE C

Have students fill in the blanks by themselves. Then go over the answers as a class. Ask students comprehension questions about the paragraph and encourage them to answer using complete sentences with *be*.

Possible questions:
Where is Elena from?
What kind of student is Yumiko?
How old is Elena?

EXERCISE D

To help students complete this exercise, give them examples about yourself. You may have to make up some of this information in case you are not studying anything right now.

EXPANSION IDEAS

Exercise B

1. Have students write sentences with the incorrect form of the verb (the one not circled).

   For example:
   1. Bella (am / (is)) a student.
   I am a student too.

Exercise C

1. In pencil, have students write a paragraph, similar to the one in Exercise C, about three students in the class they have met. Then have them erase all the *be* verbs and underline the spaces. Have them exchange their paragraphs with a partner and fill in the missing *be* verbs.

Exercise D

1. Have students interview and write sentences about a partner. Start by asking students about the questions they will need to ask in order to get the answers in the exercise. Write the questions on the board for students to refer to.

■ EXERCISE E

Ask for volunteers to write one of their sentences on the board. Correct any problems tactfully and reassure students that mistakes help everyone learn.

■ COMMUNICATE

The Communicate section allows students to practice the target grammar in more communicative, less-controlled ways through speaking and writing activities.

■ EXERCISE F

1. Have students read the example paragraph. Then ask for a volunteer to read it aloud. Ask: *Where does Jin-Hee go to school? Where is Jin-Hee from?*
2. Ask students to underline all the *be* verbs.
3. Have students complete Exercise F. Walk around and observe, making sure students are using the correct verb forms.
4. Ask for volunteers to read their paragraphs aloud.

PART TWO

The Present Tense of *Be:* Negative Statements

Part 2 introduces students to negative statements and contractions with *be*. If necessary, refer students to the Pre-lesson (page 3) for an explanation of verbs.

■ GRAMMAR IN CONTENT

This section allows students to refer to the grammar chart(s) to complete a number of controlled practice activities.

■ EXERCISE A *Track 2* 🎧

Have students read the conversation before you play the audio. Ask them how the *be* verbs in this conversation are different from the ones they studied before (They are negative forms).

E Write about yourself.   **Answers will vary.**

1. I _____ (what kind of student you are)
2. I _____ (your age)
3. I _____ (country you are from)
4. I _____ (how you feel)
5. I _____ (where you are now)

■ COMMUNICATE

F **WRITE** Write about yourself and a friend. Use affirmative sentences with *be*. Use the vocabulary from this lesson.

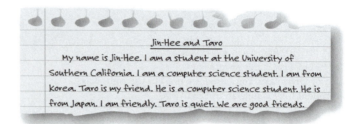

> ### Jin-Hee and Taro
> My name is Jin-Hee. I am a student at the University of Southern California. I am a computer science student. I am from Korea. Taro is my friend. He is a computer science student. He is from Japan. I am friendly. Taro is quiet. We are good friends.

PART TWO	The Present Tense of *Be*: Negative Statements

■ GRAMMAR IN CONTENT

TR2

A **Read and listen.**

> **Wrong Class**
>
> Instructor: Hola!
> Student: Professor Davidson?
> Instructor: No. I **am not** Professor Davidson. I am Professor Ortiz.
> Student: I'm confused. Is this English 205?
> Instructor: No, it **isn't**. It's Spanish 311. You **are not** in the right class.
> Student: Oh. You're right! **I'm not** in the right class. Sorry!
> Instructor: Adiós!

Hola: Spanish for "hello"   **Adiós:** Spanish for "goodbye"

10   LESSON 1 | College Success: First Day

■ EXPANSION IDEAS

Exercise F
1. Have students interview two other students in the class and write a paragraph about them.

Exercise A
1. Have students practice the conversation with a partner.

The Present Tense of *Be*: Negative Statements

Subject	*Be* + not		Contraction			
I	**am not**	a student.	**I'm not** a student.			
He She It	**is not**	from Mexico.	He She It	**isn't** **isn't** **isn't**	(OR: He**'s not**) (OR: She**'s not**) (OR: It**'s not**)	from Mexico.
You We They	**are not**	happy.	You We They	**aren't** **aren't** **aren't**	(OR: You**'re not**) (OR: We**'re not**) (OR: They**'re not**)	happy.

Note:
There is no contraction for *am not*.

B Look at the reading "Wrong Class." (Circle) the correct answers.

1. Professor Ortiz (is /(is not)) an English instructor.
2. He ((is)/ is not) a Spanish instructor.
3. The student ((is)/ is not) confused.
4. Professor Ortiz says: You (are /(are not)) in the right class.
5. The student (is /(is not)) in the right class.

C Complete the sentences about yourself. Use the correct affirmative or negative form of *be*. **Answers will vary.**

1. I ___*am not*___ an English instructor.

2. I _____ a college student.

3. Today _____ Wednesday.

4. It _____ the first day of college.

5. My instructor _____ a man.

6. My classmates _____ American.

D Rewrite the sentences. Use the negative contraction of *be*.

1. She is an instructor.   (student) ___*She isn't a student.*___

2. You are late.   (early) ___**You aren't early.**___

3. It is 8:00.   (9:00) ___**It isn't 9:00.**___

4. He is a good student.   (bad) ___**He isn't a bad student.**___

5. They are happy.   (sad) ___**They aren't sad.**___

■ EXPANSION IDEA

Grammar Chart

1. Have students close their books. Write the following contractions on the board: isn't, he's, aren't, we're, weren't, it's, I'm. Have them take out a piece of paper and write the two words that make up each contraction. Then have them write a sentence using each contraction.

■ GRAMMAR CHART

The Present Tense of Be:
Negative Statements

Go over the chart and the Note with the students. Where there is a second option for forming a contraction, say the first sentence, and then say *or . . .* and let students say the second sentence. This will keep them actively involved. As you go through the chart, refer to the examples from the reading to reinforce the rules.

■ EXERCISE B

1. Have students complete the activity. Then go over the answers as a class. If the answer is a negative sentence, say: *That's right. And is there another way to say it?* This will remind students of the option to use a contraction.

2. Once students have completed the activity and have the correct answers, have them write true statements using the incorrect answers as in Part 1, Exercise B.

   For example:
   1. Professor Ortiz (is /(is not)) an English instructor.
   Professor Ortiz is a Spanish instructor.

■ EXERCISE C

Ask for volunteers to read the sentences aloud with the correct answers before students write the answers in their books.

■ EXERCISE D

Once the class has completed the exercise, ask for volunteers to come up to the board to write one of their sentences.

■ COMMUNICATE

The Communicate section allows students to practice the target grammar in more communicative, less-controlled ways through speaking and writing activities.

■ EXERCISE E

1. Model this activity with individual students. Then help the students get into pairs. Monitor the pairs for their use of *be*.

2. For additional suggestions on doing pair work, see the Teacher's Notes on pages xvi–xviii.

Connection

Putting It Together

The purpose of this section of the lesson is to connect and extend students' understanding of the grammar, vocabulary, and content from this lesson.

■ GRAMMAR AND VOCABULARY

1. Have students work with the same partners as they did in Exercise F.

2. Model this exercise with one of the groups.

■ PROJECT

1. Help students get into groups and work on their projects.

2. Ask all group members to bring a photo to class to include in the book.

■ INTERNET

1. For this activity, pair students with less computer experience with those who have more experience.

2. Ask students to predict what they will find on the Internet.

3. Have students take notes on the piece of advice they will present to the class.

■ VOCABULARY JOURNAL

Refer to the Pre-lesson (page 6) for an explanation of the vocabulary journal.

■ C O M M U N I C A T E

E PAIR WORK Say true and false sentences. Use *be*. Take turns.

We are in class.

Right!

Mr. Harris is from Peru.

Wrong! Mr. Harris isn't from Peru. He's from the United States.

Connection   Putting It Together

GRAMMAR AND VOCABULARY Work in a group. Write true sentences about yourself. Use the grammar and vocabulary from this lesson. Put all of the papers in a pile. Each student in the group takes a turn reading one of the papers out loud. The group will listen and guess who the student is.

About Me
1. I am an engineering student.
2. I am not from China.
3. I am happy.
4. I am very nice!

PROJECT Create a class book.

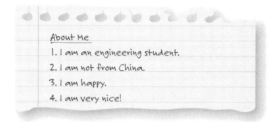

About Us
Yolanda is 25 years old. She's from Mexico. Latifa is Saudi Arabian. She is nervous about her first day at school. Chen is from China. He is a music student. We are an interesting group.

1. Work in groups of three students.
2. Write a page about the students in your group. Include photos.
3. Put your pages together with the other groups' pages to make a class book.

 INTERNET Go online. Use the keywords "advice," "first day," and "student." Find an interesting article. Share a piece of advice from the article with your class.

VOCABULARY JOURNAL Write sentences for new vocabulary you learned in this lesson.

Example: *I am nervous before tests.*

12   LESSON 1 | College Success: First Day

■ EXPANSION IDEAS

Project

1. Have students bring in additional photos or magazine clippings to illustrate their class books. If possible, display the books in the classroom after the presentations.

2. For additional suggestions on doing projects, see the Teacher's Notes on pages xvi–xviii.

Internet

1. For additional suggestions on doing Internet activities, see the Teacher's Notes on pages xvi–xviii.

PART 1
The Present Tense of *Be*:
Yes/No Questions and Short
Answers

PART 2
The Present Tense of *Be*:
Wh- Questions

Lesson ②

College Success: Filling Out Forms

Lesson ②

Overview

1. Elicit students' prior knowledge. Ask: *What do you think we will learn about in this lesson?*
2. Have students share their knowledge and personal experiences about filling out forms. Possible questions you might ask: *Did you have to fill out a form to register for this class? In what other situations have you filled out forms?* Make a list on the board of students' answers (rental application, bank account form, driver's license application, etc.)

■ CONTENT VOCABULARY

Look at the picture and form. Do you know the words?

fill out

Student Registration Form

Name	Smith	Derek
	(Last name)	(First name)

Date of birth 5/12/63   **Sex** Male ✓

Telephone number (305)555-4598   Female _____

Address 53 Tampa Street
Miami, FL 33245

E-mail address dsmith@site.net

Social security number 543-XX-1138

Signature Derek Smith   **Date** 9/15/06

Write the new words in your vocabulary journal.

■ THINK ABOUT IT

1. **What information is on Derek's form? Check (✔) the boxes.**

   ☑ name   ☑ sex   ☐ eye color   ☑ date of birth
   ☐ age   ☐ favorite food   ☑ address   ☑ signature

2. **What forms do you fill out at college? Discuss with a partner.**

13

■ CONTENT VOCABULARY

1. Direct students' attention to the registration form and vocabulary words. Ask: *What is this form for? Who filled out this form? Where does he live? How old is he?*
2. Focus on the vocabulary words: *name (first and last), date of birth, sex, telephone number, address, e-mail address, social security number,* and *signature.* Encourage students to ask questions about unfamiliar words.

■ THINK ABOUT IT

1. Have students do this activity by themselves and then share their answers with a partner.
2. Ask each pair to add three more items that are on the form to the checklist.

■ CONTENT NOTES

College Success
The topic for this lesson is College Success: Filling Out Forms. Filling out forms is a very common procedure in the United States for a number of services: opening a bank account, renting an apartment or house, taking classes, getting an ID card or license, or requesting information. Because it is such an integral part of everyday life, it is important that students understand how to fill out forms properly. Since forms request information, they are a natural context for reviewing question formation.

PART ONE

The Present Tense of *Be: Yes/No* Questions and Short Answers

Part 1 introduces students to *yes/no* questions and short answers with *be*.

■ GRAMMAR IN CONTENT

This section exposes students to a theme-based reading that includes examples of the target structure. Students can refer to the grammar chart(s) to complete the controlled practice activities.

■ EXERCISE A *Track 3*

1. Ask students to look at the picture. Ask the following questions: *Who is in the picture? Where are they? What are they doing?*
2. Play the audio and have students follow along.
3. Ask the following questions: *How is Igor feeling? Why?*

■ GRAMMAR CHARTS

The Present Tense of Be: Yes/No *Questions and Short Answers with* Be

Go over the chart with the students. Go over the Notes. Say the first question and have students repeat. Then read only the *be* verb in the next question so that students must say the rest. As you go through the chart and Notes, refer to the examples from the reading to reinforce the rules.

■ EXERCISE B

Have students complete the activity and check their answers with a partner.

■ GRAMMAR IN CONTENT

A Read and listen.

The Registration Form (Part 1)

Igor:	Is this the history department office?
Stacy:	Yes, it is. Are you a new student?
Igor:	Yes, I am. My name is Igor. I'm Russian.
Stacy:	Welcome, Igor. I'm Stacy. Here is a new student registration form.
Igor:	Um . . . thanks.
Stacy:	Are you OK?
Igor:	Well . . . no, I'm not. This form is confusing.
Stacy:	No problem. I can help you.
Igor:	Great. Thanks!

confusing: not clear; hard to understand

help: assist; support

The Present Tense of *Be: Yes/No* Questions

Be	Subject	
Am	I	right?
Is	he / she / it	a student?
Are	you / we / they	tired?

Note:
Yes/No questions only ask for Yes/No answers.

Short Answers with *Be*

Affirmative			Negative		
	Subject	Be		Subject + Be + Not	
	I	am.		I'm not.	
Yes,	he / she / it	is.	No,	he isn't. OR he's not. / she isn't. OR she's not. / it isn't. OR it's not.	
	you / we / they	are.		you aren't. OR you're not. / we aren't. OR we're not. / they aren't. OR they're not.	

Note:
Do not contract forms of *be* after yes.
Example: *Yes, I am.* (NOT: ~~Yes, I'm.~~)

B Look at the dialogue "The Registration Form (Part 1)." Underline the questions with *be*. Circle the short answers.

■ EXPANSION IDEAS

Exercise A
1. Have students practice the dialogue in pairs.
2. Have them practice the dialogue again inserting their own names and personal information (i.e., ethnicity [*Russian*] and how they are feeling [*confused*]).

Grammar Charts
1. Have students work with a partner to practice the information in the charts. Have one student ask the other student a question from the chart and have the other student answer.

For example:
Student 1: *Am I right?*
Student 2: *Yes, you are.* or *No, you're not.*
Student 1: *Is he a student?*
Student 2: *Yes, he is.* or *No, he isn't.*

After a few minutes, have students switch roles.

C Look at the dialogue "The Registration Form (Part 1)." (Circle) the correct short answers.

1. Are Igor and Stacy in a classroom?   Yes, they are. / (No, they aren't.)
2. Are they in the history department office?   (Yes, they are.) / No, they aren't.
3. Is Igor a new student?   (Yes, he is.) / No, he isn't.
4. Is the registration form confusing for Igor?   (Yes, it is.) / No, it isn't.
5. Is Spanish Igor's first language?   Yes, it is. / (No, it isn't.)

D Look at the student ID cards. Answer the questions.

 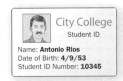

1. Are Yan and Antonio instructors? _____ *No, they aren't.*
2. Are they students? **Yes, they are.**
3. Is Yan 20 years old? **No, she isn't.**
4. Is her student ID number 10023? **Yes, it is.**
5. Is Antonio's birthday April 9? **Yes, it is.**
6. Is his student ID number 10045? **No, it isn't.**
7. Is he a City College student? **Yes, he is.**

E Write short answers to the questions. **Answers will vary.**

1. Are you a teacher? _____
2. Are you from the United States? _____
3. Are you a science student? _____
4. Are you in class now? _____

F PAIR WORK Ask your partner the questions in exercise E. Write down his or her answers. Tell your class about your partner.

■ EXERCISE C

Have pairs of students check their answers with one another by asking and answering the questions.

■ EXERCISE D

1. Go over the questions and short answers as a class.
2. Ask students additional comprehension questions about the ID cards and encourage them to answer you using complete sentences.

   Possible questions:
   What is Yan's student ID number?
   What school does Antonio go to?
   What year was Yan born in?

■ EXERCISE E

Have students share their answers with one another by asking and answering the questions. Monitor students for their use of short answers with *be*.

■ EXERCISE F

For this exercise, students will expand on Exercise E by writing down their partners' answers. When they are finished, ask students to stand up and tell the class something about their partners.

■ EXPANSION IDEA

Exercise D

1. Have students take out a piece of paper and make an ID card with their own personal information. Then collect the ID cards and pass them out to different students in the class. Have the students read the ID cards and return them to their owners. They will be able to do this quickly if they learned their classmates' names in Lesson 1; otherwise, they may ask their classmates *Yes/No* questions to find out who they are.

For example:

Student 1: *Is your name Maria Rios?*
Student 2: *No, it's not.*
(move on)
Student 1: *Is your date of birth 4/15/73?*
Student 3: *No, it isn't.*
(move on)
Student 1: *Is your student ID number 1597873?*
Student 4: *Yes, it is.*
(Student number 1 gives Maria her ID card back and sits down.)
This process continues until everyone is sitting down with his or her own ID card.

■ EXERCISE G

Before you play the audio, have students look at the conversations and guess what might go on the lines. You may want to have them write their guesses below or above the lines and then see if they are correct after they listen to the recording. Check answers by calling on different students to play the roles.

■ EXERCISE H

Look at the example with students and ask them why the word *Is* is used. After students have completed the exercise, have students go over the answers and ask why they chose the form of the verb they did.

■ COMMUNICATE

The Communicate section allows students to practice the target grammar in more communicative, less-controlled ways through speaking and writing activities.

■ EXERCISE I

Have students do the activity without writing anything down. Then ask them to go back and write from memory the answers their partner gave them.

■ EXERCISE J

Help students get started on this activity by modeling it with a group of volunteers. Make sure the students understand how the game works before you have them do it on their own. Encourage them to think of famous people that everyone in the class is likely to be familiar with.

G Listen. Complete the conversation.

TR4

1. Instructor: __Are__ __you__ an art student?
          (1)   (2)
   Herman: Yes, I __am__.
              (3)
2. Akiko: __is__ she a biology student?
       (4)
   Sofia: __Yes__, __she__ __is__.
       (5)   (6) (7)
3. Ricardo: __Are__ __they__ professors?
          (8)   (9)
   Toshi: __No__, __they're__ not.
        (10)   (11)
4. Yang-sook: __Is__ __it__ 10:30?
               (12)   (13)
   Instructor Jones: __No__, __it__ __isn't__.
               (14) (15) (16)

H Write *Yes / No* questions.

1. your school / large   *Is your school large?*
2. English / difficult   **Is English difficult?**
3. your instructor / nice   **Is your instructor nice?**
4. this class / interesting   **Is this class interesting?**
5. you / tired today   **Are you tired today?**

■ COMMUNICATE

I PAIR WORK Ask your partner the questions from exercise H.

J GROUP WORK Work in groups of four students. One student thinks of a famous person. The other students ask *Yes/No* questions with *be*. Guess the person. Take turns.

Is it a woman?

Is he an actor?

Is he Tom Cruise?

No, it isn't.

Yes, he is.

Yes, he is!

16   LESSON 2 | College Success: Filling Out Forms

■ EXPANSION IDEA

Exercise G *Track 4*

1. Have students write two conversations like the ones in Exercise G. Have them underline the question words and answers just like in the exercise. Ask for volunteers to come to the board and write one of their conversations with the question and answer words deleted. Then have the class try to complete the conversations.

■ **GRAMMAR IN CONTENT**

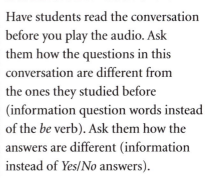

A Read and listen.

TR5

> **The Registration Form (Part 2)**
>
> Stacy: **What is** your name?
> Igor: Igor Petrov.
> Stacy: OK. Write it here. **What's** your date of birth?
> Igor: It's January 8, 1973. Excuse me, **what** time is it?
> Stacy: It's 10:15.
> Igor: Oh no! I'm late for class.
> Stacy: **When's** your class?
> Igor: 10:00.
> Stacy: **Where's** your class?
> Igor: It's in the Johnson building.
> Stacy: **Who's** the instructor?
> Igor: Mr. Craig.
> Stacy: You should go to your class. We can fill out the form later.
> Igor: OK. Thanks.

late: not on time

The Present Tense of *Be: Wh-* Questions

Meaning of *Wh-* Words	*Wh-* Word	*Be*	Subject	Answer		
who — people	Who	are	they?	My friend.	OR	She's my friend.
what — things	What	is	your name?	Eduardo.	OR	My name is Eduardo.
where — places	Where	is	the office?	Room 205.	OR	It's in Room 205.
when — time	When	is	the exam?	May 25.	OR	It's May 25.
how — description	How	are	you?	Fine.	OR	I'm fine.

Notes:
• *Wh-* words ask for information.
• You can make the following contractions with *wh-* words: *What is* = *What's*, *Where is* = *Where's*, *How is* = *How's*, *Who is* = *Who's*, *When is* = *When's*.

PART TWO

The Present Tense of *Be: Wh-* Questions

Part 2 introduces students to *wh-* questions with *be.*

■ GRAMMAR IN CONTENT

This section allows students to refer to the grammar chart(s) to complete a number of controlled practice activities.

■ EXERCISE A *Track 5*

Have students read the conversation before you play the audio. Ask them how the questions in this conversation are different from the ones they studied before (information question words instead of the *be* verb). Ask them how the answers are different (information instead of *Yes/No* answers).

■ GRAMMAR CHARTS
Meaning of Wh- *Words and The Present Tense of* Be: Wh- *Questions*

Go over the charts with the students. After you read each question, ask students the meaning of the *Wh-* word (e.g., *Who* means "people"). Go over the Notes. Refer to the examples from the reading to reinforce the rules.

■ EXPANSION IDEA

Grammar Chart
1. Write the following chart on the board:

Wh- Words	Meaning	Possible Answers
who	people	*teacher,*
what	things	*friend,*
where	places	*John*
when	time	
how	description	

2. Have students work alone to add words to the third column. Then have them form groups to share their answers and add more to their own charts.

EXERCISE B

1. Have students complete the activity.
2. Go over the questions and answers as a class.
3. Have students practice asking and answering the questions with a partner.

EXERCISE C

Ask for volunteers to read the questions and answers aloud once the class has completed the activity.

B Look at the dialogue "The Registration Form (Part 2)." (Circle) the correct answers.

1. What is the student's name?   a. a student   (b.) Igor   c. Mr. Craig
2. What is the student's date of birth?   (a.) 1/8/73   b. the office   c. 132 Brent Avenue
3. What is the problem?   (a.) He's late.   b. Igor   c. Russian
4. When is the class?   (a.) 10:00   b. 5:00   c. Mr. Craig
5. Where is the class?   (a.) the Johnson building   b. Russia   c. 132 Post Street
6. Who is the instructor?   (a.) Mr. Craig   b. Stacy   c. history

C Look at the student registration form. Match the questions to the correct answers.

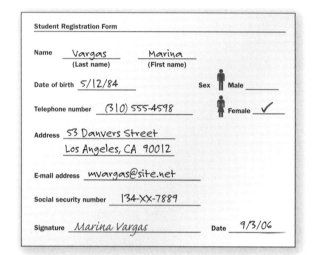

| Student Registration Form |
| Name   Vargas (Last name)   Marina (First name) |
| Date of birth 5/12/84   Sex ♂ Male _____ |
| Telephone number (310) 555-4598   ♀ Female ✓ |
| Address 53 Danvers Street   Los Angeles, CA 90012 |
| E-mail address mvargas@site.net |
| Social security number 134-XX-7889 |
| Signature Marina Vargas   Date 9/3/06 |

___h___ 1. What is her first name?
___b___ 2. What is the date?
___d___ 3. What is her date of birth?
___a___ 4. What is her last name?
___f___ 5. What is her address?
___g___ 6. What is her e-mail address?
___e___ 7. What is her telephone number?
___c___ 8. What is her social security number?

a. Vargas
b. 9/3/06
c. 134-XX-7889
d. 5/12/84
e. (310) 555-4598
f. 53 Danvers Street, Los Angeles, CA 90012
g. mvargas@site.net
h. Marina

EXPANSION IDEA

Exercise C

1. Have students create registration forms with their own (or invented) personal information, or have students fill out actual forms used by the school. Then collect the forms and pass them out to different students in the class. Have the students walk around the room and ask information questions to try to find the person whose form they are holding.

For example:

Student 1: *What is your date of birth?*
Student 2: *January 11, 1987.* (wrong person) (move on)
Student 1: *What is your telephone number?*
Student 3: *(830) 555-2857* (wrong person) (move on)
Student 1: *What city do you live in?*
Student 4: *Flower Mound.* (correct person)

D Complete the questions. Use a *wh-* word.

1. ___What___ is your name?   John.
2. ___Who___ is your instructor?   Ms. Smith.
3. ___What___ is the class?   Biology 205.
4. ___When___ is the test?   It's tomorrow.
5. ___How___ are the students?   Very smart.
6. ___Where___ is the class?   It's in the science building.

E Read the dialogue. Write *wh-* questions.

Doric: Hi! (What) ___What is your name?___
(1)

Tom: My name is Tom Davison. What's yours?

Doric: Doric. (Who) ___Who is your instructor?___
(2)

Tom: Mr. Delgado is my English instructor. He's nice.

Doric: (How) ___How are the classes?___
(3)

Tom: My classes are very interesting. I like them. Oh! I have to go. I have an appointment with Mr. Delgado.

Doric: (When) ___When is your appointment?___
(4)

Tom: It's at 12:30. See you!

■ C O M M U N I C A T E

F **WRITE** Write five *wh-* questions to ask your teacher. Then ask the questions and write the answers.

Interview Questions for My Teacher
1. What is your first name?
2. Where are you from?
3. When is the final exam?

■ **EXERCISE D**

Once the class has completed the exercise, ask for volunteers to come up to the board to write the correct questions. Read each question out loud and have the class call out the answer.

■ **EXERCISE E**

Ask for volunteers to come to the front of the class and present the conversation. Encourage students to have fun "acting" and to applaud each pair. Make a note of any pronunciation problems you hear so you can discuss them with the whole class after the presentations.

■ **COMMUNICATE**

The Communicate section allows students to practice the target grammar in more communicative, less-controlled ways through speaking and writing activities.

■ **EXERCISE F**

1. Before students write their questions, have a discussion with them about what is appropriate to ask. Remind them that there is a respect level between teachers and students and that in college, they need to be careful not to cross the line. Come up with a list of questions that should not be asked:

Examples of taboo questions:
How old are you?
What is your social security number?
How much do you weigh?

2. Have students take turns asking you their questions. Since many of the questions are likely to be similar, continue only as long as someone has a different question to ask.

■ **EXPANSION IDEA**

Exercises E and F

1. Have students use questions and answers they have from the teacher interviews in Exercise F to write out a conversation similar to the one in Exercise E.

Connection

Putting It Together

The purpose of this section of the lesson is to connect and extend students' understanding of the grammar, vocabulary, and content from this lesson.

■ GRAMMAR AND VOCABULARY

1. Have students work alone to write their questions for the first column.

2. Model this exercise by walking around the class and asking three students the two sample questions. Show students how to write the answers in the columns.

3. For additional suggestions on doing group work, see the Teacher's Notes on pages xvi–xviii.

■ PROJECT

1. Help students form groups and provide materials and/or suggestions for finding information they need for their project.

■ INTERNET

1. For this activity, pair students with less computer experience with those who have more experience.

2. Make a list on the board of different schools students might search for.

3. Remind students how to use a search engine to find their information.

■ VOCABULARY JOURNAL

Refer to the Pre-lesson (page 6) for an explanation of the vocabulary journal.

GRAMMAR AND VOCABULARY Write five more questions. Use the grammar and vocabulary from this lesson. Ask three of your classmates the questions. Write their answers.

Question	Classmate #1	Classmate #2	Classmate #3
What's your name?			
Are you a nursing student?			

PROJECT Create a school quiz.

1. Work with a group.
2. With your group, think of *Yes/No* and *wh-* questions to ask about your school.
3. Find out the answers to the questions. Look through the school catalog and ask staff members questions.
4. Create a multiple-choice exam about your school.
5. Give the test to the other groups.

```
                    School Quiz

1. Who is the President of our University?
a) Ann Lawrence    b) Alan Brown

2. Is the library in the Johnston Building?
a) Yes, it is.    b) No, it isn't.

3. What are the school colors?
a) Red and Blue    b) Brown and Gold
```

 INTERNET Go online. Search for a local college or university. Find admissions information. How do you apply to the college? What forms do you need to fill out? Report back to your class.

VOCABULARY JOURNAL Write sentences for new vocabulary you learned in this lesson.

Example: My date of birth is 9/3/86.

■ EXPANSION IDEAS

Project

1. For additional suggestions on doing projects, see the Teacher's Notes on pages xvi–xviii.

Internet

1. Have students use the information they learned from the Internet to write a short paragraph on what they need to do to apply to a certain school.

2. For additional suggestions on doing Internet activities, see the Teacher's Notes on pages xvi–xviii.

PART 1
Singular and Plural Nouns

PART 2
Spelling and Pronunciation of
Regular Plural Nouns

Lesson ③

College Success: The Classroom

■ CONTENT VOCABULARY

Look at the picture. Do you know the words?

Write the new words in your vocabulary journal.

■ THINK ABOUT IT

What's in your classroom? Check (✔) the items you see. Add more items. Answers will vary.

- ☐ a notebook
- ☐ dictionaries
- ☐ pencils
- ☐ an eraser

- ☐ a window
- ☐ a table
- ☐ a door
- ☐ chairs

- ☐ _____
- ☐ _____
- ☐ _____
- ☐ _____

21

Overview

1. Elicit students' prior knowledge. Ask: *What will we learn about in this lesson?* (the classroom)
2. Have students share their knowledge about and personal experiences in different classrooms in which they have studied. Possible questions you might ask: *Where did you study before you came to this school? Are classrooms different in different countries? What was your favorite classroom? Why?*

■ CONTENT VOCABULARY

1. Direct students' attention to the pictures. Ask: *What do you see in the picture?* (textbook, whiteboard, highlighter, pen, pencil, eraser, window, table, door, chair, clock, notebook) *Do we have the same things in our classroom?* (encourage students to look around and say what is the same and what is different)
2. Have students tell a partner what items they brought with them to class.

■ THINK ABOUT IT

1. Have students do this activity by themselves and then share their answers with a partner.
2. Ask each pair to add four things that they see in the classroom to the list.

■ CONTENT NOTES

College Success

The topic for this lesson is College Success: The Classroom. Many colleges and universities offer a course called College Success that all freshmen must take. This class is designed to help prepare them for their college experience.

In order to be successful in college, students need to become comfortable with the classroom. When students feel comfortable in the classroom, they are more likely to make friends, practice their English, ask you questions, and learn what they need to know to succeed.

You can help your students become more comfortable in the classroom by:

1. helping them get to know their classmates.
2. helping them get to know you.
3. making sure they understand the class rules and your expectations.
4. being available for help before, during, and after class.

PART ONE

Singular and Plural Nouns

Part 1 introduces students to singular and plural nouns. If necessary, refer students to the Pre-lesson (page 1) for an explanation of nouns.

■ GRAMMAR IN CONTENT

This section exposes students to a theme-based reading that includes examples of the target structure. Students can refer back to the grammar chart(s) to complete the controlled practice activities.

■ EXERCISE A Track 6 🎧

1. (books closed) Ask students *What should you bring to class every day?* (pencil, paper, etc.) Make a list on the board.

2. (books open) Explain that the illustration in Exercise A is part of a syllabus, a list of the materials you need and the topics you will study in a class. Play the audio and ask students to listen.

3. Have students look at the syllabus list. Ask: *Which words have a in front of them? Why do you think these words have a in front of them? Which words have an -s on the end? Which words have an in front of them?* Help the students come up with the rules by looking at the examples on the syllabus.

■ GRAMMAR CHART
Singular and Plural Nouns

Go over the chart with the students. Go over the Notes. For each note, ask students for more examples. (The last note gives the most common irregular plural forms, but students may know other animal examples such as *sheep/sheep* or *goose/geese*.)

■ GRAMMAR IN CONTENT

🎧 **A** Read and listen.

TR6

English Composition 101
Instructor: Frank Jackson
Room: Lynn Campus, L430
Time: 9:00–11:00

Please bring these items to class every day:

☑ a notebook   ☑ pens   ☑ a dictionary   ☑ questions
☑ pencils   ☑ a highlighter   ☑ an eraser

Singular and Plural Nouns	
Singular (One)	**Plural (More Than One)**
a book	books
an eraser	erasers

Notes:
- Use *a* and *an* with singular nouns. Example: *a car, an apple*
- Do not use *a* and *an* with plural nouns. Example: *a cars, an apples*
- Use *a* before nouns that start with a consonant sound like *book, pen,* and *desk*. Use *an* before nouns that start with a vowel sound like *eraser, item,* and *instructor*.
- Put an *-s* at the end of most nouns to make them plural. Example: *one book, two books*
- You can put a number before plural nouns: Example: *I have three books.*
- Some plural nouns do not end in *-s*. They have irregular plural forms. Common irregular plural nouns are *child/children, foot/feet, man/men, mouse/mice, tooth/teeth,* and *woman/women.*

B Look at "English Composition 101." <u>Underline</u> all of the singular nouns. ⟨Circle⟩ all of the plural nouns.

■ EXPANSION IDEAS

Exercise A

1. Draw the following table on the board. Ask students to work with a partner to add more words to each column.

Singular (a)	Singular (an)	Plural	Irregular plural
a book	an eraser	pens	tooth/teeth

2. Call out the following list of words and ask students to say *singular* or *plural*. Start out by asking the whole class to respond. Then call on individual students.

T: books	S: plural
T: a table	S: singular
T: a computer	S: singular
T: pens	S: plural
T: two notebooks	S: plural
T: students	S: plural
T: a keyboard	S: singular
T: desks	S: plural
T: an eraser	S: singular
T: women	S: plural

C Write *a* or *an*.

1. _a_ pen   4. _a_ table   7. _an_ apple   10. _a_ college
2. _a_ window   5. _an_ eraser   8. _a_ chair   11. _an_ hour
3. _an_ elevator 6. _a_ door   9. _a_ library   12. _a_ year

D Write the plural of the nouns.

1. elevator ____elevators____   4. pen ____pens____
2. apple ____apples____   5. highlighter ____highlighters____
3. woman ____women____   6. college ____colleges____

E Write a sentence. Use *It's* and a singular noun or *They're* and a plural noun.

1. What is it?
____It's a table.____

4. What are they?
____They're windows.____

2. What are they?
____They're chairs.____

5. What are they?
____They're notebooks.____

3. What is it?
____It's a clock.____

6. What is it?
____It's an apple.____

■ **EXERCISE B**

Have students do the exercise. Then say the different items on the list and ask students whether they are singular or plural.

■ **EXERCISE C**

As you go over answers, ask students why they chose *a* or *an*. Practice pronunciation by having students repeat the noun phrases as well as simple sentences (*It's a pen*) after you. Demonstrate linking *an* to the noun after it: *I'd like an apple.*

■ **EXERCISE D**

As you go over the answers, ask students what the spelling rule is for each answer. (Example: elevators rule: add an *-s*)

■ **EXERCISE E**

After students have finished writing the answers, have them practice answering and asking the questions with a partner.

■ **EXPANSION IDEA**

Exercises C, D and E

1. Have students make a list in their notebooks of all the new vocabulary words they are learning in this lesson. Since this lesson is about singular and plural nouns, have them make their list in two columns. Including a gloss of the word in their native language can help students remember the word's meaning.

NOUNS		
Singular	**Plural**	**Translation**
book	books	libro
pen	pens	pluma
man	men	hombre

■ EXERCISE F

1. Have students read the direction line and example in the art. Ask: *What words do we use with it's?* (singular nouns) *What words do we use with they're?* (plural nouns)

F PAIR WORK Student A closes his or her eyes. Student B chooses one or more items from the box below and puts the item(s) in Student A's hands. Student B says "What is it?" or "What are they?" Student A guesses "It's . . ." or "They're . . ." Take turns.

What are they?

They're pens.

one or more pens	one or more notebooks
one or more pencils	one or more textbooks
one or more highlighters	one or more erasers

PART TWO	Spelling and Pronunciation of Regular Plural Nouns

PART TWO

Spelling and Pronunciation of Regular Plural Nouns

Part 2 encourages students to think about and practice the spelling and pronunciation of regular plural nouns. See the Appendix at the back of the student book for more spelling information.

■ GRAMMAR CHART

Spelling of Regular Plural Nouns

(books closed) Write the following chart on the board and ask students to complete it with the plural form of each singular noun. (Don't fill in the column with the heading *Rule* yet.)

Singular	Plural	Rule
book teacher		
bus box		
dictionary library		
shelf knife		
photo tomato		

After students are done, have them share their answers with a partner. Ask for volunteers to come up and write the answers in the chart.

■ EXERCISE A

1. Have students complete the exercise and share their answers with a partner.

2. Go over the answers as a class. Ask for volunteers to spell the correct answers aloud.

■ GRAMMAR IN CONTENT

Spelling of Regular Plural Nouns

Base Form	Plural Form	Rule
book teacher	books teachers	For most plural nouns: Add -s
bus box	buses boxes	If the noun ends in s, z, x, ch, sh: Add -es
dictionary library	dictionaries libraries	If the noun ends in a consonant + y: Change y to i and add -es
shelf knife	shelves knives	For some nouns that end in f or fe: Change the f or fe to -ves
photo tomato	photos tomatoes	If the noun ends with a consonant + o, some words take -s and others take -es.

A Write the plural form of each noun.

1. computer *computers*
2. student **students**
3. dish **dishes**
4. party **parties**
5. pencil **pencils**
6. leaf **leaves**
7. comedy **comedies**
8. clock **clocks**
9. life **lives**

■ EXPANSION IDEA

Exercise F

1. Have students do the same exercise but with their eyes open, walking around the room and pointing at things. For example, a pair of students is standing in front of the door.

Student A: *What is this?* (Student A points at the door.)

Student B: *It's a door*

2. For additional suggestions on conducting pair work activities, see the Teacher's Notes on pages xvi–xviii.

B Complete the sentences with the plural form of a word from the box.

city	country	university	~~day~~	class	test

1. Monday and Wednesday are _____*days*_____.

2. Harvard and Oxford are _____**universities**_____.

3. Biology 203 and English 105 are _____**classes**_____.

4. The TOEFL and the SAT are _____**tests**_____.

5. Japan and Brazil are _____**countries**_____.

6. Tokyo and São Paulo are _____**cities**_____.

Pronunciation of Regular Plural Nouns

There are three ways of pronouncing the final -s and -es.

For Nouns That End in . . .	Pronounce the Third Person -s:
the sounds f, k, p, t, or th	/s/ as in "books" and "pens"
the sounds b, d, g, l, m, n, ng, r, v, and all vowels	/z/ as in "teachers" and "boards"
s, se, ss, sh, ch, ge, ce, and x	/əz/ as in "classes" and "colleges"

C Listen. Check (✔) the plural sound you hear at the end of each word.

TR7

	/s/ as in "books"	/z/ as in "teachers"	/əz/ as in "classes"
1.			✔
2.			✔
3.		✔	
4.			✔
5.	✔		
6.	✔		
7.		✔	
8.		✔	

■ **EXERCISES A and B**

1. Have students complete the exercises and share their answers with a partner.

2. To go over the answers as a class, ask for volunteers to spell the correct answers aloud. Ask students: *What are some other universities/courses/tests?* etc.

■ **PRONUNCIATION CHART**
Pronunciation of Regular Plural Nouns

Go over the pronunciation chart with students. As you go over each rule, have the students help you come up with additional examples.

■ **EXERCISE C** *Track 7*

1. Prepare students for listening by reading the following words. As you read each word, ask students which sound they hear (/s/, /z/, or /ez/). (pens /z/, trucks /s/, watches /ez/).

2. Have students do the listening exercise and then go over the answers as a class. If students have trouble hearing the difference between /s/ and /z/, reassure them that the more important difference is between those two sounds and /əz/ since /əz/ adds an extra syllable to the plural form.

■ EXERCISE D

1. Have each student first write a list of plural nouns from the lesson.
2. Divide the class into pairs and have them give each other plural nouns to spell.
3. After the "spelling tests," have students spell words aloud for their partners to pronounce. Monitor their pronunciation of the alphabet.

Connection

Putting It Together

The purpose of this section of the lesson is to connect and extend students' understanding of the grammar, vocabulary, and content from this lesson.

■ GRAMMAR AND VOCABULARY

1. Have students find a partner that they have not worked with before in this lesson.
2. Go over the instructions with students and make sure they understand what they are supposed to do.

■ PROJECT

1. Write *Spelling Bee* on the board and talk about what it is (a spelling competition where participants are eliminated when they misspell a word).
2. Go over the directions and help students get started with their teams.
3. Moderate the spelling bee and keep track of points.

■ INTERNET ACTIVITIES

1. Prepare students by asking them what jobs they are interested in.
2. Have students share their completed lists with the class.

■ VOCABULARY JOURNAL

Refer to the Pre-lesson (page 6) for an explanation of the vocabulary journal.

D PAIR WORK First, practice spelling plural nouns: Student A says a plural noun from this lesson and Student B spells the noun. Take turns. Next, practice pronouncing plural nouns: Student A spells a noun from the lesson and Student B says the noun. Take turns.

Connection   Putting It Together

GRAMMAR AND VOCABULARY Work with a partner. Identify the items below. Use the grammar and vocabulary from this lesson.

Next, choose five different classroom items with your partner. Draw pictures of the items. Ask another pair to guess what the pictures are.

PROJECT Have a spelling bee.

1. The class works in two groups.
2. Each group chooses ten nouns from this lesson.
3. The groups find objects and/or pictures for each of the nouns. Some of the objects/pictures should show only one of the item, and some should show two or more of the item.
4. A member of Group A holds up one of the objects or pictures.
5. A member of Group B must identify the object(s) correctly using *a / an* or the plural *-s*, then spell the word.
6. If Group B uses *a / an* or *-s* correctly and pronounces and spells the word correctly, they get one point.
7. Take turns. The group with the most points wins.

INTERNET Go online. Choose a job you are interested in. What equipment does this job use? Use the name of the job (for example, "artist") and "equipment" as the keywords. Make a list of the items you find. Place *a* or *an* before singular items and make sure there is a plural *-s* at the end of regular plural nouns.

VOCABULARY JOURNAL Write sentences for new vocabulary you learned in this lesson.

 Example: *My classroom has six tables.*

■ EXPANSION IDEA

Internet

1. Have students illustrate their equipment list with drawings, pictures cut out of magazines, or pictures printed from a computer before sharing it with the class.
2. For additional suggestions on doing projects, see the Teacher's Notes on pages xvi–xviii.

College Success: Finding Your Way Around

■ CONTENT VOCABULARY

Look at the pictures. Do you know the words?

give directions

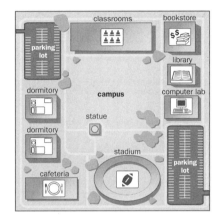

classrooms
bookstore
parking lot
library
dormitory
campus
computer lab
statue
dormitory
stadium
parking lot
cafeteria

map

Write the new words in your vocabulary journal.

■ THINK ABOUT IT

Answers will vary.

1. What places are there in your school or college? Write a list with a partner.

   library,

2. Is your school or college large? Are there many buildings? Is it difficult to find your way around? Discuss with a partner.

27

■ CONTENT NOTES

College Success

The topic of this lesson is College Success: Finding Your Way Around. Many students are nervous about being on a large college campus where they don't know their way around. This lesson is an opportunity for you to make your students feel comfortable on their campus; for example, take your class on a tour of the campus or certain buildings, or assign them to visit different buildings and bring information back to the class.

Overview

1. Elicit students' prior knowledge. Ask: *What do you think we will learn about in this lesson?*

2. Have students share their knowledge about and personal experiences in attending or visiting a college campus, either in the U.S. or other countries. Possible questions you might ask are: *Did you study at a college or university in your country? If so, what was the campus like? Was it big or small?*

■ CONTENT VOCABULARY

1. Direct students' attention to the pictures and the new vocabulary words. Ask: *What do you see in the picture?* Help students understand the vocabulary they are not familiar with.

2. If students are studying on a campus now, ask them where each of these places is.

   For example:
   Do we have a parking lot here? Where is it?
   Do we have a bookstore here? Where is it?

■ THINK ABOUT IT

1. Have students do this activity with a partner and then share their answers with a pair sitting next to them.

2. Have each new group of four discuss the questions together.

Part 1 introduces students to *this*, *that*, *these*, and *those*.

■ GRAMMAR IN CONTENT

This section exposes students to a theme-based reading that includes examples of the target structure. Students can refer to the grammar chart(s) to complete the controlled practice activities.

■ EXERCISE A   *Track 8*

1. Ask students to look at the picture. Ask the following questions: *Who are the people in this picture? What do you think is happening?*
2. Play the audio and have students follow along.
3. Compare students' predictions with the actual conversation.

■ GRAMMAR CHART
This, That, These, Those

Go over the chart with the students. Go over the Notes. As you go through both of these, refer back to the examples from the reading to reinforce the rules.

PART ONE	This, That, These, Those

■ GRAMMAR IN CONTENT

A **Read and listen.**

Is This Wendell Hall?

Student:	Excuse me. What building is **this**?
Secretary:	**This** is Wendell Hall.
Student:	Is the main office in **this** building?
Secretary:	No. **That's** across from Stevens Hall.
Student:	**This** campus is confusing!
Secretary:	Take **this**.
Student:	What's **that**?
Secretary:	**This**? It's a map of the campus. Here. Take two.
Student:	Thanks. **These** maps are helpful.

This, That, These, Those

Near Speaker	Not Near Speaker
Singular	
This is a map. **This** map is helpful.	**That** is a map. **That** map is helpful.
Plural	
These are maps. **These** maps are helpful.	**Those** are maps. **Those** maps are helpful.

Notes:
- The contraction for *That is* = *That's*.
- There is no contraction for *This is*, *These are*, or *Those are*.

■ EXPANSION IDEA

Grammar Chart

1. Have students practice the grammar with a partner using the sentence patterns found in the chart.

For example:

Student 1: *This is a pencil* (holds up the pencil from his desk). *This pencil is yellow.*

Student 2: *That is a clock* (points to a clock across the room). *That clock says it's two o'clock.*

Student 1: *Those are students* (points to another pair of students). *Those students are our classmates.*

Student 2: *These are books* (points to the books on his desk). *These books are mine.*

B Complete each sentence with *This, That, These,* or *Those.*

1. ___These___ are textbooks.

3. ___This___ is the computer lab.

2. ___That___ is a catalog.

4. ___Those___ are restrooms.

C Complete the sentences. Use *This, That, These,* or *Those* and *be.*

1. ___This___ ___is___ the bookstore.
2. ___These___ ___are___ the books for your class.

3. ___This___ ___is___ the cafeteria.
4. ___Those___ ___are___ the vending machines.
5. ___This___ ___is___ my lunch.

6. Ssshh! ___This___ ___is___ the library.
7. ___That___ ___is___ the checkout desk.
8. ___Those___ ___are___ the computers.

9. ___This___ ___is___ the football stadium.
10. ___Those___ ___are___ the bleachers.
11. ___This___ ___is___ my ticket for the next game.

■ **EXERCISE B**

As you go over the answers, have students tell you why they selected the form of adjective they did. (Example: *These* are textbooks . . . because the books are near.)

■ **EXERCISE C**

As you go over the answers, have students tell you why they selected the form of adjective AND the form of *be* they did. (Example: *This is* the bookstore . . . because they are in the bookstore and there is only one bookstore.)

■ **EXPANSION IDEAS**

Exercise B

Write the following sentence starters on the board. Call on students to complete the sentences with items from the classroom and point to the items as they say the sentences.

1. This is a _____.
2. Those are _____.
3. These are _____.
4. That is a _____.

Exercise C

Write the sentence starters above on the board, but leave out the *be* verbs. Ask students to complete the sentences with items from the classroom and the correct form of the *be* verb.

■ COMMUNICATE

The Communicate section allows students to practice the target grammar in more communicative, less-controlled ways through speaking and writing activities.

■ EXERCISE D

Model this exercise with various students and then ask for two volunteers to model it before you have students do it on their own. Encourage students to stand up and walk around the room as they point to and talk about different objects and people.

■ EXERCISE E

Model this exercise with various students and then ask for two volunteers to model it before you have students do it on their own. As a variation, bring various small objects to class. Put one object or more than one of the same type of object in a large paper bag. Have students reach into the bag, and without looking, try to identify the object(s). Repeat with different objects and different students until everyone has had a chance to reach into the bag.

PART TWO

Prepositions of Location

Part 2 introduces students to prepositions of location.

■ GRAMMAR IN CONTENT

This section allows students to refer to the grammar chart(s) to complete a number of controlled practice activities.

■ GRAMMAR CHART

Prepositions of Location

Go over the chart with the students. Go over each of the pictures as you explain the chart. Give some of your own examples using items and people in the classroom.

D **PAIR WORK** Student A points to object(s) in class. Student B says what the object(s) is/are. Use *be* and *This*, *That*, *These*, or *Those*. Take turns.

That's a clock.

E **PAIR WORK** Close your eyes. Your partner will put something in your hand. Guess what the object(s) is/are. Use *This is* or *These are*. Take turns.

PART TWO	Prepositions of Location

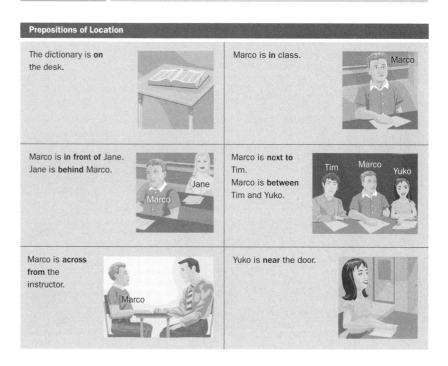

Prepositions of Location

The dictionary is **on** the desk.

Marco is **in** class. Marco

Marco is **in front of** Jane. Jane is **behind** Marco. Marco Jane

Marco is **next to** Tim. Marco is **between** Tim and Yuko. Tim Marco Yuko

Marco is **across from** the instructor. Marco

Yuko is **near** the door.

■ EXPANSION IDEA

Grammar Chart

1. Have students give you examples of these different prepositions once you have explained them. For example, the first sentence in the chart presents on. Ask the class to come up with sentences using on. Then have students get into small groups and assign each group a different preposition. Ask the groups to work together to create three or four new sentences using their preposition. Then write their sentences on the board or read them aloud for the class.

A Check (✔) *True* or *False*. Answers will vary.

		True	False			True	False
1.	I am in class.	☐	☐	5.	My instructor is across from me.	☐	☐
2.	My pens are on my desk.	☐	☐	6.	I am next to the wall.	☐	☐
3.	My textbook is in my bag.	☐	☐	7.	I am between two students.	☐	☐
4.	The whiteboard is behind me.	☐	☐	8.	I am in front of a male student.	☐	☐

B Look at the picture. Complete the sentences. Use prepositions of location.

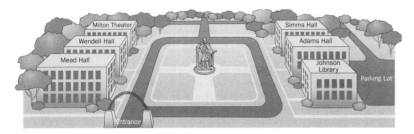

1. Simms Hall is __next to__ Adams Hall.

2. Mead Hall is __in front of__ the entrance.

3. The flag is __on__ Mead Hall.

4. The statue is __in__ the courtyard.

5. Adams Hall is __across from__ Wendell Hall.

6. Johnson Library is __near__ the parking lot. **Answers will vary.**

7. Wendell Hall is __between__ Mead Hall and the Milton Theater.

8. The parking lot is __behind__ the library.

■ COMMUNICATE

C PAIR WORK Work with a partner. One partner describes the location of a partner, using prepositions of location. The other partner guesses the person. Take turns.

He is between Mika and Irina. He is behind Carlo. He is in front of me.  It's Pavel!

■ EXPANSION IDEAS

Exercise A

1. Have students rewrite the false statements, making them true.

Exercise C

1. Do the same activity, but this time with the whole class instead of small groups.

■ EXERCISE A

To prepare students for this true/false exercise, come up with some of your own examples first and say them aloud, asking the students if each one is true or false.

For example:

1. *I am in front of the class. True or false?*

2. *Abdul is next to Jong-Ho. True or false?*

■ EXERCISE B

Have students say the sentences about the campus map with a partner before writing the answers in their books. Have them point to the two locations in their books and then decide what the correct preposition is. Once they both agree, have them write the answer in their books.

■ COMMUNICATE

The Communicate section allows students to practice the target grammar in more communicative, less-controlled ways through speaking and writing activities.

■ EXERCISE C

Go over the directions and the examples, and model the exercise with a group of students before you have the students do it on their own. Once students get into groups, make sure they all know each other so they can use each other's names for this exercise.

EXERCISE D

1. Go over the model with students and have them underline all the prepositions.
2. Have students choose a place to write about and begin working on their paragraphs.

● Connection

Putting It Together

The purpose of this section of the lesson is to connect and extend students' understanding of the grammar, vocabulary, and content from this lesson.

■ GRAMMAR AND VOCABULARY

1. Model this activity for students using the example in the book.
2. As a class, come up with some different places students might use in this exercise.
3. Ask for a volunteer to choose one of the places on the board and model it for the class. Have the class guess what place the student is talking about.
4. Have students get in pairs and give tours of at least three different places.

■ PROJECT

1. Explain to students what their final product will include and look like.
2. Help students get into groups and work on their project.
3. When groups finish, help them prepare for their presentations.

■ INTERNET

1. Talk about the words students could use in a search engine to find their maps.
2. If the class is in a computer lab, have students show you their maps before they print them.
3. Instruct students to practice using prepositions of location as they prepare to talk about their maps.

■ VOCABULARY JOURNAL

Refer to the Pre-lesson (page 6) for an explanation of the vocabulary journal.

D **WRITE** Choose a place you know (for example, the town where you live or your campus). Write about it. Use prepositions of location. Tell your class about the place.

My House

I live in Springfield. I like my house. It is small. It has three rooms. My house is next to a store. It is also across from a park.

Connection   Putting It Together

GRAMMAR AND VOCABULARY Choose a place on your campus or in your school. Pretend you are giving a tour of this place to a new student. Explain where to find different things in this place. Your classmates will guess the place. Use the grammar and vocabulary from this lesson.

Those are the dictionaries. The notebooks are next to the dictionaries. ESL books are on that shelf. The cashier is near the door.

 You are in the bookstore!

PROJECT **Create a map of your school.**

1. Work in small groups.
2. Discuss the different buildings and offices on your campus.
3. Draw an outline of the buildings and offices. Make sure everyone in your group agrees on the locations.
4. Use the outline to draw a map of your school on a large poster.
5. Present your map to the class. Talk about the places in your school.
6. The other students will tell your group if anything on your map is in the wrong place.

 INTERNET **Go online. Find a map of your campus or town. Print it out. Show it to your class and talk about the map.**

VOCABULARY JOURNAL **Write sentences for new vocabulary you learned in this lesson.**

Example: *There are many books in the library.*

■ EXPANSION IDEAS

Grammar and Vocabulary

1. Give students note cards and have them write information about a place on campus.
2. Collect the note cards and pass them out to students making sure they do not get their own cards.
3. Have students read their cards and guess what place is being described.
4. Then have them share their cards with a partner and see if the partner agrees on the place.

5. Ask for some volunteers to read their cards aloud and have the class guess the places.

Project

1. Put the completed posters around the room and each day focus on a different poster. Talk about the buildings on campus and for what reasons students might go to each.

PART 1
There Is/There Are

PART 2
Is There/Are There Questions and
Short Answers

Lesson ⑤

College Success:
People and
Programs

Overview

1. Elicit students' prior knowledge. Ask: *What do you think we will learn about in this lesson?*

2. Have students get into small groups and make a list of college programs they could study. You may have to help them get started by coming up with a few programs as a class (*business, history, education,* etc.). Ask for groups to share their lists by writing the programs they thought of on the board.

■ CONTENT VOCABULARY

Look at the pictures. Do you know the words?

Thomson University
Admissions Office

Click below to find more information on the courses at Thomson University.

art

business

computer science

engineering

nursing

undergraduate: a student in any of the first four years of college

international: a student who is not from the country in which he or she is going to school

part-time: a student who is taking less than a full course load

full-time: a student who is taking a full course load

Write the new words in your vocabulary journal.

■ THINK ABOUT IT

Answers will vary.

1. How many students are there at your school or college? ⟨Circle⟩ the closest number.

   10   100   1,000   10,000   20,000

2. How many students are there in your class? Circle the closest number.

   5   10   25   50   100

3. Are there more men or more women in your class? Circle your answer.

   more men   more women

33

■ CONTENT VOCABULARY

1. Direct students' attention to the Thomson University Web page and courses offered. Talk about each of the five programs listed on the site using the target grammar. Ask: *Is there a medical program at Thomson University?* (nursing) *Is there a business program?* (business studies) *Is there a program at Thomson that looks interesting to you?*

2. Direct students' attention to the photo and vocabulary words. Ask: *Are you part-time or full-time students? Are you international students?*

■ CONTENT NOTES

College Success
The topic of this lesson is College Success: People and Programs. Helping students learn more about their school is a good way to make them feel a part of things, which can increase their chances of success. This is a great time to teach students some school history, as well as tell them about the different opportunities available to them, such as programs and services that are offered.

■ THINK ABOUT IT

1. Have students do this activity by themselves and then share their answers with a partner.

2. Go over the answers as a class. Encourage students to use complete sentences, for example, *There are ten students in our class.*

There Is/There Are

Part 1 introduces students to *There is* and *There are*.

■ GRAMMAR IN CONTENT

This section exposes students to a theme-based reading that includes examples of the target structure. Students can refer to the grammar chart(s) to complete the controlled practice activities.

■ EXERCISE A *Track 9*

1. Ask students to look at the picture. Ask the following questions: *What university is this? Do you know where Harvard is?*
2. Have students read the information about Harvard silently. Play the audio and have students follow along.
3. Point out the vocabulary words *famous* and *examination,* and have students locate them in the reading.
4. Ask the following questions: *How many international students go to Harvard? How many programs are there for undergraduate students?*

■ GRAMMAR CHART
There Is/There Are

1. Go over the chart with the students. Go over the Notes. As you go through both of these, refer back to the examples from the reading to reinforce the rules.
2. As you go over each sentence structure, point to objects or people in the room and begin sentences for students to finish. For example, go over the first structure and example in the chart, and then point to a map and say: *There is . . .* (student: *a map on the wall.*)

■ GRAMMAR IN CONTENT

A **Read and listen.**

TR9

A World-Famous University

Harvard University is a famous American university. It is in Cambridge, Massachusetts. Here are some facts about the university.

- **There are** 6,562 students in the undergraduate school.
- **There are** 545 international students.
- **There are** 40 programs for undergraduate students. **There are** programs in mathematics, chemistry, art, languages, and sociology.
- **There is** a waiting list for most classes.
- **There is** a final examination for every class.

famous: very well known
examination: test

There Is/There Are		
Singular		
There + is	**Subject**	**Location**
There is	a nursing program	at my college.
There is	one library	on campus.
Plural		
There + are	**Subject**	**Location**
There are	ten students	in my class.
There are	some books	on the desk.

Notes:
- The contraction for *there is* is *there's*. There is no contraction for *there are*.
- An adjective can be placed before either a singular or a plural noun. Example: *There is an **excellent** college in this city. There are **excellent** colleges in this city.*
- Don't confuse *there are* and *they are*.

■ EXPANSION IDEA

Reading

1. Have students work with a partner to practice the information in the reading. Have one student begin a sentence with *There is* or *There are* and have the other student complete the sentence with a phrase from the reading.

For example:
Student 1: *There is . . .*
Student 2: *a waiting list for most classes.*
Student 1: *There are . . .*
Student 2: *545 international students.*

B Look at the reading "A World-Famous University." (Circle) the right answers.

1. (There is /(There are)) 40 programs for undergraduate students.
2. (There is /(There are)) 6,562 students in the undergraduate school.
3. (There is /(There are)) 545 international students.
4. ((There is)/ There are) a final exam for each course.

C Look at the pie chart. Complete the sentences.

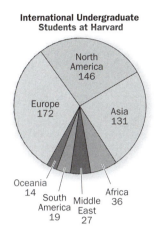

International Undergraduate
Students at Harvard

1. _____There are 27 students_____ from the Middle East.

2. _____**There are 36 students**_____ from Africa.

3. _____**There are 172 students**_____ from Europe.

4. _____**There are 14 students**_____ from Oceania.

5. _____**There are 146 students**_____ from North America.

6. _____**There are 19 students**_____ from South America.

7. _____**There are 131 students**_____ from Asia.

8. _____**There are 545 students**_____ international

undergraduate students at Harvard.

■ **EXERCISE B**

Have students complete the activity and check their answers with a partner.

■ **EXERCISE C**

Have students complete the activity and check their answers with a different partner.

■ **EXPANSION IDEA**

Exercise C

1. Conduct a classroom survey to find out where students are from by having students raise their hands.

2. Write the names of the countries on the board and tally the number of students from each country.

3. Have students write sentences using *There is* and *There are* about their class.

Ask for volunteers to come to the board to write the correct sentences. If there are mistakes in the sentences, ask for other volunteers to come up and fix the mistakes.

■ **EXERCISE E**

Have students share information about their rooms by reading the sentences aloud to each other and telling their partners whether each sentence is true or false for them.

■ **COMMUNICATE**

The Communicate section allows students to practice the target grammar in more communicative, less-controlled ways through speaking and writing activities.

■ **EXERCISE F**

Have students share their paragraphs in pairs. Then ask them to make two suggestions to improve their partners' paragraphs, for example, *You could add one more sentence about your major.*

D Write sentences. Use *There is* and *There are.*

1. 7,000 students / at his college   There are 7,000 students at his college.
2. many majors / at the college   **There are many majors at the college.**
3. an instructor / for every course   **There is an instructor for every course.**
4. 12 dorms / on the campus   **There are 12 dorms on the campus.**
5. elevators / in his dorm   **There are elevators in his dorm.**
6. a security guard / in his dorm   **There is a security guard in his dorm.**

E Think about your bedroom or dorm room. Are the sentences true or false? (Circle) the right answer.   Answers will vary.

1. There are two beds in the room.	True	False
2. There is a window next to my bed.	True	False
3. There is one pillow on my bed.	True	False
4. There is a dresser in the room.	True	False
5. There are three windows in the room.	True	False
6. There is a table next to my bed.	True	False
7. There is a computer in the room.	True	False
8. There are photographs in the room.	True	False

■ **C O M M U N I C A T E**

F **WRITE** Write about your school or college. Use *There is/There are* sentences.

Middleton College

There is a fine arts program at my college. The program is large. There are 300 students in this program. There are 22 instructors. There are majors in photography, painting, and sculpture. I am a photography major.

■ **EXPANSION IDEAS**

Exercise D

1. Have students write sentences about their own school using *There is* and *There are.*
2. Have students get into small groups and share their sentences.
3. Ask for volunteers from each group to write their most original sentences on the board.

Exercise E

1. Have students rewrite the false statements, making them true.

Exercise F

1. Have students type their paragraphs on the computer and insert a picture of their school, classroom, or dormitory.

■ GRAMMAR IN CONTENT

TR10

A Read and listen.

The Right Program?

Receptionist:	This is the admissions office. Can I help you?
Marie:	Yes. I have a few questions. <u>Is there</u> a psychology program at the university?
Receptionist:	(Yes, there is.)
Marie:	<u>Are there</u> many international students in the program?
Receptionist:	(Yes, there are.) There are over 40 international students in the program.
Marie:	<u>Is there</u> a part-time program?
Receptionist:	(No, there isn't.)
Marie:	Oh, that's too bad. This isn't the right program for me.

admissions office: office in a school that helps people apply to the school

Is There/Are There Questions and Short Answers				
Singular				
Is + there	Subject	Location	Affirmative	Negative
Is there	a library	on campus?	Yes, there is.	No, there isn't.
Plural				
Are + there	Subject	Location	Affirmative	Negative
Are there	students	in the classroom?	Yes, there are.	No, there aren't.

Notes:
- It is common to use *any* with *Are there* questions.
  Example: *Are there any night classes?*
- For negative answers, we usually use the contractions *isn't* and *aren't*.

B Look at the dialogue "The Right Program?" <u>Underline</u> the questions with *Is there* and *Are there*. (Circle) the short answers.

■ EXPANSION IDEA

Exercise B
1. Have students rewrite the conversation using information about their own school.

Is There/Are There Questions and Short Answers

Part 2 introduces students to *Is there/Are there* questions and short answers.

■ GRAMMAR IN CONTENT

This section allows students to refer to the grammar chart(s) to complete a number of controlled practice activities.

■ EXERCISE A *Track 10*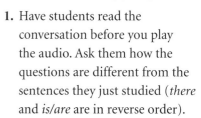

1. Have students read the conversation before you play the audio. Ask them how the questions are different from the sentences they just studied (*there* and *is/are* are in reverse order).
2. Play the recording.
3. Ask students the three questions from the conversation that use *Is there/Are there* and have them answer you with the short answers.

■ GRAMMAR CHART
Is There/Are There *Questions and Short Answers*

Go over the charts with the students. Go over the Notes. As you go through both of these, refer to the examples from the reading to reinforce the rules.

■ EXERCISE B

Once students have completed the activity and have the correct answers, have them practice the conversation with a partner.

Ask for volunteers to read the
questions and answers aloud once
the class has completed the activity.

■ **EXERCISE D**

Once the class has completed the
exercise, ask for volunteers to come
up to the board to write the correct
questions.

C Answer the questions. Use short answers.

Fast Facts about Parkhurst College							
Programs	Undergraduate	Yes		Facilities	Library	Yes	
	Graduate		No		Academic Advising Office	Yes	
	Part-time		No		Career Counseling Office	Yes	
					Computer Services	Yes	
Majors	Mathematics		No		Student Parking		No
	Science	Yes			Dorms		No
	Social Sciences	Yes					
	Languages	Yes					
	Engineering		No				
	Music		No				
	Nursing	Yes					

1. Is there a library at Parkhurst College? _____ Yes, there is.

2. Are there dorms at the college? _____ No, there aren't.

3. Are there graduate programs at the college? _____ No, there aren't.

4. Is there a mathematics program at the college? _____ No, there isn't.

5. Is there a music program at the college? _____ No, there isn't.

6. Is there a nursing program at the college? _____ Yes, there is.

7. Is there a Career Counseling Office at the college? _____ Yes, there is.

8. Are there part-time programs at the college? _____ No, there aren't.

D Complete the questions with *Is there* or *Are there*.

1. _____Is there_____ an application form?

2. _____Is there_____ a waiting list?

3. _____Are there_____ graduate programs?

4. _____Is there_____ a business program?

5. _____Are there_____ students from South America?

6. _____Is there_____ a part-time program?

7. _____Are there_____ dorms on campus?

8. _____Are there_____ computer labs on campus?

■ **EXPANSION IDEAS**

Exercise C

1. Have students make a chart like
the one in Exercise C and fill out
the Yes/No columns with true
information about their school. They
may have to walk around the campus
and ask questions to get the correct
information.

Exercise D

1. Have students ask a partner the
questions and have the partner give
short answers that are true for the
school he or she is attending.

E **PAIR WORK** Ask and answer questions about your dorm, house, or apartment. Take turns.

1. a closet? 2. vending machines? 3. an elevator? 4. parking spaces?

5. a telephone? 6. two beds? 7. a computer? 8. a washing machine?

F **PAIR WORK** Student A looks at the picture on this page. Student B looks at the picture on page 227. Find the differences. Ask and answer *Is there/Are there* questions. (Hint: There are six differences.)

Student B differences:

1. There's a teacher at the desk.
2. There are pens on the desk.
3. There is a book on the desk.
4. There isn't a clock next to the blackboard.
5. There are three windows.
6. There is an eraser near the blackboard.

■ **COMMUNICATE**

The Communicate section allows students to practice the target grammar in more communicative, less-controlled ways through speaking and writing activities.

■ **EXERCISE E**

Model this activity with the students before you have students work in pairs.

■ **EXERCISE F**

This activity may be tricky for students if they have not done information gap activities before. Model it so that students understand how it is done. Explain to students that they will be looking at different pictures, and have them make a list of the six differences they find by talking to their partners.

■ **EXPANSION IDEA**

Exercise E

1. Have students use the list of questions to interview classmates. When they find two students with the same response (*yes* or *no*), they can move on to the next question. Have them share the names of the students with the same answer, for example, *Su and Mario have telephones in their bedrooms*

2. For additional suggestions on doing pair work, see the Teacher's Notes on pages xvi–xviii.

Connection

Putting It Together

The purpose of this section of the lesson is to connect and extend students' understanding of the grammar, vocabulary, and content from this lesson.

■ GRAMMAR AND VOCABULARY

This is an information gap activity in which each partner has different information to share.

1. Go over the example and explain how this activity will work.
2. Pair students and divide each pair into *A*s and *B*s or *1*s and *2*s.
3. Have the *A*s or *1*s look at the picture on page 227 and have the *B*s or *2*s look at the picture on page 40 in their books.
4. Walk around and help students with the information gap.
5. When students are finished, talk about the differences as a class.

■ PROJECT

1. Draw a pie chart on the board to show students what one looks like.
2. Go over each step of the project and make sure students understand what they are supposed to do.
3. For additional suggestions on doing projects, see the Teacher's Notes on pages xvi–xviii.

■ INTERNET

1. Make a list on the board of different schools students might search for.
2. Remind students how to use a search engine to find their information.

■ VOCABULARY JOURNAL

Refer to the Pre-lesson (page 6) for an explanation of the vocabulary journal.

GRAMMAR AND VOCABULARY **Work with a partner. Partner A looks at the picture on this page. Partner B looks at the picture on page 227. Ask and answer questions to find out how your partner's picture is different from yours. How many differences can you find? Make notes on the differences. Use the grammar and vocabulary from this lesson.**

 Is there a music student in your picture?

 Yes, there is. Actually, there are two music students in my picture.

PROJECT **Create a pie chart about your classmates.**
1. Work with your class.
2. Find out what countries your classmates are from.
3. Count how many students there are from each country.
4. Create a pie chart to show the results. Use the pie chart on page 35 as an example.
5. Make sentences about the results.

INTERNET **Go online. Search for a college or university that you are interested in. Find out how many students there are at this university. What programs does the university have? Report back to your class.**

VOCABULARY JOURNAL **Write sentences for new vocabulary you learned in this lesson.**

Example: I am a part-time student. I only take classes two days a week.

■ EXPANSION IDEAS

Grammar and Vocabulary

1. Have students write sentences about the pictures.

Project

1. Ask for groups to read their sentences with *there is/there are* aloud, for example, *There are two students from Taiwan in the class.*

Internet

1. Have students take the information they learned from the Internet and write a short paragraph of five sentences using *There is* or *There are* to report their information to the class.
2. For additional suggestions on doing Internet activities, see the Teacher's Notes on pages xvi–xviii.

A Complete the conversation. Use the affirmative or negative form of *be*.

Carmen: Hi Bella.

Bella: Hi Carmen. It __'s__ 4:00. The first day of school __is__ over!
         (1)   (2)

Carmen: I __'m__ so glad. I __'m__ really tired.
            (3)   (4)

Bella: Really? I __'m not__ tired. I __'m__ excited. My English class __is__ wonderful.
                     (5)   (6)   (7)
         There are only six students in the class. The class __isn't__ very big.
                                                               (8)

B Match each question with the correct answer.

Students can check answers on pages 235–236.

1. __c__ Is your name Ella?   a. Tokyo.
2. __a__ Where are you from?   b. Room 303.
3. __e__ Is your teacher good?   c. Yes, it is.
4. __b__ Where is the class?   d. No, I'm not.
5. __d__ Are you happy?   e. Yes, he is.

C (Circle) the correct answers.

I am ((a)/ an) student at the University of California, Los Angeles.
    (1)
My university is very large. It has 30,000 (student /(students)),
                                                          (2)
121 (program /(programs)), and 12 ((libraries)/ librarys). My school has
          (3)   (4)
(a student /(students)) from 90 (countrys /(countries)). I live in ((a)/ an)
        (5)   (6)   (7)
dormitory. I take math and science (class /(classes)). I really like my university.
                                                (8)

D Complete the sentences with *this, that, these, those,* and *be.* Use the information in parentheses.

1. _____**This is**_____ the classroom. (near)
2. _____**These are**_____ my classmates. (near)
3. _____**That is**_____ my instructor. (not near)
4. _____**This is**_____ the library. (near)
5. _____**Those are**_____ textbooks. (not near)

Review
Lessons 1–5

The purpose of this lesson is to help students review the language and concepts they have learned in the last five lessons. Encourage them to go back to the lessons and review the grammar charts to help them complete the review exercises.

■ EXERCISE A

1. Have students do this activity by themselves and then share their answers with a partner.
2. Go over the answers as a class.

■ EXERCISE B

Help students understand how to do this activity by writing the following on the board:

Are you a student?
What do you do?

Then say the following answer and ask students what the correct question is.

Yes, I am.

■ EXERCISE C

Have students do this activity by themselves and then share their answers with a partner.

■ EXERCISE D

Model the activity first. Ask students which words they can use with something that is near (*this* and *these*) and with something that is not near (*that* and *those*). Then indicate the classroom and say, *This or these . . . the classroom.* Students should respond, *This is the classroom.*

■ EXPANSION IDEA

Exercise C

1. Have students work in a group to talk about why they chose the answers they did. Ask them to talk about which rule they used to choose their answer. For example: *The first one is* a *because it is in front of a consonant* s.

■ EXERCISE E

1. Have students do this activity by themselves and then share their answers with a partner.
2. Have students practice the conversation with a partner.

■ LEARNER LOG

1. Help students understand how to complete the Learner Log by going over it with them and offering examples of the grammar structures.
2. If students checked "I Need More Practice" for any of the structures, suggest that they review those lessons. If possible, meet with students individually to discuss their Learner Logs and make suggestions for ways to get more practice with the structures.

E Complete the sentences and questions. Use *there is, there are, is there,* or *are there.*

Reiko: Hello? Mama? It's Reiko.

Mama: Reiko! How are you? Tell me about school.

Reiko: I'm fine. School is great. __There__ __are__ students from all over the world
(1)
here. __There__ __are__ five Japanese people in my dorm. __There__ __is__
(2)   (3)
one woman from our city!

Mama: Really? __Is__ __there__ a club for Japanese students?
(4)

Reiko: Yes, __there__ __is__.
(5)

Mama: Is the campus nice?

Reiko: Yes, it is. __There__ __are__ many beautiful buildings. __There__ __are__ four
(6)   (7)
dorms. My dorm is near the library.

Mama: __Is__ __there__ a telephone in your room?
(8)

Reiko: Yes, __there__ __is__.
(9)

Mama: Then you must call us more often!

LEARNER LOG Check (✔) *Yes* or *I Need More Practice.*

Lesson	I Can Use . . .	Yes	I Need More Practice
1	Affirmative and Negative Statements with *Be*		
2	*Yes/No* Questions and Short Answers and *Wh-* Questions and Short Answers with *Be*		
3	Singular and Plural Nouns; Spell and Pronounce Regular Plural Nouns		
4	*This, That, These, Those;* Prepositions of Location		
5	*There Is/There Are* *Is There/Are There* Questions and Short Answers		

■ EXPANSION IDEA

Learner Log

1. Have students form groups and generate a list of ideas for what they can do if they checked the "I Need More Practice" column in the Learner Log. Have each group share its best ideas with the class.

You might also want to ask students what helped them learn the topics for which they checked the "Yes" column.

PART 1
The Simple Present Tense:
Affirmative Statements

PART 2
Spelling and Pronunciation of
Third-Person -s Form

PART 3
The Simple Present Tense:
Negative Statements

Lesson 6

Science: The Brain

Lesson 6

Overview

Elicit students' prior knowledge. Ask: *What do you think we will learn about in this lesson?*

■ CONTENT VOCABULARY

Look at the picture. Do you know these words?

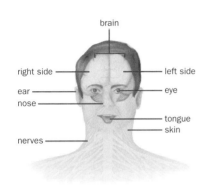

- brain
- right side
- left side
- ear
- nose
- eye
- tongue
- skin
- nerves

hear

see

smell

taste

Write the new words in your vocabulary journal.

■ CONTENT VOCABULARY

1. Direct students' attention to the anatomical drawing and vocabulary words. Discuss the vocabulary words.
2. Write the word *Senses* on the board. Go over each of the labeled pictures with students. Ask: *What do you smell with?* (nose) *What do you taste with?* (mouth or tongue) *What do you see with?* (eyes) *What do you hear with?* (ears)

■ THINK ABOUT IT

Check (✔) the correct answer(s).

The brain helps us:

✔ see   ✔ hear   ✔ smell   ✔ think   ✔ taste

■ THINK ABOUT IT

1. Have students do this activity by themselves and then share their opinions with a partner.
2. Talk about the students' opinions as a class. Help students understand that the brain helps us do all these things and more. (See Content Notes below for more information.)

43

■ CONTENT NOTES

Science

The topic for this lesson is Science: The Brain. The content of the activities in the lesson focuses on the idea that the brain controls all of our senses.

Note: It is not necessary to explain (or understand for that matter) the technical nature of the brain and how it works in order to teach this lesson well.

The Simple Present Tense: Affirmative Statements

Part 1 introduces students to affirmative statements in the simple present tense.

■ GRAMMAR IN CONTENT

This section exposes students to a theme-based reading that includes examples of the target structure. Students can refer to the grammar chart(s) to complete the controlled practice activities.

■ EXERCISE A *Track 11* 🎧

1. Ask students to look at the picture. Ask the following questions: *What is this woman doing? What do you think she hears? What do you think she sees? What do you think she smells?*

2. Play the audio and have students follow along.

3. Ask the following questions: *What does Jana hear? What does Jana see? What does Jana smell? What is she eating? How does it taste? How much does the brain weigh?*

■ GRAMMAR CHART

The Simple Present Tense: Affirmative Statements

1. Go over the chart and the Notes with the students. As you go through both of these, refer to the examples from the reading to reinforce the rules.

2. Practice saying affirmative sentences in the simple present tense. Write *see/sees the sun* on the board. Call out different subjects such as *we, she,* and *they* and call on students to say a sentence combining the subject you called out and the verb phrase on the board.

For example:

She sees the sun. Repeat with all three verbs making sure students use the *–s* ending with third-person singular subjects, for example, *He weighs three pounds.* (This should elicit a few laughs.)

PART ONE **The Simple Present Tense: Affirmative Statements**

■ GRAMMAR IN CONTENT

🎧 **A** **Read and listen.**
TR11

The Busy Brain

Every day Jana **hears** her alarm clock. She **sees** the sun. She **smells** coffee. She **tastes** her cereal. How are these things possible?

The nerves in our nose, skin, tongue, eyes, and ears **take in** information. Then the nerves **send** this information to the brain.

The brain is important in many ways. Yet it **weighs** only about three pounds.

information: knowledge, news, facts

The Simple Present Tense: Affirmative Statements

Subject	Verb	
I You We They	**see**	the sun.
He She	**smells**	the coffee.
It	**weighs**	three pounds.

Notes:
• Use the simple present tense:
1. to talk about things that happen often. Example: *I go to work at 9:00 a.m.*
2. to talk about things that are true. Example: *The brain weighs about three pounds.*
• Add *-s* or *-es* to the verb only with a third-person singular object (*he, she,* or *it*).
• "You" is both singular and plural.
• These words have an irregular form: *go/goes, do/does, have/has* (see Lesson 7).

44   LESSON 6 | Science: The Brain

■ EXPANSION IDEA

Reading

1. Have students rewrite the first paragraph of the reading in the first person by changing the subjects to *I* and supplying their own information about what they hear, see, smell, and taste in the morning.

2. Have students share their paragraphs with a partner.

3. Have students write the paragraph again using their partner's information and third-person singular *-s*.

Examples:

Everyday, I hear my husband wake up. I see my dog sleeping. I smell the rain. I eat my eggs. They taste delicious.

Everyday, Kara hears her cat in the morning. She sees the clouds. She smells breakfast. She drinks her coffee. It tastes sweet.

B Read the sentences from the reading "The Busy Brain." Circle the correct word.

1. Jana (hear / (hears)) the alarm clock.
2. She (see / (sees)) the sun.
3. She (smell / (smells)) coffee.
4. The nerves ((send) / sends) information to the brain.
5. The brain (weigh / (weighs)) only about three pounds.

C Complete the sentences with the correct form of the verb in parentheses.

1. I (smell) ___smell___ flowers.   4. I (hear) ___hear___ birds.

2. He (smell) ___smells___ hot dogs.   5. She (hear) ___hears___ music.

3. They (smell) ___smell___ garbage.   6. We (hear) ___hear___ thunder.

■ **EXPANSION IDEA**

Exercise C

1. Have students write more sentences about each of the pictures. The sentences do not have to involve the senses but should help students practice present tense.
2. Have students form small groups and share their sentences.
3. Assign each group one of the pictures to write a paragraph about, using the sentences each group member wrote individually.
4. Ask for a volunteer from each group to share the group's paragraph aloud.

■ EXERCISE D

Ask for volunteers to write the correct sentences on the board. If there are mistakes in the sentences, ask for other volunteers to come up and fix the mistakes.

■ COMMUNICATE

The Communicate section allows students to practice the target grammar in more communicative, less-controlled ways through speaking and writing activities.

■ EXERCISE E

Have students complete the first column by themselves before asking their partners the questions.

■ EXERCISE F

Have students write their paragraphs. Then ask them to go back and circle the verbs. Have them look back at the grammar charts to make sure they used the correct form of each verb.

D Correct the mistakes. Rewrite the sentences.

1. Every morning Ben bring Maria coffee.

   Every morning Ben brings Maria coffee.

2. She smell the coffee and wake up.

   She smells the coffee and wakes up.

3. They makes breakfast.

   They make breakfast.

4. Ben wash the dishes and Maria packs their lunches.

   Ben washes the dishes and Maria packs their lunches.

5. They leaves for work together.

   They leave for work together.

■ COMMUNICATE

E **PAIR WORK** Imagine you are in your favorite place. Complete the chart with information about it. Ask your partner about his or her favorite place and put the information in the chart. Tell the class about your favorite place and your partner's favorite place.

	Me	My Partner
1. What do you hear?		
2. What do you see?		
3. What do you smell?		
4. What do you taste?		
5. How do you feel?		

F **WRITE** Use the information in exercise E to write a paragraph about your favorite place and your partner's favorite place. Use the simple present tense.

■ EXPANSION IDEA

Exercise E

1. Have students walk around the room and interview other students, using the questions from the chart.

■ GRAMMAR IN CONTENT

Simple Present Spelling of Third-Person -s Form		
Base Form	**Spelling with *He*, *She*, or *It***	**Rule**
see	sees	Most verbs: Add -s
teach	teaches	Verbs that end in *sh*, *ch*, *x*, *z*, or *ss*: Add -es
study	studies	Verbs that end in consonant + *y*: Change *y* to *i* and add -es

A Circle the correct word.

1. Marco (studys /(studies)) biology.
2. He ((takes)/ takies) classes all day.
3. At night he ((works)/ workes) in the university.
4. He (hurryes /(hurries)) to the lab after classes.
5. He (cleanes /(cleans)) the laboratory.
6. He also (washs /(washes)) the equipment.
7. Marco ((tries)/ trys) to study after work.
8. But he often (falles /(falls)) asleep.

B Write sentences about someone you know. Use the third-person form of the verb.
Answers will vary.

1. (live) _____
2. (watch) _____
3. (speak) _____
4. (study) _____
5. (eat) _____
6. (work) _____

Spelling and Pronunciation of Third-Person -s Form

Part 2 introduces students to the spelling and pronunciation of the third-person -s form.

■ GRAMMAR IN CONTENT

This section allows students to refer to the grammar chart(s) to complete a number of controlled practice activities.

■ GRAMMAR CHART

Simple Present Spelling of Third Person -s Form

Go over the chart with the students.

■ EXERCISE A

When students are finished, ask for volunteers to read the correct sentence and then spell the word correctly.

■ EXERCISE B

Ask for volunteers to write their sentences on the board.

■ EXPANSION IDEA

Grammar Chart

1. Have students label the rules A, B, C. Then have them look at each verb in Exercise A and write the letter of the corresponding spelling rule at the end of each sentence. Go over the answers and repeat the process for Exercise B.

2. Write the following chart on the board:

Rule A	Rule B	Rule C
see	teach	study

Have students list appropriate verbs under each rule. Tell them to start with the verbs in Exercises A and B. When they are finished, they can think of more verbs to add to their lists.

■ GRAMMAR CHART

The Simple Present Tense: Pronunciation of Verbs in the Third-Person -s Form

Go over the chart with students, modeling the pronunciation and having them repeat after you.

■ EXERCISE C *Track 12*

1. Play the audio and have students check the sounds they hear.
2. Go over the answers as a class and practice the pronunciation.
3. If students are having trouble hearing the difference between the /s/ and /z/ sounds, assure them that it is much more important to hear (and say) the /əz/ sound since it adds an extra syllable to a word. Reinforce this idea by clapping syllables in the verbs in the third column with and without the *–es* ending, for example, *teach* (one clap), *teaches* (two claps).

■ EXERCISE D *Track 13*

Have students practice alone and with a partner before you play the recording.

The Simple Present Tense: Pronunciation of Verbs in the Third-Person -s Form	
Verbs That End In . . .	Pronounce the Third-Person -s:
the sounds *f, k, p,* or *t*	/s/ as in "eats"
the sounds *b, d, g, l, m, n, ng, r, v, y, a, e, i, o, u*	/z/ as in "lives"
ss, sh, ch, ce, se, ge, or *x*	/əz/ as in "teaches"

C Listen. Check (✔) the *-s* sound you hear.

TR12

	/s/ as in "eats"	/z/ as in "lives"	/əz/ as in "teaches"
1.		✔	
2.			✔
3.		✔	
4.	✔		
5.	✔		
6.		✔	
7.			✔
8.	✔		
9.			✔
10.	✔		

D Read each sentence aloud. Make sure you pronounce the third-person *-s* in the verb correctly. Then listen to the sentences to check your pronunciation.

TR13

1. Every day Jana **hears** her alarm clock.
2. She **sees** the sun.
3. She **feels** the water in the shower.
4. She **smells** coffee. She **tastes** her breakfast.
5. The brain **takes in** the information.
6. The brain **weighs** only about three pounds.

■ EXPANSION IDEA

Grammar Chart

1. Have students label the pronunciation rules A, B, C. Then have them look at each verb in Exercise D and write the letter of the corresponding pronunciation rule at the end of each sentence.

2. Write the following chart on the board:

Rule A	Rule B	Rule C
eat	lives	teaches

Have students list appropriate verbs under each rule. Tell them to start with the verbs in Exercises A and B on page 47. When they are finished, they can come up with more verbs to add to their lists.

■ GRAMMAR IN CONTENT

A Read and listen.

TR14

Right Brain vs. Left Brain

The brain has two sides. Some scientists think right-brain and left-brain people **do not think** alike.

For example, Stacy loves numbers. She studies mathematics. She is organized. She **doesn't study** the arts. She is a left-brain person.

Tomek loves photography. He studies art. He **doesn't like** mathematics. He is creative. He is a right-brain person.

Stacy and Tomek **don't think** alike. But they are good friends.

alike: the same

organized: ordered, arranged

creative: having artistic skill or imagination

The Simple Present Tense: Negative Statements

Subject	Do Not (Don't)/ Does Not (Doesn't)	Base Verb	
I You We They	do not (don't)	study	science.
He She It	does not (doesn't)	like	photography.

Notes:
• The contraction for *do not* is *don't.*
• The contraction for *does not* is *doesn't.*

■ **EXPANSION IDEA**

Exercise A

1. Have students write a short paragraph about themselves, explaining why they think they are left-brained or right-brained. Have them use the paragraphs in the reading as examples.

2. Have students find a partner who is the same as them (left-brained or right-brained). Have the students share their paragraphs with one another and talk about their similarities and differences.

The Simple Present Tense: Negative Statements

Part 3 introduces students to negative statements in the simple present tense.

■ **GRAMMAR IN CONTENT**

This section exposes students to a theme-based reading that includes examples of the target structure. Students can refer to the grammar chart(s) to complete the controlled practice activities.

■ **EXERCISE A** *Track 14*

1. Ask students to raise their hands if they enjoy art and music more than science and math. Ask students who prefer science and math to raise their hands.

2. Play the audio and have students follow along.

3. Ask students if they think they are left-brained or right-brained. Ask them to give reasons for their opinions.

■ **GRAMMAR CHART**

The Simple Present Tense: Negative Statements

1. Go over the chart and the Notes with the students.

2. Practice saying negative sentences in the simple present tense. Write *not + study/studies science* on the board. Call out different subjects such as *we, he,* and *you* and have students say a sentence combining the subject you called out and the verb phrase on the board, for example, *He doesn't study science.* Repeat with both verb phrases in the chart, making sure students use the *-s* ending with third-person singular subjects, for example, *She doesn't like photography.* (Note: *It* as a subject will not work very well with these verb phrases.)

■ EXERCISE B

Have students circle the correct verb form and share their answers with a partner before you go over the answers as a class.

■ EXERCISE C

1. Give students a few examples about yourself to get them started.
2. Ask for volunteers to share one of their sentences with the class. Repeat the sentences to reinforce the use of the third-person singular -s ending: *Did everyone hear? Tanya doesn't need cigarettes.*

■ EXERCISE D

1. Have pairs of students look at each other's sentences from Exercise C and write new sentences about their partners, using the third-person singular -s ending.
2. Ask volunteers to read one of their sentences aloud. Monitor students' pronunciation of the verb endings.

B Look at the reading "Right Brain vs. Left Brain." (Circle) the correct answer.

1. The brain ((has) / does not have) two sides.
2. Right-brain and left-brain people (think /(do not think)) alike.
3. Stacy ((likes)/ doesn't like) numbers.
4. Tomek (likes /(doesn't like)) mathematics.
5. Stacy and Tomek (think /(don't think)) alike.

C Write negative sentences about yourself. Use the verbs provided and the simple present tense. Answers will vary.

1. (study) _____
2. (live) _____
3. (need) _____
4. (enjoy) _____
5. (use) _____
6. (read) _____

D PAIR WORK Look at the sentences your partner wrote for exercise C. Make negative sentences about your partner. Answers will vary.

1. (study) _____
2. (live) _____
3. (need) _____
4. (enjoy) _____
5. (use) _____
6. (read) _____

E PAIR WORK Find ten things that are different about you and your partner.

I speak Spanish.   I don't speak Spanish.

F WRITE Write sentences about yourself and your partner. Share the list with your class.

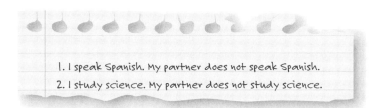

1. I speak Spanish. My partner does not speak Spanish.
2. I study science. My partner does not study science.

G WRITE Write a paragraph about things your partner does that you don't do. Use *but* to link the differences.

About Us

Francis studies photography, but I don't. I like history, but Francis doesn't. We both like math.

■ COMMUNICATE

The Communicate section allows students to practice the target grammar in more communicative, less-controlled ways through speaking and writing activities.

■ EXERCISE E

Remind students to put their pens or pencils down. Tell them that this is a speaking activity, and that they will have a chance to write in the next exercise.

■ EXERCISE F

After they write, ask pairs to come to the front of the room and each read two of their sentences.

■ EXPANSION IDEA

Exercise E

1. Have students get into groups of five or six. Have one person say something he or she likes or doesn't like. The other group members must respond with either a negative or an affirmative statement.

For example:

Student 1: *I like to study music.*
Student 2: *I don't like to study music.*
Student 3: *I like to study music, too.*
Student 4: *I don't like to study music.*

Student 5: *I don't like to study music either.*
Student 6: *I like to study music.*

Explain to students that we use *too* when we agree with positive statements and *either* when we agree with negative statements.

Connection

Putting It Together

The purpose of this section of the lesson is to connect and extend students' understanding of the grammar, vocabulary, and content from this lesson.

■ GRAMMAR AND VOCABULARY

1. Go over the directions and the example so that students understand what to do.

2. For additional suggestions on doing pair work, see the Teacher's Notes on pages xvi–xviii.

■ PROJECT

1. Go over the directions as a class. Explain that the groups will be creating displays in separate areas of the classroom.

2. On the day the projects are presented, assign each group an area of the classroom to set up their "place." Have students move around the room to experience the different "places," taking turns being the "tour guides" that stay with their own group's display to assist visitors.

3. For additional suggestions on doing projects, see the Teacher's Notes on pages xvi–xviii.

■ INTERNET

1. Remind students how to use a search engine to find the information.

2. Have students write down the Web address of the Web site with the most interesting information about the brain to share with the class.

■ VOCABULARY JOURNAL

Refer to the Pre-lesson (page 6) for an explanation of the vocabulary journal.

GRAMMAR AND VOCABULARY Work with a partner. Think of something you can see, hear, taste, or touch. Give your partner a clue about this thing. Keep giving more clues until your partner guesses the thing correctly. Use the grammar and vocabulary from this lesson.

> You see this at the beach. There is a lot of it on the beach. It's brown. It's soft.

> It's sand!

PROJECT Create a place.

1. Work with a group. Decide on a place together.
2. With your group, brainstorm a list of things you hear, see, feel, smell, and taste in this place.
3. Think of ways you can help your classmates hear, see, feel, smell, and taste these things. For example, for things you hear, you might make a recording or make the sound yourself. For things you see, you might bring in a photograph or draw a picture of things you might see at this place. Assign different students to prepare different things.
4. Set up your "place" in the classroom. Ask your classmates to say what they hear, see, feel, smell, and taste.
5. Ask your classmates to guess the place.

 INTERNET Go online. Look for more information about the brain. Use the keywords "brain" and "information" or "brain" and "facts." Tell your classmates what you learned.

VOCABULARY JOURNAL Write sentences for new vocabulary you learned in this lesson.

Example: *I hear my alarm clock every morning.*

■ EXPANSION IDEA

Internet

1. Have students try out some of the keywords other students use.

2. For additional suggestions on doing Internet activities, see the Teacher's Notes on pages xvi–xviii.

Health: Nursing

Overview

1. Elicit students' prior knowledge. Ask: *What do you think we will learn about in this lesson?*
2. Have students share their knowledge and personal experiences about going to the doctor or hospital. Possible questions you might ask include: *When do you go to the doctor? Have you ever been to the hospital? If so, what for?*

■ CONTENT VOCABULARY

Direct students' attention to the picture and the vocabulary words. Ask: *What do you see in the picture?* Help students understand the vocabulary they are not familiar with.

■ THINK ABOUT IT

1. Have students discuss the questions with a partner and then share their answers with a pair sitting next to them.
2. Have each new group of four discuss the questions together.

■ CONTENT VOCABULARY

Look at the pictures. Do you know the words?

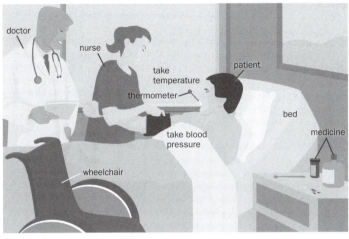

doctor
nurse
take temperature
thermometer
patient
bed
medicine
take blood pressure
wheelchair

hospital room

Write the new words in your vocabulary journal.

■ THINK ABOUT IT

Discuss these questions with a partner.

1. Where do nurses work?
2. What do nurses do?

53

■ CONTENT NOTES

The topic for this lesson is Health: Nursing. Nursing is a popular career among immigrant students because nurses are in high demand and training programs are widely available and relatively short. Below are the three different types of nursing degrees:

Diploma in Nursing: Three-year program at a hospital
Associate Degree in Nursing (ADN): Two-year program at a community college
Bachelor of Science in Nursing (BSN): Four to five year program at colleges and universities

Nurses
• provide care;
• alert other health care professionals when assistance is necessary;

• educate patients by explaining procedures and treatments;
• teach patients and families how to eat healthier;
• teach patients how to take care of themselves (take medicines, change bandages, and operate health care equipment); and
• give physical care when patients cannot take care of themselves.

Hospital nurses
• help plan patient discharge;
• help patients adapt to their conditions; and
• help patients work toward full recovery.

Nurses who work in community settings
• educate the community about transmittable illnesses, violence, obesity, and tobacco use; and
• provide maternal-child education.

PART ONE

Irregular Verbs: *Have, Go, Do*

Part 1 introduces students to the irregular verbs: *have, go,* and *do.* If necessary, refer students to the Pre-lesson (page 3) for an explanation of verbs.

■ GRAMMAR IN CONTENT

This section exposes students to a theme-based reading that includes examples of the target structure. Students can refer to the grammar chart(s) to complete the controlled practice activities.

■ EXERCISE A *Track 15*

1. Ask students to look at the picture. Ask the following questions: *Who is the person in the picture? What is he doing? Are there a lot of male nurses?*
2. Play the audio and have students follow along.
3. Have students make a list of the five things Mark does as a nurse.

■ GRAMMAR CHART
Irregular Verbs: Have, Go, Do

Go over the chart with the students. As you go through the chart, refer to the examples from the reading to reinforce the rules.

■ EXERCISE B

As you go over the answers, have students tell you why they selected the form of verb they did. (Example: Mark *has* a job . . . because Mark is *he* or *third-person singular* and we add *-s/-es* if the subject is *third-person singular.*)

■ EXERCISE C

1. Explain that some of the sentences are correct and some are not. Have students rewrite the sentences that are not correct.
2. Ask for volunteers to write their corrected sentences on the board.

PART ONE   Irregular Verbs: *Have, Go, Do*

■ GRAMMAR IN CONTENT

A Read and listen.

TR15

Mark's Job

Mark **has** a great job. He is a nurse. He works in a hospital. He **goes** to the hospital in the morning. He **does** many things. For example, he takes care of the patients. He takes their blood pressure and gives them medicine. He helps them into and out of wheelchairs. He helps the doctors. He often **goes** home late. He loves his job.

Irregular Verbs: *Have, Go, Do*

I / You / We / They . . .	He / She / It . . .
. . . **have** a job.	. . . **has** a job.
. . . **go** to class every day.	. . . **goes** to class every day.
. . . **do** homework at the library.	. . . **does** homework at the library.

B Look at the reading "Mark's Job." Complete the sentences.

1. Mark ____*has*____ a job.
2. He ____**goes**____ to the hospital in the morning.
3. He ____**does**____ many things.
4. He often ____**goes**____ home late.

C Read the sentences. If the sentence is correct, write "correct." If there is a problem, rewrite the sentence correctly.

1. Jake has a job in a hospital. _____*correct*_____
2. Jenn have a job in an office. ____**Jenn has a job in an office.**____
3. She goes to work by car. ____**correct**____
4. They has a lot of work to do. ____**They have a lot of work to do.**____
5. Jake have lunch in the cafeteria. ____**Jake has lunch in the cafeteria.**____
6. They goes home at 5:00. ____**They go home at 5:00.**____

■ EXPANSION IDEA

Exercise A

1. Have students rewrite the paragraph, changing Mark and He to *I*. Ask students whether or not they think they would enjoy working as a nurse.

D Complete the sentences. Use the correct form of *have, go,* or *do.*

Aisha and Sabina are roommates. They live

together. They ___have___ a nice apartment and
             (1)

they ___have___ good jobs. They both work in St.
        (2)

Mary's hospital. They ___go___ to work together
                        (3)

every morning.

Aisha is a doctor. She ___does___ many things
                        (4)

each day. She ___has___ many patients to take
                (5)

care of. Sabina is a nurse. She ___does___ many things for the patients and the
                                  (6)

doctors.

Sabina ___goes___ home at about 5:00 every day. She ___goes___ to the
          (7)   (8)

supermarket after work. She cooks dinner. Aisha ___goes___ home at about 7:00. They
                                                   (9)

___have___ dinner together every night. Sabina cooks. Aisha ___does___ the dishes.
   (10)   (11)

■ C O M M U N I C A T E

E **WRITE** Write a paragraph about the job of someone you know. Use *have, go,* and
do in the paragraph. Answer these questions:

• What job does the person have?
• Where does he or she go every day?
• What does he or she do?

Tell your class about the job.

---

1. Have students fill in the blanks with the correct forms of *have, go,* and *do.* Call on students to read their paragraphs aloud with the correct answers.

2. Reinforce vocabulary collocations by writing phrases containing the irregular verbs on the board as students say them, for example, *have good jobs* and *go to work.*

■ **COMMUNICATE**

The Communicate section allows students to practice the target grammar in more communicative, less-controlled ways through speaking and writing activities.

■ **EXERCISE E**

Model this exercise on the board using a person you know.

For example:

My friend Joshua is a bank teller. Everyday he goes to the bank. He helps customers make deposits and withdrawals. He counts money. He puts money in the ATM. Joshua likes his job.

■ **EXPANSION IDEA**

Exercise E
1. If students in the class have jobs, have them interview each other and write paragraphs. Otherwise, ask students to imagine they have a job before they answer their classmates' questions. Ask for volunteers to share their paragraphs with the class.

PART TWO

Prepositions of Time: *In, On, At*

Part 2 introduces students to prepositions of time.

■ EXERCISE A *Track 16* 🎧

1. Have students cover up the reading with a piece of paper and look at the picture.
2. Ask students what they see in the picture and write the sentences they say on the board.
3. Do not tell students why you are doing it, but underline all the prepositions in the sentences on the board.
4. Have students listen to the recording with the reading still covered.
5. After students have heard the recording, ask them: *What does Linda do?*
6. Have students uncover the reading and read it to themselves to see how much they remember.

■ GRAMMAR CHART

Prepositions of Time: In, On, At

1. Go over the chart with the students. As you go through the chart, refer to the reading for examples.
2. For each section of the chart, ask students questions that will allow them to practice the form. For example, to practice the use of *in*, ask: *When do you eat breakfast?* They should respond: *in the morning.* To practice the use of *on*, ask: *When is New Year's Day?* They should respond: *on January 1.*

■ EXERCISE B

Have students choose the correct preposition for each sentence and check their answers with a partner.

■ GRAMMAR IN CONTENT

🎧 **A** **Read and listen.**

TR16

Just Relax!

John: You need to relax more.

Linda: When? I take classes **in the morning**. I work at the hospital **in the afternoon**. I get home **at 6:00** every day. I do housework **in the evening**. I study **at night** and **on the weekend**. There is no time to relax!

relax: to stop working and enjoy oneself

Prepositions of Time: *In, On, At*	
Preposition	**Explanation**
in the morning **in** the afternoon **in** the evening **in** March **in** 2006	Use **in** with parts of the day and with months and years.
on Monday **on** weekends **on** January 3	Use **on** with days of the week, groups of days, and dates.
at 3:30 **at** night	Use **at** with times of day and with "night."

Note:
We often use "it" to talk about time, days, months, and years. Example: *It is April 8. It is 5:00.*

B **Complete the sentences. Use *in, on,* or *at*.**

1. John goes to school ___*on*___ Monday, Wednesday, and Friday.
2. His classes are ___**in**___ the afternoon.
3. His first class starts ___**at**___ 1:00.
4. John has an appointment with his advisor ___**on**___ September 4.

■ EXPANSION IDEA

Exercise B

1. Write the following questions on the board and divide the class into small groups to ask and answer them. Instruct students to use *in, on,* or *at* in their answers.

Questions:

When is your birthday?

What time do you do your homework?

What time do you usually go to bed?

When do you work?

When did you start studying English?

5. The appointment is __in__ the morning.

6. The appointment is __at__ 9:00.

C Read Linda's schedule. Complete the sentences. Use *in, on,* or *at* and the correct information.

Schedule	Monday	Tuesday	Wednesday	Thursday	Friday
8:00–9:30	Anatomy	Biology	Anatomy	Biology	Anatomy
10:00–11:30	Study	Psychology	Study	Psychology	Study
12:00–12:30	Lunch	Lunch	Lunch	Lunch	Lunch
1:00–5:00	Work at the hospital	Work at the hospital	Work at the hospital	Work at the hospital	Work at the hospital

1. Linda's classes start __at__ __8:00__ every day.

2. She has biology class __on__ __Tuesday__ and __Thursday__.

3. She has anatomy class __on__ __Monday__, __Wednesday__, and __Friday__.

4. She eats lunch __at__ __12:00__ every day.

5. She finishes work __at__ __5:00__.

D Complete the sentences with information about yourself.   Answers will vary.

1. My birthday is in _____.

2. My birthday is on _____.

3. I get up at _____.

4. I have English class on _____.

5. My English class is at _____.

6. I get home at _____.

7. I _____ in the evening.

8. I _____ on the weekend.

■ C O M M U N I C A T E

E **WRITE** Write your schedule for an average weekend. What do you do? Tell your class about your schedule.

Have students complete the sentences about Linda's schedule aloud with a partner before writing the answers in their books. Once both partners agree, have them write the answers in their books.

■ **EXERCISE D**

Have students complete the sentences and share their answers with a partner.

■ **COMMUNICATE**

The Communicate section allows students to practice the target grammar in more communicative, less-controlled ways through speaking and writing activities.

■ **EXERCISE E**

1. Help students get started by drawing a blank weekend schedule on the board. Include some times and some labels such as *morning, afternoon,* and *evening.*

2. Have students stand up and read their schedule aloud to the class.

■ **EXPANSION IDEAS**

Exercise C

1. Have students copy the schedule and fill in their own personal information.

2. Then have them switch schedules with a partner.

3. Have students write five sentences similar to the ones in Exercise C about their partner's schedule.

Exercise D

1. Have students work with the same partners and interview them to complete the sentences as in Exercise D.

2. Have students ask you questions about yourself to elicit the answers in Exercise D. For example, students ask: *When is your birthday?* You respond: *My birthday is in July.*

Connection

Putting It Together

The purpose of this section of the lesson is to connect and extend students' understanding of the grammar, vocabulary, and content from this lesson.

■ GRAMMAR AND VOCABULARY

1. Ask students what is happening in the pictures.
2. Explain to students that they will write a paragraph about the person in one of the pictures.

■ PROJECT

1. Go through each step of the project with students, making sure they understand what they are supposed to do.
2. When students have finished their schedules, pair them with another student to do the third step.

■ INTERNET

1. Have students do this activity alone or in pairs.
2. Provide the names of local hospitals to help students search for information.
3. Have students report the information they find to the class.

■ VOCABULARY JOURNAL

Refer to the Pre-lesson (page 6) for an explanation of the vocabulary journal.

GRAMMAR AND VOCABULARY Choose one of the pictures. Write a paragraph about the picture. Make up information about the person's job and schedule. Use the grammar and vocabulary from this lesson.

paramedic

nurse

doctor

PROJECT Create and discuss a schedule.

1. Fill in the schedule with your own activities and appointments for this week.
2. Work with a partner. Imagine you want to study together this week.
3. Discuss your schedules and find a few times when you both can meet to study.

	Monday	Tuesday	Wednesday	Thursday	Friday	Saturday	Sunday
8:00 – 10:00							
10:00 – 12:00							
12:00 – 2:00							
2:00 – 4:00							
4:00 – 6:00							
6:00 – 8:00							

 INTERNET Go online. Search for a hospital near where you live. Find information about the hospital. Tell your class about what you learned.

VOCABULARY JOURNAL Write sentences for new vocabulary you learned in this lesson.

Example: *Sick people take medicine.*

■ EXPANSION IDEAS

Project

1. Show students how to create their schedule on the computer using a table in Word or a spreadsheet in Excel.
2. For additional suggestions on doing projects, see the Teacher's Notes on pages xvi–xviii.

Internet

1. Have students find the hospital that is closest to their home in case of an emergency.
2. Discuss ways to get to the hospital; for example, talk about how to call an ambulance or a taxi.

PART 1
The Simple Present Tense:
Yes/No Questions and Short
Answers

PART 2
Simple Present *Wh-* Questions

Lesson ⑧

Media: Television

Lesson ⑧

■ CONTENT VOCABULARY

Look at the pictures. Do you know these words?

reality show

sitcom

watch TV inside

news

sports

play outside

nature

game show

turn on/off

Write the new words in your vocabulary journal.

■ THINK ABOUT IT

Do you watch television? If so, do you watch: **Answers will vary.**

____ less than one hour
a day?

____ one to two hours
a day?

____ more than two
hours a day?

59

Overview

1. Elicit students' prior knowledge. Ask: *What do you think we will learn about in this lesson?*

2. Have students get into small groups and make a list of television programs they watch in English. Ask for groups to share their lists by going to the board and writing the names of the programs.

■ CONTENT VOCABULARY

1. Ask: *How often do you watch television? What else do you do in your free time?*

2. Direct students' attention to the pictures and vocabulary words. Describe and give examples of any of the TV genres that are unfamiliar to students.

■ THINK ABOUT IT

1. Have students check the phrase that describes their TV viewing habits and then share their answers with a partner.

2. Go over the answers as a class.

■ CONTENT NOTES

Media

The topic for this lesson is Media: Television. Television and movies are a large part of American culture and affect the way people from other countries perceive Americans.

Possible discussion topics:
1. differences between television in America and in other countries

2. students' initial opinions of Americans based on American TV programs

3. students' opinions about children watching television

4. students' opinions about sex and violence on television

Part 1 introduces students to simple present *yes/no* questions and short answers.

■ GRAMMAR IN CONTENT

This section exposes students to a theme-based reading that includes examples of the target structure. Students can refer to the grammar chart(s) to complete the controlled practice activities.

■ EXERCISE A *Track 17*

1. Ask students to close their books. Write the word *interview* on the board and ask students what it means. They may come up with different types of interviews, such as job interviews or surveys, but be sure they also think about a television or radio host asking questions of a celebrity, a politician, or an expert in some field.

2. Play the audio. Ask students what the interview was about.

3. Have students open their books and read the interview.

■ GRAMMAR CHARTS

***The Simple Present Tense:
Yes/No Questions and
Affirmative and Negative
Short Answers***

Go over the charts with the students. As you review the charts, refer to the examples from the reading to reinforce the rules.

PART ONE	The Simple Present Tense: *Yes/No* Questions and Short Answers

■ GRAMMAR IN CONTENT

A Read and listen.

TR17

Interview with a Media Professor: Part 1

Interviewer: **Do** American children **watch** a lot of television?

Dr. Teleno: **Yes,** they **do.** Most of them watch three hours or more of TV a day.

Interviewer: **Do** you **think** television is bad for children?

Dr. Teleno: **Yes, I do.** Some programs are not good for children. Some children watch too much television. These children don't read enough. They also don't play outside enough.

Interviewer: **Do** some programs **help** children learn?

Dr. Teleno: **Yes,** they **do.** Some programs help children read.

enough: plenty, as much as needed

The Simple Present Tense: *Yes/No* Questions

Do/Does	Subject	
Do	I you we they	watch TV?
Does	he she it	

Affirmative and Negative Short Answers

Yes	Subject	Do/Don't	No	Subject	Do/Don't
Yes,	you I we they	do.	No,	you I we they	don't.
	he she it	does.		he she it	doesn't.

■ EXPANSION IDEA

Exercise A

1. Have students practice the interview with a partner. Then have partners switch roles so that they practice both parts of the interview.

2. Have students form small groups and discuss the following questions:
   1. Do children watch a lot of television?
   2. Do you think television is bad for children? If so, why?
   3. Do you think some programs help children learn? If so, which ones?
   4. What kinds of programs are bad for children?

B Look at the dialogue "Interview with a Media Professor: Part 1." Answer the questions with short answers.

1. Do American children watch a lot of television? _____ Yes, they do.
2. Do they watch one hour of TV a day? _____ No, they don't.
3. Do they watch three hours of TV a day? _____ Yes, they do.
4. Does Dr. Teleno think television is bad for children? _____ Yes, he does.
5. Do some programs help children learn? _____ Yes, they do.

C PAIR WORK Answer the questions about yourself. Use short answers. Then ask your partner the questions. Complete the chart with short answers. Answers will vary.

	Me	My Partner
1. Do you like television?		
2. Do you watch the news?		
3. Do you watch sitcoms?		
4. Do you watch reality shows?		
5. Do you eat dinner with the television on?		
6. Do you study with the television on?		
7. Do you watch too much television?		

D Put the words in the correct order.

1. at night / you / do / watch television _____ Do you watch television at night ?
2. no / don't / I _____ No , _____ I don't .
3. send e-mails / you / do / at night _____ Do you send e-mail at night ?
4. don't / no / I _____ No , _____ I don't .
5. study / do / at night / you _____ Do you study at night ?
6. I / do / yes _____ Yes , _____ I do !

EXERCISE B

1. Have students write short answers based on the interview and check their answers with a partner.
2. Give students a chance to practice saying short answers by asking the questions aloud and calling on different students to respond.

EXERCISE C

1. Have students complete the chart with information about themselves first and then with information they get from interviewing a partner.
2. Ask each pair to share their responses with another pair of students.
3. Conduct a class discussion by polling the class on their answers, for example, ask: *How many of you study with the television on? Really? Only two people study with the television on? Sandy, why do you like the television on when you study?*

EXERCISE D

1. Ask for volunteers to write their sentences on the board. If there are mistakes in the sentences, ask for other volunteers to come up and fix the mistakes.
2. Have students practice asking and answering the questions in pairs.

EXPANSION IDEAS

Exercise B

1. Have students write an interview similar to the one on page 60, but with their own opinions.

Exercise C

1. Have students write two more questions like the ones in Exercise C.
2. Have students individually ask five students in the class their two questions.
3. Have students report their findings to the class.

■ EXERCISE E

1. Have volunteers ask you their questions. Give them short answers about yourself.

2. Ask the volunteers who supplied the questions to write them on the board.

3. Ask students to close their books and have pairs ask each other the questions on the board. This will encourage students to look up at their partners when speaking.

■ COMMUNICATE

The Communicate section allows students to practice the target grammar in more communicative, less-controlled ways through speaking and writing activities.

■ EXERCISE F

Have students get up and walk around the room for this activity. Model the exercise with a few students before you ask students to do it on their own. Explain to students that they must find a person who says *Yes, I do* before they can write anything in the chart. Encourage them not to write the same name down for every question. In fact, you might tell them they can only ask each classmate one question.

E Write *Yes/No* questions.

1. you / have / a television _____ Do you have a television?

2. you / rent / videos _____ **Do you rent videos?**

3. you / watch / television in the evening **Do you watch television in the evening?**

4. you / like / sitcoms _____ **Do you like sitcoms?**

5. your wife / like / sports _____ **Does your wife like sports?**

6. she / control / the remote control _____ **Does she control the remote control?**

■ COMMUNICATE

F GROUP WORK What do your classmates do on the weekend? Ask your classmates *Yes/No* questions using the words in the chart. For each question, find a student who answers "Yes, I do." Write the student's name in the chart. Then report back to your class.

Do you . . .		Student's Name
	. . . watch TV?	
	. . . use the Internet?	
	. . . exercise at a gym?	
	. . . jog?	
	. . . garden?	
	. . . play an instrument?	

■ EXPANSION IDEA

Exercise E

1. Have students walk around the room and interview classmates using the questions from Exercise E.

■ GRAMMAR IN CONTENT

A Read and listen.

TR18

Interview with a Media Professor: Part 2
Interviewer:	Do your children watch TV during the week?
Dr. Teleno:	No, they don't.
Interviewer:	**When do** they watch television?
Dr. Teleno:	They only watch television on weekends.
Interviewer:	**Why do** they watch TV only on weekends?
Dr. Teleno:	I want my children to do their homework and play outside.
Interviewer:	**What do** your children watch?
Dr. Teleno:	My daughter likes cartoons.
Interviewer:	**What does** your son like?
Dr. Teleno:	He likes nature programs.
Interviewer:	**Where do** they watch TV?
Dr. Teleno:	In the living room.

The Simple Present Tense: *Wh-* Questions

Wh- Word	Do/Does	Subject	Base Verb	Answers		
What	do	you	watch?	The news.	OR	I watch the news.
Where	does	she	live?	In California.	OR	She lives in California.
When	do	we	eat?	At 7:00.	OR	We eat at 7:00.
Who	does	he	love?	Marta.	OR	He loves Marta.
How	do	you	feel?	Good.	OR	I feel good.
Why	do	you	study?	(Because) I want good grades.		

Note:
When *Who* or *What* is the subject of a question, don't add *do* or *does* before the verb.
Example: *Who watches television?* (NOT: ~~Who does watch television?~~)

B Look at the dialogue "Interview with a Media Professor: Part 2." Complete the questions. Then write answers to the questions.

1. When ___do___ Dr. Teleno's children watch TV? _____Only on weekends._____

2. Why __do__ her children watch television only on weekends?
   _____**Because they do their homework and play outside.**_____

3. What __do__ her children watch? _____**Cartoons and nature programs.**_____

■ **EXPANSION IDEAS**

Exercise A
1. Have students practice the interview with a partner.

Grammar Chart
1. Have students practice the questions and answers with a partner using the short and long answers from the chart. Then have them practice again, giving their own answers.

Simple Present *Wh-* Questions
Part 2 introduces students to simple present *wh-* questions.

■ **GRAMMAR IN CONTENT**

This section allows students to refer to the grammar chart(s) to complete a number of controlled practice activities.

■ **EXERCISE A** *Track 18*
1. Have students read the conversation before you play the recording.
2. Play the recording.
3. Ask students the following questions requiring short *yes/no* answers.

Do Dr. Teleno's children watch TV during the week? (Yes, they do.)
Do they watch TV on Tuesdays? (No, they don't.)
Does his daughter watch the news? (No, she doesn't.)
Does his son watch nature programs? (Yes, he does.)
Do they watch TV in the bedroom? (No, they don't.)

■ **GRAMMAR CHART**
The Simple Present Tense:
Wh- Questions

Go over the chart with the students. Go over the Note. As you go through both of these, refer to the examples from the reading to reinforce the rules.

■ **EXERCISE B**

Once students have completed the activity and have the correct answers, have them practice the questions and answers with a partner.

Once students have completed the
activity and have the correct answers,
have them practice the questions and
answers with a different partner.

Once students have completed the
activity and have the correct answers,
have them practice the questions and
answers with a different partner.

4. What **does** her son like? _____ **Nature programs**

5. Where **do** the children watch TV? _____ **In the living room**

C Complete the questions. Write *wh-* words.

1. **Q:** _Who_ do you live with? **A:** I live with my husband and son.

2. **Q:** _What_ do you study? **A:** I study computer science.

3. **Q:** _Why_ do you study computer science? **A:** Because I love computers.

4. **Q:** _How_ do you relax? **A:** I watch television.

5. **Q:** _What_ do you watch? **A:** I watch reality TV programs.

6. **Q:** _Where_ does your husband work? **A:** He works in an office.

7. **Q:** _How_ does he relax? **A:** He reads the newspaper and watches the news.

8. **Q:** _What_ does your son watch on TV? **A:** He watches cartoons.

D Complete the dialogue. Write *wh-* questions.

A: There's an interesting program on TV. It's about kangaroos.

B: Really? _Where do kangaroos live_ ?
(1)

A: Kangaroos live in Australia, Tasmania, and New Guinea.

B: _____ **What do they eat** _____ ?
(2)

A: They eat grass and leaves.

B: _____ **When do they eat** _____ ?
(3)

A: They eat in the late afternoon and early evening.

B: _____ **What do they do** _____ during the day?
(4)

A: During the day they rest in the shade.

B: _____ **How do they** _____ get from one place to another?
(5)

A: They hop!

B: _____ **How do they** _____ communicate?
(6)

A: They thump their feet.

EXPANSION IDEAS

Exercise C

1. Have students walk around the room and ask different classmates the questions from Exercise C. Have students give real answers instead of the ones in the book.

Exercise D

1. Have students work with a partner to write a short dialogue. Give them the following topics as options:

- the weather in their country
- the current president of the United States
- their school
- a class they are taking

Ask for volunteers to perform their dialogue for the class.

E **PAIR WORK** Write questions. Ask a partner each question. Write your partner's answers. **Answers will vary.**

1. When / get up?

    Question: _____ *When do you get up?*

    Answer: _____ *Petra gets up at 7:00.*

2. What / eat for breakfast?

    Question: _____ **What do you eat for breakfast?**

    Answer: _____

3. Who / live with?

    Question: _____ **Who do you live with?**

    Answer: _____

4. How / get to school?

    Question: _____ **How do you get to school?**

    Answer: _____

5. What / do on weekends?

    Question: _____ **What do you do on weekends?**

    Answer: _____

6. When / study?

    Question: _____ **When do you study?**

    Answer: _____

■ **COMMUNICATE**

F **PAIR WORK** Ask your partner, "What do you do on the weekend?" Then interview your partner with *wh*- questions to find out more. Take notes.

What do you do on the weekend?

Where do you go shopping?

I study and go shopping.

■ **EXERCISE E**

1. Model this activity with students, using the example.
2. Have students unscramble the questions by themselves before you direct them to ask each other the questions.

■ **COMMUNICATE**

The Communicate section allows students to practice the target grammar in more communicative, less-controlled ways through speaking and writing activities.

■ **EXERCISE F**

1. Help students brainstorm some other possible questions they might ask their partners about the weekend.
2. Show students how to take notes as opposed to writing down the whole sentence his or her partner says.

■ **EXPANSION IDEA**

Exercise F

1. Have students write a paragraph about their partner based on the information they gathered in Exercise F.

Connection

Putting It Together

The purpose of this section of the lesson is to connect and extend students' understanding of the grammar, vocabulary, and content from this lesson.

■ GRAMMAR AND VOCABULARY

1. Go over the examples in the book.
2. As a class, discuss some other possible questions students might ask their partners.

■ PROJECT

1. Since this is a class project, do the first two steps together as a class.
2. For step 2, ask for a volunteer to write down the number of votes on the board.
3. Have each student make a bar graph with the information learned from the class poll.
4. If possible, tape the bar graphs to the classroom walls and invite students to walk around and see their classmates' work.
5. For additional suggestions on doing projects, see the Teacher's Notes on pages xvi–xviii.

■ INTERNET

1. For this activity, you may want to make suggestions about good Web sites for students to visit.
2. Have students work alone or in pairs to find the information.
3. Ask students to share their answers with the class to see if they found the same information.

■ VOCABULARY JOURNAL

Refer to the Pre-lesson (page 6) for an explanation of the vocabulary journal.

GRAMMAR AND VOCABULARY Work with a partner. Ask your partner questions about his or her television habits. Use the grammar and vocabulary from this lesson.

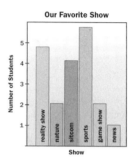

Do you like television?
When do you watch television?
Yes, I do.

PROJECT Create a bar graph about favorite TV shows.

1. With your class, discuss the following kinds of programs: reality shows, sitcoms, news, sports, nature shows, and game shows.
2. For each kind of show, take a vote: Who likes this kind of show best? Count the number of students who say it is their favorite.
3. Make a bar graph to show the results of your vote.

Our Favorite Show

Number of Students (y-axis: 1–5)

reality show, nature, sitcom, sports, game show, news

Show

 INTERNET Go online. Find out what is on television tonight. Use the keywords "television schedule." Imagine you will watch television tonight. Choose the programs you will watch.

VOCABULARY JOURNAL Write sentences for new vocabulary you learned in this lesson.

Example: *I think sitcoms are funny.*

■ EXPANSION IDEAS

Grammar and Vocabulary

1. Have students make a list of five interview questions they can ask their classmates about television viewing habits.
2. Have students walk around and interview three students, writing the answers down.
3. Ask for volunteers to share what they learned about their classmates.

Internet

1. Have each student take the information they learned from the Internet and write a short paragraph about American TV watching habits.
2. For additional suggestions on Internet activities, see the Teacher's Notes on pages xvi–xviii.

PART 1
The Present Tense of *Be* vs. the Simple Present Tense: Statements

PART 2
The Present Tense of *Be* vs. the Simple Present Tense: *Yes/No* Questions and Short Answers

PART 3
The Present Tense of *Be* vs. the Simple Present Tense: *Wh-* Questions

Lesson 9

Biology: Studying Animals

■ CONTENT VOCABULARY

Look at the pictures. Do you know the words?

chimpanzee

elephant

nest

nuts

fruits

mice

leaves

insects

Write the new words in your vocabulary journal.

■ THINK ABOUT IT

Discuss these questions with a partner.

1. Do animals think?
2. What animal is most like people?

67

Lesson 9

Overview

Elicit students' prior knowledge. Ask: *What do you think we will learn about in this lesson?*

■ CONTENT VOCABULARY

1. Direct students' attention to the pictures and vocabulary words. Ask: *Have you seen any of these animals before? If so, where? Why do you think the fruits, nuts, and leaves are pictured here?*
2. In small teams, have students come up with 1) more animal words they know, and 2) names of different insects.

■ THINK ABOUT IT

Have students answer the questions with a partner and then share their ideas with the class.

■ CONTENT NOTES

Biology

The topic for this lesson is Biology: Studying Animals. In this lesson, students will learn about the following researchers and the animals they study.

Jane Goodall: chimpanzees
Cynthia Moss: elephants
Sue Savage-Rumbaugh: chimpanzees

Note: It is not necessary to explain (or understand for that matter) technical aspects of animal biology in order to teach this lesson well. The lesson will explain everything students need to know. If students want more information about the researchers, they can gather it at the end of the lesson during the Internet activity.

PART ONE

The Present Tense of *Be* vs. the Simple Present Tense: Statements

Part 1 introduces students to the present tense of *be* vs. statements in the present tense.

■ GRAMMAR IN CONTENT

This section exposes students to a theme-based reading that includes examples of the target structure. Students can refer to the grammar chart(s) to complete the controlled practice activities.

■ EXERCISE A *Track 19*

1. Ask students to look at the pictures. Ask the following question: *Do you know who these women are?*
2. Play the audio and have students follow along.
3. Ask the following questions: *Who are Jane and Cynthia? What do they study? What does Jane Goodall study? What does Cynthia Moss study? Where do they study animals?*

■ GRAMMAR CHART

The Present Tense of Be *vs. the Simple Present Tense: Statements*

1. Go over the chart and the Note with the students. As you go through both of these, refer to the examples from the reading to reinforce the rules.
2. Ask students for additional examples using the structures in the chart. For example, go over the first example in the chart, *I am a biology professor,* and write the words *I am* on the board. Get students started by saying, *I am an English teacher.* Then have students provide examples, such as *I am a student; I am from Thailand;* and so on.

■ GRAMMAR IN CONTENT

A Read and listen.

TR19

Jane Goodall

Cynthia Moss

Two Famous Animal Researchers

Jane Goodall and Cynthia Moss **are** animal researchers. They **study** animals in Africa. Jane Goodall **studies** chimpanzees in Tanzania. Cynthia Moss **studies** elephants in Kenya.

Goodall and Moss **do** important work. Their work **helps** us understand chimpanzees and elephants.

researcher: person who studies something

The Present Tense of *Be* vs. the Simple Present Tense: Statements		
	Present Tense of *Be*	**Simple Present Tense**
Affirmative	I **am** a biology professor. He **is** a researcher.	I **teach** biology. He **studies** elephants.
Negative	I **am not** a researcher. He **is not** a biology professor.	I **do not** study elephants. He **does not** teach biology.

Note:
Don't use *be* with a simple present tense verb.
Example: *I study English.* (NOT: ~~I am study English.~~)

B Look at each sentence. Is the sentence the present tense of *be* or the simple present tense? Circle the correct answer.

1. Jane Goodall is an animal researcher. (Present Tense of *Be*) / Simple Present Tense
2. Goodall and Moss study animals in Africa. Present Tense of *Be* / (Simple Present Tense)
3. She works with chimpanzees in Tanzania. Present Tense of *Be* / (Simple Present Tense)
4. Goodall and Moss do important work. Present Tense of *Be* / (Simple Present Tense)

68   LESSON 9 | Biology: Studying Animals

■ EXPANSION IDEA

Exercise A

1. Have students rewrite the first paragraph of the reading in first person, changing the subjects to *I* and supplying their own information about what and where they study.

2. Have students share their paragraphs with a partner.

3. Have students write the paragraph again using their partner's information. Remind them to use the third-person singular *-s* ending.

C Read the sentences comparing two animal researchers. Fill in the blanks with the correct form of the underlined word(s).

1. I study chimpanzees. Dr. Ito _____studies_____ mice.

2. I do not study mice. Dr. Ito _____does not study_____ chimpanzees.

3. He works with laboratory animals. I _____do not work_____ with wild animals.

4. He does not work with wild animals. I _____do not work_____ with laboratory animals.

5. I am from the United States. He _____is_____ from Japan.

6. I am not from Japan. He _____is not_____ from the United States.

7. He speaks Japanese. I _____speak_____ English.

8. He does not speak English. I _____don't speak_____ Japanese.

9. I am married. He _____is_____ single.

10. I am not single. He _____is not_____ married.

D Correct the composition. Cross out wrong words. Add missing words. (Hint: There are five more mistakes.)

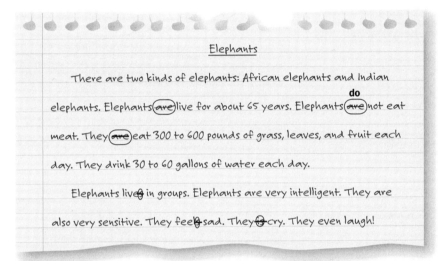

Elephants

There are two kinds of elephants: African elephants and Indian elephants. Elephants ~~are~~ live for about 65 years. Elephants ~~are~~ **do** not eat meat. They ~~are~~ eat 300 to 600 pounds of grass, leaves, and fruit each day. They drink 30 to 60 gallons of water each day.

Elephants live~~s~~ in groups. Elephants are very intelligent. They are also very sensitive. They feel~~s~~ sad. They ~~is~~ cry. They even laugh!

■ **EXERCISE C**

Have students complete the activity and check their answers with a partner.

■ **EXERCISE D**

Give students time to find all six mistakes. Then ask for volunteers to write the mistakes and their corrections to them on the board.

■ COMMUNICATE

The Communicate section allows students to practice the target grammar in more communicative, less-controlled ways through speaking and writing activities.

■ EXERCISE E

1. Do a brainstorm with the class to show students how to generate ideas before they write.
2. Have students write their paragraphs using the target grammar structures.
3. Ask for volunteers to share their paragraphs with the class.

PART TWO

The Present Tense of *Be* vs. the Simple Present Tense: *Yes/No* Questions and Short Answers

Part 2 introduces students to *yes/no* questions and short answers with the present tense of *be* and the simple present tense.

■ GRAMMAR IN CONTENT

■ EXERCISE A *Track 20*

1. Have students read and listen to the interview.
2. Have pairs practice the conversation.

■ GRAMMAR CHART

The Present Tense of Be *vs. the Simple Present Tense: Yes/No Questions and Short Answers*

1. Review the chart and the Note with the students. As you go through, refer them to the examples from the reading to reinforce the rules.
2. Practice the question and answer structures with students. Ask questions such as: *Roger, are you a soccer player? Amy, is Hany an artist? Nathan, do you study nursing?* Monitor students' short answers for accuracy.

■ C O M M U N I C A T E

E WRITE Write a paragraph about an animal you know. What is the animal? What does it look like? What does it do? Use the present tense of *be* and the simple present tense. Tell your class about the animal. **Answers will vary.**

PART TWO	The Present Tense of *Be* vs. the Simple Present Tense: *Yes/No* Questions and Short Answers

■ G R A M M A R   I N   C O N T E N T

 A Read and listen.

TR20

Sue Savage Rumbaugh and Kanzi

Question:	Who is Sue Savage Rumbaugh?
Answer:	She's an animal researcher.
Question:	Who is Kanzi?
Answer:	Kanzi is a chimpanzee she works with.
Question:	**Is** he intelligent?
Answer:	Yes, he **is.**
Question:	**Does** Kanzi **understand** language?
Answer:	Yes, he **does.**
Question:	**Does** he **speak?**
Answer:	No, he **doesn't** speak.
Question:	How does he talk to people?
Answer:	He uses a special keyboard.
Question:	Why does she work with chimpanzees?
Answer:	Because chimpanzees and humans have similar brains.

keyboard: a row of keys

The Present Tense of *Be* vs. the Simple Present Tense: *Yes/No* Questions and Short Answers

	Yes/No Questions	Short Answers		
The Present Tense of Be	Are you a biology professor? Is he a biology professor?	Yes, I am. Yes, he is.	OR OR	No, I'm not. No, he isn't.
The Simple Present Tense	Do you **teach** biology? Does he **teach** biology?	Yes, I do. Yes, he does.	OR OR	No, I don't. No, he doesn't.

Note:
Don't use *be* with a simple present tense verb in a question.
Example: *Do you teach biology?* (NOT: ~~Are you teach biology?~~)

■ EXPANSION IDEAS

Exercise E
1. Have students type their paragraphs on the computer.
2. Have students search for a picture of their animal and insert it into the document.

Grammar Chart
1. Have students practice the questions and answers from the chart with each other.
2. Have students ask their classmates *yes/no* questions that are not in the chart and get their answers. (Are you a chef? Are you a secretary? Do you study math?)

B Look again at the dialogue "Sue Savage Rumbaugh and Kanzi." Answer the questions. Use short answers.

1. Is Sue Savage Rumbaugh an animal researcher? _____ Yes, she is. _____

2. Is Kanzi an animal researcher? _____ No, he isn't. _____

3. Is Kanzi a chimpanzee? _____ Yes, he is. _____

4. Does he speak? _____ No, he doesn't. _____

5. Does he understand language? _____ Yes, he does. _____

6. Do humans and chimpanzees have similar brains? _____ Yes, they do. _____

C Fill in the missing words in the questions and answers. Use *am, is, are, do, does, don't,* or *doesn't.*

1. _Are_ you a biologist? Yes, I _am_ .

2. _Do_ you work in a laboratory? No, I _don't_ .

3. _Do_ you study animals? Yes, I _do_ .

4. _Do_ you study chimpanzees? Yes, I _do_ .

5. _Are_ chimpanzees smart? Yes, they _are_ .

6. _Do_ chimpanzees live alone? No, they _don't_ .

7. _Do_ they live in groups? Yes, they _do_ .

8. _Is_ your work interesting? Yes, it _is_ .

■ C O M M U N I C A T E

D **PAIR WORK** Choose an animal. Your partner will ask *Yes/No* questions to try to guess the animal. Take turns. Answers will vary.

Does the animal live in North America? — Yes, it does.

Is it large? — No, it isn't.

Does it live in trees? — Yes, it does.

Is it a squirrel? — Yes, it is!

Have students practice asking and answering the questions with a partner.

Once students have completed the activity, go over the answers as a class and practice the intonation.

■ **COMMUNICATE**

The Communicate section allows students to practice the target grammar in more communicative, less-controlled ways through speaking and writing activities.

■ **EXERCISE D**

1. First, model the activity with a few students.

2. After students have worked together for about ten minutes, ask for volunteers to come up to the front of the class and answer questions about their animal.

■ **EXPANSION IDEA**

Exercise C

1. Have students work in pairs to ask and answer the questions. First, have Student A ask the questions and Student B give the answers. Have student B cover the exercise in the book while answering the questions. Then have students switch roles.

The Present Tense of *Be* vs. the Simple Present Tense: *Wh-* Questions

Part 3 introduces students to *wh-* questions using the present tense of *be* and the simple present tense.

■ GRAMMAR CHART

The Present Tense of Be *vs. the Simple Present Tense:* Wh- *Questions*

1. Go over the chart and the Note with the students.
2. Write several subjects on the board. For example, write: *the cafeteria, Anna and Jim, you, Buenos Aires, my books,* and *the moon.* Call on students to answer questions with *Where is* and *Where are.* For example, ask: *Where is the cafeteria?* Then have volunteers ask questions using the subjects you wrote on the board or new ones they think of.
3. Next, write a number of verbs and verbs plus objects on the board. For example, write: *study the map, work, go shopping.* Call on students to answer questions with *Where does* and *Where do.* For example, ask: *Where does your best friend work?* Then have volunteers ask questions using the verbs you wrote on the board or new ones.

■ EXERCISE A

Have students complete this exercise with a partner.

■ EXERCISE B

1. First, have students share their answers with a partner.
2. Then review the answers as a class. Give students speaking time by directing Student A to call on Student B to answer the first question. After Student B answers, he or she should then call on Student C to answer the next question, and so on.

The Present Tense of *Be* vs. the Simple Present Tense: *Wh-* Questions	
Wh- Questions with Present Tense of *Be*	*Wh-* Questions in the Simple Present Tense
Where is she? Where are they?	Where does she live? Where do they live?

Note:
Don't use *be* with a simple present tense verb in a question.
Example: *Where do they live?* (NOT: ~~*Where are they live?*~~)

A Look at the dialogue "Sue Savage Rumbaugh and Kanzi" on page 70. <u>Underline</u> the *wh-* questions with *be.* (Circle) the *wh-* questions in the simple present tense.

B Fill in the missing word in each question. Use *is, am, are, do,* or *does.*

1. **Q:** Where ___do___ chimpanzees live?

   A: Chimpanzees live in 21 African countries.

2. **Q:** What ___is___ the Afrikaans word for "chimpanzee"?

   A: Sjimpansee.

3. **Q:** What ___do___ chimpanzees eat?

   A: Fruits, nuts, leaves, insects, and sometimes meat.

4. **Q:** How ___do___ they communicate?

   A: With sounds and their bodies.

5. **Q:** Where ___are___ baby chimpanzees born?

   A: In a nest.

6. **Q:** How ___does___ a mother chimpanzee carry her baby?

   A: She carries the baby near her belly.

7. **Q:** How ___does___ a chimpanzee show love?

   A: Chimpanzees kiss and hug.

8. **Q:** How ___are___ chimpanzees and humans similar?

   A: The genes of chimpanzees and humans are 98% the same.

■ EXPANSION IDEA

Exercise B

1. Have students write questions similar to the ones in the exercise but with different topics.

For example:

1. *Where do elephants live?*
2. *What do dogs eat?*

C Make questions for each statement.

1. **A:** My name is Svetlana.

   Q: What _____ *is your name* _____?

2. **A:** I speak Russian.

   Q: What language _____ **do you speak** _____?

3. **A:** I am from Ukraine.

   Q: Where _____ **are you from** _____?

4. **A:** I get to school by bus.

   Q: How _____ **do you get to school** _____?

5. **A:** I study biology.

   Q: What _____ **do you study** _____?

6. **A:** I study biology because I love animals.

   Q: Why _____ **do you study biology** _____?

7. **A:** My favorite animals are elephants and tigers.

   Q: What _____ **are your favorite animals** _____?

8. **A:** Ms. Jacobs is my instructor.

   Q: Who _____ **is your instructor** _____?

COMMUNICATE

D **PAIR WORK** Create questions to ask your partner. Begin your questions with the words provided. Take turns asking questions. Tell the class what you learned about your partner. **Answers will vary.**

1. What is . . . ?	4. Where do . . . ?
2. Who is . . . ?	5. How do . . . ?
3. Where is . . . ?	6. When do . . . ?
	7. Why do . . . ?

E **WRITE** Imagine you are going to interview a zookeeper. What questions would you ask him/her? Write a list of your questions. **Answers will vary.**

Ask for volunteers to write the questions on the board.

■ **COMMUNICATE**

The Communicate section allows students to practice the target grammar in more communicative, less-controlled ways through speaking and writing activities.

■ **EXERCISE D**

Help students think of a few questions they might want to ask their partner.

■ **EXERCISE E**

When students are finished, have them hand their papers to a partner and have the partner check the grammar.

■ EXPANSION IDEAS

Exercise C

1. Have students interview their classmates using the questions they wrote for Exercise C.

Exercise E

1. Ask for a volunteer to sit at the front of the class and role-play the zookeeper. Have students take turns asking the zookeeper their questions. Keep the atmosphere light so that the zookeeper feels free to invent answers to the questions.

Putting It Together

The purpose of this section of the lesson is to connect and extend students' understanding of the grammar, vocabulary, and content from this lesson.

■ GRAMMAR AND VOCABULARY

1. As a class, brainstorm as many animals as possible in one or two minutes and list them on the board.
2. Divide the class into pairs to ask and answer questions about animals. Encourage students to make up answers if they need to.
3. For additional suggestions on doing pair work, see the Teacher's Notes on pages xvi–xviii.

■ PROJECT

1. Go through each step with the students, making sure they understand what they are to do.
2. For additional suggestions on doing projects, see the Teacher's Notes on pages xvi–xviii.

■ INTERNET

1. Have students do this activity alone or in pairs.
2. Remind students how to use a search engine to find information.
3. Have students write down at least two new facts that they learned from the Internet about each researcher and report them to the class.

■ VOCABULARY JOURNAL

Refer to the Pre-lesson (page 6) for an explanation of the vocabulary journal.

GRAMMAR AND VOCABULARY Ask and answer questions about the animals in this lesson. Use the grammar and vocabulary from this lesson.

What does a kangaroo eat?   Grass.

PROJECT Be an animal researcher.

1. Work in small groups.
2. Choose an animal you want to learn about.
3. Brainstorm a list of questions about this animal with your group.
4. Assign one or more questions to each student to research.
5. Research your question. Use the library and the Internet.
6. Report back to your group on what you learned.

 INTERNET Go online. Search for more information on the work of Jane Goodall, Cynthia Moss, or Sue Savage Rumbaugh. Tell your class about what you found out. Answers will vary.

VOCABULARY JOURNAL Write sentences for new vocabulary you learned in this lesson. Answers will vary.

Example: _Birds keep eggs in their nests._

■ EXPANSION IDEAS

Grammar and Vocabulary

1. Have students choose one of the animals to write a short paragraph about.

Project

1. Have students use the information they learned about their animal to make a poster with pictures and information to present to the class.

PART 1
Adverbs of Frequency

PART 2
Questions with *How Often:*
Frequency Expressions

Lesson 10

Health: Stress

■ CONTENT VOCABULARY

Look at the pictures. Do you know the words?

worried

in a rush

headache

stomachache

relax

exercise

sleep

go out with friends

Write the new words in your vocabulary journal.

■ THINK ABOUT IT

Discuss these questions with a partner. Answers will vary.

1. What things make people feel stress?
2. What helps people relax?

75

Lesson 10

Overview

1. Elicit students' prior knowledge. Ask: *What do you think we will learn about in this lesson?*
2. Write the word *stress* on the board. Help students understand the meaning of this word.

■ CONTENT VOCABULARY

1. Direct students' attention to the pictures and vocabulary words. Ask: *What is happening in the top group of pictures? Why?*
2. Ask: *What is happening in the bottom group of pictures? How is this group of pictures related to the first group of pictures? What do you do to relieve stress?*

■ THINK ABOUT IT

1. Have students think about these questions by themselves and then share their answers with a partner.
2. Go over the answers as a class.

■ CONTENT NOTES

Health

The topic for this lesson is Health: Stress. Stress is defined as *mental or physical strain caused by pressure.* Synonyms for *stress* are *tension* or *anxiety.*

Possible discussion topics include the following:

1. Do different things cause stress in different cultures?
2. Is stress ever good for you?
3. What causes physical stress?
4. What causes mental stress?

PART ONE

Adverbs of Frequency

Part 1 introduces students to the use of adverbs of frequency.

■ GRAMMAR IN CONTENT

This section exposes students to a theme-based reading that includes examples of the target structure. Students can refer to the grammar chart(s) to complete the controlled practice activities.

■ EXERCISE A *Track 21*

1. Ask students to look at the photo and describe what they see.
2. Play the audio and have students follow along in the book. Ask students what causes stress for John.

■ GRAMMAR CHART
Adverbs of Frequency

1. Go over the chart and the Notes with the students. As you go through both of these, refer to the reading to reinforce the grammar rules and the meaning of the different adverbs.
2. Write a two-column T-chart on the board. Label the left column "Be" and the right column "Adverb." Write several forms of the verb *be* in the left column, and ask students to supply adverbs of frequency for the right column. Now, create a sentence using one of the combinations in the chart; for example, with the words *are* and *usually,* you could say, *The students in this class are usually on time.* Ask volunteers to create sentences using the remaining chart combinations.
3. Next, write another two-column chart on the board, and label the left column "Adverb" and the right column "Verb." Write several adverbs of frequency in the left column, and ask students to supply

---

■ GRAMMAR IN CONTENT

A **Read and listen.**

TR21

Stress

    John is a computer science student. He **often** feels stress. He and his wife wake up at 6:30. They get their children ready for school. Then he takes the train to school. He **usually** studies on the train. He is **often** late for class. He goes to school all day and works in the evening. He **usually** gets home after 8:00. He **rarely** relaxes. He **rarely** sleeps well.

    Stress is a problem for many people. It **sometimes** causes medical problems. It affects the heart and brain in many ways.

ready: prepared
cause: to make something happen
affect: to change

Adverbs of Frequency

Frequency Words		Examples with *Be*	Examples with the Simple Present Tense
▲ 100%	Always	He is **always** late.	I **always** study in the library.
	Usually	You are **usually** early.	He **usually** wakes up at 7:00.
	Often	They are **often** busy.	She **often** works late.
	Sometimes	We are **sometimes** in a rush.	They **sometimes** relax at home.
	Rarely	My mother is **rarely** angry.	I **rarely** exercise.
▼ 0%	Never	I am **never** wrong.	The shop is **never** closed.

Notes:
- Use adverbs of frequency to say how often something happens.
- Put adverbs of frequency after the verb *be*. Example: *I am **always** early.*
- Put adverbs of frequency before all other verbs. Example: *She **usually** works late.*

■ EXPANSION IDEAS

Exercise A
1. Have students rewrite the paragraph, inserting adverbs of frequency similar in meaning to those in the grammar chart.
2. Have students rewrite the paragraph, inserting adverbs of frequency opposite in meaning to those in the grammar chart.

Grammar Chart
1. Have students write sentences about themselves, using adverbs of frequency.

B Look at the reading "Stress." Compare yourself to John. Use the frequency words that are true for you. Answers will vary.

1. John **often** feels stress.   I _____ feel stress.

2. He is **often** late for class.   I am _____ late for class.

3. He **usually** gets home after 8:00.   I _____ get home after 8:00.

4. He **rarely** relaxes.   I _____ relax.

5. He **rarely** sleeps well.   I _____ sleep well.

C Rewrite each sentence. Put the adverb of frequency in the right place.

1. Zoya is late for class. (usually) _____ Zoya is usually late for class.

2. She is on time. (rarely) _____ **She is rarely on time.**

3. She is tired in the morning. (always) _____ **She is always tired in the morning.**

4. Karl is on time. (usually) _____ **Karl is usually on time.**

5. He is late. (rarely) _____ **He is rarely late.**

6. He is tired in the morning. (never) _____ **He is never tired in the morning.**

D Rewrite each sentence. Put the adverb of frequency in the right place.

1. Zoya studies at night. (always) _____ Zoya always studies at night.

2. She watches television. (sometimes) _____ **She sometimes watches television.**

3. She goes to bed late. (usually) _____ **She usually goes to bed late.**

4. She hears the alarm clock. (rarely) _____ **She rarely hears the alarm clock.**

5. She gets up late. (often) _____ **She often gets up late.**

6. She misses her bus. (often) _____ **She often misses her bus.**

verbs for the right column. Repeat the procedure described in number 2, giving an example sentence and having students generate additional sentences.

■ EXERCISE B

Have students complete the activity and compare their answers with a partner's answers.

■ EXERCISE C

Ask for volunteers to come to the board to write the correct sentences. If there are mistakes in the sentences, ask for other volunteers to come up and fix the mistakes.

■ EXERCISE D

Ask for volunteers to come to the board to write the correct sentences. If there are mistakes in the sentences, ask for other volunteers to come up and fix the mistakes.

■ EXPANSION IDEAS

Exercise B

1. Have students practice saying the sentences about John and about themselves with a partner. Have student A read the sentence about John and student B read the sentence about himself/herself. Then, have students switch roles.

Exercises C & D

1. Have students rewrite the sentences using *I* and the adverb that accurately describes their habits.

■ EXERCISE E

Have students complete the test and add up their scores. Then ask for a show of hands about how much stress they have in their lives, according to the scoring guide at the bottom of the test.

■ COMMUNICATE

The Communicate section allows students to practice the target grammar in more communicative, less-controlled ways through speaking and writing activities.

■ EXERCISE F

When students have completed the writing, have them get into small groups and share their paragraphs.

E Take this stress test. Choose the adverbs of frequency that are true for you. Then add up the number of each of your answers to find your score. **Answers will vary.**

The Stress Test

1. I _____ feel nervous.
   1—always   2—usually   3—sometimes   4—rarely   5—never

2. I _____ feel worried.
   1—always   2—usually   3—sometimes   4—rarely   5—never

3. I am _____ in a rush.
   1—always   2—usually   3—sometimes   4—rarely   5—never

4. People _____ tell me to relax.
   1—always   2—usually   3—sometimes   4—rarely   5—never

5. I _____ get headaches.
   1—always   2—usually   3—sometimes   4—rarely   5—never

6. I _____ have stomachaches.
   1—always   2—usually   3—sometimes   4—rarely   5—never

7. I _____ have sleep problems.
   1—always   2—usually   3—sometimes   4—rarely   5—never

8. I am _____ sad.
   1—always   2—usually   3—sometimes   4—rarely   5—never

8–16 There is a lot of stress in your life.
17–24 There is an average amount of stress in your life.
25–40 There is very little stress in your life.

■ COMMUNICATE

F WRITE Describe a typical day for you. Use each adverb of frequency at least once. Tell your class about your typical day. **Answers will vary.**

My Typical Day

I usually wake up at 7:30. Then I take a shower and get dressed. I often eat cereal for breakfast. I never take the bus to school. I always walk. I sometimes

■ EXPANSION IDEA

Exercise E

1. Have students share their answers with a partner. Have the partner make suggestions about how his or her partner can improve stress. For example:

Student A: *I always feel nervous.*
Student B: *Nervous about what?*
Student A: *Nervous about coming to English class.*
Student B: *Maybe you could make some friends in class so you aren't so nervous.*

■ GRAMMAR IN CONTENT

TR22

A Read and listen.

Doctor's Orders

Patient:	I feel stress all the time.
Doctor:	You need to take care of yourself. **How often** do you get eight hours of sleep?
Patient:	**Every day.**
Doctor:	Great. **How often** do you eat a well-balanced meal?
Patient:	Maybe **once or twice a week.**
Doctor:	You must eat healthy meals **three times a day.** **How often** do you exercise?
Patient:	**Three or four times a month.**
Doctor:	That's not good. Your body needs exercise **every day.** And you must relax more.
Patient:	You're right doctor. I need to change my habits.

well balanced: healthy combination

Questions with *How Often*	Frequency Expressions	
How often do you go to the doctor? How often do you exercise? How often do you go out with friends?	once twice three times	a day / a week / a month / a year
	every day, every night, every week, every month	

Note:
You can answer *How often* questions with just a frequency expression or with a full sentence that has a frequency expression. Example:
Q: *How often do you go to the doctor?*
A: *Once a year.*   OR   *I go to the doctor once a year.*

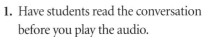

PART TWO

Questions with *How Often;* Frequency Expressions

Part 2 introduces students to *How often* questions and the use of frequency expressions.

■ **GRAMMAR IN CONTENT**

This section allows students to refer to the grammar chart(s) to complete a number of controlled practice activities.

■ **EXERCISE A** *Track 22*

1. Have students read the conversation before you play the audio.
2. Play the audio.
3. Ask students the following questions:

   How often does the patient get eight hours of sleep? (Every day.)

   How often does the patient eat a well-balanced meal? (Once or twice a week.)

   How often does the patient exercise? (Three or four times a month.)

■ **GRAMMAR CHARTS**
Questions with How Often; *Frequency Expressions*

1. Go over the charts and the Note with the students. As you go through both of these, refer back to the examples of question and answer structures in the reading.
2. Ask students questions about themselves and how often they do the things mentioned in the chart.

■ EXPANSION IDEAS

Exercise A

1. Have students practice the conversation with a partner.
2. Have students practice the conversation with a partner but this time using their own answers.

Grammar Chart

1. Have students practice the questions and answers with a partner.

■ EXERCISE B

When students have completed the activity and have the correct answers, have them practice the questions and answers with a partner.

■ EXERCISE C

When students have completed the activity, have them practice the questions and answers with a different partner.

■ EXERCISE D *Track 23*

1. Before you play the audio, go through the questions with students and make sure they understand what they will be listening for.
2. When students have finished listening and made their answer choices, play the audio again, pausing after information that answers each question so that students can check their answers.

B Look again at the dialogue "Doctor's Orders." Answer the questions.

1. How often does the patient get eight hours of sleep? _____ *every day*
2. How often does she eat a well-balanced meal? _____ **once or twice a week**
3. How often does the doctor want her to eat a healthy meal? **three times a day**
   _____
4. How often does she exercise? _____ **three or four times a month**
5. How often does the doctor want her to exercise? _____ **every day**

C Answer the questions. Compare your answers with a partner. **Answers will vary.**

1. How often do you get eight hours of sleep? _____
2. How often do you exercise? _____
3. How often do you eat vegetables? _____
4. How often do you drink coffee or tea? _____
5. How often do you go out with friends? _____

D Listen to the woman talk about her schedule. (Circle) the correct answers.

TR23

1. How often does she clean the house?
   a. once a week   (b. twice a week)   c. every day
2. How often does she do the laundry?
   a. every day   b. once a week   (c. four times a week)
3. How often does she cook dinner?
   (a. every day)   b. every week   c. every month
4. How often does she take her kids to soccer practice?
   a. once a week   b. twice a week   (c. three times a week)
5. How often does she drink a cup of coffee?
   a. once a day   b. three times a day   (c. six times a day)
6. How often does she have trouble sleeping?
   (a. every night)   b. once a week   c. twice a week

■ EXPANSION IDEA

Exercise C

1. Have students walk around the room and ask different classmates the questions from Exercise C. Have students note the answers they receive and then report what they have learned about their classmates to the class.

E PAIR WORK Look at Kenji's busy schedule. Ask your partner a *How often* question about it. Your partner will answer with a frequency expression. Take turns. **Answers will vary.**

How often does Kenji do laundry? He does laundry twice a week.

	Monday	Tuesday	Wednesday	Thursday	Friday	Saturday	Sunday
Go to School	X		X		X		
Go to Work	X	X	X	X	X		
Study	X	X	X	X	X	X	X
Clean His Apartment						X	
Do Laundry			X				X
Cook Dinner	X	X	X	X	X		X
Go Out with Friends						X	

■ COMMUNICATE

F WRITE Write a schedule of your weekly activities. Use the chart in exercise E as a model. Then write a paragraph about your weekly schedule and present it to your class. Your classmates will ask you *How often* questions about other activities you haven't included. **Answers will vary.**

■ EXERCISE E

Model this activity with the students using the example and then have students work in pairs.

■ COMMUNICATE

The Communicate section allows students to practice the target grammar in more communicative, less-controlled ways through speaking and writing activities.

■ EXERCISE F

Tell students to write a blank schedule just like Kenji's and fill in the boxes for the days of the week with *X*s. If there are other things they do during the week that are not on Kenji's list, encourage them to write them in the left column.

■ EXPANSION IDEAS

Exercise E

1. Have students interview a partner and write a paragraph about his or her partner's weekly schedule.

Exercise F

1. Have students type their schedules and paragraphs on a computer and arrange the materials on construction paper or poster boards to present to the class.

Connection

Putting It Together

The purpose of this section of the lesson is to connect and extend students' understanding of the grammar, vocabulary, and content from this lesson.

■ GRAMMAR AND VOCABULARY

1. Help students come up with the questions they will need to ask to fill out their charts.
2. Tell students they can only write a person's name once.
3. Have students stand up and walk around the room to ask their classmates questions.

■ PROJECT

1. Remind students about the dialogue they read on page 79 and tell them to use this as a model.
2. Help students prepare for their presentations.
3. For additional suggestions on doing projects, see the Teacher's Notes on pages xvi–xviii.

■ INTERNET

1. Remind students how to use a search engine to find the information.
2. Have students share their answers with the class to see if they found the same information.

■ VOCABULARY JOURNAL

Refer to the Pre-lesson (page 6) for an explanation of the vocabulary journal.

GRAMMAR AND VOCABULARY Complete the chart. Add some ideas of your own. Use the grammar and vocabulary from this lesson. Answers will vary.

Find Someone Who . . .	Name
. . . exercises every day.	
. . . sleeps less than six hours a day.	
. . . goes on vacation once a year.	
. . . reads a newspaper every day.	
. . . often gets headaches.	
. . . is usually happy.	
. . . is often late for class.	
. . . always does his or her homework.	

PROJECT Write and perform a play.

1. Work in groups of three.
2. Discuss healthy habits and unhealthy habits.
3. Write a script about a patient with unhealthy habits at a doctor's office. Student A is the patient, student B is the doctor, and student C is the nurse.
4. Perform your play for the class.

 INTERNET Go online. Find out ways to help reduce stress. Use the following keywords: "stress" and "help." Tell your class what you learned.

VOCABULARY JOURNAL Write sentences for new vocabulary you learned in this lesson.

Example: *I am always in a rush to get to work in the morning.*

82   LESSON 10 | Health: Stress

■ EXPANSION IDEA

Internet

1. Have each student take the information they learned from the Internet and write a short paragraph about how to help people with stress.

2. For additional suggestions on doing Internet activities, see the Teacher's Notes on pages xvi–xviii.

Review 6-10

A Circle the correct answers.

Alba is pregnant. She (play /(plays)) classical music for her baby every day.
(1)
She (sing /(sings)) to her baby. Why does she do this? She (know /(knows)) about
(2)   (3)
a theory called *The Mozart Effect*. Some researchers say music (help /(helps))
(4)
babies' brains develop. Other researchers ((do not)/ does not) believe in *The*
(5)
Mozart Effect. However, Alba (do not /(does not)) care. She and her baby
(6)
((listen)/ listens) to music every day. It (help /(helps)) her feel calm and happy.
(7)   (8)

B Circle the correct answers.

Aiko is a nursing student in her sophomore year. She (go /(goes)) to school
(1)
(in /(on)) Monday, Wednesday, and Friday. She (do /(does)) her training at
(2)   (3)
a hospital ((on)/ at) Tuesday and Thursday. She studies ((at)/ in) night and
(4)   (5)
(in /(on)) the weekend. She (have /(has)) a busy week, but she relaxes with
(6)   (7)
friends (at /(on)) Sunday evenings. She meets these friends every Sunday
(8)
(on /(at)) 6:00 for dinner and a movie.
(9)

C Circle the correct answers.

Q: (When /(What)) do you do on the weekend?   **A:** I relax.
(1)
Q: (What /(Where)) do you relax?   **A:** At home.
(2)
Q: ((How)/ Where) do you relax?   **A:** I watch a lot of TV.
(3)
Q: ((Do)/ Does) you watch educational programs?   **A:** No, I (do /(don't)).
(4)   (5)
Q: ((Do)/ Does) you watch soap operas?   **A:** Yes, I ((do)/ don't).
(6)   (7)
Q: ((Who)/ How) do you watch TV with?   **A:** My husband.
(8)

Review 6-10

Lessons 6-10

The purpose of this lesson is to help students review the concepts they have learned in the last five lessons. Encourage them to go back to the lessons and review the grammar charts to help them complete the review exercises.

■ EXERCISE A

1. Have students do this activity by themselves and then share their answers with a partner.
2. Go over the answers as a class.

■ EXERCISE B

1. Have students do this activity by themselves and then share their answers with a partner.
2. Go over the answers as a class.

■ EXERCISE C

1. Have students do this activity by themselves and then share their answers with a partner.
2. Go over the answers as a class.

■ EXPANSION IDEA

Exercise C

1. Have students interview a partner using the questions from Exercise C.

EXERCISE D

1. Have students do this activity by themselves and then share their answers with a partner.
2. Have students practice the conversation with a partner.

EXERCISE E

Have students do this activity with a partner.

LEARNER LOG

1. Help students understand how to complete the Learner Log by going over it with them and offering examples of the grammar structures.
2. If students checked "I Need More Practice" for any of the structures, suggest that they review those lessons. If possible, meet with students individually to discuss their Learner Logs and make suggestions for ways to get more practice with the structures.

D Complete the sentences. Use *do, does, am, is, are,* or the correct form of the missing verb.

Question: Where __do__ dolphins live?
(1)

Answer: Dolphins __are__ in most oceans and seas.
(2)

Question: __are__ dolphins intelligent?
(3)

Answer: Yes, they __are__.
(4)

Question: __are__ they like humans?
(5)

Answer: Yes, they __are__. They __are__ very friendly with humans.
(6)   (7)

E Look at Fatima's class schedule. Complete the sentences. Use each word or phrase in the box once.

How often   twice a week   (every day)   always   rarely   never

	Monday	Tuesday	Wednesday	Thursday	Friday
Intro to Teaching	X		X		X
Child Development		X		X	
Technology in Education	X		X		X

1. Fatima goes to school __every day__.
2. She takes "Child Development" __twice a week__.
3. She __always__ goes to "Child Development" on Tuesday and Thursday.
4. She __never__ takes "Intro to Teaching" on Thursday.
5. __How often__ does she take "Child Development"?
6. She __rarely__ has free time during the week!

LEARNER LOG Check (✔) *Yes* or *I Need More Practice.*

Lesson	I Can Use . . .	Yes	I Need More Practice
6	The Present Tense: Affirmative and Negative Statements		
7	Irregular Verbs: *Have, Go, Do*; Prepositions of Time: *On, In, At*		
8	Simple Present *Yes/No* Questions; Short Answers and *Wh-* Questions		
9	Present Tense of *Be* vs. Simple Present Tense: Statements		
10	Adverbs of Frequency; Questions with *How Often*; Frequency Expressions		

EXPANSION IDEA

Learner Log
1. Have students form groups and generate a list of ideas for what they can do if they checked the "I Need More Practice" column in the Learner Log. Have each group share its best ideas with the class.

PART 1
The Present Progressive Tense:
Affirmative
PART 2
Spelling of Verbs in the *-ing* Form
PART 3
The Present Progressive Tense:
Negative

Lesson 11

Education: Learning Styles

Overview

Elicit students' prior knowledge. Ask: *What do you think we will learn about in this lesson?*

■ CONTENT VOCABULARY

Look at the pictures. Do you know the words?

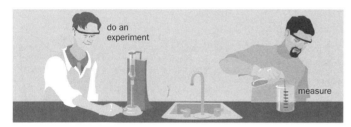

Write the new words in your vocabulary journal.

CONTENT VOCABULARY

1. Direct students' attention to the first drawing and vocabulary words. Ask: *How old are the students in this picture? What are they doing?*
2. Direct students' attention to the second drawing and ask: *What class are these students in? What are the students wearing? Why?*

■ THINK ABOUT IT

Check (✔) what you are doing right now. Answers will vary.

I am . . .

reading. ____   listening to something. ____

thinking. ____   looking at something. ____

■ THINK ABOUT IT

Have students do this activity by themselves and then share their answers with a partner. Write the following dialogue on the board for them to practice:

Student A: What are you doing right now?

Student B: I am _____.

What are *you* doing right now?

Student A: I am _____.

Model the dialogue for students, demonstrating the correct intonation.

85

■ CONTENT NOTES

Education

The topic for this lesson is Education: Learning Styles. Point out that understanding their learning style may help students find a faster way to improve their English.

Ask students what they do when they study for a test. Do they write down everything they need to know? Do they read over the material in their books and memorize it? Do they practice by speaking aloud, using flash cards, or working with another student? Do they listen to tapes or CDs?

Explain to students that if they are doing well in class, whatever learning styles they are using are working. On the other hand, if they are not doing well, they may want to try different learning styles to find out what works for them.

PART ONE

The Present Progressive Tense: Affirmative

Part 1 introduces students to affirmative statements in the present progressive tense.

■ GRAMMAR IN CONTENT

This section exposes students to a theme-based reading that includes examples of the target structure. Students can refer to the grammar chart(s) to complete the controlled practice activities.

■ EXERCISE A Track 24

1. Ask students to look at the picture. Ask the following questions: *Who is this woman? What is she doing? How old are her students?*

2. Play the audio and have students follow along.

3. Ask the following questions: *What grade does the woman teach? What is Bina doing? How does she learn? What is Michael doing? How does he learn? What is Anna doing? How does she learn?*

■ GRAMMAR CHART

The Present Progressive Tense: Affirmative

Go over the chart with the students. In each section of the chart, read the sentences with the full form of *be,* and then say, "Or . . ." and have students supply the contraction form. Repeat the procedure for all possible subjects. Go over the Notes. As you go through the chart and Notes, refer to the examples from the reading to reinforce the rules.

■ EXERCISE B

Have students complete the activity and check their answers with a partner.

■ GRAMMAR IN CONTENT

A Read and listen.

TR24

Learning Styles

I'm an elementary school teacher. I **am teaching** a first grade class right now. The children **are learning** about autumn. Different students **are learning** in different ways. Bina learns best with her eyes. She **is looking** at pictures of autumn. Michael learns well with his ears. He**'s listening** to a story about autumn. Anna learns best with her hands. She**'s touching** leaves. Researchers call these different ways of learning "learning styles."

autumn: the season between summer and winter (also called fall)

The Present Progressive Tense: Affirmative

Subject	*Be*	Verb + *-ing*	Contraction
I	am	thinking.	I'm thinking.
He She It	is	learning.	He's learning.
You We They	are	listening to music.	They're listening to music.

Notes:

- Use the present progressive to talk about something happening (or not happening) right now.
- To form the present progressive tense of a verb, add *-ing* to the end of most verbs. For verbs with special spellings in the present progressive, see Part Two of this lesson.
- Use "It" with the present progressive to talk about weather. Example: *It is raining.*

B Look at the reading "Learning Styles." (Circle) the correct form of the verb.

1. The teacher (is teach / (is teaching)) a class.
2. The students (is learning / (are learning)) about autumn.
3. Bina (looks / (is looking)) at a book.
4. Michael (am listening to / (is listening to)) a story.
5. Anna (are touching / (is touching)) leaves.

■ EXPANSION IDEAS

Exercise A

Have students close their books. On the board, write the sentences from the paragraph without the present progressive verbs. Have students fill in the blanks.

1. I _____ a first grade class right now.
2. The children _____ about autumn.
3. Different students _____ in different ways.
4. She _____ at pictures of autumn.
5. He _____ to a story about autumn.
6. She _____ leaves and a pumpkin.

Exercise B

1. Ask students what is wrong with the incorrect answers. For example, in number 1, *is teach* is wrong because the main verb needs to be in the progressive form (*-ing*) to show present action.

C What is happening right now? Check (✔) the true sentences. **Answers will vary.**

1. My instructor is talking. ___
2. The students are listening. ___
3. I am standing. ___
4. I am holding a pen. ___
5. A student is drinking water. ___
6. Some students are reading. ___
7. It is raining outside. ___
8. I am thinking about lunch. ___

D Complete the paragraph. Use the present progressive affirmative of the verbs.

Right now, Mr. Hudson (teach) _____ *is teaching* _____ the class. I
(1)
(listen) _____ **am listening** _____ to Mr. Hudson's lecture. It's very interesting.
(2)
The other students (think) _____ **are thinking** _____ about the lesson.
(3)
Zara (ask) _____ **is asking** _____ a question. Mr. Hudson
(4)
(write) _____ **is writing** _____ the answer on the board. Two students
(5)
(talk) _____ **are talking** _____ .
(6)

E Write present progressive sentences with the words provided.

Tomoko and Bill learn best with their eyes.

1. Tomoko / look at / a chart
   _____ *Tomoko is looking at a chart.* _____

2. Bill / watch / a DVD _____ **Bill is watching a DVD.**

Tomoko   Bill

Carlo and Claudia learn best with their ears.

3. Carlo / listen to / a CD
   Carlo is listening to a CD.

4. Claudia / listen to / a lecture _____ **Claudia is listening to a lecture.**

Carlo   Claudia

Jenn and Yakov learn best with their hands.

5. Jenn / do / an experiment
   Jenn is doing an experiment.

6. Yakov / touch / a rock _____ **Yakov is touching a rock.**

Jenn   Yakov

EXERCISE C

Have students complete the activity based on what is happening in their classroom. Go over the answers as a class.

EXERCISE D

1. Have students complete the activity and then go over their answers with a partner.
2. Call on students to tell you their answers and write the two parts of the present progressive verbs on the board to reinforce the form.
3. If students gave the full form of the progressive verbs as answers, have them do the activity again using contractions.
4. Model the pronunciation of the sentences in the activity using contractions and have students practice the pronunciation.

EXERCISE E

1. Ask for volunteers to come to the board and write the sentences.
2. If there are mistakes, put an X next to each sentence that has a mistake and ask for other students to come up and fix the mistakes.
3. Reinforce the idea of different learning styles by asking, for example, "Which students learn best with their ears?" Students should respond, "Carlo and Claudia learn best with their ears."

■ EXPANSION IDEA

Exercise D

1. Have students write a paragraph about their classroom and what is happening, similar to the paragraph in Exercise D.

■ EXERCISE F

1. Show a transparency of this paragraph or write it on the board with the mistakes not corrected.

2. When students have found all of the mistakes in their books, ask for volunteers to come to the board and fix the mistakes.

■ COMMUNICATE

The Communicate section allows students to practice the target grammar in more communicative, less-controlled ways through speaking and writing activities.

■ EXERCISE G

1. Model this activity with students.

2. Once students have had a chance to practice with their groups, ask for volunteers to come up to the front of the class to pretend to do something. Have students guess what their classmate is doing.

3. As a variation, write several actions on slips of paper and put them in small paper bags—one bag for each group, or one bag for the volunteers who come to the front of the class. Have students take a slip from the bag and perform the action.

PART TWO

Spelling of Verbs in the *-ing* Form

Part 2 introduces students to the spelling of verbs in the *-ing* form.

■ GRAMMAR CHART

Spelling of Verbs in the -ing *Form*

Go over the chart with the students. In the last section, point out that only the first rule in the bullet list is an exception to the rule in the first section. The remaining three rules follow the pattern of "most verbs" as in the first section.

F **Correct the student paragraph. There are eight more mistakes.**

■ COMMUNICATE

G **GROUP WORK** Work in groups of four. One student pretends to do something. The other students guess what the student is doing. Take turns. Answers will vary.

You're taking a photo!

That's right.

PART TWO	Spelling of Verbs in the *-ing* Form

Spelling of Verbs in the *-ing* Form

Base Form	*-ing* Form	Rules:
work eat	working eating	For most verbs: Add *-ing*.
live write	living writing	For verbs that end in a consonant + *e*: Drop the *e* and add *-ing*. Do not double the consonant. Wrong: ~~writting~~
sit plan	sitting planning	For one-syllable verbs that end in *one* vowel + one consonant: Double the consonant and add *-ing*.
say sleep listen think	saying sleeping listening thinking	Do not double the last consonant before *-ing* when the verb: • ends in *w, x,* or *y*. • ends in two vowels and then one consonant. • has more than one syllable (when the stress is on the first syllable). • ends in two or more consonants.

■ EXPANSION IDEA

Grammar Chart

1. Dictate the following words to students:

walking

hitting

eating

watching

helping

baking

turning

waking

winning

playing

2. Have students look back at the rules in the chart to see if they spelled the words correctly.

3. Call on students to come to the board and write the words.

A Write the *-ing* form of the verbs.

1. take   _taking_
2. read   _reading_
3. smile   _smiling_

4. stop   _stopping_
5. ride   _riding_
6. write   _writing_

7. sit   _sitting_
8. use   _using_
9. sleep   _sleeping_

B Look at the picture of the school yard. Complete the sentences with the present progressive form of one of the verbs in the box. Use the correct spelling.

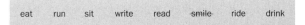

eat   run   sit   write   read   ~~smile~~   ride   drink

Pedro   Jack   Duong   Mikey   Bianca   Lilly   Darell

1. The teacher _is smiling_.
2. Bianca _is eating_ a sandwich.
3. Darell _is drinking_ milk.
4. Duong _is running_.
5. Lilly _is writing_ in her notebook.
6. Pedro and Jack _are riding_ bicycles.
7. Mikey and Lily _are sitting_ on the ground.
8. Mikey _is reading_ a book.

■ COMMUNICATE

C GROUP WORK The class forms two teams. Team A says a verb. Someone from Team B writes the progressive form of the verb on the board. The first team to spell ten words correctly wins. Answers will vary.

■ **EXPANSION IDEA**

Exercise B

1. Have students work in pairs to write sentences about what is going on outside their classroom, similar to the activity in Exercise B.

2. Ask for a volunteer from each group to come to the board and write one of their sentences.

■ **EXERCISE A**

Have students check their spelling with a partner when they are finished.

■ **EXERCISE B**

When students have completed the activity, go over the answers as a class.

■ **COMMUNICATE**

The Communicate section allows students to practice the target grammar in more communicative, less-controlled ways through speaking and writing activities.

■ **EXERCISE C**

1. Put students into two teams and have each team create a list of 15 words to give to the other team. Tell students that each word can only be used once, so if the other team uses one of their words first, they must cross it off their list.

2. Have each group choose a reader (the person who will read the verbs) and a writer (the person who will write the correct progressive form on the board. (Note: The whole team can help the reader spell the word correctly, but only the writer will write.)

3. Decide which team will go first and play the game.

4. As a variation, put the teams in two lines facing the board "relay race style." The first person in line is the writer and will go to the back of the line after taking a turn. The new person at the front of the line is the new writer, and so on.

PART THREE

The Present Progressive Tense: Negative

Part 3 introduces students to negative statements with the present progressive tense.

■ GRAMMAR IN CONTENT

This section exposes students to a theme-based reading that includes examples of the target structure. Students can refer to the grammar chart(s) to complete the controlled practice activities.

■ EXERCISE A *Track 25*

1. Ask students to look at the picture. Ask the following questions: *What does the child have in his hands? What is he doing?*
2. Play the audio and have students follow along.
3. Write the following questions on the board as headings for two columns:

   What is Enrico doing?
   What is Enrico not doing?

   Have students copy the headings onto paper and work with a partner to write sentences in each column.

■ GRAMMAR CHART

Present Progressive Negative Statements with Be; *Negative Contractions with* Be

Go over the chart with the students. Say the sentences and have students repeat. Where there are two contraction forms, say the sentence with the first form and have students repeat. Then say, "Or . . ." with a rising intonation so that students will supply the second sentence.

■ EXERCISE B

Have students share their answers in pairs before you review them as a class.

■ GRAMMAR IN CONTENT

TR25 **A** **Read and listen.**

Learning by Doing

Ming-Shan is learning about math. He **is not sitting** in math class. He **is not listening** to a teacher. He's **not doing** homework. How is he learning about math? Ming-Shan is measuring sugar. He's helping his mother bake a cake.

bake: to cook something in an oven, for example bread or cakes

Present Progressive Negative Statements with *Be*; Negative Contractions with *Be*			
Subject	***Be* + Not**	**Verb + *-ing***	**Contraction**
I	am not	sleeping.	I'm not sleeping.	
He She It	is not	working.	He isn't working. OR He's not working. She isn't working. OR She's not working. It isn't working. OR It's not working.
You We They	are not	listening.	You aren't listening. OR You're not listening. We aren't listening. OR We're not listening. They aren't listening. OR They're not listening.

B **Look at these sentences about the reading "Learning by Doing."** (Circle) **true or false.**

1. Ming-Shan is learning about math.   (True)   False
2. He's not doing homework.   (True)   False
3. He is listening to a teacher.   True   (False)
4. He's not helping his mother bake a cake. True   (False)
5. Ming-Shan is measuring sugar.   (True)   False
6. He is sitting in a classroom.   True   (False)

■ EXPANSION IDEAS

Exercise A

1. Have students write sentences about themselves similar to the ones in the reading but changing the topic to what they are doing and not doing in the classroom right now. For example:

I am writing in my book.
I am not looking at the teacher.

Exercise B

1. Have students work with a partner to make the false statements true.

C Write *true* or *false.* If false, write a negative sentence.

1. I am drinking coffee. _____ *False. I am not drinking coffee.*

2. I am learning grammar. _____ **True**

3. It is raining. _____ **Answers will vary.**

4. I am doing an exercise. _____ **True**

5. My instructor is writing on the board. _____ **Answers will vary.**

6. My instructor is sleeping. _____ **False**

7. The person in front of me is reading a newspaper.

   _____ **Answers will vary.**

8. The person behind me is talking. _____ **Answers will vary.**

■ COMMUNICATE

D **PAIR WORK** **Student A looks at the picture on this page. Student B looks at the picture on page 227. Talk about your pictures. Find the five differences. Use the present progressive.** **Answers will vary.**

 John is reading in my picture. 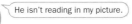 He isn't reading in my picture.

■ **EXERCISE C**

Ask for volunteers to write their sentences on the board.

■ **COMMUNICATE**

The Communicate section allows students to practice the target grammar in more communicative, less-controlled ways through speaking and writing activities.

■ **EXERCISE D**

Model this activity with a pair of students. Have one student look at this page in the book, and have the other student open to page 227. Explain that the students are looking at pictures that are similar, but not exactly the same. Make sure students do the activity by speaking to each other, not by showing each other their pictures.

■ **EXPANSION IDEA**

Exercise D

1. Have students work in pairs to write sentences about the two pictures after they have done the activity.

Connection

Putting It Together

The purpose of this section of the lesson is to connect and extend students' understanding of the grammar, vocabulary, and content from this lesson.

■ GRAMMAR AND VOCABULARY

If you already did this as an expansion exercise, you can have students do the following variation:

Before students write, ask half of the class to get up and do things in the classroom while the other half takes notes. Then have the groups switch roles. This will give the students something interesting to write about.

■ PROJECT

1. Go through each step with the students, making sure they understand the project.
2. A school catalogue or Web site might be good sources of photos. Students may also draw pictures of things they see happening.
3. For additional suggestions on doing projects, see the Teacher's Notes on pages xvi–xviii.

■ INTERNET

1. For this activity, pair students with less computer experience with those who have more experience.
2. Suggest some Web sites to visit such as CNN, NBC, or *The New York Times*.

■ VOCABULARY JOURNAL

Refer to the Pre-lesson (page 6) for an explanation of the vocabulary journal.

GRAMMAR AND VOCABULARY Look around your classroom. Write a paragraph about what you, your instructor, and your classmates are doing or not doing. Use the grammar and vocabulary from the lesson. Read your paragraph to the class.

PROJECT Create a photo collage of school activities.

1. Work in groups of three students.
2. Find or take photos of people doing things at school.
3. Create a collage of these activities.
4. What are the people doing in the pictures? Label each activity.
5. Show your collage to the class.

They are talking. He is walking. We are listening.

 INTERNET Go online. Find news stories with photographs. Use the key word "news." What is happening in the photographs? Tell your classmates.

VOCABULARY JOURNAL Write sentences for new vocabulary you learned in this lesson.

Example: *I am thinking about my homework.*

■ EXPANSION IDEA

Internet

1. Have students share the information they found on the Internet with the entire class. If a printer is available, you may want to have them print out their pictures and then describe them to the class.

PART 1
The Present Progressive Tense:
Yes/No Questions and Short
Answers

PART 2
The Present Progressive Tense:
Wh- Questions

Lesson ⑫

Computer Science: Computer Literacy

Overview

1. Elicit students' prior knowledge. Ask: *What do you think we will learn about in this lesson?*
2. Have students share their knowledge and personal experiences about using computers. Possible questions you might ask: *Do you have a computer at your house? If so, what do you use it for? Do you have an e-mail address? If so, who do you send e-mails to? How fast do you type? Have you ever taken any computer classes?*

■ CONTENT VOCABULARY

Look at the pictures. Do you know the words?

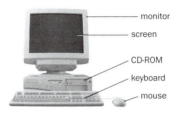

monitor
screen
CD-ROM
keyboard
mouse

desktop computer

laptop computer

Internet

e-mail

printer

Write the new words in your vocabulary journal.

■ THINK ABOUT IT

Check (✔) what you can use a computer to do.

I can use a computer to . . .

write papers. ✔   do research. ✔   play music. ✔

send e-mail. ✔   play computer games. ✔   (what else?). **Answers will vary.**

93

■ CONTENT VOCABULARY

Direct students' attention to the pictures and the labeled vocabulary words. Ask: *What do you see in the picture?* Help students understand the vocabulary they aren't familiar with. If you have a computer in your classroom, use it to talk about the vocabulary. Ask: *What is the difference between a desktop computer and a laptop computer?*

■ THINK ABOUT IT

1. Have students do this activity with a partner and then share their answers with a pair sitting next to them.
2. Have each group of four share how they use the computer. For example, they might say: *Three of us use the computer for research. One of us uses the computer to play music.*

■ CONTENT NOTES

Computer Science

The topic for this lesson is Computer Science: Computer Literacy. While many of your students may be familiar with computers and their uses, some of them may not be. All of your students should have at least a little experience from the Internet activities in each lesson of this textbook.

This lesson gives you an opportunity to talk about the importance of computers in our society. As a brainstorming activity, have the students get into small groups and list every place they can think of that computers are used (for example: ATM machines at banks and cash registers at restaurants and stores).

PART ONE

The Present Progressive Tense: *Yes/No* Questions and Short Answers

Part 1 introduces students to *yes/no* questions in the present progressive tense and to short answers.

■ GRAMMAR IN CONTENT

This section exposes students to a theme-based reading that includes examples of the target structure. Students can refer to the grammar chart(s) to complete the controlled practice activities.

■ EXERCISE A *Track 26*

1. Ask students to look at the picture. Ask the following questions: *Who are the two people in the picture? Where are they? What do you think they are talking about?*
2. Play the audio and have students follow along.
3. Ask the following questions: *Is the computer working? Is the student using it? What is he doing on the computer?*

■ GRAMMAR CHARTS

The Present Progressive Tense: Yes/No Questions and Short Answers

Go over the charts with the students. As you go through the charts, refer to the examples from the reading to reinforce the rules.

■ EXERCISE B

1. Have students refer to the charts as they write short answers to the questions.
2. Say the questions, and call on students to say their answers.

■ GRAMMAR IN CONTENT

A Read and listen.

TR26

In the Computer Lab

Lab assistant:	Is this computer **working**?
Student:	Yes, it **is**.
Lab assistant:	**Are** you **using** it?
Student:	Yes, I **am**.
Lab assistant:	**Are** you **doing** research?
Student:	No, I'm not.
Lab assistant:	**Are** you **writing** a paper?
Student:	No, I'm not. I'm playing a computer game.
Lab assistant:	Sorry. No computer games in the lab.
Student:	Oh, OK. I'm sorry!

The Present Progressive Tense: *Yes/No* Questions

Be	Subject	Verb + -ing
Am	I	standing?
Is	he she it	working?
Are	you we they	writing?

Short Answers

Affirmative

Yes	Subject	Be
	I	am.
Yes,	he she it	is.
	you we they	are.

Negative

No	Subject + Be + Not
	I'm not.
No,	he isn't. OR he's not. she isn't. OR she's not. it isn't. OR it's not.
	you aren't. OR you're not. we aren't. OR we're not. they aren't. OR they're not.

B Look at the dialogue "In the Computer Lab." Give a short answer for each question.

1. Is the computer working? _____ Yes, it is. _____
2. Is the student using it? _____ **Yes, he is.** _____
3. Is he doing research? _____ **No, he isn't.** _____
4. Is he writing a paper? _____ **No, he isn't.** _____
5. Is he playing a computer game? _____ **Yes, he is.** _____

94 LESSON 12 | Computer Science: Computer Literacy

■ EXPANSION IDEAS

Exercise A

1. Have students practice the conversation with a partner.

Grammar Charts

1. Have students practice asking and answering the questions with a partner. One student will ask a question from the first chart and the other student will answer using the second chart. Model this for students until they understand what to do.

C Look at the picture. Write *yes/no* questions and short answers about it.

Elena   Hanif   Tan

Ivanna

1. (Ivanna / stand next to the printer)

   Q: _Is Ivanna standing next to the printer_ ? A: _____Yes, she is_____ .

2. (Elena and Hanif / use laptops)

   Q: _____**Are Elena and Hanif using laptops**_____ ? A: _____**Yes, they are**_____ .

3. (Hanif / sit between Elena and Ivanna)

   Q: _____**Is Hanif sitting between Elena and Ivanna**_____ ? A: _____**No, he isn't**_____ .

4. (Tan / putting a CD-ROM in the computer)

   Q: _____**Is Tan putting a CD-ROM in the computer**_____ ? A: _____**Yes, he is**_____ .

5. (Ivanna and Tan / wear blue shirts)

   Q: _____**Are Ivanna and Tan wearing blue shirts**_____ ? A: _____**Yes, they are**_____ .

6. (Elena / using the mouse)

   Q: _____**Is Elena using the mouse**_____ ? A: _____**Yes, she is**_____ .

■ COMMUNICATE

D PAIR WORK Ask and answer present progressive questions with a partner. Use the words provided. Then make up more present progressive questions to ask your partner. Take turns.

 Are we practicing the present progressive?  Yes, we are.

1. we / practice the present progressive
2. we / practice the past tense
3. I / sit next to a window
4. you / wear jeans
5. the instructor / write on the board
6. the instructor / explain the grammar

■ **EXERCISE C**

Have students write *yes/no* questions and short answers and then practice asking and answering the questions with a partner.

■ **COMMUNICATE**

The Communicate section allows students to practice the target grammar in more communicative, less-controlled ways through speaking and writing activities.

■ **EXERCISE D**

1. Point out the words in number 1 and the way they are used in the example. Model the example with a student.
2. Have students invent some present progressive questions of their own.

■ **EXPANSION IDEAS**

Exercise C

1. Ask for volunteers to write the questions and answers on the board.

Exercise D

1. Ask for volunteers to act out some of the questions they made up.

■ EXERCISE E

Model this activity by thinking of a student and having the class ask you questions about this person until they can guess who you have in mind. You may want to write some questions on the board to help them get started. For example:

Is the student male or female?
Is she wearing glasses?
Is she holding a pencil?
Is she sitting in the front of the classroom?

The Present Progressive Tense: *Wh-* Questions

Part 2 introduces students to *wh-* questions in the present progressive tense.

■ GRAMMAR IN CONTENT

This section exposes students to a theme-based reading that includes examples of the target structure. Students can refer to the grammar chart(s) to complete the controlled practice activities.

■ EXERCISE A *Track 27*

1. Have students cover up the reading with a piece of paper and look only at the picture.
2. Have students listen to the recording with the reading still covered.
3. After students have heard the recording, ask them: *What is Keiko doing? Who is she writing to? Why is she writing the e-mail?*
4. Have students uncover the reading. Play the recording again so they can follow along and see how well they remembered.

E **GROUP WORK** Work in groups of three students. One student thinks of a person in class. The others ask questions to guess the person. Take turns. Answers will vary.

Is she wearing a red shirt and blue jeans?

Is she writing in her notebook?

Yes, she is.

No, she isn't.

PART TWO	The Present Progressive Tense: *Wh-* Questions

■ GRAMMAR IN CONTENT

A **Read and listen.**
TR27

Writing an E-mail

Mai: **What are** you **doing?**
Keiko: I'm writing an e-mail.
Mai: **Who are** you **writing** to?
Keiko: I'm writing to Inez.
Mai: **Why are** you **writing** to Inez?
Keiko: We're making plans to get together.
Mai: You aren't typing anymore. What's wrong?
Keiko: You're asking too many questions. It's hard to concentrate.

concentrate: to focus, to think hard about something

The Present Progressive Tense: *Wh-* Questions

Wh- Word	*Be*	Subject	Verb + *-ing*	Answers		
Who	am	I	talking to?	Eduardo.	OR	You're talking to Eduardo.
What	are	you	doing?	Writing.	OR	I'm writing an e-mail.
Where	is	Lola	studying?	The lab.	OR	She's studying in the lab.
How	are	you	feeling?	Fine.	OR	I'm feeling fine.
Why	is	she	crying?	Because she's sad.		

Note:
The question "What . . . doing?" is often answered with a different verb.
Example: *What are you* **doing?** *I'm* **writing** *a letter.*

■ EXPANSION IDEAS

Exercise E

1. In groups, have students choose a person in the classroom and write a paragraph about him or her. For example:

She is sitting on the left side of the classroom. She is wearing black pants and a blue shirt.

Ask for a volunteer from each group to read their paragraph, and have the class guess who the paragraph is about.

Grammar Chart

1. Have students practice asking and answering the questions with a partner. One student will ask a question from the left side of the chart and the other student will give an answer from the right side of the chart. Model this for students until they understand what to do.

B Look at the dialogue "Writing an E-mail." Match the questions and answers.

   b   1. What is Keiko doing?   a. Asking a lot of questions.

   d   2. Who is Keiko writing to?   b. Writing an e-mail.

   e   3. Who is Keiko talking to?   c. They're making plans.

   c   4. Why is she writing to Inez?   d. Inez.

   a   5. What is Mai doing?   e. Mai.

C Complete each question. Use the information from the answer.

1. **Question:** What _____is Sally buying?_____

   Answer: Sally is buying a laptop computer.

2. **Question:** Where _____**is Sally buying it?**_____

   Answer: She's buying it at the mall.

3. **Question:** Who _____**is Sally speaking to?**_____

   Answer: She's speaking to a salesperson.

4. **Question:** Who _____**is she shopping with?**_____

   Answer: She's shopping with a friend.

5. **Question:** Why _____**does she need it?**_____

   Answer: She needs it for school.

D Write *wh-* questions about the underlined words in the statements.

1. Linda is sending an e-mail to John. _____Who is Linda sending an e-mail to?_____

2. Linda is looking at the screen. _____**What is Linda looking at?**_____

3. She is working in the computer lab. _____**Where is she working?**_____

4. John is sitting in his room. _____**Where is John sitting?**_____

5. He's reading Linda's e-mail. _____**What is he reading?**_____

6. He is feeling good. _____**How is he feeling?**_____

EXERCISE B

Have students check their answers with a partner and then take turns asking and answering the questions.

EXERCISE C

1. Have students do this activity orally with a partner before writing the answers in their books. Once they both agree, have them write the answers in their books.

2. Call on pairs to act out their questions and answers.

EXERCISE D

1. Ask for volunteers to come to the board and write the questions.

2. If there are mistakes, put an X next to each question that has a mistake and ask for other students to come up and fix the mistakes.

EXPANSION IDEA

Exercise B

1. Have students rewrite and practice the questions and answers in a dialogue format using complete answers instead of short ones. The dialogue should start like this:

A: *What is Keiko doing?*

B: *She is writing an e-mail.*

■ COMMUNICATE

The Communicate section allows students to practice the target grammar in more communicative, less-controlled ways through speaking and writing activities.

■ EXERCISE E

Help students get started by modeling a few examples.

E **PAIR WORK** **What's happening in your class right now? Ask and answer questions. Use *wh-* questions in the present progressive. Answers will vary.**

What's Jill doing?

She's talking.

Who is she talking to?

Tom.

Connection

Putting It Together

The purpose of this section of the lesson is to connect and extend students' understanding of the grammar, vocabulary, and content from this lesson.

Connection Putting It Together

GRAMMAR AND VOCABULARY **Look at the picture. Ask and answer questions about what is happening. Use the grammar and vocabulary from the lesson. Answers will vary.**

Computer Café

■ GRAMMAR AND VOCABULARY

1. Help students get started by asking them a few questions about the picture using grammar and vocabulary from the lesson.
2. When students are done practicing with a partner, ask for volunteers to come to the front of the room and talk about the picture.

■ PROJECT

1. Go over the directions with the students, making sure they understand what they are supposed to do.
2. For additional suggestions on doing projects, see the Teacher's Notes on pages xvi–xviii.

■ INTERNET

1. For this activity, ask students to find a partner to exchange e-mail addresses and messages with.
2. If necessary, pair students who don't have an e-mail account with those who do.

■ VOCABULARY JOURNAL

Refer to the Pre-lesson (page 6) for an explanation of the vocabulary journal.

PROJECT **Perform and narrate a silent movie.**

1. Work in small groups.
2. Decide where your movie will take place, who the characters are, and what the story is.
3. Choose a name for your movie.
4. Write the narration for each action in your movie. Use the present progressive tense.
5. Have some students from your group narrate the movie while the other students perform it for the class.

 INTERNET **Go to an Internet café or computer lab. What are people doing? Send an e-mail to a classmate about what is happening.**

VOCABULARY JOURNAL **Write sentences for new vocabulary you learned in this lesson.**

Example: *I send my mother a letter or e-mail every week.*

■ EXPANSION IDEA

Project

1. Have students type their narratives on a computer and add art to go along with the dialogue.

2. For additional suggestions on doing projects, see the Teacher's Notes on pages xvi–xviii.

PART 1
The Simple Present Tense vs.
the Present Progressive Tense:
Statements

PART 2
The Simple Present Tense vs.
the Present Progressive Tense:
Yes/No Questions

PART 3
The Simple Present Tense vs.
the Present Progressive Tense:
Wh- Questions

Lesson 13

English:
Journal Writing

Overview

Elicit students' prior knowledge.
Ask: *What do you think we will learn about in this lesson?*

■ CONTENT VOCABULARY

1. Direct students' attention to the drawing of the man and ask: *What is this man doing? What is a journal?* Discuss the word *journal* and ask the students if any of them write in journals.

2. Direct students' attention to the poem and story and discuss the differences between these types of writings.

3. Direct students' attention to the bottom set of drawings and have them help you list the different emotions on the board.

■ THINK ABOUT IT

Have students do this activity by themselves and then share their answers with a partner.

■ CONTENT VOCABULARY

Look at the pictures. Do you know the words?

ideas   memories

problems

journal

poem

drawing

story

 happy   sad   angry   scared

feelings

Write the new words in your vocabulary journal.

■ THINK ABOUT IT

Check (✔) what you can write about in a journal.

✔ memories   ✔ drawings   ✔ feelings   ✔ problems

✔ stories   ✔ things you see   ✔ things you hear   ✔ poems

<u>Answers will vary.</u>   (what else?)

99

■ CONTENT NOTES

English

The topic for this lesson is English: Journal Writing. Regular writing practice provides a useful tool to improve writing skills.

Encourage students to start writing in a journal. For example:

1. Have each student give you a notebook to use as his or her journal.

2. At a designated time every day, pass out the journals and have students write for 15 to 30 minutes on an assigned topic, such as "your weekend," "your family," "your educational experiences," or "yesterday."

3. Once a week, skim through the journals and make comments on content only.

Part 1 introduces students to statements in the simple present and present progressive tenses.

■ GRAMMAR IN CONTENT

This section exposes students to a theme-based reading that includes examples of the target structure. Students can refer to the grammar chart(s) to complete the controlled practice activities.

■ EXERCISE A *Track 28*

1. Ask students to look at the picture. Ask the following questions: *Where is this woman? What is she doing?*
2. Play the audio and have students follow along.
3. Ask students why verbs in the simple present tense are used in the first paragraph and verbs in the present progressive tense are used in the second. See if the students can help you formulate rules for using the correct tense.

■ GRAMMAR CHART

The Simple Present Tense vs. the Present Progressive Tense: Statements

Go over the chart with the students and refer back to the reading for additional example sentences. As you go through the second and third bulleted items in the Notes, write examples of incorrect sentences on the board, such as, *I am needing a piece of paper* or *She is often riding her bicycle to class.* Draw lines through the sentences to show that they are incorrect.

■ EXERCISE B

Have students complete the activity and check their answers with a partner.

■ GRAMMAR IN CONTENT

TR28

A Read and listen.

Writing in a Café

I'm an English major. I <u>write</u> in my journal every day for my composition class. I often <u>write</u> about my thoughts and feelings. Sometimes I <u>draw</u> pictures. I (don't worry) about spelling, punctuation, or grammar in my journal.
Right now I'm (sitting) in a café. I'm (looking) at people and (writing) about them. I <u>see</u> a woman across from me. She's (not drinking) her coffee. She's (writing) in a notebook. Maybe she's (writing) in her journal, too.

composition: a type of writing

punctuation: marks used to make writing clear (for example, ; , : ! ? .)

too: also

The Simple Present Tense vs. the Present Progressive Tense: Statements

	Simple Present	Present Progressive
Affirmative	He **writes** in his journal every day. We **read** the newspaper every morning.	He **is writing** in his journal now. We **are not reading** the newspaper now.
Negative	I **do not write** in my journal every day. We **do not read** the newspaper every day.	I **am not writing** in my journal now. We **are not reading** the newspaper now.

Notes:
- Use the simple present to talk about habits and things that people do or do not do again and again. Use the present progressive to talk about actions happening or not happening right now.
- Some verbs are not usually used in the present progressive tense. These verbs include *hate, hear, know, like, love, need, remember, see, taste, understand,* and *want.*
- Adverbs of frequency and time expressions are used with the simple present. They are not usually used with the present progressive. Use "now" or "right now" with the present progressive.

B Look at the reading "Writing in a Café." <u>Underline</u> the simple present tense verbs. (Circle) the present progressive tense verbs. Answers are above.

■ EXPANSION IDEAS

Exercise A

1. Have students rewrite the paragraph in the third person, changing all of the *I*s to *she*s.
2. Have students rewrite the paragraph again but this time changing all of the *I*s to *she*s and making the sentences negative.
3. Have students do either of the above exercises with a partner, orally instead of in writing.

Grammar Chart

1. Have students write sentences in the simple present tense with words that are not usually used in the present progressive tense: *hate, hear, know, like, love, need, remember, see, taste, understand, want.*

C Complete the paragraph. Use the simple present or the present progressive form of the verbs in parentheses.

Right now I (write) ___*am writing*___ in my journal. It (rain)
                          (1)

___**is raining**___ outside. I (think) ___**am thinking**___ about my family. I often
      (2)   (3)

(think) ___**think**___ about my family. I am in LA. My family is in Japan.
              (4)

I (speak) ___**speak**___ with my family every weekend. My mother (send)
                (5)

___**sends**___ me letters every week. But I still miss them. Oh! The phone
      (6)

(ring) ___**is ringing**___. Maybe my father (call) ___**is calling**___. He always
              (7)   (8)

(call) ___**calls**___ on Sunday.
              (9)

D Complete the sentences with a negative statement.

1. Raj is studying in the library now. Tanya ___*is not studying in the library now*___.

2. Tanya is writing in her journal now. Raj ___**is not writing in his journal now**___.

3. Raj is using a dictionary now. Tanya ___**is not using a dictionary now**___.

4. Tanya writes poems in her journal. Raj ___**does not write poems in his journal**___.

5. Raj draws pictures in his journal. Tanya ___**does not draw pictures in her journal**___.

6. Raj shows Tanya his journal. Tanya ___**does not show Raj her journal**___.

E Correct the journal entry. There are six more mistakes.

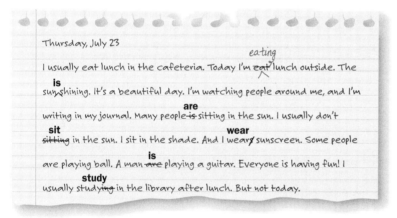

Thursday, July 23

I usually eat lunch in the cafeteria. Today I'm ~~eat~~ **eating** lunch outside. The
sun~shining. It's a beautiful day. I'm watching people around me, and I'm **is**
writing in my journal. Many people ~~is~~ **are** sitting in the sun. I usually don't
~~sitting~~ **sit** in the sun. I sit in the shade. And I wear✗ **wear** sunscreen. Some people
are playing ball. A man ~~are~~ **is** playing a guitar. Everyone is having fun! I
usually ~~studying~~ **study** in the library after lunch. But not today.

Have students complete the activity. Then go over the answers as a class.

■ **EXERCISE D**

1. Have students complete the activity and then go over the answers with a partner.
2. Ask for volunteers to write the sentences on the board.
3. If there are mistakes, write an X next to each sentence that has a mistake and ask for other students to come up and fix the mistakes.

■ **EXERCISE E**

Allow students time to find all seven of the mistakes and then go over the answers as a class.

■ **EXPANSION IDEAS**

Exercise C

1. Have students rewrite the paragraph in Exercise C in the third person, changing the *Is* to *hes.*
2. Have students rewrite the paragraph in Exercise C, using their own personal information.

Exercise E

1. Have students rewrite the paragraph, correcting all of the mistakes.

■ COMMUNICATE

The Communicate section allows students to practice the target grammar in more communicative, less-controlled ways through speaking and writing activities.

■ EXERCISE F

1. Remind students to look at Exercise E on page 101 for an example.
2. Have students share their journal entries with a partner.

■ EXERCISE G

1. Have students write in their journals and then share their journal entries with a partner.

PART TWO

The Simple Present Tense vs. the Present Progressive Tense: Yes/No Questions

Part 2 introduces students to *yes/no* questions in the simple present and present progressive tenses.

■ GRAMMAR IN CONTENT

This section exposes students to a theme-based reading that includes examples of the target structure. Students can refer to the grammar chart(s) to complete the controlled practice activities.

■ EXERCISE A *Track 29*

1. Play the audio and have students follow along.
2. Have students practice the conversation with a partner.

■ GRAMMAR CHART

The Simple Present Tense vs. the Present Progressive Tense: Yes/No Questions

Go over the chart with the students. Say the questions and model rising intonation. Call on different students to answer, using the short answers in the chart.

■ COMMUNICATE

F WRITE Write a journal entry. Write about the things happening around you. What are you doing? What are your classmates doing?   Answers will vary.

G WRITE Write a journal entry about activities you do often. Tell about any hobbies and interests you have. Do any of your friends or family members have similar hobbies or interests?

PART TWO	The Simple Present Tense vs. the Present Progressive Tense: *Yes/No* Questions

■ GRAMMAR IN CONTENT

 A Read and listen.

TR29

Interview with an English Instructor

Interviewer:	**Do** your students **write** in journals?
Professor Harris:	Yes, they **do.**
Interviewer:	**Are** they **writing** in their journals now?
Professor Harris:	Yes, they **are.**
Interviewer:	**Are** they **writing** about themselves?
Professor Harris:	Yes, they **are.** They're writing about their feelings, ideas, problems, and memories.
Interviewer:	**Do** your students **worry** about spelling and punctuation in their journals?
Professor Harris:	No, they **don't.**
Interviewer:	**Do** they **write** in their journals every day?
Professor Harris:	Yes, they **do.**

The Simple Present Tense vs. the Present Progressive Tense: *Yes/No* Questions

	Yes/No Questions	Short Answers
Simple Present	**Do** you **teach** an English class? **Does** she **teach** an English class?	Yes, I **do.** OR No, I **don't.** Yes, she **does.** OR No, she **doesn't.**
Present Progressive	**Are** you **teaching** an English class now? **Is** she **teaching** an English class now?	Yes, I **am.** OR No, I'm **not.** Yes, she **is.** OR No, she **isn't.**

■ EXPANSION IDEA

Grammar Chart

1. Have pairs of students practice asking and answering the questions in the chart. The first time have them answer *yes*, and the second time have them answer *no*.

B Look at the dialogue "Interview with an English Instructor." Answer the questions with short answers.

1. Do Professor Harris's students keep journals? ___Yes, they do.___

·2. Are they writing in their journals now? ___Yes, they are.___

3. Are they writing about themselves? ___Yes, they are.___

4. Do they worry about spelling in their journals? ___No, they don't.___

5. Do they write in their journals every day? ___Yes, they do.___

C Listen to each question. (Circle) the correct answer.

TR30

1. (a.) Yes, she does.   b. Yes, she is.
2. a. No, she doesn't.   (b.) No, she isn't.
3. a. Yes, they do.   (b.) Yes, they are.
4. (a.) No, they don't.   b. No, they aren't.
5. (a.) Yes, you do.   b. Yes, you are.
6. a. Yes, you do.   (b.) Yes, you are.

D Write questions for the answers.

1. _Is Amy sitting in the right chair?_ Yes, Amy is sitting in the right chair.

2. **Does she always sit in that chair?** Yes, she always sits in that chair.

3. **Are we listening to the instructor?** Yes, we are listening to the instructor.

4. **Do we always listen to the instructor?** Yes, we always listen to the instructor.

5. **Are you writing in your journal now?** Yes, I am writing in my journal now.

6. **Do you write in your journal everyday?** No, I don't write in my journal every day.

E Rewrite the questions correctly.

1. Is it rain now? _Is it raining now?_

2. Is it rain every day? **Does it rain every day?**

3. Does she using a computer every day?

    Does she use a computer every day?

4. She using a computer now? **Is she using a computer now?**

5. Does you often use a dictionary? **Do you often use a dictionary?**

6. You use a dictionary right now? **Are you using a dictionary right now?**

■ **EXERCISE B**

Have students check their answers with a partner when they are finished.

■ **EXERCISE C** *Track 30*

1. Prepare the class for the audio by telling students that they will need to circle the grammatically correct answers.

2. Write the following examples on the board to help students practice before they listen to the audio.
   a. *Yes, she does.*   b. *Yes, she is.*
   a. *No, she doesn't.* b. *No, she isn't.*
   Read: *Is Amanda sleeping right now?* (have students choose *a* or *b*)
   Read: *Does Amanda have a car?* (have students choose *a* or *b*)

3. Play the audio and have students circle the correct answers.

4. Play the audio a second time, pausing after each item to check students' answers.

■ **EXERCISE D**

Ask for volunteers to write the questions on the board.

■ **EXERCISE E**

Ask for volunteers to write the corrected questions on the board.

■ **EXPANSION IDEAS**

Exercise C

1. Have students work in pairs to write a new question for each of the items in Exercise C. Tell them to write a question that can be answered by only one of the answers in the item.

For example, for number 6: *Do I go to school here?* (Answer: Yes, you do.)

2. Have each pair of students work with another pair to ask and answer the questions they just wrote.

■ COMMUNICATE

The Communicate section allows students to practice the target grammar in more communicative, less-controlled ways through speaking and writing activities.

■ EXERCISE F

1. Model this activity with students until they are ready to do it by themselves.

PART THREE

The Simple Present Tense vs. the Present Progressive Tense: *Wh-* Questions

Part 3 introduces students to *wh-* questions in the simple present and present progressive tenses.

■ GRAMMAR IN CONTENT

This section exposes students to a theme-based reading that includes examples of the target structure. Students can refer to the grammar chart(s) to complete the controlled practice activities.

■ EXERCISE A *Track 31*

1. Have students read the conversation.
2. Play the audio and have students follow along.
3. Write a two-column chart on the board with the headings "Present" and "Present Progressive."
4. Have students work with a partner to decide which questions from the conversation belong in each column.
5. Ask for students to come up and write the questions in the correct columns on the board.

■ GRAMMAR CHART

The Simple Present Tense vs. the Present Progressive Tense: Wh- Questions

Go over the chart with the students. Read a question in simple present tense

F PAIR WORK Ask your partner a simple present tense *yes/no* question with a phrase in the box. Then ask your partner a present progressive *yes/no* question with the same phrase. Take turns. Ask more questions using your own phrases. Answers will vary.

read the newspaper	watch TV	speak English	write in a journal
think about grammar	wear jeans	drink coffee	use a dictionary

Do you read the newspaper every day?   Yes, I do.

Are you reading the newspaper now? No, I'm not.

PART THREE	The Simple Present Tense vs. the Present Progressive Tense: *Wh-* Questions

■ GRAMMAR IN CONTENT

A Read and listen.

Starting a Journal

Student: I want to start a journal, but I have so many questions. What **do** journal writers **write** about? When **do** they **write**? How **do** they **start**?

Professor Harris: It's simple. Think about these questions: How **are** you **feeling** right now? What **are** you **doing**? What **are** you **thinking** about? Look around you. Who **do** you **see**? What **are** people **doing**? Now get a pen and paper and write.

simple: not complicated

The Simple Present Tense vs. the Present Progressive Tense: *Wh-* Questions

Simple Present	Present Progressive
What **do** you **write** about in your journal?	What **are** you **writing** about in your journal?
What languages **does** she **speak**?	What language **is** she **speaking** now?
Where **do** they **work**?	Where **are** they **working** today?
Where **does** he **go** after school?	Where **is** he **going** now?

■ EXPANSION IDEA

Exercise A

1. Have students use the questions in the conversation as discussion questions as they work in small groups. For example:

Student 1: *What do journal writers write about?*
Student 2: *They write about their feelings.*
Student 3: *They write about what they did yesterday.*
Student 4: *They write their thoughts.*
Student 2: *When do they write?*
Student 1: *They write in the morning when they first wake up.*
Student 3: *They write when they get home from school or work.*
Student 4: *They write during their free time.*

B Look at each question. Is it the simple present or the present progressive tense? Circle the correct answer.

1. What do journal writers write about? (Simple Present) / Present Progressive
2. What are you doing? Simple Present /(Present Progressive)
3. When do they write? (Simple Present)/ Present Progressive
4. What do you see? (Simple Present)/ Present Progressive
5. What are you thinking about? Simple Present /(Present Progressive)

C Circle the correct question.

1. (a.) What does John study? b. What does John studying?
2. (a.) What language do you speak? b. What language are you speak?
3. a. Where am I go? (b.) Where am I going?
4. (a.) Where are you going now? b. Where do you going now?
5. (a.) Why are they smiling? b. Why does they smiling?
6. (a.) What are we doing? b. What do we doing?
7. a. Who does you writing about? (b.) Who are you writing about?

D Write the correct form of the verb in parentheses.

A: Who are you (write) ___writing___ about?
(1)

B: My mother. She's a nurse.

A: Where does she (work) ___work___ ?
(2)

B: She (work) ___works___ at Brookville Hospital.
(3)

A: What is she (do) ___doing___ now?
(4)

B: She's (sleep) ___sleeping___ .
(5)

A: Why is she (sleep) ___sleeping___ ?
(6)

B: She (come) ___comes___ home from the hospital very late.
(7)

■ COMMUNICATE

E GROUP WORK Think about a friend or family member. What is his/her name? Where is he/she? What is he/she doing right now? Ask your classmates about their friends or family members. Complete the chart. Answers will vary.

Name of Friend	Location of Friend	What Friend Is Doing

out loud and then ask, *When?* Students should respond with words like, *always* or *every day* or *anytime.* Then, read a question in present progressive and ask, *When?* Students should respond with words like, *right now* or *at this moment.* Continue alternating between the questions on the right and left sides of the chart.

■ EXERCISE B

Have students share their answers with a partner. Then go over the answers as a class.

■ EXERCISE C

Call on volunteers to read the correct questions.

■ EXERCISE D

1. Ask for volunteers to write the correct questions and answers on the board in the same arrangement as shown in the book.
2. Have students close their books. Ask for volunteers to practice the conversation out loud or have pairs practice it together. This reminds students to look up rather than always looking down at the book.

■ COMMUNICATE

The Communicate section allows students to practice the target grammar in more communicative, less-controlled ways through speaking and writing activities.

■ EXERCISE E

Model this activity with students so that they understand how to do it.

■ EXPANSION IDEAS

Exercise B

1. Have pairs of students quiz each other on the answers to this exercise. Have one student close his or her book while the other reads the question aloud. The students with their books closed must say whether the question is in the simple present or present progressive verb tense.

Exercise C

1. Have students work with a partner to label each correct question simple present or present progressive.

Exercise E

1. Have students write sentences based on their completed charts. For example:

Karla's friend's name is Larsen. Larsen is at work. He is taking orders from customers because he works in a restaurant.

Connection

Putting It Together

The purpose of this section of the lesson is to connect and extend students' understanding of the grammar, vocabulary, and content from this lesson.

■ GRAMMAR AND VOCABULARY

Help students get started on this writing by brainstorming on the board some of the things they might write in their letters.

■ PROJECT

1. Go through each step with the students, making sure they understand what they are supposed to do.
2. For additional suggestions on doing individual projects, see the Teacher's Notes on pages xvi–xviii.

■ INTERNET

1. Have students do this activity alone or with a partner.
2. Suggest some Web sites for students to visit such as CNN, NBC, or *The New York Times.*

■ VOCABULARY JOURNAL

Refer to the Pre-lesson (page 6) for an explanation of the vocabulary journal.

GRAMMAR AND VOCABULARY Write a letter or e-mail to someone you know. Use the grammar and vocabulary from this lesson.

> Dear Kenji,
>   Hi! I hope you are well. I miss you. What are you doing right now? Are you reading this letter in the kitchen? Is mom cooking?

PROJECT Start a writing journal.

1. Buy a notebook.
2. Each day write a journal entry in your notebook. Start each entry with the date. Then write about your thoughts, feelings, and problems.
3. Keep writing in your journal until the end of the course.
4. At the end of the course, read your journal.

 INTERNET Go online. Search the news headlines and report back to the class on what's happening today. Do these things happen often? Discuss.

VOCABULARY JOURNAL Write sentences for new vocabulary you learned in this lesson.

Example: *I wrote a poem for my boyfriend on Valentine's Day.*

Sociology: The Family

Overview

1. Elicit students' prior knowledge. Ask: *What do you think we will learn about in this lesson?*
2. Write "Family Tree" on the board and ask students if they know what it is.

■ CONTENT VOCABULARY

Look at Sarah's family tree. Do you know the words?

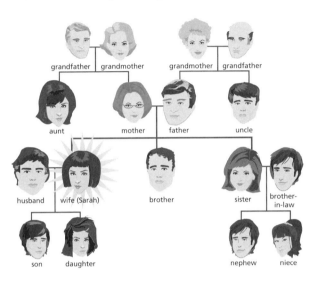

married

divorced

Write the new words in your vocabulary journal.

■ CONTENT VOCABULARY

1. Direct students' attention to the pictures and the family vocabulary words. Help students understand the vocabulary they aren't familiar with.
2. To practice the vocabulary, take an informal poll by asking students to raise their hands. Possible questions: *Who has a sister? Who has a brother? Who has a niece? Who has a son?*

■ THINK ABOUT IT

Discuss these questions with a partner. **Answers will vary.**

1. Who are the people in your family?
2. Why are families important?

■ THINK ABOUT IT

Have students do this activity with a partner and then share their answers with a pair sitting next to them.

107

■ CONTENT NOTES

Sociology

The topic for this lesson is Sociology: The Family.

The following are some possible discussion questions for this lesson:

1. Names (in the U.S. we have a first, middle, and last name) How is this different in other cultures? How does the name change in marriage? What names are given to the children?
2. What family member is the head of the household? The head of the family?
3. What family members live together?

PART ONE

Possessive Nouns

Part 1 introduces students to possessive nouns. If necessary, refer students to the Pre-lesson (page 1) for an explanation of nouns.

■ GRAMMAR IN CONTENT

This section exposes students to a theme-based reading that includes examples of the target structure. Students can refer to the grammar chart(s) to complete the controlled practice activities.

■ EXERCISE A *Track 32*

1. Ask students to look at the picture. Ask the following questions: *Who are the people in the picture? How are they related? Do they all look alike?*

2. Play the audio and have students follow along.

3. Ask the following questions: *Who does Jenn live with? What is her mother's maiden name? Whose last name does Jenn have?*

■ GRAMMAR CHART
Possessive Nouns

As you go over the chart with the students, refer to the examples from the reading to reinforce the rules.

■ EXERCISE B

When students are finished with the exercise, have them check their answers with a partner. Then ask for volunteers to write the correct possessive forms on the board.

■ GRAMMAR IN CONTENT

A **Read and listen.**

TR32

One Family

What is a family? A traditional family is a mother, a father, and their children. But families are often more complicated. For example, **Jenn's** parents are divorced. Jenn lives with her mother, her stepfather, and her **stepfather's** daughter.

Jenn's last name is Maslin. This is her **father's** last name. Her **mother's** last name is Roberts. This is her **mother's** maiden name. And her **stepfather's** and **stepsister's** last name is Brown.

traditional: usual, customary

maiden name: a woman's family name before she marries

stepfather: father by marriage

Possessive Nouns		
Nouns	**Explanation**	**Examples**
Singular nouns: Karen, brother	add apostrophe (') + s	**Karen's** house is small. Her **brother's** wife is nice.
Plural nouns that end in -s: sons, dogs	add apostrophe (') only	My **sons'** names are Dan and John. The **dogs'** dishes are empty.
Irregular plural nouns: women, children	add apostrophe (') + s	The **women's** room is to the left. The **children's** toys are on the floor.

B **Complete the sentences with the possessive form of the nouns in parentheses.**

1. (Mark) _____Mark's_____ parents are divorced.

2. Their (mother) _____mother's_____ name is Maria.

3. My (parent) _____parent's_____ house is large.

4. The (children) _____children's_____ school is across the street.

5. Diane is a (woman) _____woman's_____ name.

6. Diane and Karen are (women) _____women's_____ names.

■ EXPANSION IDEA

Exercise A

1. Have students find each possessive form in the reading and decide which rule it follows: singular, plural, or irregular.

C Look at the family tree. Complete the sentences about Ben and his family. Use possessive nouns.

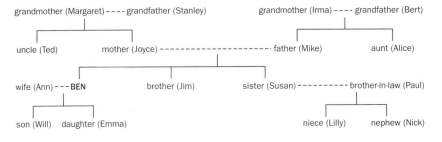

grandmother (Margaret) ---- grandfather (Stanley)   grandmother (Irma) ---- grandfather (Bert)

uncle (Ted)   mother (Joyce) -------------------- father (Mike)   aunt (Alice)

wife (Ann) --- **BEN**   brother (Jim)   sister (Susan) --------- brother-in-law (Paul)

son (Will)   daughter (Emma)   niece (Lilly)   nephew (Nick)

1. Ben is married. His _____*wife's*_____ name is Ann.

2. His _____**son's**_____ name is Will.

3. Joyce is his _____**mother's**_____ name.

4. Bert is his _____**grandfather's**_____ name.

5. Will and Emma are his _____**children's**_____ names.

6. Stanley is _____*Margaret's*_____ husband.

7. Nick is _____**Lilly's**_____ brother.

8. Lilly is _____**Nick's**_____ sister.

9. Lilly is _____**Paul's**_____ niece.

D PAIR WORK Work with a partner to make more sentences about the family tree in exercise C. **Answers will vary.**

■ C O M M U N I C A T E

E PAIR WORK Draw a family tree for your family. Then use your family tree to tell your partner about your family. **Answers will vary.**

■ **EXERCISE C**

1. When students are finished, have them practice the sentences with a partner. Show them how to point to each person on the family tree as they are reading the related sentence.

2. Ask for volunteers to write the completed sentences on the board.

■ **EXERCISE D**

1. Model this activity for students until they are ready to do it by themselves.

2. Ask for volunteers to act out some of the sentences they made up.

■ **COMMUNICATE**

The Communicate section allows students to practice the target grammar in more communicative, less-controlled ways through speaking and writing activities.

■ **EXERCISE E**

1. Help students get started on making their own family trees by starting one on the board for them. It could be yours or you could create a fictitious one.

2. Walk around and help students.

3. Once students are finished, pair them up with other students in the class to share their family trees.

■ **EXPANSION IDEAS**

Exercise C

1. Have students cover up the sentences they completed.

2. Ask for volunteers to make up sentences about the family tree and say them aloud to the class.

3. Have the rest of the class look at the tree and decide if the sentence is correct or not.

For example:

Student A: *Mike is Alice's husband.*

Class: *Yes*

Student B: *Joyce is Margaret's niece.*

Class: *No. Joyce is Margaret's daughter.*

Exercise E

1. Ask for volunteers to draw their family trees on the board and share them with the class.

PART TWO

Possessive Adjectives

Part 2 introduces students to possessive adjectives.

■ GRAMMAR IN CONTENT

This section exposes students to a theme-based reading that includes examples of the target structure. Students can refer to the grammar chart(s) to complete the controlled practice activities.

■ EXERCISE A *Track 33* 🎧

1. Have students cover up the reading with a piece of paper and look at the picture.
2. Have students listen to the recording, with the reading still covered.
3. After students have heard the recording, ask them: *Where is this family from? Who does Amato live with? How old is Amato's sister Marta?*
4. Have students uncover the reading and play the recording again so they can follow along.

■ GRAMMAR CHART
Possessive Adjectives

Go over the chart with the students. Go over the Note. As you go through the chart, refer back to the reading for examples.

■ EXERCISE B

Have students complete the exercise and then check their answers with a partner.

■ GRAMMAR IN CONTENT

A **Read and listen.**

TR33

A Family from Mexico

Amato is part of a Mexican family. His family is very close. He lives with **his** mother, father, and sister. Amato's sister is seven years old. **Her** name is Marta. **Their** father is the head of the house. **His** name is Cristo. **Their** mother is the heart of the family. **Her** name is Isabel. **Their** grandmother and grandfather also live with them. **Their** aunts, uncles, and cousins live nearby.

close: not far apart, near
head of the house: the leader of the family
nearby: close by

Possessive Adjectives

Subject Pronoun	Possessive Adjective	Example
I	my	My name is Emilio.
you	your	Your house is beautiful.
he	his	His book is on the table.
she	her	Her family is in Peru.
it	its	Its tail is white.
we	our	Our car is old.
they	their	Their last name is Markov.

Note:
Possessive adjectives replace possessive nouns. Example: *Marco's mother is here = His mother is here.*

B **Look at the reading "A Family from Mexico." Complete the sentences about Amato with possessive adjectives.**

1. Cristo is _____*his*_____ father.
2. Isabel is _____**his**_____ mother.
3. Amato has a little sister. _____**Her**_____ name is Isabel.
4. Isabel and Amato have grandparents. _____**Their**_____ grandparents live with them.

110 LESSON 14 | Sociology: The Family

■ EXPANSION IDEA

Exercise A

1. Have students underline all the possessive adjectives in the reading.
2. Then have them work with a partner to create other sentences about people/things in their classroom, using those same possessive adjectives. For example:
   Reading: <u>Her</u> name is Marta.
   New sentence: *Her name is Kimla.*
   (point to student in class named Kimla)

She is sitting on the left side of the classroom. She is wearing black pants and a blue shirt.

3. Ask for volunteers to read their new sentences aloud.

C Complete the sentences. Use the possessive adjectives that relate to each underlined subject pronoun.

1. I am a sociology student. _____My_____ name is Yakov.

2. I live with _____my_____ wife and children in a small house.

3. My children are in elementary school. They do _____their_____ homework in the living room.

4. My neighbor has a dog. It eats _____its_____ dinner in the kitchen.

5. My brother's name is Sascha. He lives with _____his_____ wife in California.

6. My sister's name is Sonia. She lives with _____her_____ husband and children in New York.

7. My mother and father live in Russia. They love _____their_____ apartment in Moscow.

8. We visit _____my_____ parents every year.

D Answer the questions. Use possessive adjectives.   Answers will vary.

1. What is your name? _____ name is _____.

2. What are your parents' names? _____ names are _____ and _____.

3. What room is your class in? _____ class is in room _____.

4. What is your instructor's name? _____ name is _____.

5. What color is your instructor's hair? _____ hair is _____.

6. What is the name of the student next to you? _____ name is _____.

7. What color is the student's eyes? _____ eyes are _____.

8. What is the title of your class's textbook? The title of _____ textbook is _____.

E PAIR WORK Ask a classmate the questions from exercise D.   Answers will vary.

■ C O M M U N I C A T E

F WRITE Write five more questions to ask your partner about students in your class. Use possessive adjectives. Ask your partner the questions.

■ **EXERCISE C**

1. Have students complete the sentences orally with a partner before writing the answers in their books. Once they both agree, have them write the answers in their books.

2. Go over the answers as a class, calling on students to read the sentences aloud.

■ **EXERCISE D**

Have students complete the sentences by themselves.

■ **EXERCISE E**

Have students practice asking and answering the questions with a partner.

■ **COMMUNICATE**

The Communicate section allows students to practice the target grammar in more communicative, less-controlled ways through speaking and writing activities.

■ **EXERCISE F**

1. Help students get started by modeling a few example questions.

2. Have students pair up with a different partner. Have them practice asking and answering the questions from Exercise D as well as the new ones they just wrote.

■ **EXPANSION IDEA**

Exercise C

1. Have students rewrite the sentences in Exercise C, making them true about themselves.

For example:
I am an ESL student. My name is Stacy.

2. Call on students to write their sentences on the board.

Putting It Together

The purpose of this section of the lesson is to connect and extend students' understanding of the grammar, vocabulary, and content from this lesson.

■ GRAMMAR AND VOCABULARY

NOTE: In order for students to do this activity, they will need photos or drawings of their family members.

1. Read the directions aloud and go over the example in the book with students.
2. Help students get into circles of four or five.
3. Sit in one circle and model the activity for the class.
4. Walk around to help each circle.

■ PROJECT

1. Go through each step with the students, making sure they understand what they are supposed to do.
2. In class, help students write the questions they will ask the family.
3. Encourage students to ask these questions to a family they know.
4. When students come back to class with the information, help them write their paragraphs and add photos.
5. For additional suggestions on doing projects, see the Teachers Notes on pages xvi–xviii.

■ INTERNET

1. Have students find a partner and decide on the family name they will research.
2. To make sure no two pairs are using the same name, have students report their names to the class.
3. Have students work together to do their research and report back to the class.

GRAMMAR AND VOCABULARY Work with four or five students. Sit in a circle. One student shows a partner a picture or drawing of the people in his or her family. This person tells the partner the names and relationships of each person in the picture. Use the grammar and vocabulary from this lesson. Take turns.

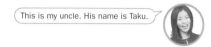

This is my uncle. His name is Taku.

The partner shows the picture to the next student in the circle and repeats the information.

This is Nori's uncle. His name is Taku.

Keep passing the picture around the circle. The last person in the circle gives the picture back to the first person and repeats the information. The first person corrects any mistakes.

This is your uncle. Your uncle's name is Taro.

No! His name is Taku!

PROJECT Make a family information book.

1. Interview three or more members of your family or a family you know.
2. Find out about their likes and dislikes; favorite book, movie, TV show; most important possession; favorite activities; etc.
3. Write a paragraph about each person. You may want to add photos.
4. Present one or more of the paragraphs to your class.

INTERNET Choose a famous family name (such as Kennedy or Gandhi). Go online. Use that last name and the word "family" as keywords. Learn more about the family. Report back to your class.

VOCABULARY JOURNAL Write sentences for new vocabulary you learned in this lesson.

Example: *My mother's sister is my aunt.*

■ EXPANSION IDEAS

Project

1. Have students type their paragraphs on the computer and scan their pictures.

Internet

1. Have students make a poster about the family name they researched, adding information they gathered as well as pictures of famous families with this last name.

■ VOCABULARY JOURNAL

Give students a few examples to get them started and them have them find five other words from this lesson to use for entries.

Literature: Shakespeare

Lesson 15

■ CONTENT VOCABULARY

Look at the pictures. Do you know the words?

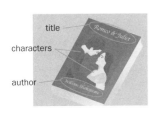

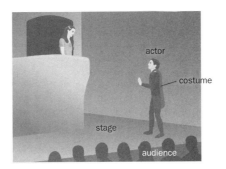

Write the new words in your vocabulary journal.

■ THINK ABOUT IT

Discuss these questions with a partner.

1. Do you know any plays by Shakespeare? If you do, choose one. What is the title of the play? Who are some of the characters in the play?
2. What is the title of your favorite book? Who is the author? Who are the characters in the book?

Overview

1. Elicit students' prior knowledge. Ask: *What do you think we will learn about in this lesson?*

■ CONTENT VOCABULARY

1. Direct students' attention to the pictures and the vocabulary words. Ask: *Do you know the play* Romeo and Juliet? *Who knows who William Shakespeare is?*
2. Have a discussion about theater and plays. Find out how much the students know about this topic and write their ideas on the board.

■ THINK ABOUT IT

1. Have students do this activity with a partner. If neither student knows Shakespeare, have them do the second question.
2. Ask for some volunteers to share what they discussed with their partners.

■ CONTENT NOTES

Literature

The topic for this lesson is Literature: Shakespeare. The following are some basic facts about Shakespeare's life:

Born: April 23, 1564 (approximate date)
Christened: April 26, 1564
Married to Anne Hathaway: November 28, 1582

First child, Susanna, christened: May 26, 1583
Twins, Hamnet & Judith, christened: February 2, 1585
Globe Theatre opened: 1599
Globe Theatre burned down: 1613
Shakespeare died: April 23, 1616

PART ONE

Object Pronouns

Part 1 introduces students to object pronouns. If necessary, refer students to the Pre-lesson (page 6) for a review of subject pronouns.

■ GRAMMAR IN CONTENT

This section exposes students to a theme-based reading that includes examples of the target structure. Students can refer to the grammar chart(s) to complete the controlled practice activities.

■ EXERCISE A *Track 34*

1. Ask students to look at the picture and describe what they think is happening.
2. Play the audio and have students follow along.
3. Have students read the story again to themselves and then ask if they have any questions.

■ GRAMMAR CHART

Subject and Object Pronouns

1. Check that students understand the grammatical terms "subject" and "object." Write a few of the simple sentences from the chart on the board and label the subjects and objects. Ask students to explain the difference; for example, they might say the subject *does* something and the object *receives* something.
2. Go over the Notes with students to show the relationships between subjects and objects and subject pronouns and object pronouns.
3. Go over the chart with the students. Point out that there are different pronoun forms for the different grammatical functions except in the cases of *you* and *it*, which have the same pronoun form for both subject and object. As you go through the chart, refer to the examples from the reading to reinforce the patterns.

■ GRAMMAR IN CONTENT

TR34

A Read and listen.

King Lear

Lear is the king of England. He decides to give his kingdom to his three daughters. First he gives **them** a test. He asks **them**: "How much do you love me?" Goneril and Regan are Lear's older daughters. They want his money and power. They tell **him** lies about their love. Lear believes **them**. Cordelia is Lear's youngest daughter. She loves Lear, but she does not talk about her love. This makes Lear angry. He throws **her** out and gives Goneril and Regan his kingdom. The king of France marries Cordelia. He brings **her** to France.

Lear lives first with Goneril and then with Regan. They both treat **him** badly. Lear realizes his mistake. He leaves their houses. He walks around in a storm and slowly loses his mind. Cordelia brings the French army to England to fight for her father. The English army wins the fight. They kill Cordelia and Lear dies from grief.

kingdom: the land and money of a king

power: control

to lose one's mind: to go mad

army: a large group that fights wars

grief: great sadness

Subject Pronouns	Object Pronouns	Examples					
I	me	I	love	him.	He	loves	me.
you	you	You	help	her.	She	helps	you.
he	him	He	calls	you.	You	call	him.
she	her	She	needs	us.	We	need	her.
it	it	It	likes	her.	She	likes	it.
we	us	We	meet	them.	They	meet	us.
they	them	They	write	you.	You	write	them.

Notes:
- Subject pronouns take the place of nouns in the subject position.
  Mary likes John. = She likes John.
- Object pronouns take the place of nouns in the object position.
  Mary likes John. = She likes him.

■ EXPANSION IDEAS

Exercise A

1. Have students work with a partner to retell the story of King Lear without looking at the book. Then, have them read it again to see what they missed.

Alternative

1. Have students work in groups of four or five. Have each person in the group tell one part of the story until they have reconstructed the whole story.

B Rewrite the sentences. Replace the underlined words with a subject or object pronoun.

1. My class and I are reading *King Lear*. _We are reading King Lear._

2. King Lear has three daughters. _He has three daughters._

3. Goneril and Regan are terrible daughters. _They are terrible daughters._

4. I don't like Goneril and Regan. _I don't like them._

5. Goneril and Regan tell Lear lies. _Goneril and Regan tell him lies._

6. He believes Goneril and Regan. _He believes them._

7. Cordelia is a good daughter. _She is a good daughter._

8. She really loves Lear. _She really loves him._

9. He treats Cordelia badly. _He treats her badly._

10. Lear makes me and my class angry. _Lear makes us angry._

C Complete the sentences with subject and object pronouns.

My name is Ms. Thompson. I'm an English Literature

instructor. _I_ teach first year students. I sometimes teach
    (1)

them a play by Shakespeare. My students are often confused
 (2)

at first. _They_ don't understand the play. They ask _me_
       (3)   (4)

many questions. _We_ discuss the play together. Then _they_
          (5)   (6)

understand _it_. Right now _we_ are reading *King Lear*.
      (7)   (8)

My students like _it_. _They_ are writing essays about their favorite character.
          (9)   (10)

Lear is an interesting character. Many students are writing about _him_. Some
                                                    (11)

students are writing about Cordelia. Most students really like _her_.
                                                 (12)

■ COMMUNICATE

D **WRITE** What is your favorite book? Write the title and the author of the book. Then write a paragraph describing the story. Read your paragraph to the class. **Answers will vary.**

■ **EXERCISE B**

1. When students are finished with the exercise, have them check their answers with a partner.

2. Then ask for volunteers to write the correct sentences on the board.

■ **EXERCISE C**

When students are finished with the exercise, ask for volunteers to read the sentences from the paragraph.

■ **COMMUNICATE**

The Communicate section allows students to practice the target grammar in more communicative, less-controlled ways through speaking and writing activities.

■ **EXERCISE D**

1. Model this activity for students by brainstorming and writing about your favorite book.

2. First write the title, author, main characters, and some plot ideas.

3. Then put that information into a short paragraph for students to follow as a model.

4. Ask for volunteers to come up to the front of the class and read their paragraphs.

5. Encourage the class to ask questions.

■ **EXPANSION IDEA**

Exercise C

1. Have students look at their completed paragraphs and underline any other nouns that could be changed into pronouns. For example, in the fourth sentence *my students* could be changed to *they*.

2. Have students write the pronouns above the words they've underlined.

3. When students are finished, ask for volunteers to read the sentences. It will be clear that the paragraph doesn't make sense with all pronouns. Ask students when nouns should be used versus when pronouns should be used.

PART TWO

Indirect Objects

Part 2 introduces students to indirect objects.

■ GRAMMAR IN CONTENT

This section exposes students to a theme-based reading that includes examples of the target structure. Students can refer to the grammar chart(s) to complete the controlled practice activities.

■ EXERCISE A *Track 35*

1. Have students cover up the reading with a piece of paper and look at the picture.

2. Have students listen to the recording, with the reading still covered.

3. Have students read the story again to themselves.

4. Model the pronunciation of the vocabulary words and have students repeat after you.

■ GRAMMAR CHART

Direct and Indirect Objects

1. Introduce the idea of sentences with two objects by writing a simple sentence with one object on the board. Ask the students to identify the subject and the object of the sentence. Next, write a simple sentence with two objects such as the first sentence in the chart. Ask the students to identify the subject. Then ask them to identify the object. They may be able to tell you that there are two objects in the sentence.

2. Go over the chart with the students. Go over the Notes. As you go through the chart, refer to the reading for examples.

■ GRAMMAR IN CONTENT

A Read and listen.

TR35

Romeo and Juliet

Romeo and Juliet's families are enemies. Romeo meets Juliet at a party. They fall in love. The next day, Friar Lawrence secretly marries them. Juliet's family plans to marry her to another man. The family makes a date for the wedding. Friar Lawrence helps Juliet. **He gives a special drink to her.** The day of her wedding comes. Juliet takes the drink. It puts her to sleep and makes her family think she is dead. Her family puts her in the family tomb. **The Friar sends a message to Romeo.** Romeo doesn't get the message. He thinks Juliet is dead. **A shopkeeper sells poison to Romeo.** He takes it to Juliet's tomb. Romeo drinks the poison and dies. Juliet wakes up. She sees Romeo and kills herself.

enemy: a person that intends harm to another
secretly: a way of doing something without others knowing
tomb: a burial room or grave
poison: a substance that harms or kills

Subject	Verb	Direct Object	*To / For* + Indirect Object
I	give	flowers	to my wife.

Subject	Verb	Indirect Object	Direct Object
I	give	my mother	flowers.

Notes:

• Some sentences have two objects after a verb: a direct object and an indirect object. An indirect object is a person or thing who receives the direct object.

• All sentences with direct and indirect objects can follow the first pattern above (subject + verb + direct object + *to/for* indirect object).

• Sentences with the following verbs can follow both of the patterns above.

To + Direct Object					*For* + Direct Object		
bring	give	tell	show		buy	do	make
e-mail	sell	send	write		cook	get	save

■ EXPANSION IDEAS

Exercise A

1. Have students work with a partner to retell the story of Romeo and Juliet without looking at the book. Then, have them read it again to see what they missed.

Alternative

1. Have students work in groups of four or five. Have each person in the group tell one part of the story until they have reconstructed the whole story.

B Use the words and phrases to make sentences with direct and indirect objects.

1. homework / is giving / the instructor / us / to

   The instructor is giving homework to us.

2. tests / he / us / gives / every week _____ **He gives us tests every week.**

3. reads / he / her / to / the book _____ **He reads the book to her.**

4. they / us / the story / told _____ **They told us the story.**

5. is showing / to / she / the photos / us _____ **She is showing the photos to us.**

6. is explaining / to / she / me / the play _____ **She is explaining the play to me.**

C Underline the direct object and (circle) the indirect object in each sentence.

1 2 3 4

5 6 7 8

"Roberto and Julietta"

1. Roberto buys <u>a ring</u> for (Julietta.)
2. Roberto reads <u>poetry</u> to (her.)
3. Roberto gives <u>the ring</u> to (her.)
4. Julietta's father sends <u>an angry e-mail</u> to (Roberto.)
5. Roberto writes <u>a letter</u> to (Julietta's family.)
6. He cooks <u>dinner</u> for her (family.)
7. He builds <u>a shed</u> for (Julietta's father.)
8. Julietta's father gives <u>his blessing</u> to (Roberto.)

D Rewrite each sentence in exercise C without *to* or *for*. Follow this sentence pattern: Subject + verb + indirect object + direct object.

1. _____ *Roberto buys Julietta a ring.*

2. _____ **Roberto reads her poetry.**

3. _____ **Roberto gives her the ring.**

4. _____ **Julietta's father sends Roberto an angry e-mail.**

---

1. Have students unscramble the sentences orally with a partner before writing the answers in their books. When both students agree, have them write the answers in their books.
2. Call on students to write the sentences on the board.

■ **EXERCISE C**

Go over the answers as a class.

■ **EXERCISE D**

1. Go over the example.
2. Once students are finished with the exercise, ask for volunteers to write the sentences on the board.

■ **EXPANSION IDEAS**

Exercise B

1. Ask volunteers to write the sentences from Exercise B on the board. Then look at each sentence as a class and ask if there is another way to say the same thing. Write the alternative version under each sentence. For example, sentence 1 could be paraphrased as: *The instructor is giving us homework.*

Exercise C

1. Have students cover up the sentences and work with a partner to retell the story.
2. Have students cover up the sentences and write a paragraph about what is happening in the pictures. Tell them to include direct and indirect objects in their sentences.

■ COMMUNICATE

The Communicate section allows students to practice the target grammar in more communicative, less-controlled ways through speaking and writing activities.

■ EXERCISE E

Help students get started by going over the example in the book. Remind students to brainstorm ideas before they start to write.

Connection

Putting It Together

The purpose of this section of the lesson is to connect and extend students' understanding of the grammar, vocabulary, and content from this lesson.

■ GRAMMAR AND VOCABULARY

When students are done practicing with a partner, ask for volunteers to come to the front of the room and talk about their plays. Alternatively, ask for the partners to come up and talk about the play their partners told them about.

■ PROJECT

1. Go through each step with the students, making sure they understand what they are supposed to do.
2. For additional suggestions on doing projects, see the Teacher's Notes on pages xvi–xviii.

■ INTERNET

To avoid duplication, consider assigning each student a specific play to find information about.

■ VOCABULARY JOURNAL

Refer to the Pre-lesson (page 6) for an explanation of the vocabulary journal.

---

5. _____ Roberto writes Julietta's family a letter.
6. _____ He cooks her family dinner.
7. _____ He builds Julietta's father a shed.
8. _____ Julietta's father gives Roberto his blessing.

■ C O M M U N I C A T E

E **WRITE** Think of a holiday that is important to you. What do you give and get on this holiday? What do you make? What special things do you do? **Answers will vary.**

About Tet
Tet is an important holiday in Vietnam. During Tet my mother cooks sticky rice cake for our family. We give children money in small, red envelopes.

Connection   Putting It Together

GRAMMAR AND VOCABULARY Talk about a play you have seen. Tell your partner about the title, the author, the characters, the actors, and the costumes. Use the grammar and vocabulary from this lesson.   **Answers will vary.**

PROJECT Write and perform a play.

1. Work with a small group.
2. Discuss and decide on characters and a story for a short play.
3. Write the play with your group.
4. Perform your play for your class.

 INTERNET Go online. Search for other plays by Shakespeare. Learn about the characters and the story of one of the plays. Tell your classmates about the play.

VOCABULARY JOURNAL Write sentences for new vocabulary you learned in this lesson.

Example: "Grammar Connection" is the title of this book.

118   LESSON 15 | Literature: Shakespeare

■ EXPANSION IDEAS

Exercise E

1. Have students type the paragraphs they wrote about their favorite holidays on the computer and add art to illustrate what they have written.

Project

1. Have students type their scripts on the computer and illustrate their plays on poster boards (like the storyboard on page 117).
2. For additional suggestions on doing projects, see the Teacher's Notes on pages xvi–xviii.

Review 11–15

A Complete the sentences with the affirmative and negative present progressive form of the verbs. Use correct spelling.

Right now, I (watch) **am watching** my daughter's class. The teacher (read)
$\underline{\text{is reading}}$ a book. She (show) **is showing** the children a picture. The
$\qquad$ (2) $\qquad$ (3)
children (not / talk) **are not talking** They (listen) **are listening** to the teacher.
$\qquad$ (4) $\qquad$ (5)
The children (not / cry) **are not crying** They (smile) **are smiling** .
$\qquad$ (6) $\qquad$ (7)

B Circle the correct answers.

Tia: Goodbye Jenn.

Nori: Where is Tia (go /(going))?
$\qquad$ (1)

Jenn: She's going to the computer lab to meet her brother.

Nori: (Are /(Is)) her brother writing a paper?
$\qquad$ (2)

Jenn: No, he (aren't /(isn't)).
$\qquad$ (3)

Nori: Is he (do /(doing)) research on the Internet?
$\qquad$ (4)

Jenn: (Yes /(No)), he isn't.
$\qquad$ (5)

Nori: What (does /(is)) he doing at the computer lab?
$\qquad$ (6)

Jenn: He's (work /(working)). He fixes computer problems for the students in
$\qquad$ (7)
the lab.

C Circle the correct answers.

Right now I am (write /(writing)) in my journal and (think /(thinking))
$\qquad$ (1) $\qquad$ (2)
about my family. They are very far away. I am in the United States. My family
is in Brazil. It is 7:00 in the evening right now in Brazil. What (do /(are))
$\qquad$ (3)
they doing right now? My mother is probably (cook /(cooking)) dinner. What
$\qquad$ (4)
(does /(is)) she cooking? (Does /(Is)) she cooking chicken and rice? My father
$\qquad$ (5) $\qquad$ (6)
usually ((reads)/ reading) the newspaper in the evening. Is he (read /(reading))
$\qquad$ (7) $\qquad$ (8)
the newspaper now? My little sister (do /(does)) her homework in the evening.
$\qquad$ (9)
I ((miss)/ missing) them so much! (Are /(Do)) they miss me?
$\qquad$ (10) $\qquad$ (11)

The purpose of this lesson is help students review the concepts they have learned in the last five lessons. Encourage them to go back in to the lessons and review the grammar charts to help them complete the review exercises.

■ EXERCISE A

1. Have students do this activity by themselves and then share their answers with a partner.
2. Go over the answers as a class by asking students to read the sentences aloud.

■ EXERCISE B

1. Have students do this activity by themselves and then share their answers with a partner.
2. Go over the answers as a class.
3. Have students practice the conversation with the correct answers.

■ EXERCISE C

1. Have students do this activity by themselves and then share their answers with a partner.
2. Go over the answers as a class by asking students to read the sentences aloud.

■ EXPANSION IDEA

Exercise C

1. Have students rewrite the paragraph in Exercise C with different verbs. For example, for verbs (1) and (2) they might write: Right now, I am *reading* my journal and *wondering* about my family. Students don't necessarily need to use synonyms as long as the sentences make sense.

■ EXERCISE D

1. Have students do this activity by themselves and then share their answers with a partner.
2. Go over the answers as a class.

■ EXERCISE E

Have students do this activity with a partner, agreeing on the correct answers before circling them in their books.

■ LEARNER LOG

1. Help students understand how to complete the Learner Log by going over it with them and offering examples of the grammar structures.
2. If students checked "I Need More Practice" for any of the structures, suggest that they review those lessons. If possible, meet with students individually to discuss their Learner Logs and make suggestions for ways to get more practice with the structures.

D Circle the correct answers.

((João) / João's) is from Brazil. (João / (João's)) parents still live in Brazil, but (1) (2)
João lives in the United States now. (He / (His)) wife is from the United States. (3)
(His / (Her)) name is Sharon. João and Sharon have a daughter. (She / (Her)) (4) (5)
name is Nina. (Our / (Their)) daughter goes to Brazil every summer. She visits (6)
her ((grandparents) / grandparent's). Her (grandparents / (grandparents')) house (7) (8)
is near the beach. She loves to visit her grandparents. (Nina / (Nina's)) trip is (9)
always over too soon.

E Circle the correct answers. If both answers are correct, circle them both.

My favorite book is *Jane Eyre* by Charlotte Bronte. Jane Eyre is an orphan. ((She) / Her) lives with her mean aunt. The aunt has three children. (1)
((They) / Them) do not like Jane. Jane does not like (they / (them)). Only a (2) (3)
servant is nice to Jane. The servant ((reads Jane stories) / (reads stories to Jane)). (4)
Years later, Jane takes a job at Thornfield Hall. Mr. Rochester is the owner of Thornfield Hall. Jane and Mr. Rochester become friends. She tells (he / (him)) about her life. Jane falls in love with (he / (him)). ((He) / Him) (5) (6) (7)
loves (she / (her)) too. ((They) / Them) are very happy. Then Mr. Rochester (8) (9)
((tells a story to Jane) / (tells Jane a story)). He already has a wife! Jane runs away (10)
from Mr. Rochester. A year later, Jane returns to (he / (him)). His first wife is (11)
dead. Jane and Mr. Rochester marry.

LEARNER LOG Check (✔) Yes or *I Need More Practice*.

Lesson	I Can Use . . .	Yes	I Need More Practice
11	Present Progressive Statements		
12	Present Progressive Question Forms		
13	Simple Present vs. Present Progressive		
14	Possessive Nouns and Adjectives		
15	Object Pronouns and Indirect Objects		

■ EXPANSION IDEAS

Exercises D & E

1. Go through each of the answer choices with students and discuss why the wrong answer is incorrect. For example, the answer for (1) cannot be Joao's because there is no noun following (1) for Joao to possess.

Learner Log

1. Have students get into groups and generate a list of ideas for what they can do if they checked the "I Need More Practice" column in the Learner Log. Have each group share its best ideas with the class.

You might also want to ask students what helped them learn the topics for which they checked the "Yes" column.

Media Studies: Fame

■ CONTENT VOCABULARY

Look at the pictures. Do you know the words?

inventor

founder

princess

drummer   guitarist   singer

keyboard player

rock group

baseball player   soccer player

athletes

Write the new words in your vocabulary journal.

■ THINK ABOUT IT

Discuss these questions with a partner. Answers will vary.

1. Who were the most famous people of the twentieth century?
2. Who are the most famous people in the world now?

121

Overview

1. Elicit students' prior knowledge. Ask: *What do you think we will learn about in this lesson?*
2. Lead students to the idea of famous people. Ask students to form groups and brainstorm a list of famous people.

■ CONTENT VOCABULARY

1. Direct students' attention to the pictures and the vocabulary words. As you go over each one, ask students if any of the people on the lists that they came up with fit these categories.
2. What other famous types of people can students think of? See if students can help you come up with some categories. (political figures, movie stars, etc.)

■ THINK ABOUT IT

Have students do this activity with a partner and then write their answers on the board.

■ CONTENT NOTES

Media Studies

The topic for this lesson is Media Studies: Fame.

Possible discussion questions:
1. *What makes a person famous?*
2. *Can you think of some famous people who have done bad things?*
3. *Would you like to be famous? If so, what would you like to be famous for?*

PART ONE

The Past Tense of *Be*: Affirmative Statements

Part 1 introduces students to the simple past of *be* in affirmative statements. If necessary, refer students to the Pre-lesson (page 3) for an explanation of verbs.

■ GRAMMAR IN CONTENT

This section exposes students to a theme-based reading that includes examples of the target structure. Students can refer to the grammar chart(s) to complete the controlled practice activities.

■ EXERCISE A *Track 36*

1. Ask students to look at the pictures and ask if they know who the people are and what they are famous for.
2. Play the audio and have students follow along.
3. Help students with the pronunciation of the names and then ask the following questions: *Who won the Nobel Peace Prize? Who played soccer? Who invented the airplane?*

■ GRAMMAR CHART

The Past Tense of Be: *Affirmative Statements*

Go over the chart with the students. Go over the Notes. As you review the chart, refer to the examples from the reading to reinforce the rules.

■ GRAMMAR IN CONTENT

A Read and listen.

TR36

Famous People of the Twentieth Century

In 1999, *Time* magazine listed the 100 most important people of the twentieth century. These are some of the people on the list:

- Wilbur and Orville Wright—They **were** the inventors of the airplane. They **were** brothers.
- Mahatma Gandhi—He **was** the leader of India in the 1920s and 1930s.
- Mother Teresa—She **was** a nun. She **was** a winner of the Nobel Peace Prize.
- Marilyn Monroe—She **was** a movie star.
- Pelé—He **was** a soccer player. He **was** the best soccer player of the twentieth century.

twentieth century: the years 1901 to 2000

nun: a female member of a religious order

The Past Tense of *Be*: Affirmative Statements		
Subject	***Be***	
I	was	born in 1983.
He She It	was	cold yesterday.
You We They	were	in Europe last week.

Notes:
- Use *was* and *were* to talk about the past.
- There are no contractions with *was* and *were* in affirmative statements (WRONG: *I's*, *we're*).
- Some past time expressions are:
  yesterday
  last (week / month / year)
  (a week / two months / six years) **ago**

■ EXPANSION IDEA

Exercise A

1. Have students add information to the reading in Exercise A. For instance, if they know more about Pelé, have them write one or two more sentences about him in the past tense.

2. Have students share their information with the class.

B Complete each sentence with *was* or *were*.

1. Wilbur and Orville Wright _____were_____ brothers.

2. Wilbur _____was_____ born in 1867. Orville _____was_____ born in 1871.

3. They _____were_____ the inventors of the airplane.

4. People _____were_____ excited about the first airplane.

5. Mahatma Gandhi _____was_____ the leader of India in the 1920s.

6. Gandhi _____was_____ born in India in 1869.

7. Marilyn Monroe _____was_____ an American movie star in the 1950s.

8. She _____was_____ very beautiful.

9. Many people _____were_____ interested in her.

C Correct the sentences. There are four mistakes.

was Jackie Robinson ~~were~~ a famous baseball player. He was African **was** American. He ~~is~~ born in 1919. He was the first African American major league baseball player.	**were** The Beatles ~~was~~ a famous rock group. They were British. They ~~are~~ **were** very popular in the 1960s. Ringo Starr was the drummer.

D Complete each sentence to make a true statement about yourself. Use a time expression (*yesterday, last . . .* , or *. . . ago*). **Answers will vary.**

1. I was born _____.

2. I was in primary school _____.

3. I was 12 years old _____.

4. I was at the movies _____.

5. I was with my best friend _____.

6. I was sick _____.

7. I was with my family _____.

8. I was at home _____.

■ **EXERCISE B**

1. When students are finished, have them check their answers with a partner.

2. Go over the answers as a class.

■ **EXERCISE C**

When students are finished, ask for volunteers to read the correct sentences from the paragraphs.

■ **EXERCISE D**

Call on students to write their sentences on the board.

■ **EXPANSION IDEA**

Exercise C

1. Have students do research to find out more information about Jackie Robinson and Ringo Starr.

The Communicate section allows students to practice the target grammar in more communicative, less-controlled ways through speaking and writing activities.

■ EXERCISE E

Have students do this exercise in small groups before they share the information with the class.

PART TWO

The Past Tense of *Be:* Negative Statements

Part 2 introduces students to the past tense of *be* in negative statements.

■ GRAMMAR IN CONTENT

This section exposes students to a theme-based reading that includes examples of the target structure. Students can refer to the grammar chart(s) to complete the controlled practice activities.

■ EXERCISE A *Track 37*

1. Have students cover up the reading with a piece of paper and look at the picture.
2. Ask students to listen to the recording, with the reading still covered.
3. Have students read the story again to themselves.
4. Find out what else students know about Princess Diana.

■ GRAMMAR CHART

The Past Tense of Be: *Negative Statements*

Go over the chart with the students. As you review the chart, refer to the reading for examples.

■ COMMUNICATE

E GROUP WORK Look at the sentences your partner wrote for exercise D. Use the sentences to tell your class about your partner.

PART TWO	The Past Tense of *Be:* Negative Statements

■ GRAMMAR IN CONTENT

A Read and listen.

TR37

A Very Famous Woman

This woman was very famous all around the world in the 1990s. Millions of people were interested in her. She **wasn't** a movie star. She **wasn't** an inventor. She **wasn't** an athlete. Who was she?

Answer: Princess Diana

famous: very well-known
million: 1,000,000
interested: wanting to know more

The Past Tense of *Be*: Negative Statements

Subject	*Was / Were* + Not		Contraction		
I	was not	in class yesterday.	I	wasn't	in class yesterday.
He She It	was not	in the U.S. last year.	He She It	wasn't	in the U.S. last year.
You We They	were not	born in the U.S.	You We They	weren't	born in the U.S.

■ EXPANSION IDEA

Reading

1. Have students think of a famous person and write a paragraph similar to the one about Princess Diana, using negative statements and not revealing the name.

2. Ask for volunteers to read their paragraphs out loud and have the class guess who the person is.

B Look at the reading "A Very Famous Woman." (Circle) the correct answers.

1. Diana ((was not) / were not) an inventor.
2. Diana ((was not) / were not) a movie star.
3. Diana ((was) / was not) a princess.
4. Millions of people ((were) / were not) interested in her.

C These sentences are not true. Rewrite each as a negative sentence. Then use the word(s) in parentheses to write a true sentence.

1. Princess Diana was Spanish. (British)

   Princess Diana wasn't Spanish. She was British.

2. Wilbur and Orville Wright were the inventors of the telephone. (airplane)

   Wilbur and Orville Wright were not the inventors of the telephone.
   They were the inventors of the airplane.

3. Jackie Robinson was born in 1940. (1919)

   Jackie Robinson was not born in 1940. He was born in 1919.

4. Pelé was a baseball player. (soccer player)

   Pelé was not a baseball player. He was a soccer player.

5. Marilyn Monroe was a teacher. (movie star)

   Marilyn Monroe was not a teacher. She was a movie star.

6. The Beatles were doctors. (a rock group)

   The Beatles were not doctors. They were a rock group.

D Complete each sentence with *was, were, wasn't,* or *weren't* to make true sentences.   **Answers will vary.**

1. I _____ in Paris last night.

2. My school _____ open yesterday.

3. We _____ in this room yesterday.

4. It _____ cold yesterday.

5. I _____ tired this morning.

6. There _____ students in this class an hour ago.

■ EXERCISE B

Go over the answers as a class.

■ EXERCISE C

1. Have students do this exercise orally with a partner before writing the answers in their books. Once both partners agree, have them write the answers in their books.
2. Call on students to write the sentences on the board.

■ EXERCISE D

Call on a few different students to read each sentence aloud, since they may not all have the same answer. Expand a bit on each student's sentence. For example, for question 1, if a student says: *I wasn't in Paris last night,* you might say: *You weren't? Where were you last night?*

■ EXPANSION IDEA

Exercise C

1. Have students talk with a partner about each person in Exercise C. Using information they have learned in previous pages of this lesson, have students say a false statement to their partners. The partners must then correct the information. For example:

Student A: *Wilbur and Orville Wright were cousins.*

Student B: *Wilbur and Orville Wright weren't cousins. They were brothers.*

■ COMMUNICATE

The Communicate section allows students to practice the target grammar in more communicative, less-controlled ways through speaking and writing activities.

■ EXERCISE E

1. Go over the examples and instructions.
2. Once students are finished, ask for volunteers to write one or two of their sentences on the board.

Connection

Putting It Together

The purpose of this section of the lesson is to connect and extend students' understanding of the grammar, vocabulary, and content from this lesson.

■ GRAMMAR AND VOCABULARY

1. Help students get started by going over the example in the book.
2. Walk around and help student pairs write their sentences and then play the guessing game with another pair.

■ PROJECT

1. Go through each step with the students, making sure they understand what they are supposed to do.
2. For additional suggestions on doing projects, see the Teacher's Notes on pages xvi–xviii.

■ INTERNET

Have students work alone or with a partner to do their Internet research.

■ VOCABULARY JOURNAL

Refer to the Pre-lesson (page 6) for an explanation of the vocabulary journal.

E WRITE Write four sentences about yourself and your life now. Use the present of *be*. Write four sentences about what was different ten years ago. Use the past of *be*.

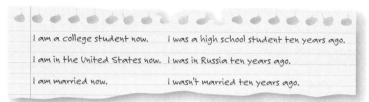

I am a college student now.	I was a high school student ten years ago.
I am in the United States now.	I was in Russia ten years ago.
I am married now.	I wasn't married ten years ago.

Connection | Putting It Together

GRAMMAR AND VOCABULARY Choose three famous people or groups of people from the past. Write four sentences about each person or group. Use the grammar and vocabulary from the lesson. Read your sentences to another pair. If they guess the person, they win a point. Take turns.

 He was born in 1940. He was in a famous band. He wasn't American.  John Lennon?

PROJECT Prepare a report about a famous person.

1. Work with a partner.
2. Choose a famous person from history you want to learn more about.
3. Look for information about the person in the library or on the Internet.
4. Prepare a report about that person.
5. Present your report to the class.

INTERNET Go online. Search for more information about some of the famous people in this lesson. Find out more about these people. Tell your classmates about what you found out.

VOCABULARY JOURNAL Write sentences for new vocabulary you learned in this lesson.

Example: *Pelé, Tiger Woods, and Lance Armstrong are athletes.*

126 LESSON 16 | Media Studies: Fame

■ EXPANSION IDEAS

Exercise E

1. After students have written some of their sentences on the board, indicate one that is an affirmative statement and ask the class how it could be changed to a negative statement. Write the negative statement under the affirmative statement.

Internet

1. Have students use the information they learned on the Internet to type a paragraph about their famous person and illustrate it with a photo or drawing. Display the illustrated paragraphs in the classroom if possible.

World History: The Twentieth Century

■ CONTENT VOCABULARY

Look at the pictures. Do you know the words?

explorer

astronaut

scientist

president   first lady

painter

fashion designer

writer

Write the new words in your vocabulary journal.

■ THINK ABOUT IT

Who are the most important kinds of people? Discuss with a partner. Put the people in order of importance. (1 = most important, 12 = least important) **Answers will vary.**

___ inventors	___ rock groups	___ teachers	___ writers
___ movie stars	___ athletes	___ explorers	___ painters
___ presidents	___ scientists	___ astronauts	___ fashion designers

127

Overview

Elicit students' prior knowledge. Ask: *What do you think we will learn about in this lesson?*

■ CONTENT VOCABULARY

Direct students' attention to the pictures and the vocabulary words. As you go over each one, ask them if they know any names of people who have that job.

■ THINK ABOUT IT

1. Have students do this activity by themselves before they share their answers with a partner.
2. Go over the answers as a class. Keep a list of student responses on the board to see if there is a consensus of opinion in the class.

■ CONTENT NOTES

World History

The topic for this lesson is World History: The Twentieth Century. Throughout this unit, students will learn about different historical figures (see the list below). It is not necessary that you know more about these figures than what is presented in this lesson.

Edmund Hillary
Neil Armstrong
Nelson Mandela
Pablo Picasso

Tenzing Norgay
Yuri Gagarin
Wilbur and
  Orville Wright

Albert Einstein
George Washington
Johann Sebastian
  Bach
Jacques Chirac

Fyodor Dostoevsky
John Adams
Ludwig
  van Beethoven
Lech Walesa

Find out what students already know by listing these people on the board or calling out the names and seeing if they know:

1. where they are from.
2. why they are famous.

PART ONE

The Past Tense of *Be*:
Yes/No Questions

Part 1 introduces students to *yes/no* questions with the past tense of *be*.

■ GRAMMAR IN CONTENT

This section exposes students to a theme-based reading that includes examples of the target structure. Students can refer to the grammar chart(s) to complete the controlled practice activities.

■ EXERCISE A *Track 38*

1. Ask students to look at the picture and talk about astronauts. Ask them if they can name any famous astronauts. Ask them what astronauts do.
2. Play the audio and have students follow along.
3. Ask the following questions: *Was Neil Armstrong an explorer? Was Yuri Gagarin an astronaut? What did Edmund Hillary and Tenzing Norgay do?*

■ GRAMMAR CHARTS

The Past Tense of Be: Yes/No *Questions and Short Answers*

Go over the charts with the students. Call on students to read the questions in the chart on the left side of the page. After a student reads a question, call on another student and say, "*Yes, ...*" using a rising intonation so the student completes the affirmative short answer. Call on another student and say, "*No, ...*" using a rising intonation so the student completes the negative short answer. After you go through the chart, refer to the examples from the reading to reinforce the rules.

■ GRAMMAR IN CONTENT

A Read and listen.

History Test

Haru:	I'm studying for my history test. It's about important "firsts" of the twentieth century. I have a couple of questions. You're a history major. Can you help me?
Paco:	Sure.
Haru:	**Were** Edmund Hillary and Tenzing Norgay the first explorers to reach the top of Mount Everest?
Paco:	**Yes, they were.**
Haru:	**Was** Neil Armstrong the first astronaut in space?
Paco:	**No, he wasn't.** He was the first astronaut to walk on the moon. Yuri Gagarin was the first astronaut (or cosmonaut, as they say in Russian) in space.

space: the area beyond Earth's atmosphere

The Past Tense of *Be*: *Yes/No* Questions		
Was/ Were	**Subject**	
Was	I	here?
Was	he she it	there?
Were	you we they	first?

The Past Tense of *Be*: Short Answers					
Affirmative			**Negative**		
Yes	**Subject**	**Was/ Were**	**No**	**Subject + *Was/Were* + Not**	
Yes,	I	was.	No,	I was not. (I wasn't.)	
	he she it	was.		he was not. (he wasn't.) she was not. (she wasn't.) it was not. (it wasn't.)	
	you we they	were.		you were not. (you weren't.) we were not. (we weren't.) they were not. (they weren't.)	

■ EXPANSION IDEA

Exercise A

1. Have students practice the conversation.
2. Have students write their own exchange about two other famous people they know about.
3. Have students perform their conversations for the class.

B Look at the dialogue "History Test." Answer the questions.

1. Were Hillary and Norgay astronauts? _____ *No, they weren't.*

2. Were Hillary and Norgay explorers? _____ **Yes, they were.**

3. Was Yuri Gagarin the first cosmonaut in space? _____ **Yes, he was.**

4. Was Yuri Gagarin the first cosmonaut on the moon? _____ **No, he wasn't.**

5. Was Neil Armstrong the first astronaut on the moon? _____ **Yes, he was.**

C Write *Yes/No* questions. Then write short answers.

1. Nelson Mandela / president of South Africa

   _____ *Was Nelson Mandela the president of South Africa* ? *Yes, he was* .

2. Wilbur and Orville Wright / inventors

   _____ **Were Wilbur and Orville Wright inventors** ? **Yes, they were** .

3. Yuri Gagarin and Neil Armstrong / athletes

   _____ **Were Yuri Gagarin and Neil Armstrong athletes** ? **No, they weren't.** .

4. Pablo Picasso / painter

   _____ **Was Pablo Picasso a painter** ? **Yes, he was** .

5. Tenzing Norgay / writer

   _____ **Was Tenzing Norgay a writer** ? **No, he wasn't.** .

■ C O M M U N I C A T E

D PAIR WORK Write a list of *Yes/No* questions to ask your partner about his or her childhood. Then ask your partner the questions. Take turns.

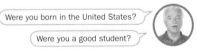 

Were you born in the United States?

Were you a good student?

No, I wasn't.

Yes, I was.

■ **EXPANSION IDEA**

Exercise B

1. Have students write three questions similar to the ones in Exercise B about other famous people.

2. Have them walk around the classroom and ask different students their questions.

■ **EXERCISE B**

1. When students are finished, have them check their answers with a partner.

2. Have students practice asking and answering the questions with a partner.

■ **EXERCISE C**

Call on students to write their questions and short answers on the board.

■ **COMMUNICATE**

The Communicate section allows students to practice the target grammar in more communicative, less-controlled ways through speaking and writing activities.

■ **EXERCISE D**

1. Have each student write five questions.

2. Have students ask and answer questions with a partner.

3. If students agree that they will not be embarrassed, have their partners describe their childhood to the class, using affirmative and negative statements in the past tense. For example: *Amy wasn't born in Panama. She moved there with her family. She was a very good student, but she didn't like to practice the piano.*

PART TWO

The Past Tense of *Be*: *Wh-* Questions

Part 2 introduces students to the past tense of *be* in *wh-* questions.

■ GRAMMAR IN CONTENT

This section exposes students to a theme-based reading that includes examples of the target structure. Students can refer to the grammar chart(s) to complete the controlled practice activities.

■ EXERCISE A *Track 39*

1. Have students cover up the reading with a piece of paper and look at the picture.
2. Have students listen to the recording with the reading still covered.
3. With the reading still covered, ask students the questions about Einstein and see if they can remember the answers.
4. Let them read to find out if they were correct.

■ GRAMMAR CHARTS
Past Tense Wh- Questions with Be *(with* Wh- *Word as Subject)*

1. Write the words *was* and *were* on the board. Read each question in the first chart aloud. After each one, ask: *Was* or *Were?* Students will indicate the word they heard and you can point to it on the board.
2. Ask students to explain why the words are used as they are in the questions. They should tell you that the form of *be* depends on the subject, so the forms are *you were*, *she was*, and so forth.
3. Call on students to read the questions in the first chart, and call on different students to read the answers.

■ GRAMMAR IN CONTENT

A **Read and listen.**

TR39

The Person of the Century

Question:	**Who was** *Time* magazine's person of the century?
Answer:	Albert Einstein.
Question:	**When was** he born?
Answer:	1879.
Question:	**Where was** he born?
Answer:	Germany.
Question:	**Why was** Einstein famous?
Answer:	He was a great scientist.

Past Tense *Wh-* Questions with *Be*

Wh-Word	Was/Were	Subject		Answer
Who	were	you	with?	My friend. OR I was with my friend.
What	was	Gagarin's	name?	Yuri. OR His name was Yuri.
Where	was	she	born?	India. OR She was born in India.
When	was	she	in Hawaii?	Last year. OR She was in Hawaii last year.
How	was	the weather	yesterday?	Cold. OR It was cold.
Why	were	you	late?	Because I was sick this morning.

Past Tense *Wh-* Questions with *Be* (with *Wh-* Word as Subject)

Wh- Word (Subject)	Was/Were	
Who	was	your teacher last year?
Who	were	the Beatles?

Note:
Who can also be used to ask about the subject. Question: *Who was with you?* Answer: *My friend.* OR *My friend was with me.*

■ EXPANSION IDEAS

Exercise A

1. Have students practice the conversation.

Grammar Charts

1. With a partner, have students practice the questions and answers in the charts.

B Look at the reading "The Person of the Century." Complete each sentence with a question word and *was* or *were*.

1. ___Who___ ___was___ *Time* magazine's person of the century? Albert Einstein.

2. ___Why___ ___was___ he famous? He was a great scientist.

3. ___Where___ ___was___ he born? Germany.

4. ___When___ ___was___ he born? 1879.

C Write past tense questions. Then write the answers. Use the information provided.

1. **Question:** Who / Fyodor Dostoevsky ___Who was Fyodor Dostoevsky?___

   Answer: nineteenth-century Russian writer
   ___He was a nineteenth-century Russian writer.___

2. **Q:** Who / the first two U.S. presidents ___Who were the first two U.S. presidents?___

   A: George Washington and John Adams ___They were George Washington and John Adams.___

3. **Q:** When / the French Revolution ___When was the French Revolution?___

   A: 1789 ___It was in 1789.___

4. **Q:** Where / Bach and Beethoven born ___Where were Bach and Beethoven born?___

   A: Germany ___They were born in Germany.___

D Put the words in order to make *wh-* questions. Then write answers about yourself when you were a child.

1. you / when / were / born ___When were you born___ ?
   _____ .

2. your / was / who / best friend ___Who was your best friend___ ?
   _____ .

3. was / what / your favorite subject in school ___What was your favorite subject in school?___ ?
   _____ .

4. your favorite food / what / was ___What was your favorite food___ ?
   _____ .

5. was / your favorite book / what ___What was your favorite book___ ?
   _____ .

4. Go over the second chart and the Note on page 130. Point out that the difference between the two charts is that the *wh-* words in the first chart ask about objects and in the second chart they ask about subjects.

■ EXERCISE B

Go over the answers as a class.

■ EXERCISE C

1. Have students do this exercise orally with a partner before writing the answers in their books. Once both partners agree, have them write the answers in their books.

2. Call on students to write the questions and answers on the board.

■ EXERCISE D

1. Call on volunteers to read the questions aloud.

2. Have students walk around the room and ask different students their questions (one student per question.)

3. Have students report to the class what they learned about their classmates.

■ CONTENT NOTES

Exercise C

1. Have students choose one of the questions in Exercise C that they know more information about. Have them write questions and answers like the ones in Exercise C about that person or historical event. Have students use their questions to quiz a partner.

■ COMMUNICATE

The Communicate section allows students to practice the target grammar in more communicative, less-controlled ways through speaking and writing activities.

■ EXERCISE E

Ask for volunteers to share their paragraphs with the class.

Connection

Putting It Together

The purpose of this section of the lesson is to connect and extend students' understanding of the grammar, vocabulary, and content from this lesson.

■ GRAMMAR AND VOCABULARY

Help students understand how to prepare for the game and how the game works. It might be a good idea to assign jobs to students, such as "question reader" and "scorekeeper."

■ PROJECT

1. Go through each step with the students, making sure they understand what they are supposed to do.
2. For additional suggestions on doing projects, see the Teacher's Notes on pages xvi–xviii.

■ INTERNET

Have students work with a partner to do their Internet research.

■ VOCABULARY JOURNAL

Refer to the Pre-lesson (page 6) for an explanation of the vocabulary journal.

E PAIR WORK Ask your partner about his or her childhood. Use the questions in exercise D. Add questions of your own. Take notes on your partner's answers. Write a paragraph about your partner's childhood.

Connection Putting It Together

GRAMMAR AND VOCABULARY With your group, write questions about people, places, and events in history. Use the grammar and vocabulary from the lesson. Each group takes turns asking another group questions. Each group that answers a question correctly gets one point.

Who was president of France in 2000?
Was it Jacques Chirac?
Yes, it was. You get one point.

PROJECT Create a history exam.

1. Work in groups.
2. Create a multiple-choice history exam to give to the other groups.
3. Ask questions about the people in Lessons 16 and 17. Use the Internet or the library to find out more information.
4. Have a class quiz. The group with the most right answers wins!

```
             Our History Exam

1. Nelson Mandela was president of South
Africa between:
a) 1994-1999  b) 1984-1989  c) 1964-1969

2. Pablo Picasso was born in:
a) Russia      b) Spain      c) Slovakia
```

 INTERNET Go online. Find information about famous twentieth-century people. Report back to your class.

VOCABULARY JOURNAL Write sentences for new vocabulary you learned in this lesson.

Example: *Van Gogh and Picasso are famous painters.*

132 LESSON 17 | World History: The Twentieth Century

■ EXPANSION IDEAS

Exercise E

1. Have students take the information they learned about their partners, type a paragraph on the computer, and add a picture.
2. Post these around your classroom as "Famous People in Our Class."

Internet

1. Have students type the information they learned from the Internet and add art.

PART 1
The Simple Past Tense of Regular Verbs: Affirmative and Negative
PART 2
Spelling and Pronunciation of the Simple Past Tense of Regular Verbs
PART 3
The Simple Past Tense of Irregular Verbs

Lesson 18

Business: Successful Business People

Lesson 18

Overview

Elicit students' prior knowledge. Ask: *What do you think we will learn about in this lesson?* Have students brainstorm in small groups.

■ CONTENT VOCABULARY

Look at the pictures. Do you know the words?

employee   manager

customer   salesperson

product

pay

millionaire

Write the new words in your vocabulary journal.

■ THINK ABOUT IT

Work with a group to make a list of the five most important companies in the world today. Do you know who started each company?

■ CONTENT VOCABULARY

1. Direct students' attention to the first drawing and ask them what is happening. Go over any new vocabulary.
2. Direct students' attention to the second drawing and ask them what is happening. Go over any new vocabulary.
3. Direct students' attention to the third drawing and ask how this drawing is related to the first two drawings. Lead students to the idea of starting a business and making lots of money.

■ THINK ABOUT IT

1. Have groups share their lists with the class and see which companies all the groups have in common.
2. Write the companies on the board and find out whether students know who started them.

133

■ CONTENT NOTES

Business

The topic for this lesson is Business: Successful Business People. Below is a list of some of the largest companies in the United States and the people who started them.

Bank of America: A. P. Giannini
Berkshire Hathaway: Warren Buffett
Chevron Texaco: Joe Cullinan
ConocoPhillips: Isaac Elder Blake
Costco Wholesale: Jeffrey Brotman
Dell: Michael Dell
Ford Motor: Henry Ford

General Motors: William C. Durant
Home Depot: Arthur M. Blank
  and Bernard Marcus
Johnson & Johnson: Robert Wood Johnson
Microsoft: Bill Gates
Pfizer: Charles Pfizer
Proctor & Gamble: William Proctor
  and James Gamble
Starbucks: Howard Shultz
State Farm Insurance: George J. Mecherle
United Parcel Service: Jim Casey
Wal-Mart: Sam Walton

PART ONE

The Simple Past Tense of Regular Verbs: Affirmative and Negative

Part 1 introduces students to the simple past tense of regular verbs in the affirmative and negative.

■ GRAMMAR IN CONTENT

This section exposes students to a theme-based reading that includes examples of the target structure. Students can refer to the grammar chart(s) to complete the controlled practice activities.

■ EXERCISE A *Track 40*

1. Ask students to look at the picture of jeans. Ask if anyone owns a pair of Levi's jeans.
2. Play the audio and have students follow along.
3. Ask students the following questions: *Where was Levi Strauss born? Where did he open his store? What did his company manufacture? Who wore the pants?*

■ GRAMMAR CHART

The Simple Past Tense of Regular Verbs: Affirmative and Negative Statements

1. Go over the chart with the students, referring to the examples from the reading to reinforce the rules.
2. Go over the reading with the students. Ask them to think of events that are finished. Start with events that happened yesterday, then last week, last month, and so on. Note students' ideas on the board using the simple past tense.

■ EXERCISE B

1. Have students complete the activity and check their answers with a partner.
2. Ask for volunteers to write the corrected false statements on the board.

■ GRAMMAR IN CONTENT

A Read and listen.

TR40

Levi Strauss

Levi Strauss was born in Germany. He **moved** to the United States in 1829. In 1853 he **opened** a store in San Francisco. Strauss **shared** his business with his nephews and **turned** it **into** a family business. Levi Strauss & Company **manufactured** the first blue jeans. The pants were popular with cowboys and farmers. Today blue jeans are popular with people around the world, and Levi Strauss & Company is still a family business.

manufacture: make

cowboy: a man who works on a cattle ranch

Affirmative Statements		
Subject	Base Form of Verb + -d/-ed	
I He She It You We They	worked	yesterday.

Negative Statements			
Subject	Did + Not	Base Form of Verb	
I He She It You We They	did not OR didn't	work	yesterday.

Note: Use the simple past to talk about events that happened and are now finished.

B Look at the reading "Levi Strauss." Is each sentence true or false? Rewrite false sentences correctly.

1. Levi Strauss was born in Italy.   True (False)
   Levi Strauss was not born in Italy. He was born in Germany.

2. He stayed in Germany.   True (False)
   He did not stay in Germany, He moved to the United States.

3. He moved to the United States in 1829.   (True) False
   _____

■ EXPANSION IDEAS

Exercise A and B

1. Have students work with a partner.
2. Ask students to make up false statements from the reading. Their partners must correct the false statements.

For example:

Student A: *Levi Strauss was born in Italy.*
Student B: *No, he wasn't. He was born in Germany.*

4. He shared his company with his nephews.   (True) False

_____

5. Levi Strauss & Company manufactured the first computers.   True (False)
   They did not manufacture the first computers. They manufactured the first blue jeans.

C Complete the paragraph with the past tense form of the verbs in parentheses.

Richard Branson is one of the most successful business people in the world.

He was born in England in 1950. He (start) _started_ his first
                                              (1)

business at the age of 16. It was a magazine for students. He (not graduate)

didn't graduate from high school. He (open) **opened**
      (2)   (3)

a record store in London. In 1972, he (create) **created** his own
                                                   (4)

record company. He (call) **called** it Virgin Records. The company was very
                             (5)

successful. In 1984, he (decide) **decided** to start an airline. In 1999, he (add)
                                     (6)

added a cell phone business to his company. Branson now owns more
   (7)

than 200 businesses. Branson also (dream) **dreamed** of adventure. He (want)
                                              (8)

wanted to fly around the world in a hot air balloon. That (not happen) **didn't happen** ,
   (9)   (10)

but in 1987 he (cross) **crossed** the Atlantic Ocean in a hot air balloon.
                           (11)

D Complete the blanks with the negative past tense form of the verbs in parentheses.

John wanted to be successful. But instead his manager
fired him. John was a bad employee.

1. He (arrive) _did not arrive_ on time for work.

2. He (work) **did not work** hard.

3. He (listen) **did not listen** to his manager.

4. He (ask) **did not ask** questions.

5. He (fix) **did not fix** problems.

6. He (finish) **did not finish** his work.

Have students complete the activity. Then go over the answers as a class. Model the pronunciation of the past tense verbs and have students repeat after you.

■ EXERCISE D

1. Have students complete the activity and then go over the answers with a partner.
2. Ask for volunteers to write the sentences on the board.
3. If there are mistakes put an *X* next to each sentence that has a mistake and ask for other students to fix the mistakes on the board.

■ EXPANSION IDEAS

_____

Exercise C

1. Direct students to work in a group. Ask them to think together of someone famous or someone they know who has started his or her own business.
2. Ask each group to write a paragraph like the one in Exercise C about the person they chose.
3. Ask for a representative from each group to read the paragraph aloud to the class.

Exercise D

1. Find out whether students agree that John was a bad employee. Ask them which of John's work problems were the most serious.

■ EXERCISE E

1. Have students complete the paragraph.
2. Go over the answers as a class and discuss the meaning of the last two sentences. Ask students why Marta doesn't dream of being a millionaire now (*she probably is one*) and why she dreams of taking a vacation (*she is probably too busy*).

■ COMMUNICATE

The Communicate section allows students to practice the target grammar in more communicative, less-controlled ways through speaking and writing activities.

■ EXERCISE F

1. Have students brainstorm some ideas before they begin writing their paragraphs.
2. Remind students to look at the model paragraphs on pages 134 and 135.

PART TWO

Spelling and Pronunciation of the Simple Past Tense of Regular Verbs

Part 2 introduces students to the spelling and pronunciation of the simple past tense of regular verbs.

■ GRAMMAR CHART

Spelling of Past Tense of Regular Verbs

1. Have students close their books. Dictate the Past Form column to them.
2. Ask for volunteers to write the words on the board.
3. Group each set of words by putting a box around them and ask students if they can think of the spelling rule. As they think of rules, supply any missing rules and give a few more examples. (See bottom of this page for more examples.)
4. Have students open their books and read the chart.

E Complete the paragraph with the simple present or the simple past tense of the verbs in parentheses.

The story of Marta's Muffins began a long time ago. Fifteen years ago Marta (work) __worked__ (1) in a bakery. She (want) __wanted__ (2) to be a chef. She (dream) __dreamed__ (3) of being successful. Now she (own) __owns__ (4) the bakery and (have) __has__ (5) ten restaurants. Ten years ago, she (dream) __dreamed__ (6) of being a millionaire. Now she (dream) __dreams__ (7) of taking a vacation.

■ COMMUNICATE

F **WRITE** Write a paragraph about yourself as a child. Use past tense affirmative and negative sentences.

PART TWO	Spelling and Pronunciation of the Simple Past Tense of Regular Verbs

Spelling of Past Tense of Regular Verbs

Base Form	Past Form	Rule
work walk	worked walked	For most verbs: Add -ed.
live dance	lived danced	For verbs that end in an e: Add -d only.
study cry	studied cried	For verbs that end in a consonant + y: Change y to i and add -ed.
play enjoy	played enjoyed	For verbs that end in a vowel + y: Add -ed.
drop hug	dropped hugged	For one-syllable verbs that end in a consonant + vowel + consonant: Double the final consonant and add -ed.
show relax	showed relaxed	For verbs that end in w or x: Do not double the consonant. Just add -ed.
happen open	happened opened	For two-syllable verbs that end in a consonant + vowel + consonant: If the first syllable is stressed, add -ed. Do not double the consonant.
prefer admit	preferred admitted	For two-syllable verbs that end in a consonant + vowel + consonant: If the second syllable is stressed, double the final consonant and add -ed.

136 LESSON 18 | Business: Successful Business People

■ EXPANSION IDEA

Grammar Chart

1. More past tense verbs that follow the spelling rules from the grammar chart.

Past Form

brushed		saved	flawed
cleaned	tapped	organized	waxed
	scrubbed	worried	watered
		carried	ordered
		stayed	committed
		obeyed	submitted

A Choose the correct spelling of the verbs in this paragraph.

To: kiya@netmail.net
From: fred@netmail.net
Re: My pay raise!

Hi! How are you? I have a funny story for you. You know I (wantid /(wanted)) a pay raise, right?
(1)
Well, I ((typed)/ typped) an e-mail to my manager. I ((asked)/ askt) him for a raise. He
(2)   (3)
(studyed /(studied)) my e-mail, and then he (replyed /(replied)). He (decidded /(decided)) to
(4)   (5)   (6)
give me a raise. I (walkd /(walked)) to my manager's office and (huged /(hugged)) him. He
(7)   (8)
((looked)/ lookd) shocked. Then he (laught /(laughed)). It was a good day! Are you having a
(9)   (10)
good day too?

Frederico

B Write the past tense form of each verb.

1. like ___liked___   7. use ___used___
2. stop ___stopped___   8. open ___opened___
3. carry ___carried___   9. fix ___fixed___
4. cook ___cooked___   10. show ___showed___
5. drop ___dropped___   11. enjoy ___enjoyed___
6. marry ___married___   12. listen ___listened___

Pronunciation of Regular Verb Past Tense Forms	
For Verbs That End In . . .	**Pronounce the Ending . . .**
the sounds *p, k, f, s, ch,* or *sh*	/t/ as in "cooked" and "helped"
the sounds *b, g, v, z, zh, th, j, m, n, ng, l, r,* or a vowel sound	/d/ as in "played" and "used"
the sounds *d* or *t*	/əd/ as in "wanted" and "needed"

■ **EXERCISE A**

1. Have students complete the exercise and then share their answers with a partner.
2. Ask for a volunteer to read the e-mail message aloud.

■ **EXERCISE B**

1. Have students check their answers with a partner when they are finished.
2. Call on volunteers to spell the words aloud.

■ **GRAMMAR CHART**
Pronunciation of Regular Verb Past Tense Forms

Go over the pronunciation with students, modeling the words in the chart and having students repeat after you.

■ **EXPANSION IDEA**

Grammar Chart

1. Have students work in pairs to write other past tense verb forms that would fit into each of the pronunciation categories. Have them write a chart with three columns and the following headings: /t/, /d/, /əd/. Ask students to come up with at least five words for each column.

2. Ask for students to write their words on the board. Tell them to write words only if they do not appear on the board already.

3. With the comprehensive list on the board, go over each word with students, helping them practice their pronunciation.

■ EXERCISE C Track 41

1. Prepare students for listening by going over the pronunciation of -ed in each of the columns.

2. Review the directions and have students fill out the chart as they listen to the recording.

3. If students have trouble hearing the difference between the past tense endings, reassure them that the most important one to hear and pronounce is the /əd/ ending since it adds an extra syllable to a word.

■ COMMUNICATE

The Communicate section allows students to practice the target grammar in more communicative, less-controlled ways through speaking and writing activities.

■ EXERCISE D

1. Model this activity for your students by saying a couple of past tense verbs. Say *walked* correctly. Say *kissed* correctly. Say *watched*, pronouncing it *watch-ed*. As you say each word, ask students whether it is correct or incorrect and have them write the word on a piece of paper.

2. Explain that this is what students will be doing with their partners, except they won't purposely pronounce the words incorrectly.

PART THREE

The Simple Past Tense of Irregular Verbs

Part 3 introduces students to the simple past of irregular verbs.

■ GRAMMAR IN CONTENT

■ EXERCISE A Track 42

1. Ask students to read the story about Anita Roddick.

2. Play the audio and have students follow along.

3. Answer any questions students have.

C Which -ed ending do you hear? Put a check (✔) in the correct column.

TR41

	/t/ as in "cooked"	/d/ as in "lived"	/əd/ as in "wanted"
1.		✔	
2.			✔
3.	✔		
4.		✔	
5.	✔		
6.			✔
7.	✔		
8.		✔	
9.			✔
10.		✔	

■ COMMUNICATE

D **PAIR WORK** Say a verb with a regular past tense form. Your partner will check your pronunciation. Your partner will write the past tense form of the verb. Check your partner's spelling. Take turns.

PART THREE	The Simple Past Tense of Irregular Verbs

■ GRAMMAR IN CONTENT

A **Read and listen.**

TR42

A Success Story

Anita Roddick is the founder of the company called The Body Shop. Roddick **began** with one store. She opened the store in England in 1976. The store **sold** beauty products. She **did not have** business experience, but she **had** good ideas. She **made** natural products. She **put** the products in special containers. People could recycle the containers. She **sold** the products with no advertising. The Body Shop **became** an international success. There are now over 1,980 Body Shop stores in 49 countries. The company has more than 77 million customers.

natural: something made by nature
container: anything used to put or keep things in
recycle: to use again

138 LESSON 18 | Business: Successful Business People

■ EXPANSION IDEA

Exercise A

1. Have students work in small groups to rewrite the paragraph about Anita Roddick, changing the irregular verbs to regular verbs in the past tense.

Possible Changes:
began: started
sold: advertised
had: possessed
made: created
put: packaged

NOTE: This may be a challenge for students but it will encourage them to think about synonyms they know that could replace certain words. Consider letting students use a dictionary or thesaurus.

Affirmative Statements				Negative Statements			
Subject	Past Form of Verb			Subject	Did + Not	Base Form of Verb	
I He She It You We They	ate	in a restaurant last night.		I He She It You We They	did not OR didn't	eat	in a restaurant last night.

Notes:

- Irregular verbs do not have the -ed ending in the past tense. Here are some common irregular verbs and their simple past forms.

be / was, were	go / went	meet / met
buy / bought	have / had	pay / paid
come / came	leave / left	put / put
do / did	make / made	see / saw
get / got	sell / sold	take / took
give / gave	speak / spoke	write / wrote

- See the appendix on page 232 for more irregular verbs and their simple past forms.

B Look at the reading "A Success Story." Fill in each blank with the past tense of one of the verbs in the box.

Anita Roddick is the founder of The Body Shop. Roddick
__began__ with one store. She __opened__ the store in England
(1)   (2)
in 1976. The store __sells__ beauty products. She __has__
(3)   (4)
good ideas. The Body Shop __became__ an international success.
(5)

become
have
sell
open
begin

C Complete each sentence with the past tense form of one of the verbs in the box.

Yesterday Jim __went__ to the electronics store. He
(1)
wanted a cell phone. He __spoke__ with a salesperson about
(2)
the different cell phones. The salesperson was very helpful. Jim
__chose__ a cheap cell phone and __took__ it to the counter.
(3)   (4)
He __bought__ the cell phone and __paid__ with a credit card.
(5)   (6)
The salesperson __put__ the cell phone in a bag.
(7)

go
buy
pay
speak
take
put
choose

■ **GRAMMAR CHART**

The Simple Past Tense of Irregular Verbs: Affirmative and Negative Statements

Go over the chart with the students. Go over the Notes. Show students the appendix on page 232, where they can find a more comprehensive list of irregular verbs and their simple past forms.

■ **EXERCISE B**

Have students fill in the blanks and then share their answers with a partner.

■ **EXERCISE C**

Have students do this exercise with a partner, discussing the correct answers before writing them in their books.

■ **EXPANSION IDEAS**

Grammar Chart/Appendix of Irregular Verbs

1. Write the following verbs on the board and have students use the appendix in the back of the book to find the simple past form:

find	fly
swim	leave
drive	wake
win	understand
catch	send

pay	cost
steal	cut

2. Have students find answers to the following questions in the appendix:

How many verbs have the same base form and irregular form? (6) Which verbs are they? (*cost, cut, hit, let, put, shut*)

How many past tense verbs end in the letters *ght*? (5) Which ones are they? (*brought, bought, caught, taught, thought*)

■ EXERCISE D

1. Ask for volunteers to write their sentences on the board.

■ COMMUNICATE

The Communicate section allows students to practice the target grammar in more communicative, less-controlled ways through speaking and writing activities.

■ EXERCISE E

1. Model this activity for students by writing five sentences on the board about yourself (four true and one false).

2. Ask students which sentence they think is false.

Connection

Putting It Together

The purpose of this section of the lesson is to connect and extend students' understanding of the grammar, vocabulary, and content from this lesson.

■ GRAMMAR AND VOCABULARY

Model this activity for students by telling the students about an experience you had at the store.

■ PROJECT

Go through each step with the students, making sure they understand what they are supposed to do.

■ INTERNET

1. As a class, brainstorm names of some successful businesses.

2. Pair up students and ask each pair to choose one of the companies listed on the board, so that no pair is looking up the same company.

3. Ask each pair to find out five interesting facts about their business to report back to the class.

D Use regular and irregular past tense verbs to complete the sentences about yourself. **Answers will vary.**

1. This morning, I _____.
2. Last night, I _____.
3. Yesterday, I _____.

■ COMMUNICATE

E **GROUP WORK** Write five sentences about your past. Four sentences should be true. One should be false. Use irregular verbs in the simple past tense. Work with a small group. Read your sentences to your group. The group will try to guess the false sentence. Take turns.

Connection   Putting It Together

GRAMMAR AND VOCABULARY Think about the last time you went to a store and bought something. Tell your partner about it. Use the grammar and vocabulary from this lesson.

> Yesterday I went to the mall. I looked in all the clothing stores. I tried on some pants but I didn't like them. The salesperson showed me a nice sweater. I bought it. I paid with a credit card.

PROJECT Write a short biography of an imaginary successful business person.

1. Work with a partner.
2. Make up a story about the life of a successful business person and the business the person started. Answer questions like the following: What is the person's name? When was he/she born? Where was he/she born? What things did he/she do in his/her life? What is the name of his/her business? What does this business do or sell?
3. Work with your partner to write a biography of this person. You may want to use the biographies on pages 134 and 138 as models.
4. Read your biography to the class.

 INTERNET Go online. Find out more about a successful business you know. Take notes on the history of the business. Tell your class what you found out.

VOCABULARY JOURNAL Write sentences for new vocabulary you learned in this lesson.

Example: *I paid for my new computer with a credit card.*

140   LESSON 18 | Business: Successful Business People

■ EXPANSION IDEA

Exercise E

1. Give each student an index card and ask them to write two sentences about themselves in the past tense.

2. Collect the cards and redistribute them, making sure that no student gets his or her own card.

3. Write the following two expressions on the board and practice saying with the students:
"Hey, that's me!"
"No, that's not me."

4. Have students walk around the room and read the sentences on the cards they're holding to classmates. The classmates must respond with one of the two expressions.

5. When a match is made, the student will take his or her original card and sit down, giving the card he or she was holding to the other student to keep walking around with.

PART 1
The Simple Past Tense: *Yes/No*
Questions and Short Answers

PART 2
The Simple Past Tense: *Wh-*
Questions

Lesson ⑲

Criminology: Crime

■ CONTENT VOCABULARY

Look at the pictures. Do you know these words?

vandalism

murder

theft

police officer

handcuffs

arrest

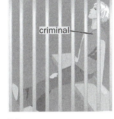

criminal

jail

fingerprint

Write the new words in your vocabulary journal.

■ THINK ABOUT IT

Discuss these questions with a partner.

1. Did you ever see a crime? If so, what was the crime? Describe what you saw.
2. Make a list of some famous criminals and famous crimes.

141

Overview

1. Elicit students' prior knowledge. Ask: *Have you ever had an experience with a police officer?* Ask students to share if they don't mind.
2. Ask students to talk with a partner about what the job of a police officer is.

■ CONTENT VOCABULARY

1. Direct students' attention to the pictures and vocabulary words.
2. Ask them what they think is happening in the pictures.
3. Help them define the words to write in their vocabulary journals.

■ THINK ABOUT IT

1. Have students think about the answers by themselves before they share their answers with a partner.
2. Go over the answers as a class, seeing if you can come up with a list of famous criminals.

■ CONTENT NOTES

Criminology

The topic for this lesson is Criminology: Crime. Throughout this unit, students will learn about different criminals in history and the crimes they committed. It is not necessary that you know any more about these criminals than what is presented in this lesson. However, this lesson gives the students a great opportunity to do research and learn more about the people mentioned.

Criminology is the scientific study of crime, criminals, criminal behavior, and corrections. In general, criminology is considered a part of sociology. Criminology uses psychology, economics, and other disciplines to examine humans and their environment.

PART ONE

The Simple Past Tense: *Yes/No* Questions and Short Answers

Part 1 introduces students to the simple past tense with *yes/no* questions and short answers.

■ GRAMMAR IN CONTENT

This section exposes students to a theme-based reading that includes examples of the target structure. Students can refer to the grammar chart(s) to complete the controlled practice activities.

■ EXERCISE A *Track 43*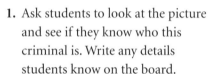

1. Ask students to look at the picture and see if they know who this criminal is. Write any details students know on the board.
2. Play the audio and have students follow along.
3. Ask the following questions: *Did the Unabomber kill anyone? How long did it take the FBI to find him? How long will he be in jail?*
4. Have students practice the conversation with a partner.

■ GRAMMAR CHARTS

The Simple Past Tense: Yes/No *Questions and Short Answers*

Go over the charts with the students. As you go through them, refer to the examples from the reading to reinforce the rules.

PART ONE | The Simple Past Tense: *Yes/No* Questions and Short Answers

■ GRAMMAR IN CONTENT

A Read and listen.

TR43

The Unabomber: An American Criminal

Student:	Who is "the Unabomber"?
Professor:	He's an American criminal. He sent people bombs in the mail.
Student:	**Did** he **kill** anyone?
Professor:	**Yes, he did.** He killed three people.
Student:	**Did** the FBI **find** him quickly?
Professor:	**No, they didn't.** It took 18 years to find him.
Student:	**Did** he **have** a trial?
Professor:	**Yes, he did.**
Student:	Is he in jail now?
Professor:	Yes, he is. He's serving a life sentence.

bomb: a weapon that explodes

FBI: the U.S. agency that looks into national crimes

trial: a legal proceeding to decide guilt or innocence

serving a life sentence: in jail for life

The Simple Past Tense: *Yes/No* Questions			Short Answers						
			Affirmative			Negative			
Did	**Subject**		**Yes,**	**Subject**	**Did**	**No,**	**Subject**	**Didn't**	
Did	I he she it you we they	see the crime?	Yes,	I he she it you we they	did.	No,	I he she it you we they	didn't.	

■ EXPANSION IDEA

Exercise A

1. Have pairs of students write their own conversations using a different famous criminal. Remind them of the criminals you talked about in the beginning of the unit, or they can choose a different one that they know about.

2. Have students perform their conversations for the class.

B Look at the dialogue "The Unabomber: An American Criminal." Answer the questions with short answers.

1. Did the Unabomber send bombs in the mail? _____ *Yes, he did.*

2. Did he kill anyone? _____ **Yes, he did.**

3. Did the FBI find him quickly? _____ **No, they didn't.**

4. Did the Unabomber have a trial? _____ **Yes, he did.**

C Look at the pictures of the bank robbery. The bank robbery happened an hour ago. Write questions about the robbery. Then write the correct short answers.

1. he have a knife

    Q: ___ *Did he have a knife?* ___ A: ___ *No, he didn't.* ___

2. he tie up people

    Q: ___ **Did he tie people up?** ___ A: ___ **Yes, he did.** ___

3. he hurt anyone

    Q: ___ **Did he hurt anyone?** ___ A: ___ **Yes, he did.** ___

4. he have brown hair

    Q: ___ **Did he have brown hair?** ___ A: ___ **No, he didn't./Don't know.** ___

5. the teller give him money

    Q: ___ **Did the teller give him money?** ___ A: ___ **Yes, she did.** ___

6. the robber put the money in a box

    Q: ___ **Did the robber put the money in a box?** ___ A: ___ **No, he didn't.** ___

7. the teller press the "emergency" button

    Q: ___ **Did the teller press the "emergency" button?** ___ A: ___ **Yes, she did.** ___

1. When students are finished, have them check their answers with a partner.

2. Have students practice asking and answering the questions with a partner.

■ **EXERCISE C**

1. Look at the pictures as a class and discuss what happened.

2. Have students work with a partner to write the questions and answers.

3. Call on pairs to read aloud their questions and answers.

■ **EXPANSION IDEAS**

Exercise B

1. Have students write a paragraph about the Unabomber, using the information they learned from the reading.

Exercise C

1. Have students write a paragraph about the bank robbery in Exercise C.

2. Have students read their paragraphs.

3. Have the partners ask *yes/no* questions about the paragraph.

■ COMMUNICATE

The Communicate section allows students to practice the target grammar in more communicative, less-controlled ways through speaking and writing activities.

■ EXERCISE D

1. Go over the directions and the example.
2. Model the exercise using a crime that your students know about. Have students ask you *yes/no* questions about the crime and the criminal.

PART TWO

The Simple Past Tense: *Wh-* Questions

Part 2 introduces students to the simple past tense in *wh-* questions.

■ GRAMMAR IN CONTENT

■ EXERCISE A *Track 44* 🎧

1. Have students look at the picture and guess what the listening will be about.
2. Have students cover the reading and listen to the recording.
3. With the reading still covered, ask them the questions from the conversation.
4. Let them read to see if their answers are correct.
5. Play the audio again and let students follow along.

■ GRAMMAR CHART

Past Tense Wh- *Questions with Answers*

1. Go over the question words with students and discuss the possible answers. For example, to answer a *who* question, you must use a person, and to answer a *where* question, you must use a place.

(continued on page 145)

■ COMMUNICATE

D **PAIR WORK** **Student A thinks of a famous crime. Student B asks *yes/no* questions to guess the crime.**

> Did the crime happen in the United States?

> Did the criminal use a gun?

> Yes, it did.

> No, he didn't.

PART TWO	The Simple Past Tense: *Wh-* Questions

■ GRAMMAR IN CONTENT

🎧
TR44

A **Read and listen.**

uniform: a special type of clothing worn by members of a certain group or profession (for example, police officers)

A Great Museum Theft

Student:	**Where did** the biggest art theft in U.S. history **happen?**
Instructor:	At the Isabella Stewart Gardner Museum in Boston.
Student:	**When did** it **happen?**
Instructor:	On March 8, 1990.
Student:	**How did** the thieves **get** the paintings?
Instructor:	They dressed in police uniforms and handcuffed the security guards.
Student:	**What did** the thieves **take?**
Instructor:	Paintings by Vermeer, Rembrandt, and Manet.
Student:	**Why did** they **take** the art?
Instructor:	Probably because the art was worth $300,000,000.
Student:	Did the police catch the thieves?
Instructor:	No, they didn't. The frames are still hanging in the museum with no paintings in them.

Wh- Questions

Wh- Word	Did	Subject	Base Verb	Answers		
What		he	study?	Business.	OR	He studied business.
Where		they	live?	In Brazil.	OR	They lived in Brazil.
When	did	she	leave?	At 9:00.	OR	She left at 9:00.
Who		I	call?	John.	OR	You called John.
How		you	do on the test?	Very well.	OR	I did very well.
Why		we	buy it?	(Because) We liked it.		

Note:

In formal written English, the *wh-* question word for *who* is *whom*. Example: *Whom did the president call?*

■ EXPANSION IDEAS

Exercise A

1. Have students practice the conversation with a partner.

Grammar Chart

1. With a partner, have students practice the questions and answers in the chart.

Wh- Word as Subject	Past Tense Verb	Answers
Who	called?	Mike. OR Mike called.
What	happened?	It rained.

B Match the questions to the answers.

b   1. Who called?
_e_   2. Why did she call?
_c_   3. Who did they arrest?
_f_   4. Why did they arrest him?
_h_   5. What did he do?
_a_   6. Where did he do it?
_d_   7. Why did he do it?
_g_   8. What did he write?

a. On the wall of the dormitory.
b. Julia called.
c. They arrested Mario.
d. Because he wanted to ask Julia to marry him.
e. She called to tell you the police arrested someone.
f. Because he vandalized school property.
g. "I love you Julia. Marry me."
h. He wrote on a wall.

C PAIR WORK One partner looks at text A. The other looks at text B on page 228. Take turns asking each other past tense *wh-* questions to find the missing information.

Text A: Crimes of the Century

The Great Train Robbery happened in **Oxford, England**
(1)
(Where?). The robbery happened on August 8, 1963.

_____**15 people**_____ (Who?) robbed the train. They took
(2)
a lot of money. They took __**2.6 million pounds**__ (How much?).
(3)
They hurt one person. They hurt the engineer. They hit him

over the head with _____**an iron bar**_____ (What?).
(4)
The police found the robbers' fingerprints. The police caught

_____**14**_____ (How many?) of the robbers.
(5)

2. Go over the first part of the chart on page 144 with the students, referring to the reading for additional examples. Call on students to read the questions on the left side of the chart. After a student reads a question, call on another student to answer.

3. Go over the second part of the chart on page 145. Point out that in questions about subjects, the word *did* is not used.

■ **EXERCISE B**

1. Look at the example with students so they understand how to find the correct answers.

2. Go over the answers as a class.

3. Have students walk around the room and practice asking and answering the questions with their classmates.

■ **EXERCISE C**

Exercise C is an information gap activity where students will have to ask each other questions to find the missing information.

1. Put students in pairs and number each person in the pair 1 or 2. Tell the 1s to turn to page 228 and tell the 2s to look at the paragraph on this page.

2. Tell partners that they both have the same paragraph but that different information is missing in each. Explain that they will have to ask questions to find the missing information.

3. When you think students are ready to do the information gap activity by themselves, have them work with their partners to complete the paragraphs.

4. When they are finished, have students compare paragraphs to check their answers.

■ **EXPANSION IDEA**

Exercise C

1. Have students work alone to write five *yes/no* and five information questions about the Great Train Robbery.

2. Ask for volunteers to write their questions on the board.

3. Indicate which questions need to be fixed (spelling, grammar, punctuation) and ask for volunteers to fix them on the board.

■ COMMUNICATE

The Communicate section allows students to practice the target grammar in more communicative, less-controlled ways through speaking and writing activities.

■ EXERCISE D

When students are finished, ask for volunteers to share what they learned about their partners' birthdays.

● Connection

Putting It Together

The purpose of this section of the lesson is to connect and extend students' understanding of the grammar, vocabulary, and content from this lesson.

■ GRAMMAR AND VOCABULARY

1. Explain to students that they will recite their conversation in front of the class.
2. Give students time to plan and practice their conversations.
3. Ask students to listen carefully to each pair in order to decide if the accused person is guilty or innocent of the crime.

■ PROJECT

1. Help students generate a list of crimes they might research.
2. Go through each step with the students, making sure they understand what they are supposed to do.
3. For additional suggestions on doing projects, see the Teacher's Notes on pages xvi–xviii.

■ INTERNET

Have students work with a partner to do their Internet research.

■ VOCABULARY JOURNAL

Refer to the Pre-lesson (page 6) for an explanation of the vocabulary journal.

■ COMMUNICATE

D PAIR WORK Ask your partner past tense *wh-* questions about his or her last birthday.

Where did you go? / I went to a club.
What did you do there? / I danced.

Connection   Putting It Together

GRAMMAR AND VOCABULARY Work with a partner. Pretend one person is a police officer. The other is a person who may have committed a crime. Decide on the crime. Then do a role play. Use the grammar and vocabulary from this lesson.

Did you kill Mr. Roberts? / No, I didn't.
Did you see Mr. Roberts on the night of the crime? / Yes, I did.
Where did you see him? / I saw him at a club downtown.

PROJECT Research a crime.

1. Work with a partner. Choose a crime you want to learn more about.
2. Look on the Internet to find information about the crime.
3. Learn all you can about the crime. Take notes on what you learn.
4. Tell your classmates which crime or criminal you and your partner learned about.
5. Let your classmates ask you and your partner questions about the crime. Use your notes to try to answer your classmates' questions.

 INTERNET Go online. Search the news headlines on the Internet. Use the keywords "news" and "crime." What crimes happened this week?

VOCABULARY JOURNAL Write sentences for new vocabulary you learned in this lesson.

Example: *People who paint public walls are vandals.*

146   LESSON 19 | Criminology: Crime

■ EXPANSION IDEAS

Exercise D

1. Have students use the information they learned about their partners' last birthdays to type a paragraph on the computer.

Internet

1. Have students share the information with the class to see how many students found the same crimes.

PART 1
The Past Tense of *Be* and the
Simple Past Tense: Statements
PART 2
The Past Tense of *Be* and the
Simple Past Tense: Questions

Lesson 20

Archaeology: Ancient Egypt

■ CONTENT VOCABULARY

Look at the pictures. Do you know the words?

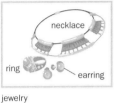

necklace
ring
earring
jewelry

rouge
lipstick

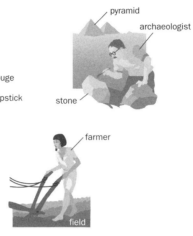

pyramid
archaeologist
stone
farmer
field

Write the new words in your vocabulary journal.

■ THINK ABOUT IT

Discuss these statements with a partner. Do you think each statement is true or false? (You will find the answers in the lesson.)   Answers will vary.

1. Most ancient Egyptians were farmers.	True	False
2. Ancient Egyptian men and women wore rouge.	True	False
3. The ancient Egyptians believed in life after death.	True	False
4. An archaeologist discovered a pharaoh's tomb in the twentieth century.	True	False

147

Lesson 20

Overview

1. Elicit students' prior knowledge. Ask: *What do you know about your culture in the past?* Ask students to work in groups of students from the same culture (if possible) to come up with some ideas.
2. Ask students to share with the class.

■ CONTENT VOCABULARY

1. Direct students' attention to the pictures and vocabulary words.
2. Ask them what all these pictures have in common.
3. Help students define the words and ask them to write them in their vocabulary journals.

■ THINK ABOUT IT

1. Have students think about the answers by themselves before they share their answers with a partner.
2. Go over the answers as a class.

■ CONTENT NOTES

Archaeology

The topic for this lesson is Archaeology: Ancient Egypt. Archaeology is the study of past human life and culture through the recovery and study of remaining materials and artifacts, such as buildings, tools, pottery, etc. The discipline of archaeology dates back to Italy in the fifteenth century when the Italians became interested in learning about ancient Greece.

Egyptology is a highly productive form of archaeology that focuses specifically on the Egyptian culture. Egyptology came about because of the wealth of materials found in the dry Egyptian climate. One of the most important artifacts uncovered there was the Rosetta stone, a tablet which had inscriptions in Greek along with Egyptian hieroglyphics, providing the key to deciphering Egyptian hieroglyphs.

PART ONE

The Past Tense of *Be* and the Simple Past Tense: Statements

Part 1 introduces students to the past tense of *be* and the simple past tense in statements.

■ GRAMMAR IN CONTENT

This section exposes students to a theme-based reading that includes examples of the target structure. Students can refer to the grammar chart(s) to complete the controlled practice activities.

■ EXERCISE A *Track 45*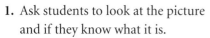

1. Ask students to look at the picture and if they know what it is.
2. Play the audio and have students follow along.
3. Ask the following questions: *What was the richest country of the ancient world? Who were the rulers of Egypt? How do archaeologists understand Egyptian culture?*
4. Go over the ideas and vocabulary in the reading.

■ GRAMMAR CHART

The Past Tense of Be *and the Simple Past Tense: Statements*

1. Go over the chart with the students. Point out that the chart has four sections: Affirmative, Negative, The Past Tense of *Be*, and The Simple Past Tense. Ask students why they think this chart separates *be* from other verbs. They will probably tell you that *be* is irregular and doesn't have the same forms or rules as other verbs.
2. As you go through the chart, refer to the examples from the reading to reinforce the rules of forming affirmative and negative statements in the past tense.

■ CONTENT VOCABULARY

TR45

A Read and listen.

Ancient Egypt

The ancient Egyptians lived about 5,000 years ago along the Nile River. Egypt was the richest country of the ancient world. Food was easy to grow. The Nile flooded every year. Farmers used the water for their fields.

The pharaohs were the rulers of Egypt. The Egyptians buried some of their pharaohs in tombs within pyramids. The builders did not have modern tools and machines. They floated large stones down the Nile River on boats. Then they carried the stones and pushed them up ramps.

Archaeologists study ancient Egyptian tombs. The paintings and objects inside the tombs help us understand ancient Egyptian culture and life.

pharaoh: a ruler of ancient Egypt
bury: to put a dead person in the ground or a grave
float: to rest or move on top of water
flood: a rising or overflowing of water

The Past Tense of *Be* and the Simple Past Tense: Statements	Affirmative	Negative
The Past Tense of *Be*	She **was** in class yesterday. We **were** at home last night.	She **was not** at home yesterday. We **were not** at school last night.
The Simple Past Tense	He **studied** in the library yesterday. They **lived** in Mexico last year.	He **did not study** at home yesterday. They **did not live** in Argentina last year.

B Look at the reading "Ancient Egypt." Complete each sentence with the correct past tense form of one of these verbs: *be, use, bury,* or *live*.

1. The Egyptians _____lived_____ about 5,000 years ago.
2. Egypt ____was____ the richest country of the ancient world.
3. Farmers ____used____ water from the Nile River for their fields.
4. Pharaohs ____were____ the rulers of Egypt.
5. The Egyptians ____buried____ some of their pharaohs in pyramids.

■ EXPANSION IDEA

Exercise A

1. Have students cover the story in their books and retell as many facts as they can remember to a partner. Have the partners work together to see how much they can remember as a pair.

C Complete the paragraphs. Use the correct past tense form of the verbs in parentheses.

Most ancient Egyptians (be) ___*were*___ farmers. They (love) ___**loved**___
                              (1)   (2)

good food and drink. They (eat) ___**ate**___ bread, fish, and vegetables. Beer
                                      (3)

(be) ___**was**___ the most popular drink.
        (4)

Both men and women (wear) ___**wore**___ jewelry such as earrings, rings, and
                                 (5)

necklaces. Egyptian women (make) ___**made**___ lipstick and rouge from red clay.
                                       (6)

D Read the sentences. Fill in the blanks with the negative form of the underlined words.

1. Most ancient Egyptians <u>had</u> very simple houses. They ___*did not have*___ a lot of furniture.

2. Cats <u>were</u> the most popular pets. Birds ___**were not**___ the most popular pets.

3. The average Egyptian <u>lived</u> to the age of 40. The average Egyptian ___**did not live**___ to the age of 60.

4. Some boys <u>went</u> to school. Girls ___**did not go**___ to school.

5. Divorce <u>was</u> legal. It ___**was not**___ illegal.

E Correct the composition. There are six more mistakes.

The Ancient Egyptians: Family and Religious Life

                                did

The ancient Egyptians ~~do~~ not wait long to marry. They usually

married   **had**   **were**

~~marryed~~ young and ~~has~~ many children. Most Egyptians ~~was~~ very

              did   **prayed**

religious. They not pray to one god. They ~~did pray~~ to many gods. They

believed

~~was believe~~ in life after death.

---

1. When students are finished, have them check their answers with a partner.
2. Go over the answers as a class by calling on students to read the sentences aloud.

■ **EXERCISE C**

1. When students are finished, have them check their answers with a partner.
2. Go over the answers as a class by calling on students to read the sentences aloud.
3. Ask students what information about ancient Egyptian culture is interesting to them.

■ **EXERCISE D**

1. Have students work with a partner to fill in the blanks.
2. Call on students to write the sentences on the board.
3. Conduct a discussion comparing the information about ancient Egyptian culture to a current culture students are familiar with.

■ **EXERCISE E**

1. Once students have found the seven mistakes, have them share their work with a partner.
2. Go over the mistakes as a class and go over the reasons the errors are grammatically incorrect.

■ **EXPANSION IDEA**

Exercise D

1. Have students think about their own culture as if it were in the past.
2. Have them write sentences similar to those in Exercise D about their own culture.

For example:
Most Vietnamese had very extravagant houses. They had a lot of furniture.

■ COMMUNICATE

The Communicate section allows students to practice the target grammar in more communicative, less-controlled ways through speaking and writing activities.

■ EXERCISE F

Model this activity for students by writing a sample paragraph on the board about a class you have taken.

PART TWO

The Past Tense of *Be* and the Simple Past Tense: Questions

Part 2 introduces students to the past tense of *be* and simple past tense questions.

■ GRAMMAR IN CONTENT

This section exposes students to a theme-based reading that includes examples of the target structure. Students can refer to the grammar chart(s) to complete the controlled practice activities.

■ EXERCISE A *Track 46*

1. Ask students if they know what the picture is.
2. Have students cover the reading and listen to the recording.
3. With the reading still covered, ask students the same questions that are written in the conversation.
4. Have students read the text to see whether they were correct.
5. Play the listening again and have students follow along.

■ GRAMMAR CHART

The Past Tense of Be *and the Simple Past Tense:* Yes/No *and* Wh- *Questions*

Go over the chart with the students, pointing out its four-part structure. As you review the chart, refer to the reading for examples.

■ COMMUNICATE

F **WRITE** Write a paragraph about a favorite class you took in the past. Answer questions such as: *What was the class? When did you take it? Was it interesting? Why was it interesting? What did you learn? Did you like the instructor? Why did you like the instructor? Were there many students in the class? Who was in the class?*

PART TWO	The Past Tense of *Be* and the Simple Past Tense: Questions

■ GRAMMAR IN CONTENT

 A **Read and listen.**

TR46

Tutankhamen's Tomb

Question:	**Who was** Tutankhamen?
Answer:	He was an Egyptian pharaoh. A British archaeologist named Howard Carter discovered his tomb.
Question:	**When did** Carter **discover** the tomb?
Answer:	He discovered it on November 4, 1922.
Question:	**Did** he **find** many things in the tomb?
Answer:	Yes, he did.
Question:	**What did** he **find** in the tomb?
Answer:	Besides Tutankhamen's body, he found jewelry, furniture, statues, clothes, and other treasures.

discover: find

treasures: valuable things

The Past Tense of *Be*: *Yes/No* and *Wh-* Questions

Yes/No Questions	*Wh-* Questions
Was she in Egypt? **Were** you in the museum?	**When was** she in Egypt? **Why were** you in the museum?

The Simple Past Tense: *Yes/No* and *Wh-* Questions

Yes/No Questions	*Wh-* Questions
Did he go on vacation? **Did** they **study** archaeology?	**Where did** he go on vacation? **Why did** they **study** archaeology?

■ EXPANSION IDEAS

Exercise F

1. Have students use the questions in Exercise F to ask a partner about a class he or she has taken.

Exercise A

1. Have students practice the conversation with a partner.
2. Have students practice it again, this time with one student covering his or her book and answering the questions.

B Look at the dialogue "Tutankhamen's Tomb." Match the questions to the correct answers.

   b   1. Was Tutankhamen an archaeologist?   a. Yes, he did.

   e   2. Who was Tutankhamen?   b. No, he wasn't.

   c   3. Who was Howard Carter?   c. An archaeologist.

   a   4. Did Carter discover Tutankhamen's tomb?   d. November 4, 1922.

   d   5. When did he discover the tomb?   e. An Egyptian pharaoh.

C Complete each question with one or more of these words: *was, were, did, who, when, how.*

1. **Q:** _When_ _did_ Tutankhamen become pharaoh?   **A:** After his father died.

2. **Q:** _Was_ Tutankhamen a young pharaoh?   **A:** Yes, he was.

3. **Q:** _When_ _did_ he become pharaoh?   **A:** He became pharaoh when he was 9 years old.

4. **Q:** _Was_ he married?   **A:** Yes, he was.

5. **Q:** _Who_ _was_ he married to?   **A:** His half-sister.

6. **Q:** _Did_ he have children?   **A:** Yes, he did. He had two children.

7. **Q:** _Were_ they boys?   **A:** No, they weren't.

8. **Q:** _Did_ he die young?   **A:** Yes, he did.

9. **Q:** _How_ old _was_ he?   **A:** He was 18 when he died.

10. **Q:** _Did_ someone kill Tutankhamen?   **A:** No one is sure.

■ COMMUNICATE

D **GROUP WORK** The class works as two teams. With your team, write a list of questions about the information you learned in this lesson. Each team takes turns testing the other team with a question. Each team that answers a question correctly gets one point. The team with the most points at the end wins the game.

■ **EXERCISE B**

1. Have students do the exercise by themselves. Then go over the answers as a class.
2. Have students walk around the room and practice asking and answering the questions with their classmates.

■ **EXERCISE C**

1. Have students work with a partner to come up with the correct answers.
2. Have students practice the questions and answers with a different partner.

■ **COMMUNICATE**

The Communicate section allows students to practice the target grammar in more communicative, less-controlled ways through speaking and writing activities.

■ **EXERCISE D**

1. Divide the class into two teams and help each team get started on writing questions about ancient Egypt. Have each team write as many questions as there are people in their group. (If they have 12 team members, students should write 12 questions.)
2. Have each team member ask the other team one question.
3. Facilitate the game and be the scorekeeper.

■ **EXPANSION IDEA**

Exercise B

1. Have students use the information on ancient Egypt from page 148 to create a matching exercise like the one in Exercise B on this page.
2. Tell students to write five questions and answers and format them as a matching activity, as in Exercise B.
3. Have students exchange their papers with a partner and complete the activities they have made for each other.

■ EXERCISE E

1. Model this activity by asking students a few questions like the ones in the exercise. Then ask the students to work in pairs.

2. When students are finished with the exercise, ask for volunteers to share what they learned about their partners.

■ EXERCISE F

Help students get started by modeling a few sentences on the board for them.

Connection

Putting It Together

The purpose of this section of the lesson is to connect and extend students' understanding of the grammar, vocabulary, and content from this lesson.

■ GRAMMAR AND VOCABULARY

1. Help students get started by writing some example questions on the board.

2. When students are finished, collect their questions and look them over, making sure they are comprehensible.

3. Pass out the questions to different students in the class to answer.

■ PROJECT

1. Go through each step with the students, making sure they understand what they are supposed to do.

2. For additional suggestions on doing projects, see the Teacher's Notes on pages xvi–xviii.

■ INTERNET

1. As a class, come up with a list of ancient civilizations.

2. Assign small groups of students different civilizations to research.

E PAIR WORK What was your partner's life like five years ago? Ask your partner questions. Use the question cues below. Add questions of your own. Take notes on your partner's answers.

1. . . . you in the United States five years ago?
2. Where . . . you?
3. . . . you live with your parents?
4. Who . . . you live with?
5. . . . you in school?
6. What . . . you study?
7. . . . you have a job?
8. . . . you have a car?

F WRITE Write a paragraph about your partner's life five years ago. Use the information from exercise E.

Connection   Putting It Together

GRAMMAR AND VOCABULARY Write five questions about ancient Egypt. Use the grammar and vocabulary from the lesson. Your partner will write answers to the questions.

PROJECT Write a story about an archaeological discovery.

1. Work in pairs. Imagine you are archaeologists in Egypt. You discover a new tomb in a pyramid.
2. Write a story about your find.
3. Read your story to the class.
4. Your classmates will ask questions about your discovery.

 INTERNET Find out some facts about the people of another ancient civilization such as the Mayans, Romans, or ancient Greeks. Where did they live? What did they do? What did they wear? Report back to your class.

VOCABULARY JOURNAL Write sentences for new vocabulary you learned in this lesson.

Example: *My wife puts red lipstick on her lips every morning.*

■ EXPANSION IDEA

Exercise E

1. Give students note cards and have them write down short answers to the questions in Exercise E. For example:
   1. no   5. yes
   2. Mexico   6. high school
   3. yes   7. no
   4. my parents   8. no

2. Have them write their initials on the bottom of the card before you collect them.

3. Before you pass the cards out to students, explain to them how the activity will work. Students will walk around the room and ask the questsions from Exercise E.

Students will answer with the answers on the note card they are holding. The goal is for the person who is asking the questions to find his or her own card. When the student asking the questions thinks he or she has found the right card, he or she will ask: *Does that card belong to A.R. (initials)?* If so, he or she can take his or her card and sit down. If not, students must move on and talk to other students. This will continue until everyone finds his or her card.

4. Model this with students until they understand what they are supposed to do.

A (Circle) the correct answers.

The twentieth century ((was)/ were) an exciting century. There were
(1)
many "firsts." For example, Wilbur and Orville Wright (was /(were)) the
(2)
inventors of the airplane. Before then, the airplane ((was)/ were) just a dream.
(3)
Jackie Robinson is another example of a twentieth-century "first." Robinson
((was)/ were) the first black baseball player in the major leagues. Before Jackie
(4)
Robinson, black people (were /(were not)) allowed to play in the major leagues.
(5)

B Complete the questions and answers with *was, were, wasn't, weren't, who, where,* or *why.*

Jane: __**Where**__ were you on New
(1)
Year's Eve?

Eve: Times Square, New York City.

Jane: __**Who**__ were you with?
(2)

Eve: A million other people!

Jane: __**Was**__ it fun?
(3)

Eve: Yes, it __**was**__. Was it a fun
(4)
New Year's for you and John?

Jane: No, it __**wasn't**__.
(5)

Eve: __**Were**__ you and John at a
(6)
party?

Jane: No, we __**weren't**__.
(7)

Eve: __**Where**__ were you?
(8)

Jane: We were at home.

Eve: __**Why**__ were you at home?
(9)

Jane: We were sick.

C Complete the sentences with the correct past tense form of the verbs in parentheses.

Bill Gates is the founder of the Microsoft Corporation. Gates (is) __**was**__ born
(1)
in Seattle in 1955. Gates (go) __**went**__ to Harvard University. While he was at
(2)
Harvard, he (write) __**wrote**__ an important computer programming book. But
(3)
Gates (not graduate) __**did not graduate**__ from Harvard. He (drop) __**dropped**__
(4)   (5)
out before his senior year. Gates (start) __**started**__ Microsoft in 1975. The
(6)
company (make) __**made**__ Gates one of the wealthiest men in the world.
(7)

Review 16–20

Lessons 16–20

The purpose of this lesson is to help students review the concepts they have learned in the last five lessons. Encourage them to go back to the lessons and review the grammar charts to help them complete the review exercises.

■ EXERCISE A

1. Have students do this activity by themselves and then share their answers with a partner.
2. Go over the answers as a class by asking students to read the sentences aloud.

■ EXERCISE B

1. Have students do this activity by themselves and then share their answers with a partner.
2. Go over the answers as a class.
3. Have students practice the conversation with the correct answers.

■ EXERCISE C

1. Have students do this activity by themselves and then share their answers with a partner.
2. Go over the answers as a class by asking students to read the sentences aloud.

■ EXPANSION IDEA

Exercise B

1. Have students work with a partner to rewrite the conversation in Exercise B, putting in information about themselves and what they did on New Year's Eve.

■ **EXERCISE D**

1. Have students work with a partner to choose the correct answers.
2. Have the students practice the conversation.

■ **EXERCISE E**

Have students do this activity with a partner, agreeing on the correct answers before they write them in their books.

■ **LEARNER LOG**

1. Help students understand how to complete the Learner Log by going over it with them and offering examples of the grammar structures.
2. If students checked "I Need More Practice" for any of the structures, suggest that they review those lessons. If possible, meet with students individually to discuss their Learner Logs and make suggestions for ways to get more practice with the structures.

D Circle the correct answers.

Paco: A thief broke into my house yesterday.

Rai: That's terrible. (Did he take / Did he took) anything?
(1)

Paco: (Yes, he did / No, he didn't.)
(2)

Rai: (When / What) did he take?
(3)

Paco: He took my television and jewelry.

Rai: (Did catch the police / Did the police catch) him?
(4)

Paco: (Yes, we did. / Yes, they did.)
(5)

Rai: (When did they catch / When did they caught) him?
(6)

Paco: This morning.

E Complete the questions and answers with the missing words.

Q: Who __was__ Cleopatra?   **A:** She __was__ the last Egyptian pharaoh.
(1)   (2)

Q: When __did__ she rule Egypt? **A:** She __ruled__ Egypt from 51 to 31 B.C.
(3)   (4)

Q: __Was__ she very intelligent? **A:** Yes, she __was__.
(5)   (6)

Q: __Did__ she have children?   **A:** Yes, she __had__ four children.
(7)   (8)

Q: __How__ did she die?   **A:** She killed herself.
(9)

Q: __Who__ ruled Egypt after she died? **A:** The Romans.
(10)

LEARNER LOG Check (✔) Yes or I Need more Practice.

Lesson	I Can Use . . .	Yes	I Need More Practice
16	Past of *Be*: Statements		
17	Past of *Be*: Questions		
18	Simple Past Tense Statements		
19	Simple Past Tense Questions		
20	Past of *Be* vs. Simple Past Tense		

■ **EXPANSION IDEAS**

Exercise D

1. Go through each of the answers with students and discuss the grammatical reason why the wrong answer is incorrect. For example, the answer to (1) can't be *Did he took* because in *yes/no* questions about the past, we use *did* plus the base form of the verb.

Learner Log

1. Have students form groups and generate a list of ideas for what they can do if they checked the "I Need More Practice" column in the Learner Log. Have each group share its best ideas with the class.

Marketing: Advertising

Overview

1. Elicit students' prior knowledge. Write the words *advertising* and *marketing* on the board. Ask students if they know the meanings of these words.
2. Once students understand the meanings, ask them for examples of advertising (ads in the paper, commercials, etc.).

■ CONTENT VOCABULARY

Look at the pictures. Do you know the words?

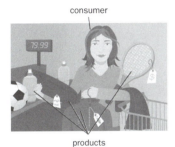

consumer

products

clothes

food

advertisement

money

furniture

Write the new words in your vocabulary journal.

■ THINK ABOUT IT

Discuss these questions with a partner.

1. Where do you see advertisements? Write a list.
2. Do people buy things because of advertisements?
3. Did you ever buy something because of an advertisement? If so, what?

■ CONTENT VOCABULARY

1. Direct students' attention to the pictures and vocabulary words.
2. Ask them what all these pictures have in common. (Most are things you can buy.)
3. Help them define new words to write in their vocabulary journals.

■ THINK ABOUT IT

1. Have students think about the answers by themselves before they share their answers with a partner.
2. Have each pair join another pair and share their ideas.

155

■ CONTENT NOTES

Marketing

The topic for this lesson is Marketing: Advertising. *Marketing* involves the techniques used to persuade consumers to buy products or subscribe to services. *Advertising* is the paid promotion of goods, services, companies, and ideas by a specific sponsor. Marketers consider advertising to be part of an overall promotional strategy for a product or service.

Students who decide to study marketing could find careers in:

advertising
market research
product (brand) management
public relations
retailing
sales
sales promotion

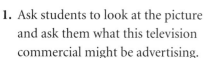

PART ONE

Count and Noncount Nouns

Part 1 introduces students to count and noncount nouns.

■ GRAMMAR IN CONTENT

This section exposes students to a theme-based reading that includes examples of the target structure. Students can refer to the grammar chart(s) to complete the controlled practice activities.

■ EXERCISE A *Track 47* 🎧

1. Ask students to look at the picture and ask them what this television commercial might be advertising.
2. Play the audio and have students follow along.
3. The reading mentions three techniques used to sell products. Ask students what these techniques are. See if they can come up with any specific jingles, "perfect" people, or cartoons used to advertise a product.

■ GRAMMAR CHART

Count and Noncount Nouns

Go over the chart with the students. As you go through the chart, refer to the examples from the reading to reinforce the rules. Ask students to provide additional examples of each type of noun.

■ GRAMMAR IN CONTENT

 A Read and listen.

TR47

Advertising Techniques

Advertisements use many techniques to sell (products.) Here are a few.

Some advertisements use short (songs) called "jingles." Jingles often stay in people's minds long after the commercial is over. There are jingles for everything from (hamburgers) to laundry detergent.

Advertisements often show "perfect" people using the (product.) The consumer often wants to be like the person they see using the makeup, wearing the clothes, or eating the food.

Advertisements often use cartoon characters to sell (products) to children. For example, one company uses a cartoon tiger to sell their cereal. Another uses a cartoon rabbit to sell chocolate milk.

technique: a special way of doing something
perfect: the best possible
cartoon character: a funny drawing of a person, animal, or object

Count Nouns		Noncount Nouns
Singular	**Plural**	water
		rice
a book	books	furniture
an apple	apples	
a computer	computers	

Notes:
- Count nouns are nouns that can be counted. Count nouns have a singular and a plural form.
- Use *a* or *an* with singular count nouns. To form the plural of most count nouns, add *-s* or *-es*.
- Noncount nouns are not usually counted. They have no plural form and no indefinite article. They take a singular verb.
  Correct: *Snow is cold.* Wrong: ~~Snows are cold.~~

■ EXPANSION IDEA

Exercise A

1. Have students look for all the count nouns in the reading. Refer them to the appendix on page 230 for spelling rules for plural nouns.
2. Have students work in pairs to share answers and create a list that includes both singular and plural forms. Write this partial list on the board to help students get started:

<u>Singular</u>	<u>Plural</u>
advertisement	advertisements
technique	techniques

3. Ask for volunteers to complete the lists on the board.

Kinds of Noncount Nouns

Type A: Nouns that do not have separate parts.
Examples: milk, water, cheese, coffee

Type C: Nouns that are categories of things.
Examples: fruit, furniture, money, clothes

Type B: Nouns with too many parts to count.
Examples: rice, snow, sugar, hair

Type D: Nouns that are ideas (you can't touch them).
Examples: love, crime, information, music

B Look at the reading "Advertising Techniques." Find and (circle) five count nouns. Find and underline five noncount nouns. Answers on page 156.

C Are the underlined nouns in "Think Before You Spend" count nouns or noncount nouns? Write "C" above the count nouns and "NC" above the noncount nouns.

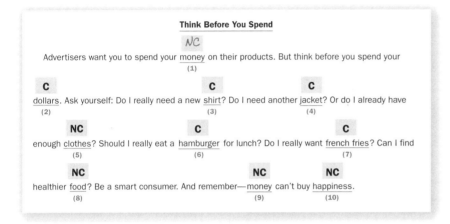

Think Before You Spend

NC
Advertisers want you to spend your money on their products. But think before you spend your
(1)

C   *C*   *C*
dollars. Ask yourself: Do I really need a new shirt? Do I need another jacket? Or do I already have
(2)   (3)   (4)

NC   *C*   *C*
enough clothes? Should I really eat a hamburger for lunch? Do I really want french fries? Can I find
(5)   (6)   (7)

NC   *NC*   *NC*
healthier food? Be a smart consumer. And remember—money can't buy happiness.
(8)   (9)   (10)

D Some of the sentences have mistakes. Find the mistakes and correct them.

1. I drink ~~coffees~~ *coffee* every morning.
2. She wants ~~a~~ rice.
3. He needs a pen.
4. You have three books.
5. They love ~~a~~ music.
6. Brush your hair~~s~~.

Kinds of Noncount Nouns

Go over the chart with the students. Ask students to think of at least one more example of each type of noncount noun. (For example, Type A: gasoline; Type B: salt; Type C: homework; Type D: beauty.)

■ **EXERCISE B**

When students are finished, have them check their answers with a partner.

■ **EXERCISE C**

1. Have students work with a partner to complete the exercise.
2. Put two columns on the board, *count* and *noncount.*
3. Have students write the words from both Exercises B and C under the correct columns.

■ **EXERCISE D**

1. Once students have found the mistakes, have them share with a partner.
2. Ask for volunteers to write the corrected sentences on the board.
3. Go over the sentences as a class and discuss the grammatical problems in the errors in the exercise.

■ **EXPANSION IDEA**

Have students list all the nouns they have learned in the chapter. Show students what the list should look like:

Singular	Plural	Noncount
book	books	water
apple	apples	rice

■ COMMUNICATE

The Communicate section allows students to practice the target grammar in more communicative, less-controlled ways through speaking and writing activities.

■ C O M M U N I C A T E

E PAIR WORK Look through a magazine or newspaper. Make a list of the things you see advertised. Use a dictionary if necessary. Divide the list into two columns. Put all of the count nouns in one column and all of the noncount nouns in the other.

■ EXERCISE E

1. Bring newspapers to class or ask students to bring newspapers so they can do the activity in class. Alternatively, show students some examples and assign the activity for homework.

2. Show students what the list should look like:

Things Advertised in the Paper	
Count	Noncount
computers	food

PART TWO	A/An, Some, Any

■ G R A M M A R   I N   C O N T E N T

TR48

A Read and listen.

Advertise Here?
1-800-555-4321

Advertising Is Everywhere

Studies show that Americans see about 3,000 ads each day. There are advertisements on television, in newspapers, and on the radio. But they are turning up in **some** new places too. For example, **some** stores now have advertisements on their floors. **Some** public bathrooms now have ads. There are even ads on **some** fruit.

Are there **any** advertisements in space? Not yet, but soon there may be. The Russian space program launched a rocket in 2000 with **an** ad for Pizza Hut. There are also **some** companies trying to put ads in space that we can see from Earth.

ads: short form of "advertisements"

turn up: appear

launch: to send up in the air

PART TWO

A/An, Some, Any

Part 2 introduces students to *a/an*, *some*, and *any*.

■ GRAMMAR IN CONTENT

This section exposes students to a theme-based reading that includes examples of the target structure. Students can refer to the grammar chart(s) to complete the controlled practice activities.

A/An, Some, and *Any*			
	Affirmative Statements	Negative Statements	Questions
Singular Count Nouns	I ate a carrot. I ate an apple.	I didn't eat a carrot. I didn't eat an apple.	Do you want a carrot? Do you want an apple?
Plural Count Nouns	I ate some carrots.	I didn't eat any carrots.	Do you want any carrots? Do you want some carrots?
Noncount Nouns	I ate some bread.	I didn't eat any bread.	Do you want any bread? Do you want some bread?

Notes:
- *A/an* means "one." Use *a* before a consonant sound. Use *an* before a vowel sound.
- *Some* means "an indefinite amount."
- *Any* is the negative form of *some*. Either *any* or *some* can be used in yes/no questions.

■ EXERCISE A *Track 48*

1. Ask students what they see in the picture. (It's a billboard on the moon offering advertising space.)

2. Have students follow along while you play the recording.

■ GRAMMAR CHART

A/An, Some, and Any

1. Go over the chart with the students. Go over the Notes. As you go through the chart, refer to the reading for examples.

■ EXPANSION IDEA

Exercise A

1. Have students underline the *count* nouns and circle the *noncount* nouns.

2. Practice the pronunciation of *an* + noun, demonstrating the way the /n/ sound is linked with the vowel sound that follows it; for example, *an apple* is pronounced as if it were one word, *anapple*.

B Complete with *a/an* or *some*.

1. _some_ stores
2. _a_ store
3. _some_ money
4. _a_ dollar
5. _an_ advertisement
6. _some_ advertisements

C Listen and complete the sentences with *a/an*, *some*, or *any*.

TR49

Woman: Look at all of these dirty clothes! I have _a_ (1) family, _a_ (2) job, and _a_ (3) busy house. I don't have _any_ (4) spare time. I need _some_ (5) help! I need _an_ (6) answer!

Announcer: This is _a_ (1) job for Suds Bright! All you need is _a_ (2) washing machine and _some_ (3) Suds Bright detergent. You don't need _any_ (4) bleach. You don't need _any_ (5) stain removers. Suds Bright does it all!

D Complete the sentences and questions with *a/an*, *some*, or *any*. (For some items, either *some* or *any* is correct.)

Daughter: Dad, I need _some_ (1) clothes. Can I have _some_ (2) money?

Father: Did your mother give you _any_ (3) money for clothes last week?

Daughter: Yes, she did. But I bought _a_ (4) jacket. I don't have _any_ (5) money left.

Father: Maybe it's time for you to look for _a_ (6) job.

Daughter: Um . . . Forget it. I don't need _any_ (7) money. I guess I don't really need more clothes.

■ C O M M U N I C A T E

E **PAIR WORK** What did your partner have for breakfast this morning? Ask *yes/no* questions with *a/an* and *some/any* to find out.

■ EXERCISE B

Have students do the exercise by themselves. Then go over the answers as a class.

■ EXERCISE C *Track 49*

1. Prepare students for listening by going through the sentences and asking them to predict what might belong in the spaces.
2. Have students listen and fill in the blanks.
3. Go over the answers as a class, referring to the grammar chart on page 158 as necessary.

■ EXERCISE D

Have students do the exercise by themselves and then go over the answers by practicing the conversation with a partner.

■ COMMUNICATE

The Communicate section allows students to practice the target grammar in more communicative, less-controlled ways through speaking and writing activities.

■ EXERCISE E

1. Prepare students for this activity by making a list of possible breakfast foods on the board.
2. Discuss whether each food word is a count or noncount noun.
3. Model the activity with a few students before having students do the exercise in pairs.

■ EXPANSION IDEA

Exercise C

1. Have small groups of students choose or invent a product and write an advertisement similar to the second set of sentences in Exercise C.

2. Ask for a volunteer from each group to read the group's ad aloud.

■ EXERCISE F

1. Prepare students for this activity by making a list of things they might have at home.
2. Discuss whether each word is a count or noncount noun.
3. Model the activity with a few students before having students do the exercise in pairs.

Connection

Putting It Together

The purpose of this section of the lesson is to connect and extend students' understanding of the grammar, vocabulary, and content from this lesson.

■ GRAMMAR AND VOCABULARY

1. Bring newspapers or magazines to class for students to use.
2. Model this activity for the class by first going over the example in the book and then by giving another example from a newspaper. Ask for a few volunteers to practice with you.

■ PROJECT

1. Go through each step with the students, making sure they understand what they are supposed to do.
2. For additional suggestions on doing projects, see the Teacher's Notes on pages xvi–xviii.

■ INTERNET

1. Have students do the exercise alone or with a partner.
2. Have students share their lists in pairs or small groups and check each other's grammar.

■ VOCABULARY JOURNAL

Refer to the Pre-lesson (page 6) for an explanation of the vocabulary journal.

F **PAIR WORK** What items does your partner have at home? Ask "Do you have . . ." questions with *a/an* or *some/any* and the words below. Then ask more questions with words of your own.

computer	apples	plants
curtains	carpet	air conditioner

Connection | Putting It Together

GRAMMAR AND VOCABULARY Work with a partner. Look through a magazine or newspaper. Your partner will look through a different magazine or newspaper. Take turns telling about the advertisements you see and answering questions about them. Use the grammar and vocabulary from this lesson.

> There are some ads for clothes in my magazine.

> Are there any ads for sneakers?

> Yes. There's an ad for blue and white sneakers. In the ad there's a woman running through a garden. There are flowers and some trees around her.

PROJECT Create an advertisement.

1. Work in groups of three or four.
2. Write an ad for one of the following products: Snaffle Soda, Meow Cat Food, or Luscious Lipstick. Include grammar from this lesson.
3. Show your ad to your class.

INTERNET Go to your three favorite online stores. Make a list of the things you see advertised. Divide the list into two columns. Put all of the count nouns in one column and all of the noncount nouns in the other.

VOCABULARY JOURNAL Write sentences for new vocabulary you learned in this lesson.

Example: *I am a smart consumer. I buy things I need.*

■ EXPANSION IDEAS

Project

1. Have students create and illustrate their advertisements on the computer.

Internet

1. Have students go to different Web sites that they often visit (search engines, e-mail sites, etc.) and see what kinds of products are advertised there.

Business: Tourism

■ CONTENT VOCABULARY

Look at the pictures. Do you know the words?

souvenirs

tourist

GREETINGS FROM SPRINGFIELD

Van Gogh
4/1 - 8/15

museum

beach

park

a postcard

travel agent

traffic

Write the new words in your vocabulary journal.

■ THINK ABOUT IT

Discuss these questions with a partner. Answers will vary.

1. What are five popular cities for tourists to visit?
2. What can tourists see and do in these cities?
3. Do tourists like to visit the place where you live? What can they do and see there?

161

Lesson ㉒

Overview

1. Elicit students' prior knowledge. Write *tourism* on the board. Ask students if they know the meaning of this word.
2. Once students understand the meaning, ask them why tourism is important. Ask them if they have ever been tourists and, if so, where.

■ CONTENT VOCABULARY

1. Direct students' attention to the pictures and vocabulary words.
2. Ask them what all these pictures have in common. (All have something to do with travel.)
3. Help students define the words and ask them to write them in their vocabulary journals.

■ THINK ABOUT IT

After students discuss the questions with a partner, discuss them as a class to discover whether there is any consensus about the five most popular cities in the world for tourists to visit.

■ CONTENT NOTES

Business

The topic for this lesson is Business: Tourism. Tourism is an important part of the economy for most countries in the world. In most parts of the world, tourism is a great source of income and many countries could not survive without it.

Travel and tourism, which includes transportation, catering, accommodations, recreation, and travel services, is the world's largest industry and generator of jobs. In 1999, in the United States alone, domestic and international travelers spent $519 billion dollars.

PART ONE

Quantity Expressions

Part 1 introduces students to quantity expressions with count and noncount nouns.

■ GRAMMAR IN CONTENT

This section exposes students to a theme-based reading that includes examples of the target structure. Students can refer to the grammar chart(s) to complete the controlled practice activities.

■ EXERCISE A *Track 50*

1. Play the audio and have students follow along.
2. Ask the following questions:
   How is the weather in Malaga?
   How much sunshine is there?
   How much rain is there?
   What can you do in Malaga?

■ GRAMMAR CHART

Quantity Expressions: Count and Noncount Nouns

1. Go over the charts with the students. Go over the Notes. As you review the charts and the Notes, refer to the examples from the reading to reinforce the rules.
2. Since the sentences in the charts are about cars and traffic, ask students about cars and traffic in your city or area. For example, ask: *Are there many cars on campus? Is there a lot of traffic downtown?*

■ GRAMMAR IN CONTENT

TR50

A Read and listen.

Welcome to Malaga

Welcome to Malaga, Spain. I'm the hotel manager here at Hotel Malaga. Malaga is a beautiful city in southern Spain. The weather is wonderful. There is always **a lot of** sunshine. There is **not much** rain. There are **many** things to see and do in our city. For example, there are **many** beaches, **a lot of** restaurants, and **a few** interesting museums.

I want to make sure our guests have the best possible visit. How do I do this? I ask them **some** questions. I learn about their interests. Then I give them **a lot of** advice.

advice: directions or opinions about what to do

Quantity Expressions: Count Nouns (Plural)

Affirmative			Negative		
	Quantity Expression	Plural Count Noun		Quantity Expression	Plural Count Noun
There are	a lot of many some a few no	cars.	There aren't There are not	a lot of many any	cars.

Quantity Expressions: Noncount Nouns

Affirmative			Negative		
	Quantity Expression	Plural Noncount Noun		Quantity Expression	Plural Noncount Noun
There is	a lot of some a little no	traffic.	There isn't There is not	a lot of much any	traffic.

Notes:
- Use *many* with count nouns and *a lot of* with count and noncount nouns to talk about a large amount or number.
- Use *a little* with noncount nouns and *a few* with count nouns to talk about a small amount.
- Use *not many* with count nouns and *not much* with noncount nouns to talk about a very small amount or number.

■ EXPANSION IDEA

Exercise A

1. Using Exercise A as an example, have students write a paragraph about the city they are from or the city they live in now.

B Complete each sentence with *many* or *much*.

"Hi! I want to travel to Europe. I have __many__ questions.
(1)
I want to visit __many__ European countries. I want to see
(2)
__many__ museums. I don't have __much__ money. I don't have
(3)   (4)
__much__ time. I like cities with __many__ things to do. But I
(5)   (6)
don't like cities with __much__ traffic and noise. I don't have __many__ ideas. Do you?"
(7)   (8)

C Complete each sentence with *a few* or *a little*.

"Son, I have __a little__ advice for you. Buy __a few__
(1)   (2)
bilingual dictionaries. Bring __a few__ warm sweaters.
(3)
Spend __a little__ time on the beaches in Portugal. Try
(4)
__a little__ coffee in Italy. Learn __a little__ Spanish in
(5)   (6)
Spain. Eat __a little__ French food in France. Send us __a few__ postcards.
(7)   (8)
And bring home __a few__ souvenirs for me."
(9)

D Write true sentences about your city or neighborhood. Use quantity words or phrases. **Answers will vary.**

1. (beaches) _____

2. (history) _____

3. (restaurants) _____

4. (parks) _____

5. (shops) _____

6. (crime) _____

■ C O M M U N I C A T E

E **WRITE** Write a paragraph about your city or neighborhood. Use count and noncount nouns and quantity expressions. Use the vocabulary from this lesson.

■ **EXPANSION IDEAS**

Exercise B

1. Have students write a short paragraph, like the one in Exercise B, about a place they'd like to travel to and what they'd like to see and do there. Ask them to use the words *much* and *many*.

Exercise C

1. Have students write a short paragraph of advice, like the one in Exercise C, giving advice to someone who might travel to their native country. Ask them to use the terms *a few* and *a little*.

■ **EXERCISE B**

1. Have students complete the exercise by themselves.
2. Ask them to go over their answers with a partner, discussing why they chose the answers they did.

For example: "*The first one is* many *because* questions *is a count noun and it's plural.*"

■ **EXERCISE C**

1. Have students complete the exercise by themselves.
2. Have them go over their answers with a partner, discussing why they chose the answers they did.

For example: "*The first one is* a little *because* advice *is a noncount noun.*"

■ **EXERCISE D**

1. Model the exercise for the class using the first item, *beaches*. For example: *There are not many beaches in my neighborhood.*
2. After students finish the exercise, ask for volunteers to write one of their sentences on the board.

■ **COMMUNICATE**

The Communicate section allows students to practice the target grammar in more communicative, less-controlled ways through speaking and writing activities.

■ **EXERCISE E**

If students already wrote about their city in the expansion activity, have them write about their neighborhood in this exercise.

Part 2 introduces students to *how many/how much.*

■ GRAMMAR IN CONTENT

This section exposes students to a theme-based reading that includes examples of the target structure. Students can refer to the grammar chart(s) to complete the controlled practice activities.

■ EXERCISE A *Track 51*

1. Ask students if they know what city is in the picture.
2. Have students cover up the reading and listen only as you play the recording.
3. With the reading still covered, ask students the questions from the conversation.
4. Play the recording one more time, letting students look at the reading while they listen.
5. Have students practice the conversation with a partner.

■ GRAMMAR CHART

How many/How much

Go over the chart and the Notes with the students, referring to the reading for examples. After you look at the first section of the chart, write several plural count nouns on the board. Ask volunteers to ask questions using the nouns along with *How many.* For example, if you write *students* on the board, someone might say, *How many students are there in this class?* Look at the second section of the chart and repeat the procedure with noncount nouns.

■ GRAMMAR IN CONTENT

A **Read and listen.**

TR51

Facts about New York City

Question:	**How many** people are there in New York City?
Answer:	There are about 7.5 million people.
Question:	**How many** restaurants are there?
Answer:	There are about 19,500 restaurants.
Question:	**How many** tourists visit each year?
Answer:	About 35 million.
Question:	**How much** money do tourists spend each year?
Answer:	About 15 billion dollars.
Question:	**How much** traffic is there in New York City?
Answer:	There is a lot of traffic.
Question:	**How much** crime is there?
Answer:	There isn't a lot of crime. New York City is one of the safest large cities in America.

How Many/How Much		
How Many	**Plural Count Noun**	
How many	restaurants people	are there in New York?
How Much	**Noncount Noun**	
How much	traffic crime	is there in New York?

Notes:

• Use *how many* to ask about the quantity of count nouns. Use *how much* to ask about the quantity of noncount nouns.

• Use *how much* to ask about the cost of something. When asking about cost, use *how much* without a noun. Example: *How much money is a train ticket?*

■ EXPANSION IDEA

Exercise A

1. Have students work in small groups to rewrite the conversation in Exercise A, using information they know about the city they live in or the city the school is in.

B Complete the questions with *many* or *much*.

1. How __many__ steps are there in the Statue of Liberty? 354.
2. How __many__ windows are there in the Statue of Liberty's crown? 25.
3. How __much__ steel is there in the statue? 250,000 pounds.
4. How __many__ people visit the statue each year? 4 million.
5. How __much__ is a ticket to the Statue of Liberty and Ellis Island? It's free.
6. How __much__ traffic is there on Ellis Island? There is no traffic on Ellis Island.

C Complete each question with *how many* or *how much* and one of the phrases in the box.

did you visit	did you see	~~did you meet~~	did you buy
did you hear	did you spend	did you learn	did you write
did you have	did you take		

1. __How many__ people __did you meet__ ?
2. __How much__ money __did you spend__ ?
3. __How much__ music __did you hear__ ?
4. __How many__ museums __did you visit__ ?
5. __How much__ art __did you see__ ?
6. __How much__ French __did you learn__ ?
7. __How many__ postcards __did you write__ ?
8. __How many__ souvenirs __did you buy__ ?
9. __How many__ photographs __did you take__ ?
10. __How much__ fun __did you have__ ?

■ COMMUNICATE

D **PAIR WORK** Ask your partner about the city or neighborhood he or she grew up in. Ask as many *how many/how much* questions as possible. Your partner should use as many count and noncount nouns and quantity expressions as possible. Take turns.

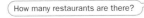

How many restaurants are there?   There are many restaurants.

---

1. Look at the example as a class. Have students do the exercise by themselves. Then go over the answers as a class.
2. Have students practice asking and answering the questions in pairs.

■ EXERCISE C

1. Go over the first example with students and explain what they need to do.
2. When students are finished, go over the answers as a class. Reinforce vocabulary collocations by writing the verb+noun combinations from the exercise on the board. For example, after you go over question 2, write *spend money* on the board.

■ COMMUNICATE

The Communicate section allows students to practice the target grammar in more communicative, less-controlled ways through speaking and writing activities.

■ EXERCISE D

1. First go over the example in the book.
2. Then ask for a volunteer to tell you a little about the neighborhood he or she grew up in. Ask *how many/how much* questions about the neighborhood.
3. Tell the class a little about the neighborhood you grew up in and have students ask you questions about it using *how many/how much*.
4. Have students do the activity with a partner.

■ EXPANSION IDEA

Exercise D

1. Have students write paragraphs about the neighborhoods they grew up in.
2. Have students make a list of questions they might ask other students about the neighborhoods they grew up in.
3. Direct them to walk around the room and ask their questions to different students.

Connection

Putting It Together

The purpose of this section of the lesson is to connect and extend students' understanding of the grammar, vocabulary, and content from this lesson.

■ GRAMMAR AND VOCABULARY

1. First go over the example in the book.

2. Then ask for a volunteer to tell you a little bit about his or her vacation. Ask questions.

3. Tell the class about a vacation you have taken. Have the students ask you questions about your vacation.

4. Have students do the activity with a partner.

■ PROJECT

1. Go through each step with the students, making sure they understand what they are supposed to do.

2. For additional suggestions on doing projects, see the Teacher's Notes on pages xvi–xviii.

■ INTERNET

1. Have students talk to each other to find a partner who wants to research the same city or country.

2. Have students do the Internet research in pairs and share information with the class.

■ VOCABULARY JOURNAL

Refer to the Pre-lesson (page 6) for an explanation of the vocabulary journal.

GRAMMAR AND VOCABULARY Work with a partner. Tell your partner about your last vacation. Your partner will ask questions to learn more about your vacation. Take turns. Use the grammar and vocabulary from this lesson.

I was in New York last year. I went to Broadway shows, great restaurants, and interesting museums.

How many museums are there in New York?

There are a lot! I went to four or five.

PROJECT Create a tourist brochure for your town or city.

1. Work in pairs.
2. Imagine you work for the tourist information office where you live.
3. Prepare a brochure telling tourists about the places to go and things to see in your town or city. Be sure to use some quantity expressions in your brochure. You may wish to illustrate your brochure with photographs or drawings.
4. Present your brochure to the class.

 INTERNET Is there a country or city you would like to visit? Go online. Search for information about this place. Tell your class what you learned.

VOCABULARY JOURNAL Write sentences for new vocabulary you learned in this lesson.

Example: *I always send my mother a postcard when I travel.*

■ EXPANSION IDEAS

Grammar and Vocabulary

1. Have students write a paragraph about their vacation or have them write a paragraph about their partner's vacation.

Internet

1. Have students make a poster about the city or country they researched on the Internet.

2. Ask them to present their finished posters to the class.

PART 1
Can: Affirmative and Negative
PART 2
Can: Yes/No Questions and
Short Answers

Lesson (23)

Health Sciences: Physical Therapy

■ CONTENT VOCABULARY

Look at the pictures. Do you know the words?

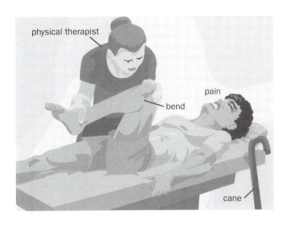

physical therapist

bend

pain

cane

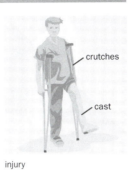

crutches

cast

injury

knee

break

bone

leg

Write the new words in your vocabulary journal.

■ THINK ABOUT IT

Discuss these questions with a partner. Answers will vary.

1. What are the different ways people can get injured or hurt? Make a list. Use a dictionary if necessary.
2. Have you ever been injured or hurt? How did it happen? How did you get better? Tell your partner about it.

167

■ CONTENT NOTES

Health Sciences

The topic for this lesson is Health Sciences: Physical Therapy. Health sciences usually include courses and programs in health care, wellness, and physical education. Specific courses might include:

Dental Assisting

Nurse's Aide

Occupational
  Therapy

Physical
  Therapy

Dental Hygiene

Nursing

Physical
  Education

Respiratory
  Therapy

Physical therapy is the treatment of injury or physical dysfunction through the use of therapeutic exercise as well as the application of heat, light, water, and massage. Common conditions treated by physical therapy are stroke, arthritis, fractures, and nerve damage. A physician will prescribe physical therapy for a patient and a physical therapist will carry out the treatment. The job of a physical therapist is to try to prevent further pain or injury by training different muscles to take over for the ones that have been damaged.

Overview

1. Elicit students' prior knowledge. Write *physical therapy* on the board. Ask students if they know the meaning of this phrase.
2. Once students understand the meaning, ask them if any of them have ever had physical therapy.
3. Ask students to help you make a list on the board of reasons people might go to physical therapy. (car accident, on-the-job accident, repetitive motions that cause pain, etc.)

■ CONTENT VOCABULARY

1. Direct students' attention to the pictures and vocabulary words.
2. Ask students what they see in each of the pictures.
3. Help students define the words and ask them to write them in their vocabulary journals.

■ THINK ABOUT IT

1. After students have discussed the first question with a partner, have them talk to other pairs around them to compare their lists. Then ask students to add to their lists two more ways that people can get injured or hurt.
2. After students have discussed the second question, ask for volunteers to tell the class about their partner's injuries.

PART ONE

Can: Affirmative and Negative

Part 1 introduces students to *can*: affirmative and negative.

■ GRAMMAR IN CONTENT

This section exposes students to a theme-based reading that includes examples of the target structure. Students can refer to the grammar chart(s) to complete the controlled practice activities.

■ EXERCISE A *Track 52*

1. Ask students what is happening in the picture.
2. Have students read the paragraphs first before you play the recording.
3. Play the recording and have students follow along.
4. Ask the following questions: *What does Sonia do? What is wrong with Keisha? Can she walk? Can she run? Can she play soccer?*

■ GRAMMAR CHART

Can: *Affirmative and Negative*

Go over the chart and the Notes with students. As you review the chart, read the first example sentence aloud; for instance, say, *I can run.* Then read only the subjects and call on students to finish the sentences. Refer to the reading for additional examples.

■ EXERCISE B

1. Have students complete the exercise by themselves.
2. Ask students to go over their answers with a partner.

■ GRAMMAR IN CONTENT

A Read and listen.

TR52

A Physical Therapist at Work

    I'm Sonia. I'm a physical therapist. The people I work with have injuries or pain. Some of them have broken bones, and some have sports injuries. These problems make it hard for my patients to move parts of their body. I help their bodies move better and become stronger.
    Right now I'm working with Keisha. She's a soccer player. She has a knee injury. She **can walk** with a cane now, but she **can't run** and she certainly **can't play** soccer yet. I **can help** her with therapy, exercise, and advice. Her knee is getting better every day. She **can't wait** to get back to the soccer field.

Can: Affirmative and Negative

Affirmative			Negative		
Subject	**Can**	**Base Verb**	**Subject**	**Cannot / Can't**	**Base Verb**
I You He She It We They	can	run.	I You He She It We They	cannot can't	swim.

Notes:
* *Can* expresses ability and possibility.
* The negative form of *can* is *cannot*. The contraction is *can't*.

B Look at the reading "A Physical Therapist at Work." Complete the sentences with *can* or *can't*.

1. Keisha has a knee injury. She ___*can't*___ play soccer now.
2. She ___**can**___ walk with a cane.
3. She ___**can't**___ run.
4. Sonia ___**can**___ help Keisha.
5. Keisha ___**can't**___ wait to play soccer again.

■ EXPANSION IDEAS

Exercise A

1. Ask students to think of a time when they were injured. Have them rewrite the second paragraph of the reading from their own point of view at the time, saying what they can and can't do. (NOTE: Have them write in present tense, as if they were injured now.)

2. Have students make lists of physical activities they can and can't do and share their lists in small groups. Give examples:

I Can	I Can't/Cannot
walk	*ski*
run	*play golf*
play basketball	

Grammar Chart

1. Write two columns on the board:

C Listen to the dialogue. (Circle) what Namiko can and can't do.

TR53

1. She (can /(can't)) walk without crutches.
2. She ((can)/ can't) drive.
3. She (can /(can't)) ride her bike.
4. She (can /(can't)) exercise.
5. She (can /(can't)) move her leg.
6. She (can /(can't)) scratch an itch.
7. She ((can)/ can't) relax more now.
8. She (can /(can't)) do many chores around the house.

D Write a sentence about what each person can or can't do. Use the words and phrases in the box. **Answers will vary.**

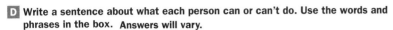

| cook | repair a computer | dance | play the violin | drive | cut hair |

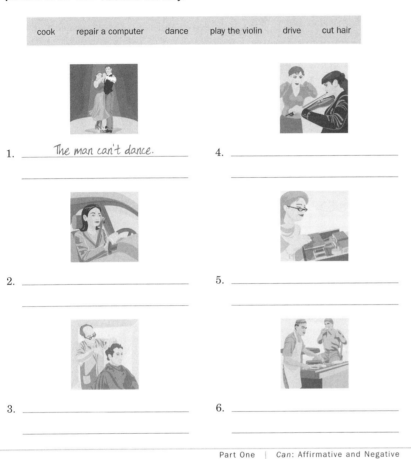

1. _The man can't dance._

4. _____

2. _____

5. _____

3. _____

6. _____

■ **EXERCISE C** *Track 53*

1. Ask students what they see in the picture.
2. Go through the sentences and ask students to predict what Namiko can and can't do.
3. Play the audio and have students circle the correct answers.

■ **EXERCISE D**

1. Go over the first example with students and explain the directions.
2. When students are finished, ask for volunteers to write their sentences on the board.

■ **EXPANSION IDEA**

Exercise C

1. Demonstrate the differences in pronunciation between *can* and *can't* by saying the sentences in Exercise C and having students repeat them after you. (In spoken English, *can* is usually pronounced quickly and with the reduced vowel /ə/. In contrast, *can't* is pronounced with the full, clear vowel sound /æ/ and, of course, the /t/ sound at the end.) Point out that when people are speaking quickly, it is difficult to hear the /t/ sound of *can't*, so it's important to listen for the vowel sound.

2. Have students practice the sentences in Exercise C, using the pronunciation of *can* and *can't* that you just demonstrated.

The Communicate section allows students to practice the target grammar in more communicative, less-controlled ways through speaking and writing activities.

■ EXERCISE E

1. Focus students' attention on the final goal of this activity, which is for their classmates to think of a job that might be good for them. When students are making their lists, they need to focus on things they can do that are job-related.

2. Help students get started by writing two lists on the board of things that you can and can't do.

I Can	I Can't/Cannot
speak English	*do math*
explain things clearly	*operate machines*

■ EXERCISE F

Many of your students may not feel they have any unusual talents, so discuss this as a class first and see if you can help students come up with things they can do.

PART TWO

Can: Yes/No Questions and Short Answers

Part 2 introduces students to *yes/no* questions and short answers with *can*.

■ GRAMMAR IN CONTENT

■ EXERCISE A Track 54

1. Ask students what is happening in the picture.
2. Have students cover up the reading and listen only as you play the recording.
3. With the reading still covered, ask students the questions from the conversation.

E GROUP WORK Make a list of things you can do. Make another list of things you can't do. Tell your group about the things you can and can't do. Your group will discuss your skills and decide on a good job for you.

F GROUP WORK Do you have any unusual talents? Can you stand on your head? Can you write with your feet? Tell the class what you can do. If possible, show your group.

PART TWO	*Can:* Yes/No Questions and Short Answers

■ GRAMMAR IN CONTENT

A Read and listen.

TR54

Mr. Rivera

Physical Therapist:	Mr. Rivera had a stroke a few months ago.
Interviewer:	**Can** he **walk?**
Physical Therapist:	No, he **can't.**
Interviewer:	**Can** he **move** his legs?
Physical Therapist:	Yes, he **can.** He can move them a little.
Interviewer:	**Can** physical therapy **help?**
Physical Therapist:	Yes, it **can.** It can help his legs become stronger.

stroke: a blocked or broken blood vessel in the brain that can cause difficulty moving and speaking and sometimes death

Can: Yes/No Questions and Short Answers

Can	Subject	Base Form of Verb		Short Answers	
Can	I	carry	the books?	Yes, I **can.**	No, I **can't.**
	you			Yes, you **can.**	No, you **can't.**
	he			Yes, he **can.**	No, he **can't.**
	she			Yes, she **can.**	No, she **can't.**
	it			Yes, it **can.**	No, it **can't.**
	we			Yes, we **can.**	No, we **can't.**
	they			Yes, they **can.**	No, they **can't.**

■ EXPANSION IDEA

Exercise E

1. After doing the reading and going over the grammar chart, have students work in pairs to write a conversation between a job interviewer and a job applicant, using information from the lists they wrote in Exercise E. Write the first lines on the board for them:

Applicant: *I would like to apply for a job.*
Interviewer: *Can you_____?*

2. Ask for volunteers to read their conversation for the class.

B Look at each picture. Write a *yes/no* question with *can* and the verb given. Then write an answer.

1. (ski)

Q: _Can he ski?_

A: _Yes, he can._

4. (sew)

Q: **Can he sew?**

A: **No, he can't.**

2. (sing)

Q: **Can she sing?**

A: **Yes, she can.**

5. (run)

Q: **Can he run?**

A: **No, he can't.**

3. (ride a bicycle)

Q: **Can he ride a bicycle?**

A: **No, he can't.**

6. (swim)

Q: **Can she swim?**

A: **Yes, she can.**

■ **COMMUNICATE**

C **GROUP WORK** Review the words in the chart. Ask your classmates *yes/no* questions with *can* and the words in the chart. When you find a student who answers "Yes, I can" to a question, put the student's name in the chart.

Can you . . .	Student's Name	Can you . . .	Student's Name	Can you . . .	Student's Name
Hello! Bonjour! Ni hao! . . . speak three languages?		. . . juggle?		. . . whistle?	
. . . write with your left hand?		. . . do yoga?		. . . touch your toes?	

■ **EXPANSION IDEA**

Class project for Exercise C

1. Have a volunteer go to the board and make a tally of how many students in the class can do each of the things listed in the chart in Exercise C.

2. Have other volunteers write sentences on the board describing their class.

For example:

Four people can do yoga.
Twenty-five people can't do yoga.

Twelve people can whistle.
Seventeen people can't whistle.

4. Play the recording one more time and let students look at the reading while they listen.

5. Have students practice the conversation with a partner.

■ **GRAMMAR CHART**

Can: Yes/No *Questions and Short Answers*

Go over the chart with the students, reading each question aloud and calling on students to give the short answers. As you go through the chart, refer to the reading for additional examples.

■ **EXERCISE B**

1. Have students work with a partner to write the questions and answers.

2. Have pairs of students practice the questions and answers by saying them aloud to each other.

■ **COMMUNICATE**

The Communicate section allows students to practice the target grammar in more communicative, less-controlled ways through speaking and writing activities.

■ **EXERCISE C**

1. Go over the directions and each of the questions with students and make sure they understand the vocabulary.

2. Model this activity by walking around to different students and asking them questions. When a student says, "Yes, I can," write his or her name in your book.

3. Tell students they may only write a student's name once.

4. When students are finished, ask them questions to find out who can do what. For example: *Who can speak three languages?*

Connection

Putting It Together

The purpose of this section of the lesson is to connect and extend students' understanding of the grammar, vocabulary, and content from this lesson.

■ GRAMMAR AND VOCABULARY

1. First go over the example in the book.
2. Then model the activity by asking students questions about what they *can* and *can't* do.
3. Next have volunteers ask you questions.
4. Finally, have two volunteer students ask questions of one another. Model this until you feel students are prepared to do it by themselves.

■ PROJECT

1. Go through each step with students, making sure they understand what they are supposed to do.
2. Demonstrate by listing things on the board that you can do and asking a student what he or she would like to learn from you. Teach him or her the skill.
3. For additional suggestions on doing projects, see the Teacher's Notes on pages xvi–xviii.

■ INTERNET

1. Have students work with a partner to do their Internet research.
2. Ask students to share what they learn with the class to see if they found the same or different information.

■ VOCABULARY JOURNAL

Refer to the Pre-lesson (page 6) for an explanation of the vocabulary journal.

GRAMMAR AND VOCABULARY Work with a partner. Ask your partner what things he/she can do. Use the words and phrases in the box. Also ask questions of your own. Your partner will give short answers and then give you more information. Use grammar and vocabulary from this lesson.

| dance | sew | ride a bicycle | see without glasses | cook | ski | ride a horse | play the guitar |

Can you cook?

No, I can't. But my husband can. He cooks Spanish food and some Italian food. I can bake, though. I can make a delicious chocolate cake.

PROJECT Teach a New Skill/Learn a New Skill

1. Work with a partner.
2. Write a list for your partner of things that you can do. These should be skills you can teach your partner in class. Use a dictionary if necessary.
3. Your partner will choose a skill he or she would like to learn.
4. Teach your partner the skill.
5. Your partner will perform his or her new skill for the class. Take turns.

> **Things I Can Do**
>
> I can say "hello" in Chinese.
> I can do a handstand.
> I can do a push-up.
> I can use sign language.
> I can tell a good joke.
> I can sing a lullaby.

 INTERNET Use the Internet to find out more about the job of a physical therapist. Use the keyword phrase "physical therapist job profile." Look for information about the education physical therapists need, the kinds of work they do, and how much money they make. Share what you learn with a partner.

VOCABULARY JOURNAL Write sentences for new vocabulary you learned in this lesson.

Example: *My grandfather walks with a cane.*

172 LESSON 23 | Health Sciences: Physical Therapy

■ EXPANSION IDEAS

Grammar and Vocabulary

1. Have students write sentences about their partners using the information they learned.
2. Ask for volunteers to write their sentences on the board.

Internet

1. Have students make a poster about what a physical therapist does, incorporating art and any interesting techniques they learned about.

Science: In the Laboratory

■ CONTENT VOCABULARY

Look at the pictures. Do you know the words?

laboratory

experiment

Write the new words in your vocabulary journal.

■ THINK ABOUT IT

Work with a partner.

1. Pretend to use or put on a piece of laboratory equipment. Your partner will guess the equipment. Take turns.
2. What are important safety rules in a laboratory? Discuss with a partner.

173

Overview

1. Elicit students' prior knowledge. Write *laboratory* on the board. Ask students if they know the meaning of this word. Explain that this is where scientists work.
2. Once students understand the meaning, ask them to help you make a list of things they might see in a laboratory.

■ CONTENT VOCABULARY

1. Direct students' attention to the pictures and vocabulary words.
2. Ask students what is happening in each of the pictures.
3. Help them define the words to write in their vocabulary journals.

■ THINK ABOUT IT

1. Tell students to use the new words they just learned to act out the actions in question 1.
2. Have students share with the class the safety rules they discussed with their partner. Make a list on the board.

■ CONTENT NOTES

Science

The topic for this lesson is Science: In the Laboratory. Below is a list of possible fields that scientists might work in. The less common ones have been defined.

Chemical Engineering
Cybernetics and Systems
Ethology (the zoological study of animal behavior)
Forensic Entomology (using insect evidence to uncover circumstances)

Geosciences (the study of Earth and other planets)
Health Physics
Hydrology (the study of water)
Mammalogy
Neuropathology
Nuclear Science
Ocean Engineering
Parasitology (the study of parasites)
Photobiology (the study of the interaction of light with living organisms)

PART ONE

Imperatives

Part 1 introduces students to imperatives.

■ GRAMMAR IN CONTENT

This section exposes students to a theme-based reading that includes examples of the target structure. Students can refer to the grammar chart(s) to complete the controlled practice activities.

■ EXERCISE A *Track 55*

1. Review the safety rules that students came up with in the Think About It section.
2. Play the audio and have the students follow along.
3. Ask students which rules in this exercise are different from the ones they had come up with.

■ GRAMMAR CHART
Imperatives

Go over the chart and the Notes with the students. As you go through the chart, refer to the examples from the reading to reinforce the rules.

■ EXERCISE B *Track 56*

1. Ask students what makes a command affirmative and what makes it negative. (The word *don't* makes it negative.) Tell students they will be listening for affirmative and negative commands and will circle what they hear.
2. Play the recording and have students complete the activity.
3. Have students share their answers with a partner before you play the recording again.

■ GRAMMAR IN CONTENT

A **Read and listen.**
TR55

LABORATORY SAFETY RULES

1. **Read** the rules carefully.
2. **Wear** rubber gloves and safety glasses at all times.
3. **Wear** shoes or sneakers. **Do not wear** sandals.
4. **Don't eat** or drink in the laboratory.
5. **Keep** your hands away from your face and body during experiments.
6. **Clean** all work areas after experiments.
7. **Turn off** all equipment after experiments.
8. **Wash** your hands after each experiment.

rule: a statement about what must be done   during: at the time of
sandals: shoes that do not cover the toes

Imperatives			
Affirmative		**Negative**	
Base Form of Verb		***Don't***	Base Form of Verb
Close	the door.	Don't	close	the door.

Notes:

- Use imperatives to:
  - a) Give directions or instructions.   Example: *Turn left at the corner.*
  - b) Give warnings.   Example: *Be careful!*
  - c) Give advice.   Example: *Relax a little.*
  - d) Give orders.   Example: *Don't be late!*
  - e) Make polite requests (with *please*).   Example: *Please open the window.*
- The subject of imperative statements is always "you," but the subject is not often included in the statement.
- Add "please" to the beginning or the end of an imperative to make a polite request: Please close the door. Close the door, please.

B **Listen to each imperative.** (Circle) *Affirmative* or *Negative*.
TR56

1. (Affirmative) Negative   4. Affirmative (Negative)
2. Affirmative (Negative)   5. Affirmative (Negative)
3. (Affirmative) Negative   6. (Affirmative) Negative

■ EXPANSION IDEAS

Grammar Chart

1. Have students work with a partner to write a command for each of the five ways imperatives can be used (listed in the Notes). Tell them to read the examples and then come up with one or two of their own for each.

Examples:
Give directions: *Turn right at the stop sign.*
Give warnings: *Don't touch the hot plate.*

Exercise B

1. Use the recording from Exercise B as dictation.
2. Play each command separately and have students write what they hear.
3. Have students share their answers with a partner. Then call on volunteers to write the sentences on the board.
4. Have the class check for mistakes.

C Match the statements to the correct imperative.

_c_ 1. I need to remember this experiment.   a. Clean it up.

_e_ 2. I need to look at this slide.   b. Wear rubber gloves.

_d_ 3. I need a flame.   c. Take notes.

_a_ 4. I spilled water on the table.   d. Light the Bunsen burner.

_b_ 5. These chemicals are dangerous.   e. Use a microscope.

D Write a negative imperative for each picture. Use a word or phrase from the box for each sentence.

| use your cell phone | eat | ~~drink~~ | wear sandals | chew gum | take off your safety glasses |

1. _____Don't drink_____

    in the lab.

2. ____Don't use your cell phone____

    in the lab.

3. _____Don't eat_____

    in the lab.

4. _____Don't chew gum_____

    in the lab.

5. __Don't take off your safety glasses__

    in the lab.

6. ____Don't wear sandals____

    during an experiment.

LAB RULES

1.   4.

2.   5.

3.   6.

E Write laboratory safety rules with the words provided. Decide if each should be an affirmative or a negative imperative.

1. come / to the laboratory late ___Don't come to the laboratory late.___

2. smoke / in the laboratory ___Don't smoke in the laboratory.___

3. take / notes on experiments ___Take notes on experiments.___

4. smell / the chemicals ___Don't smell the chemicals.___

5. take / laboratory equipment home ___Don't take laboratory equipment home.___

6. follow / instructions ___Follow instructions.___

Have students complete the activity by themselves. Then go over the answers as a class.

■ **EXERCISE D**

1. Go over the first example with students and explain what they are supposed to do.
2. When students are finished, ask for volunteers to write their sentences on the board.

■ **EXERCISE E**

1. Have students work with a partner to write the statements.
2. Ask for volunteers to write the safety rules on the board.
3. At this point, students may ask about using *do* to form affirmative commands, as in *Do take notes on experiments*. You can explain that *do* is sometimes used to emphasize a contrast with *don't*, but it is not a necessary part of affirmative commands.

■ **EXPANSION IDEA**

Exercise C

1. Have pairs of students use the information in Exercise C to write a conversation. This is what the conversation should look like:

Student A: *I need to remember this experiment.*

Student B: *Take notes.*

Student A: *I need to look at this slide.*

Student B: *Use a microscope.*

■ COMMUNICATE

The Communicate section allows students to practice the target grammar in more communicative, less-controlled ways through speaking and writing activities.

■ EXERCISE F

1. Put students in groups of four and have them list ten rules: five affirmative and five negative.
2. When students are finished, have them share their lists. Make a master list of class rules on the board or on poster paper. Vote on which rules are the most important.

■ EXERCISE G

After students have written their lists, have each pair share its ideas with another pair.

<table>
<tr><td colspan="2" align="center">PART TWO</td></tr>
</table>

Polite Requests with *Could you/Would you*

Part 2 introduces students to polite requests with *could you/would you.*

■ GRAMMAR IN CONTENT

This section exposes students to a theme-based reading that includes examples of the target structure. Students can refer to the grammar chart(s) to complete the controlled practice activities.

■ EXERCISE A *Track 57*

1. Play the recording and have students follow along.
2. Ask students how the requests in this conversation are different from the imperatives they just studied. Discuss when you would use imperatives and when you would use these polite requests.

■ COMMUNICATE

F **GROUP WORK** Imagine a new student is joining your class. Write a list of classroom rules for the student to follow.

G **PAIR WORK** Work with a partner. Look at the three situations. Brainstorm a list of imperatives to give advice for each situation.

How to Take Care of a Cold	How to Prepare for a Test	How to Prepare for a Job Interview
Get a lot of rest.		

<table>
<tr><td>PART TWO</td><td>Polite Requests with Could You/Would You</td></tr>
</table>

■ GRAMMAR IN CONTENT

TR57

A Read and listen.

Lab Partners

Lab Partner 1:	**Could you** light the Bunsen burner?
Lab Partner 2:	Sure.
Lab Partner 1:	**Would you** pour the chemicals into the test tubes?
Lab Partner 2:	Um . . . OK.
Lab Partner 1:	**Could you** heat the chemicals please?
Lab Partner 2:	Hey! **Would you** please help me do the experiment?

Polite Requests with *Could You/Would You*

Could/ Would	You	Base Form of Verb		Short Answers
Could Would	you	help	me?	Of course. Sure. OK.

Notes:
- Use *could you* and *would you* to ask someone to do something.
- *Please* is often used with *could you* and *would you*. *Please* can come after the subject or at the end of the question. Example: *Could you please close the door?* OR *Could you close the door, please?*

■ EXPANSION IDEA

Exercise E (page 175)
1. Have the class agree on what the class rules should be.
2. Have a group of students volunteer to create this list on the computer, adding art where necessary.
3. If necessary for your population, have students help translate the rules into as many languages as necessary.

4. Post the rules in the class and make copies so that every time a new student enters the class, he or she gets a copy.

NOTE: Having students create this list and take ownership of it will make it much easier for you to enforce the class rules.

B Match the sentences with the requests.

_b_ 1. I need your last name.

_f_ 2. I don't understand this question.

_e_ 3. These chemicals are dangerous.

_h_ 4. Raj needs the microscope.

_g_ 5. These are for the instructor.

_a_ 6. I can't hear you.

_d_ 7. We need a flame.

_c_ 8. I can't find my notes.

a. Could you speak louder?

b. Could you please spell it?

c. Would you please show me yours?

d. Could you light the Bunsen burner?

e. Would you lend me your rubber gloves?

f. Could you please explain it to me?

g. Would you give them to her, please?

h. Could you let him use it?

C Write a polite request for each picture. Use the verbs in the box.

> hold   lend   ~~open~~   turn on   close   be quiet

1. _Can you please open the door?_

4. **Can you please be quiet?**

2. **Can you please turn on the light?**

5. **Can you please lend me a pen?**

3. **Can you please close the window?**

6. **Can you please hold this?**

■ **GRAMMAR CHART**

Polite Requests with
Could You/Would You

Go over the chart and the Notes with the students. As you go through the chart, refer to the reading for examples.

■ **EXERCISE B**

Go over the example with students and have them complete the exercise by themselves. Then go over the answers as a class.

■ **EXERCISE C**

1. Have students work with a partner to write polite requests using *could you, would you,* and *please.*

2. Call on students to share what they have written.

■ **EXPANSION IDEA**

Exercise C

1. Have each student draw a picture similar to those in Exercise C. Have them put their name on the back of the paper.

2. Collect the pictures and pass them out, making sure no student gets his or her own picture.

3. Ask students to write a polite request under each picture.

4. Have students pass their pictures to another student and have those students write another polite request under the picture.

5. Do this as many times as you think students can come up with creative, new requests.

6. Give the pictures back to the students who drew them and ask for volunteers to share the requests.

■ COMMUNICATE

The Communicate section allows students to practice the target grammar in more communicative, less-controlled ways through speaking and writing activities.

■ EXERCISE D

1. First go over the example in the book.
2. Then model the activity by saying the following: *You are at the post office and you need to fill out a form. The person standing next to you is using the pen. What do you say? (Could I please borrow the pen?)*

Connection

Putting It Together

The purpose of this section of the lesson is to connect and extend students' understanding of the grammar, vocabulary, and content from this lesson.

■ GRAMMAR AND VOCABULARY

1. First go over the example in the book.
2. As a class, discuss some ideas for what a teacher might say.
3. Model this activity using some of the expressions students have suggested until you feel students are prepared to do it by themselves.

■ PROJECT

1. Go through each step with the students, making sure they understand what they are supposed to do.
2. Have each pair of students contribute one "How to . . ." page to include in the class book.
3. Consider providing a binder that students can use to make the book.
4. For additional suggestions on doing projects, see the Teacher's Notes on pages xvi–xviii.

■ COMMUNICATE

D **PAIR WORK** Think of a situation in which you would use a polite request. Tell your partner the situation. Your partner will say the polite request. Take turns.

You are very hot. The window is closed. A person is standing next to the window.   Would you open the window, please?

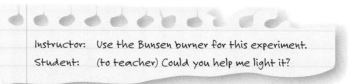

Connection **Putting It Together**

GRAMMAR AND VOCABULARY Work with a partner. Student A is a student. Student B is a teacher. The teacher uses an imperative to tell the student to do something. The student responds by asking a question beginning with *would you* or *could you*. Write five sentences and responses. Use the grammar and the vocabulary from this lesson.

> Instructor: Use the Bunsen burner for this experiment.
> Student: (to teacher) Could you help me light it?

PROJECT **Create a class How-To book.**

1. Work with a partner. Discuss something you both know how to do and the steps involved in doing it. For example, how to fix something, how to cook a particular recipe, or how to do a particular experiment.
2. Write "How to [insert your topic]" at the top of a piece of paper.
3. Work together to write the steps involved in doing the activity you chose.
4. Put your page together with your classmates' to form a How-To book.

 INTERNET **Go online. Find a list of lab rules at a school. Type the words "lab safety rules" in an Internet search engine. Write down three of the rules you see. Tell your class what you learned.**

VOCABULARY JOURNAL Write sentences for new vocabulary you learned in this lesson.

Example: *I wear rubber gloves when I wash the dishes.*

■ EXPANSION IDEA

Internet

1. Have students make a class poster with the rules they find on the Internet.

■ INTERNET

1. Have students work alone or with a partner to do their Internet research.
2. Have students share what they learn with the class to see if they found the same or different information.

■ VOCABULARY JOURNAL

Refer to the Pre-lesson (page 6) for an explanation of the vocabulary journal.

Lesson 25

Cultural Anthropology: Gestures

Lesson 25

Lesson 25

■ CONTENT VOCABULARY

Look at the pictures. Do you know the words?

rude

polite

You're welcome.
Thank you.

smile

bow

kiss and hug

yawn

shake hands

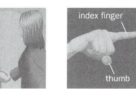
index finger
thumb
point

Write the new words in your vocabulary journal.

■ THINK ABOUT IT

Discuss these questions with a partner. Answers will vary.

1. Imagine you meet someone for the first time. How do you greet that person?
2. Imagine you meet a good friend. How do you greet him/her?

179

Overview

1. Elicit students' prior knowledge by making a few gestures to see if students know what they mean.
   1. (wave) Hi, Hello.
   2. (nod your head) Yes.
   3. (shake your head) No.
   4. (wiggle your hand) So-so.
2. Write the word *gestures* on the board. Explain to students that this is the word for the types of movements you just made.

■ CONTENT VOCABULARY

1. Direct students' attention to the pictures and vocabulary words.
2. Ask students what is happening in each of the pictures.
3. Help them define the words to write in their vocabulary journals.

■ THINK ABOUT IT

After students discuss the questions in pairs, discuss them as a class to see if there are any cultural differences in the ways people greet each other.

■ CONTENT NOTES

Cultural Anthropology

The topic for this lesson is Cultural Anthropology: Gestures. Cultural anthropology is the study of the development of human cultures. These studies are done using ethnologic,* ethnographic,* linguistic, social, and psychological data.

Gestures are defined as motions made to express thought or emphasize speech. The content of this lesson will focus on the idea that different cultures use different gestures for expression and that it's important to respect these cultures by learning their gestures.

*ethnology—the comparison of human societies
*ethnography—the practice of scientists participating in and observing the social and cultural life of a group over a period of time

PART ONE

Should/Should Not

Part 1 introduces students to *should/should not*.

■ GRAMMAR IN CONTENT

This section exposes students to a theme-based reading that includes examples of the target structure. Students can refer to the grammar chart(s) to complete the controlled practice activities.

■ EXERCISE A *Track 58* 🎧

1. Have students look at the pictures and ask what the difference is between the two.
2. Play the audio and have the students follow along.
3. Practice the gestures discussed in the reading.

■ GRAMMAR CHART

Should/Should Not

Go over the chart with the students. Go over the Notes. As you go through the chart, refer to the examples from the reading to reinforce the rules.

■ GRAMMAR IN CONTENT

🎧 **A** **Read and listen.**

TR58

pointing gesture in the U.S.

pointing gesture in Asia

Gestures Around the World

Gestures have different meanings in different countries. For example, the "OK" sign is a common gesture in the United States. But you **shouldn't** use it in many other countries. It is rude in Germany, Russia, and many South American countries. In Japan it means "money." In France it means "zero."

Do you want to point to something? In the United States, you **should** use your index finger. However, you **should not** do this in Asia. In Asia, this gesture is rude. Instead, you **should** point with an open hand. In Germany, you should use your thumb.

To show respect to neighbors, friends, and classmates from different cultures, you **should** learn the meanings of gestures in different countries.

gesture: a body movement to show a feeling or an idea
instead: in place of
respect: great approval and appreciation

Should/Should Not

Should			Should Not		
Subject	Should	Base Verb	Subject	Should not/ Shouldn't	Base Verb
I You He She It We They	should	go.	I You He She It We They	should not shouldn't	stay.

Note:
Use *should* to give advice.

■ EXPANSION IDEAS

Exercise A

1. Have students work with a small group and talk about the gestures used in their countries. If possible, try to put students from different cultures in each group. Have students discuss the gestures for:

1. OK
2. pointing at something
3. hello
4. goodbye

Grammar Chart

1. Have students work with a partner to make a list of things they should and shouldn't do every day.

For example:
I should study.
I should practice speaking in English.
I shouldn't be late to class.

B Look at the reading "Gestures Around the World." Read each sentence and (circle)
True or *False.*

1. You shouldn't use the American "OK" sign in South America. (True) False
2. You should point with your thumb in the United States. True (False)
3. You should point with an open hand in Asia. (True) False
4. You should learn the meanings of gestures in different countries. (True) False

C Look at the pictures. Then make sentences with the words provided and *should* or
shouldn't.

1. You ___*shouldn't*___ yawn in public in Argentina.

2. You ___**shouldn't**___ show the bottom of your feet in Thailand.

3. You ___**should**___ eat with your right hand in Indonesia.

4. You ___**should**___ take off your shoes in a home in Saudi
Arabia.

5. You ___**shouldn't**___ shout in Japan.

6. You ___**should**___ greet friends with a kiss in Brazil.

■ **EXERCISE B**

Have students go over their answers
with a partner.

■ **EXERCISE C**

Have students complete the activity
by themselves. Then go over the
answers as a class.

■ **EXPANSION IDEAS**

Exercise B

1. Have students make the false
statement true.

Exercise C

1. Have students work with a partner to
write more statements about gestures
in different cultures like the ones in
Exercise C.
2. Have them write three statements
with *should* and three with *shouldn't.*
Ask for volunteers to write their
statements on the board.

■ COMMUNICATE

The Communicate section allows students to practice the target grammar in more communicative, less-controlled ways through speaking and writing activities.

■ EXERCISE D

Help students get started by writing a few examples on the board for your native country. For example:

You should greet people by shaking hands.
You shouldn't bow.

■ EXERCISE E

When the groups are finished with their lists of advice, have one member from each group share what they talked about.

PART TWO

Should: Yes/No Questions and Short Answers

Part 2 introduces students to *yes/no* questions and short answers with *should*.

■ GRAMMAR IN CONTENT

This section exposes students to a theme-based reading that includes examples of the target structure. Students can refer to the grammar chart(s) to complete the controlled practice activities.

■ EXERCISE A *Track 59*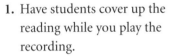

1. Have students cover up the reading while you play the recording.
2. Ask students the following questions: *Should Jim bow to the president of the company? Should Jim stand near the president? Should Jim make eye contact? Should Jim stare?*
3. Play the recording again and let students follow along in their books.

■ C O M M U N I C A T E

D WRITE Imagine a friend is going to your native country. Write a list of things your friend should do and shouldn't do to be polite.

Things You Should Do | Things You Shouldn't Do
You should greet people with a kiss on the cheek. | Don't come to a party without a gift.

E GROUP WORK Make a list of advice for each situation. Use *should* and *shouldn't*. Does your group agree on everything? Are there any cultural differences?

1. Your friend has a job interview tomorrow. What should and shouldn't he or she do at the interview?
2. Your friend is meeting his girlfriend's parents for the first time. What should and shouldn't he do?

| PART TWO | ***Should*: Yes/No Questions and Short Answers** |

■ G R A M M A R   I N   C O N T E N T

 A Read and listen.

TR59

Advice for a Business Trip

Jim: I have a business meeting in Japan next month. Could you give me some advice?
Mai: Sure.
Jim: My meeting is with the president of a company. **Should I bow?**
Mai: Yes, you **should**. This shows respect.
Jim: **Should I stand** near him?
Mai: No, you **shouldn't**. It's rude to stand very close to people in Japan.
Jim: **Should I make** eye contact?
Mai: Well, a little eye contact is OK, but you **shouldn't** stare. That's rude.

eye contact: a look directly in the eyes of another person
stare: to look at someone or something steadily

182   LESSON 25 | Cultural Anthropology: Gestures

■ EXPANSION IDEAS

Exercise E

1. Have the class agree on advice for situations 1 and 2.
2. Divide the class into two groups and assign one of them to list the advice for 1 and the other the advice for 2.
3. Have each group create their list on a computer or on a poster, adding art where possible.
4. Post the advice in the classroom.

Exercise A

1. Have students practice the conversation with a partner.
2. Have students rewrite the conversation using information about a culture they are familiar with.
3. Ask for volunteer pairs to present their conversations to the class.

182   *Grammar Connection 1* Teacher's Edition

Should: Yes/No Questions and Short Answers

Should	Subject	Base Form of Verb	Short Answers: Affirmative		Negative	
Should	I you he she it we they	go?	Yes,	I you he she it we they should.	No,	I you he she it we they shouldn't.

B Look at the dialogue "Advice for a Business Trip." Pretend Jim is taking a business trip to your native country. Answer the questions with short answers.

1. Should he bow to the president of the company? ___**Yes, he should.**___

2. Should he stand near the president of the company? ___**No, he shouldn't.**___

3. Should he make eye contact? ___**Yes, he should.**___

4. Should he stare? ___**No, he shouldn't.**___

C John is meeting Svetlana's Russian family tomorrow. He has many questions. Write *yes/no* questions with *should.* Then complete the short answers.

John: I'm very nervous about meeting your family. I don't know anything about Russian gestures and customs.

Svetlana: What do you want to know?

John: (arrive on time) ___*Should I arrive on time?*___

Svetlana: Yes, ___*you should*___.

John: (kiss your father) ___**Should I kiss your father?**___

Svetlana: No, ___**you shouldn't**___. Give him a firm handshake.

John: (use your father's first name) ___**Should I use your father's first name?**___

Svetlana: No, ___**you shouldn't**___. Use his full name.

John: (take off my shoes) ___**Should I take off my shoes?**___

Svetlana: Yes, ___**you should**___. My parents will give you slippers to wear in the house.

John: (bring a gift) ___**Should I bring a gift?**___

Svetlana: Yes, ___**you should**___. Maybe bring flowers.

■ GRAMMAR CHART

Should: Yes/No *Questions and Short Answers*

Go over the chart with the students. As you go through the chart, refer to the reading for examples.

■ EXERCISE B

Have students complete the exercise by themselves. Then go over the answers as a class.

■ EXERCISE C

1. Have students work with a partner to write the questions and answers.
2. Have the pairs practice the conversation.
3. Call on different pairs to read parts of the conversation aloud for the class.

■ EXPANSION IDEA

Exercise C

1. Have students rewrite the conversation using information about a culture they are familiar with.

2. Ask for volunteer pairs to perform their conversations for the class.

COMMUNICATE

The Communicate section allows students to practice the target grammar in more communicative, less-controlled ways through speaking and writing activities.

■ EXERCISE D

1. Model this activity by practicing with a volunteer. Ask the student questions about meeting his or her family for the first time.
2. Then ask a volunteer to model asking you questions about meeting your family.
3. Have students do the activity with a partner.

Connection

Putting It Together

The purpose of this section of the lesson is to connect and extend students' understanding of the grammar, vocabulary, and content from this lesson.

■ GRAMMAR AND VOCABULARY

1. First go over the situations in the book.
2. Choose one of the situations and model this activity with some students.
3. If students are all from the same culture, have them do the exercise to see if they agree on the rules for polite behavior.

■ PROJECT

1. Go through each step with the students, making sure they understand what they are supposed to do.
2. When grouping students, consider that groups of students from the same culture could write a guidebook about their native country, whereas groups of students from different cultures can make a guidebook about the country they are living in now.

■ COMMUNICATE

D PAIR WORK Imagine you are going to meet your partner's family. Ask *should* questions using the following words and phrases. Then ask more questions of your own. Your partner will give short answers. Take turns.

| bring a gift | shake hands | kiss | take off my shoes | bow | stand close |

Connection   Putting It Together

GRAMMAR AND VOCABULARY Work with a partner from a different country. Read the four situations below. Choose one. Tell your partner about the kind of behavior that would be appropriate in the situation in your country. Ask questions to find out if the same behavior would be appropriate in your partner's country. Use the grammar and vocabulary from this lesson.

1. A woman is meeting her boyfriend's parents for the first time.
2. A man is at a friend's wedding.
3. A woman is at a job interview.
4. A man is at a party. He sees a woman he would like to meet.

PROJECT Create a gesture and behavior guide.

1. Work in a small group.
2. Create a guide for new immigrants or visitors to your country or the country where you live now.
3. Include information about polite and rude gestures and behavior.
4. Show your guide to the class.

 INTERNET Use the Internet to learn more about polite behavior and gestures in another country. Choose a country you are interested in learning about. Use the keywords "etiquette" and "[name of the country]." Tell your classmates what you learned.

VOCABULARY JOURNAL Write sentences for new vocabulary you learned in this lesson.

Example: *In my country, it is rude to point with your index finger.*

■ EXPANSION IDEA

Internet
1. Have students make posters using the information they find on the Internet to display in the classroom.

3. For additional suggestions on doing projects, see the Teacher's Notes on pagese xvi–xviii.

■ INTERNET

1. Have students work with a partner to do Internet research about a country they are both interested in.

2. Have students share their information with the class.

■ VOCABULARY JOURNAL

Refer to the Pre-lesson (page 6) for an explanation of the vocabulary journal.

A Circle the correct answers.

Wife: Hi, honey. I'm calling from a furniture store.

Husband: Why? We don't need (some /(any)) furniture.
(1)

Wife: But the store is having ((a)/ an) great sale.
(2)

Husband: Are there (a /(any)) chairs? David needs ((a)/ an) chair for his room.
(3)   (4)

Wife: Oh, that's right. Yes. There are (any /(some)) chairs.
(5)

Husband: Did you bring some ((money)/ monies)?
(6)

Wife: I only have ten (dollar /(dollars)).
(7)

Husband: Use ((a)/ some) credit card.
(8)

Wife: OK. Then I can buy ((a)/ some) couch too. It's beautiful. You'll love it. Bye!
(9)

Husband: Wait! We don't need a couch. Hello . . . ? Hello . . . ?

B Circle the correct answers.

Tourist: Hi, I need ((a little)/ a few) information about this city.
(1)

Hotel Manager: Of course. Would you like (a little /(a few)) suggestions? This
(2)
city has ((many)/ much) museums and ((many)/ much) parks.
(3)   (4)

Tourist: Actually, I think I need ((a little)/ a few) coffee first.
(5)

Hotel Manager: There are (a little /(a few)) nice cafés on this street.
(6)
(How many /(How much)) Spanish do you know?
(7)

Tourist: I only know (a little /(a few)) words.
(8)

Hotel Manager: Well, "café con leche" means coffee with ((a little)/ a few) milk.
(9)

C Write an imperative and a polite request using each set of words provided.

	IMPERATIVE	POLITE REQUEST
1. in / come	Come in.	Would you come in, please?
2. a seat / take	Take a seat.	Would you take a seat, please?
3. open / your book	Open your book.	Would you open your book, please?
4. with a partner / work	Work with a partner.	Would you work with a partner, please?
5. turn off / the equipment	Turn off the equipment.	Would you turn off the equipment, please?

■ EXPANSION IDEAS

Exercise A

1. Have students rewrite the conversation by changing the nouns and phrases following the articles and quantity expressions. For example, in the first conversation, they might change the phrase *from a furniture store to an office supply store.*

Exercise C

1. After the imperatives and polite requests are on the board, ask for two volunteers to come to the front of the room. Explain that the class must do whatever the volunteers say. Have the volunteers take turns saying the imperative phrases and the polite requests in any order. Everyone in the class should listen and do or pantomime the actions they hear.

Lessons 21-25

The purpose of this lesson is to help students review the concepts they have learned in the last five lessons. Encourage them to go back to the lessons and review the grammar charts to help them complete the review exercises.

■ EXERCISE A

1. Have students do this activity by themselves and then share their answers by practicing the conversation with a partner.
2. Go over the answers as a class by asking students to read the conversation aloud.

■ EXERCISE B

1. Have students do this activity by themselves and then share their answers by practicing the conversation with a partner.
2. Go over the answers as a class by asking students to read the conversation aloud.

■ EXERCISE C

1. Look at the examples as a class.
2. Have students do the activity by themselves and then share their answers with a partner.
3. Go over the answers as a class by asking students to write their imperatives and polite requests on the board.

■ EXERCISE D

1. Have students work with a partner to choose the correct answers.

2. Have the students practice the conversation. You may need to point out that the pronunciation of *can* is not reduced in short answers.

3. Go over the answers as a class by calling on students to read parts of the conversation aloud.

■ EXERCISE E

1. Have students work with a partner to choose the correct answers.

2. Have the students practice the conversation.

3. Go over the answers as a class by calling on students to read parts of the conversation aloud.

■ LEARNER LOG

1. Help students understand how to complete the Learner Log by going over it with them and offering examples of the grammar structures.

2. If students checked "I Need More Practice" for any of the structures, suggest that they review those lessons. If possible, meet with students individually to discuss their Learner Logs and make suggestions for ways to get more practice with the structures.

D Circle the correct answers.

Jake: Why is your knee in a brace?

Ann: I had knee surgery last month.

Jake: I had knee surgery a few years ago. My physical therapist helped strengthen the muscles in my leg. Now I (**can** / can't) do most of the things I did before the surgery.
(1)

Ann: (You can / **Can you**) walk without pain?
(2)

Jake: Yes, I (**can** / can't). I can also run, and I (**can** / can't) play sports.
(3)   (4)

Ann: (**Can** / Can't) you drive?
(5)

Jake: No, I (can / **can't**). But I didn't drive before my knee surgery either!
(6)

E Circle the correct answers.

Mu Kong: Please come for dinner tonight. My parents want to meet you.

Mike: OK, thanks. (I should / **Should I**) bring a gift?
(1)

Mu Kong: (**Yes,** / No,) you should. Bring a small gift like fruit or tea.
(2)

Mike: (**Should I wrap the gift?** / Wrap the gift should I?)
(3)

Mu Kong: Sure. But you (**should wrap** / wrap should) the gift in gold and red. These are lucky colors.
(4)

Mike: (I shake / **Should I shake**) hands with your parents?
(5)

Mu Kong: Yes, (**you should** / you shouldn't).
(6)

Mike: (**Should** / Should not) I make eye contact?
(7)

Mu Kong: (Yes / **No**), you shouldn't. You should lower your eyes when you greet them.
(8)

LEARNER LOG Check (✔) *Yes* or *I Need More Practice.*

Lesson	I Can Use . . .	Yes	I Need More Practice
21	Count and Noncount Nouns; *An, Some, Any*		
22	Quantity Expressions; *How Many/How Much*		
23	Imperatives; Polite Requests with *Could You/Would You*		
24	*Can*: Affirmative and Negative; *Can*: *Yes/No* Questions		
25	*Should*: Affirmative and Negative; *Should*: *Yes/No* Questions		

■ EXPANSION IDEAS

Exercises D and E

1. Have students choose the conversation in either Exercise D or E and memorize it with a partner. Then have them perform it for the class.

Learner Log

1. Have students get into groups and generate a list of ideas for what they can do if they checked the "I Need More Practice" column in the Learner Log. Have each group share its best ideas with the class.

Lesson ㉖

Criminology: The Courtroom

■ CONTENT VOCABULARY

Look at the picture. Do you know the words?

judge
juror
jury
witness
lawyer
court reporter
courtroom

trial

Write the new words in your vocabulary journal.

■ THINK ABOUT IT

Have you seen trials on television? Think about and discuss these questions with a partner.

1. What people are at a trial?
2. Are there rules in a courtroom? What are some courtroom rules?

187

Overview

Elicit students' prior knowledge. Ask: *What do you think we will learn about in this lesson?*

■ CONTENT VOCABULARY

1. Direct students' attention to the pictures and the courtroom words. Help students understand the vocabulary they aren't familiar with.
2. Ask students if they have ever seen the inside of a courtroom. Discuss the different reasons that people go to court (traffic ticket, jury duty, etc.)

■ THINK ABOUT IT

Have students do this activity with a partner and then share their answers with a pair sitting next to them.

■ CONTENT NOTES

Criminology

The topic for this lesson is Criminology: The Courtroom. Criminology is the study of crime, criminals, criminal behavior, and corrections. The focus of this lesson will be on the courtroom and the rules governing behavior in the courtroom. Although rules may vary from state to state and courtroom to courtroom, below are some general rules that apply to most courtrooms:

• Dress appropriately. No shorts, tank tops, jogging/sweat suits, or sleeveless shirts are permitted in the courtroom

• Do not read newspapers, magazines, or other items unless they are official papers
• Do not bring food, bottles, paper cups, or beverage containers into the courtroom
• Do not prop feet up on tables, chairs, or benches
• Do not talk or make noise that might interfere with court procedure
• Do not smoke

PART ONE

Must/Must Not

Part 1 introduces students to *must* and *must not*.

■ GRAMMAR IN CONTENT

This section exposes students to a theme-based reading that includes examples of the target structure. Students can refer to the grammar chart(s) to complete the controlled practice activities.

■ EXERCISE A *Track 60*

1. Ask students to look at the picture and ask the following questions: *Who is the person in the picture? What is she doing? Why?*
2. Play the audio and have students follow along in the text.
3. Ask the following *yes/no* questions to check comprehension: *Can lawyers speak with the jurors? Can lawyers sit while they are speaking in court? Can witnesses lie? Can jurors make a decision before the end of the trial?*

■ GRAMMAR CHART

Must/ Must Not

Go over the chart with the students. Go over the notes. As you go through the chart, refer to the examples from the reading to reinforce the rules.

■ EXERCISE B

1. Have students write the rules by themselves.
2. When students are finished, have them compare their answers with a partner.
3. Then ask for volunteers to write the rules on the board.

■ GRAMMAR IN CONTENT

A **Read and listen.**

TR60

Courtroom Rules

Different people in the courtroom **must follow** different rules. For example, lawyers **must not speak** with the jurors. They **must stand** when they speak in court. Witnesses **must answer** questions. They **must not lie**. Jurors **must not read** newspapers during the trial. They **must not talk** to anyone about the trial. Jurors **must not make** decisions until the end of the trial.

It is important to follow courtroom rules. These rules keep courtrooms organized and they keep trials fair.

decision: a choice, conclusion

organized: to be in order, arranged

Must/Must Not

Subject	*Must*	Base Verb	Subject	*Must Not*	Base Verb
I You He / She / It We They	must	listen.	I You He / She / It We They	must not mustn't	speak.

Notes:

- Use *must* to talk about something that is very important or necessary. We also use *must* to talk about rules and laws. Example: *You must stop at a red light.*
- Use *must not* to talk about something that you are not allowed to do because it is against rules or laws. (You don't have a choice.) Example: *You must not cheat on the test.*

B Look at the reading "Courtroom Rules." Write one rule for each of the following people.

1. Lawyers: _____ Lawyers must not speak with the jurors.

   Lawyers: _____ **Lawyers must stand when they speak in court.**

2. Witnesses: _____ **Witnesses must answer questions.**

3. Jurors: _____ **Jurors must not make decisions until the end of the trial.**

■ EXPANSION IDEA

Exercise B

1. Have students write one more rule for each of the people listed in Exercise B.

C Fill in the blanks with *must* or *mustn't*.

1. Lawyers ___must___ be in the courtroom on time.

2. Lawyers ___must___ listen to the judge.

3. Lawyers ___mustn't___ argue with the judge.

4. Jurors ___must___ come to the trial every day.

5. Jurors ___must___ listen carefully.

6. Jurors ___mustn't___ talk in the courtroom.

D Look at this poster found outside a courtroom. Then complete each sentence with *must* or *mustn't* and one of the verbs in the box.

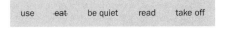

| use | eat | be quiet | read | take off |

1. You ___mustn't eat___ food in the courtroom.

2. You ___mustn't read___ newspapers in the courtroom.

3. You ___must be quiet___ in the courtroom.

4. You ___mustn't use___ cell phones in the courtroom.

5. You ___must remove___ hats and coats before entering the courtroom.

■ COMMUNICATE

E GROUP WORK With your group, write two or three sentences about what you must and must not do in each of the following places or situations. Use a dictionary if necessary.

when you are driving
when you are taking a test
when you are in the library
when you are on an airplane

---

1. Go over the example with students and remind them of the *mustn't* contraction. Practice the pronunciation of *mustn't*.

2. When students are finished, call on volunteers to read the rules aloud.

■ EXERCISE D

1. Go over each picture with the students and ask them what they see. Go over the example.

2. When students are finished, ask for volunteers to write the rules on the board.

■ COMMUNICATE

The Communicate section allows students to practice the target grammar in more communicative, less-controlled ways through speaking and writing activities.

■ EXERCISE E

1. When the groups are finished, ask one person from each group to share the rules they came up with with the class.

2. If you plan to do the expansion activity, divide the class into at least four groups to do Exercise E.

■ EXPANSION IDEA

Exercise E

1. Divide the class into four groups and assign each group one of the ideas listed in the exercise. Each group will be responsible for creating a comprehensive list of rules to present to the class.

2. Since each group has already discussed the rules, form new groups that have at least one member from each of the old groups.

3. Have the new groups use the computer to create a list of rules for their place or situation. Ask the groups to create a poster of the rules that they can present to the class.

Part 2 introduces students to *have to* and *don't have to*.

■ GRAMMAR IN CONTENT

This section exposes students to a theme-based reading that includes examples of the target structure. Students can refer to the grammar chart(s) to complete the controlled practice activities.

■ EXERCISE A *Track 61*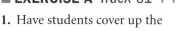

1. Have students cover up the reading with a piece of paper and look at the picture.
2. Ask students what they think a court reporter does. Make a list on the board. Accept all answers even if you think they may be incorrect.
3. Have students listen to the recording with the reading still covered.
4. After students have heard the recording, ask them if they were correct about the job of a court reporter.
5. Play the recording again so students can follow along in the book.

■ GRAMMAR CHART
Have to/Don't Have to

Go over the chart with the students. Go over the Notes. As you review the chart, refer to the reading for additional examples.

■ GRAMMAR IN CONTENT

A Read and listen.

TR61

A Court Reporter

I'm a court reporter. I write down everything people say during a trial. I **have to be** in court every day of the trial. I **have to listen** to the trial very carefully.

Court reporters **have to concentrate.** They also need good grammar and punctuation. I like my job. It's an interesting job, and I **don't have to work** long hours. My sister is a lawyer. She **has to work** all the time.

concentration: total attention to something

Have To/Don't Have To

Subject	Have To/ Has To	Base Verb	Subject	Do Not/ Does Not	Have To	Base Verb
I You We They	have to	listen.	I You We They	do not don't	have to	listen.
He She It	has to		He She It	does not doesn't		

Notes:

• We use *have to* to say that something is necessary. *Have to* is less formal and less urgent than *must*. It is also more common in spoken English. Example: *I need stamps. I **have to** go to the post office.*

• We use *don't have to* to say that something is not necessary. There is a choice. Example: *I have stamps. I **don't have to** go to the post office.*

■ EXPANSION IDEA

Exercise A and Grammar Chart

1. Have students write two short paragraphs about things they have to do and don't have to do today.
2. Model the activity by writing two short paragraphs on the board about things you have to do and don't have to do today.

For example:
Today, I have to teach class. After class, I have to grade papers. Then I have to go to a meeting.

I don't have to cook dinner tonight because my family is going out to dinner. I don't have to grade papers after class since I will do it after school. And I don't have to go to bed early because tomorrow is Saturday!

B Read each sentence. (Circle) the correct choice.

1. I don't have any money. I ((have to) / don't have to) go to the bank.
2. You can keep this video for three days. You (have to / (don't have to)) bring it back tomorrow.
3. Please leave your drink outside. You (don't have to / (must not)) drink in the courtroom.
4. The rent is due on the first day of the month. You ((have to) / don't have to) pay the rent on time.
5. Today is Wednesday. The museum is free on Wednesdays. You ((don't have to) / must not) pay today.

C Complete the sentences with *have to, has to, don't have to,* or *doesn't have to* to make true sentences. **Answers will vary.**

1. I _____ speak English in class.
2. My instructor _____ teach at night.
3. I _____ do homework for this class.
4. My instructor _____ teach grammar.
5. I _____ go to school on the weekend.
6. I _____ take a final exam for this class.

D Write sentences using the words provided, *have to* or *don't have to,* and the information in the chart.

Have to . . .	Lawyers	Jurors
be citizens		X
have a law degree	X	
come to court every day of a trial	X	X
speak in court	X	

1. lawyers / citizens _____ Lawyers don't have to be citizens. _____
2. jurors / citizens _____ Jurors have to be citizens. _____
3. lawyers / have a law degree _____ Lawyers have to have a law degree. _____
4. jurors / have a law degree _____ Jurors don't have to have a law degree. _____
5. lawyers / come to court every day _____ Lawyers have to come to court every day. _____
6. jurors / come to court every day _____ Jurors have to come to court every day. _____
7. lawyers / speak in court _____ Lawyers have to speak in court. _____

1. Have students do this exercise with a partner. Tell the pairs of students to make sure they agree on the correct answer before they circle it in their books.
2. Go over the answers as a class.

■ **EXERCISE C**

1. Have students do this exercise orally with a partner before writing the answers in their books. Once they both agree, have them write the answers in their books.
2. Ask for volunteers to write the sentences on the board.

■ **EXERCISE D**

1. Ask students *yes/no* questions about the information in the chart. For example: *Do jurors have to be citizens?* (Yes, they do.) *Do jurors have to have a law degree?* (No, they don't.)
2. Go over the example with students and have them complete the exercise by themselves.
3. Ask for volunteers to write the sentences on the board.

■ **EXPANSION IDEA**

Exercise C

1. Have students rewrite the sentences in Exercise C, making them all false.

■ COMMUNICATE

■ EXERCISE E

1. As a class, brainstorm a list of possible jobs students might want to have. Write all the ideas on the board.

2. Explain that students will choose any job they would like to have and make two lists: one of things a person with this job has to do and another of things this person doesn't have to do.

3. Go over the example with students to help them get started.

4. When students are finished, have them compare their lists in pairs. Then call on different pairs to tell the class how the jobs they chose are similar and different.

Connection

Putting It Together

The purpose of this section of the lesson is to connect and extend students' understanding of the grammar, vocabulary, and content from this lesson.

■ GRAMMAR AND VOCABULARY

Go over the directions and help students get started by modeling a few examples.

■ PROJECT

1. Go through each step with the students, making sure they understand what they are supposed to do.

2. For additional suggestions on doing projects, see the Teacher's Notes on pages xvi–xviii.

■ INTERNET

1. Have students work with a partner to do the Internet research.

2. Encourage students to share what they learned as well as their opinions about the responsibilities of jurors.

■ COMMUNICATE

E What job do you want? Make a list of five things a person with this job has to do and five things the person doesn't have to do. Then compare your list with a partner. How are your jobs similar? How are they different?

> I want to be a nurse.
> A nurse has to wear a uniform.

> I want to be a teacher.
> A teacher doesn't have to wear a uniform.

Connection   Putting It Together

GRAMMAR AND VOCABULARY Work with a partner. Each person chooses one of the places below and writes a list of as many rules for behavior in that place as he or she can. Use the grammar and, where appropriate, the vocabulary from this lesson.

| a courtroom | an airport | a church, temple, or mosque |

Exchange lists with your partner. Do you agree with all the rules on your partner's list? Are there any rules missing? Discuss with your partner.

PROJECT Create a classroom handbook.

1. Work with a group.
2. Brainstorm ideas about proper classroom behavior for students. Discuss what students:
   • must / have to do
   • must not do
   • don't have to do
3. Create a handbook for new students with your group. You may wish to illustrate the handbook.
4. Present your handbook to your class.

 INTERNET Look on the Internet for more information about the responsibilities of a juror. Use the keyword phrase "juror handbook." Share what you learned with your classmates.

VOCABULARY JOURNAL Write sentences for new vocabulary you learned in this lesson.

Example: *A juror mustn't speak in court.*

192   LESSON 26 | Criminology: The Courtroom

■ EXPANSION IDEA

Exercise E

1. Have students use the information from their lists to write two paragraphs about what a person with the job they chose has to do and doesn't have to do.

■ VOCABULARY JOURNAL

Refer to the Pre-lesson (page 6) for an explanation of the vocabulary journal.

Business: Opening a Restaurant

Lesson 27

Overview
Elicit students' prior knowledge. Ask: *What do you think we will learn about in this lesson?* Have students brainstorm in small groups.

■ CONTENT VOCABULARY

Look at the pictures. Do you know the words?

hire

check

Write the new words in your vocabulary journal.

■ THINK ABOUT IT

Discuss these questions with a partner.   Answers will vary.

1. What kinds of people work in a restaurant?
2. What do these people do?

■ CONTENT VOCABULARY

1. Direct students' attention to the drawings and ask them what they see in each one.
2. Help students define new vocabulary words for their vocabulary journals.

■ THINK ABOUT IT

1. Have pairs make two lists, one of the different job titles people have in restaurants (host, food server, chef, cook, manager, etc.) and the other of what those people do (seat people, take orders, make food, etc.)
2. After students finish, write headings for the two lists on the board and ask for students to come up and add their ideas.

193

■ CONTENT NOTES

Business

The topic for this lesson is Business: Opening a Restaurant. Below are some different ways to open a restaurant that you can discuss with your students.

1. Opening a restaurant: buy an existing restaurant, start your own restaurant, buy a franchise.

2. Financing the restaurant: use your own money, get a loan, get investors.
3. Finding a location: buy, lease, or rent a building.

Part 1 introduces students to *be going to:* affirmative and negative statements.

■ GRAMMAR IN CONTENT

This section exposes students to a theme-based reading that includes examples of the target structure. Students can refer to the grammar chart(s) to complete the controlled practice activities.

■ EXERCISE A *Track 62*

1. Have students look at the picture and ask them to guess what the woman is thinking.
2. Play the audio and have students follow along.
3. Ask students the following questions: *What kind of restaurant is the woman going to open? Is she going to have live music? How is she going to get the money?*

■ GRAMMAR CHART

Be Going To: *Affirmative and Negative Statements*

1. Go over the chart with the students. Get students involved by reading the first sentence with the subject *I.* Then continue by saying only the subject and letting students supply the correct form of *be* before you finish saying the sentence.
2. Go over the Notes and ask students for additional examples of Note 1 and Note 2, for example, *I'm going to graduate next year* and *It's very cloudy. It's going to rain.* As you go through the chart and the Notes, refer to the examples from the reading to reinforce the rules.

■ GRAMMAR IN CONTENT

A **Read and listen.**

TR62

Planning a New Restaurant

I'm **going to open** a Mexican restaurant. It's **not going to be** like any other restaurant in the neighborhood. The food **is going to be** delicious. The restaurant **is going to be** fun and friendly. There **is** even **going to be** a mariachi band. My customers **are going to love** it.

Today I'm **going to go** to the bank. I need to get a loan for my restaurant. I'm **going to show** the bank manager my business plan. I have to convince him that my restaurant **isn't going to fail.** I'm **going to prove** that it's **going to be** a big success.

mariachi: a kind of traditional Mexican music

loan: borrowed money that must be paid back with interest

business plan: a description of a business and its goals

convince: to make someone believe something is true

prove: show

Be Going To									
Affirmative					**Negative**				
Subject	*Be*	Going To	Base Verb		Subject	*Be*	*Not*	Going To	Base Verb
I	am				I	am			
He					He				
She	is				She	is			
It		going to	order.		It		not	going to	drink.
You					You				
We	are				We	are			
They					They				

Notes:

• We use *be going to:*
  1. to talk about the future when plans were made before this moment.
     Example: *I'm going to get married next September.*
  2. to make strong predictions about the future based on current information.
     Example: *I didn't study for the test. I'm going to fail!*
• In informal speech, *going to* is often pronounced as "gonna."

■ EXPANSION IDEA

Exercise A

1. Have students work with a partner to rewrite the paragraphs, changing only the information that is necessary to describe a restaurant they would like to open.

2. Ask for volunteers to read their paragraphs for the class.

Future Time Expressions

	tomorrow . . .	next . . .	in . . .
tomorrow	. . . morning	. . . week	. . . five minutes
tonight	. . . afternoon	. . . month	. . . an hour
	. . . evening	. . . year	. . . three days
	. . . night	. . . Monday	. . . two weeks

B Look at the pictures. Then complete each sentence with the correct form of *be going to* and a phrase from the box.

> clear the table   look at the menus   ~~pour water into the glass~~
> set the table   pay the check   eat

1. The waiter *is going to pour water into the glass.*

2. The waiter **is going to clear the table.**

3. The men **are going to look at the menus.**

4. The woman **is going to pay the check.**

5. The man and woman **are going to eat.**

6. The server **is going to set the table.**

---

3. Point out the Future Time Expressions chart on this page and give (or ask students for) examples using several of the expressions.

■ EXERCISE B

1. Look at the pictures as a class and talk about what is happening in each one.
2. Go over the example and have students complete the exercise on their own.
3. Ask for volunteers to write the completed sentences on the board.

■ EXPANSION IDEA

Grammar Chart

1. Have students write a statement using *be going to* for each of the future time expressions.

For example:

Tomorrow, I'm going to go shopping.
Tonight, I'm going to cook dinner.
Tomorrow morning, I'm going to ride my bike to school.

■ EXERCISE C

Have students complete the activity. Then call on students to read their sentences aloud. You may want to chat a bit with students about their answers, for example, *Oh, you are going to eat lunch after class? What are you going to have for lunch?*

■ EXERCISE D

1. Have students complete the sentences and then share their plans with a partner.
2. Ask for volunteers to write their sentences on the board.

■ COMMUNICATE

The Communicate section allows students to practice the target grammar in more communicative, less-controlled ways through speaking and writing activities.

■ EXERCISE E

Go over the sample paragraph and then have students work alone to write their own paragraphs.

■ EXERCISE F

1. Go over the examples in the book.
2. Model the activity with a few volunteers until you think students are ready to do it by themselves.

C Complete each sentence with *am going to* or *am not going to* to make true sentences about yourself. **Answers will vary.**

1. I _____ eat lunch after class.
2. I _____ do homework tonight.
3. I _____ take a test tomorrow.
4. I _____ see my friends this weekend.
5. I _____ be 22 next year.
6. I _____ graduate in two years.

D Complete each sentence with true information about yourself. **Answers will vary.**

Tonight, _____

Tomorrow, _____

Next weekend, _____

Next year, _____

■ COMMUNICATE

E **WRITE** Where are you going to be in ten years? What are you going to be doing? Make predictions about your life, using *going to* and *not going to*.

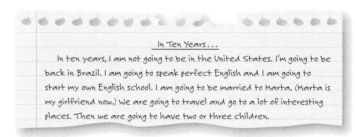

In Ten Years...

In ten years, I am not going to be in the United States. I'm going to be back in Brazil. I am going to speak perfect English and I am going to start my own English school. I am going to be married to Marta. (Marta is my girlfriend now.) We are going to travel and go to a lot of interesting places. Then we are going to have two or three children.

F **PAIR WORK** Pretend that one of you wants to get together sometime this week. The other person doesn't want to get together and keeps making excuses. Take turns.

Can you meet me on Saturday night?

Can you meet me on Sunday morning?

Sorry. On Saturday night I'm going to the library to study.

No. On Sunday morning I'm going to the gym to exercise.

■ EXPANSION IDEA

Exercise E

1. Have students walk around the room and read their paragraphs to different students.

2. Ask for volunteers to share something they learned about a classmate.

■ GRAMMAR IN CONTENT

A Read and listen.

TR63

Meeting with the Bank Manager
Elisa:	I'm here to talk with you about getting a loan for a restaurant.
Manager:	**Are** you **going to buy** one of the restaurants in town?
Elisa:	No, **I'm not.** I'm going to open a new restaurant.
Manager:	**Where are** you **going to open** the restaurant?
Elisa:	In this neighborhood. I found a nice building on Center Street.
Manager:	**Are** you **going to lease** the building?
Elisa:	Yes, **I am.** I'm very happy with the lease. It's a good price for the location.
Manager:	That sounds good. Alright, Ms. Ramirez, let's look at your business plan . . .

lease: rent for a period of time

location: spot, site

Be Going To: Yes/No Questions

Be	Subject	Going To	Base Verb
Am	I		
Is	he		
	she		
	it	going to	help?
	you		
Are	we		
	they		

Be Going To: Short Answers

	Affirmative			Negative	
Yes	Subject	Be	No	Subject + Be + Not	
	I	am.		I'm not.	
	he			he isn't. OR he's not.	
	she	is.		she isn't. OR she's not.	
Yes,	it		No,	it isn't. OR it's not.	
	you			you aren't. OR you're not.	
	we	are.		we aren't. OR we're not.	
	they			they aren't. OR they're not.	

Be Going To: Wh- Questions

Wh- Word	Be	Subject	Going To	Base Verb
Who	are	you		hire?
What	am	I		do?
Where	is	she		go?
When	is	he	going to	work?
Why	are	we		leave?
How	are	they		pay?

Note:

When "who" or "what" is the subject of an information question, don't use a subject pronoun after *be*. Example: *Who is going to open a restaurant?*

■ **EXPANSION IDEA**

Exercise A

1. Have students practice saying the conversation with a partner.

Be Going To: Questions

Part 2 introduces students to *be going to* questions.

■ **GRAMMAR IN CONTENT**

This section exposes students to a theme-based reading that includes examples of the target structure. Students can refer to the grammar chart(s) to complete the controlled practice activities.

■ **EXERCISE A** *Track 63*

1. Have students look at the picture and ask them what they think is happening.
2. Play the audio and have students follow along.
3. Ask students what Elisa is talking to the manager about and what she plans to do.

■ **GRAMMAR CHARTS**

Be Going To: *Yes/No Questions and Short Answers and Wh- Questions*

1. Go over the first two charts with the students. Have pairs of students practice the *yes/no* questions and short answers as you circulate and monitor their usage of the structures.
2. Go over the third chart, forming sentences with several of the *wh-* words, subjects, and base verbs. Then, ask several *wh-* questions with *be going to* that students can answer, such as, *Where are you going to go after class?* Call on different students to answer your questions.
3. Go over the Note. As you go through the charts and the Note, refer to the examples from the reading to reinforce the rules.

1. Have students look at the schedule with you and ask them information questions such as: *What is Elisa going to do on Saturday?*
2. Go over the example with students and have them complete the exercise by themselves.
3. Have students work with a partner to practice asking and answering the questions.
4. Ask for volunteers to write the questions and answers on the board.

■ **EXERCISE C**

Exercise C is an information gap activity. Have one student in each pair look at the Partner A calendar on page 199 while the other looks at the Student B calendar on page 228. Point out that the *wh-* words that students will use to ask their questions are given in parentheses.

B Look at Elisa's schedule for the week. Write *yes/no going to* questions with the words provided. Then give true answers.

1. She / work on the business plan on Monday
   Q: _Is she going to work on the business plan on Monday_ ? A: _Yes, she is_ .
2. She / talk with her accountant on Wednesday
   Q: **Is she going to talk with her accountant on Wednesday** ? A: **No, she isn't** .
3. She / fill out the loan application on Wednesday
   Q: **Is she going to fill out the loan application on Wednesday** ? A: **Yes, she is** .
4. She and the bank manager / meet on Thursday
   Q: **Are she and the bank manager going to meet on Thursday** ? A: **Yes, they are** .
5. She and the chef / discuss the menu on Friday
   Q: **Are she and the chef going to discuss the menu on Friday** ? A: **Yes, they are** .
6. She / buy a computer on Friday
   Q: **Is she going to buy a computer on Friday** ? A: **No, she isn't** .
7. She / work on Sunday
   Q: **Is she going to work on Sunday** ? A: **No, she isn't** .

C **PAIR WORK** It is now a week before the opening of Elisa's restaurant. One person looks at the Partner A calendar and statements on the following page. The other looks at the Partner B calendar and statements on page 228. Take turns asking each other *wh-* questions with *going to* to find the missing information in your statements.

■ **EXPANSION IDEA**

Exercise C

1. Have students use the information they learned in Exercise C to write a paragraph about what Elisa is going to do to open her restaurant.

Partner A Questions   Answers will vary.

1. On Monday she is going to order _____. (What?)

2. On Wednesday she is going to get _____. (What?)

3. On Friday she is going to pick up the menu from _____. (Where?)

4. On Sunday she is going to _____. (What?)

D Complete the dialogue with *wh- going to* questions.

Ali: I'm excited. I'm going out tonight.

Betsy: Really? *Where are you going to go* ?

Ali: I'm going to go to a new Mexican restaurant downtown.

Betsy: Who are you going to go with ?

Ali: I'm going to go with my family.

Betsy: What are you going to order ?

Ali: I'm going to order burritos.

Betsy: What time are you going to meet ?

Ali: We're going to meet at 8:00.

Betsy: Why are you going to eat there ?

Ali: We're eating there because we love Mexican food.

■ COMMUNICATE

E **PAIR WORK** Ask your partner *yes/no* and *wh-* questions about his or her plans for the future. Use phrases from the box.

| get married | open a business | live in the U.S. | have children | work in an office | travel |

■ **EXERCISE D**

1. Go over the example with students and have them complete the exercise by themselves.

2. Have them work with a partner to practice asking and answering the questions.

3. Ask for volunteers to perform the dialogue for the class.

■ **COMMUNICATE**

The Communicate section allows students to practice the target grammar in more communicative, less-controlled ways through speaking and writing activities.

■ **EXERCISE E**

1. Go over the phrases and examples as a class.

2. Ask students for examples of the questions they will ask. (*Are you going to go to a business? Where are you going to travel?*)

3. When students have finished, ask them *yes/no* and *wh-* questions about their partners.

For example: *Martin, is Sandra going to get married?*

■ **EXPANSION IDEA**

Exercise E

1. Have students write paragraphs about their partners based on what they learned in Exercise E.

Connection

Putting It Together

The purpose of this section of the lesson is to connect and extend students' understanding of the grammar, vocabulary, and content from this lesson.

■ GRAMMAR AND VOCABULARY

1. Go over the directions and ask students which *wh-* word they will use to ask about each topic, for example, *who* to ask about the name of a person.
2. Have students imagine the situation and write their sentences.
3. Have students take turns asking about each other's plans as you circulate and monitor their use of the language.

■ PROJECT

1. Go through each step with the students, making sure students understand what they are supposed to do.
2. Explain that both partners need to be involved in making the presentation.

■ INTERNET

1. As a class, brainstorm some restaurants students might look for online.
2. Have students work alone or in pairs and then report back to the class about their plans.

■ VOCABULARY JOURNAL

Refer to the Pre-lesson (page 6) for an explanation of the vocabulary journal.

GRAMMAR AND VOCABULARY Imagine you are going to go out to eat this weekend. Complete the following sentences. Then ask your partner questions to find out about his or her plans. Take turns.   Answers will vary.

I am going to go to _____. (name of restaurant)

I'm going to go with _____. (name of person)

I'm going to go on _____. (day)

I'm going to go at _____. (time)

I'm going to order _____. (food)

PROJECT   Start your own business.

1. Work with a partner. Imagine you will open a business together.
2. Discuss the following questions.
   a. What kind of business are you going to open?
   b. What is your business going to sell?
   c. Where are you going to open your business?
   d. Who are you going to hire?
   e. How are you going to find customers?
   f. How are you going to get the money for the business?
3. Present your idea to the class. Give your classmates a chance to ask you questions about your business.

 INTERNET   Go online. Find Web sites for restaurants in your area. Look at the menus. Decide which restaurant you would most like to go to. Plan a visit to the restaurant. When are you going to go? Who are you going to go with? What are you going to order?

VOCABULARY JOURNAL   Write sentences for new vocabulary you learned in this lesson.

   Example: *We're done with our meal. Can we have the check?*

■ EXPANSION IDEA

Internet
1. Have each pair make a poster about the restaurant they researched and the plans they made.
2. Have them get pictures or a menu from the Internet to add to their poster.
3. Have them present their posters to the class.

Medicine: Today and Tomorrow

■ CONTENT VOCABULARY

Look at the pictures. Do you know the words?

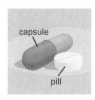

medicine

robot

examination

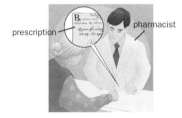

transplant

Write the new words in your vocabulary journal.

■ THINK ABOUT IT

Which of the following do you think are true or possible now? Discuss each statement with a partner.   Answers will vary.

1. There is a cure for cancer.
2. Robots can do surgery.
3. People can choose the sex of their baby before it is born.

201

Overview

Elicit students' prior knowledge. Ask: *What do you think we will learn about in this lesson?* Have students brainstorm in small groups.

■ CONTENT VOCABULARY

1. Direct students' attention to the drawings and ask them what they see in each one.
2. Help students define new vocabulary words for their vocabulary journals.

■ THINK ABOUT IT

1. Have pairs discuss the statements and then share their ideas with a pair sitting next to them.
2. Discuss the ideas as a class.

■ CONTENT NOTES

Medicine

The topic for this lesson is Medicine: Today and Tomorrow. The focus is on what doctors are able to do now and what they might be able to do in the future.

PART ONE

Will: Affirmative and Negative Statements

Part 1 introduces students to *will* used in affirmative and negative statements.

■ GRAMMAR IN CONTENT

This section exposes students to a theme-based reading that includes examples of the target structure. Students can refer to the grammar chart(s) to complete the controlled practice activities.

■ EXERCISE A *Track 64*

1. Have students look at the picture and ask them who the woman is and what she is doing.
2. Play the audio and have students follow along in their books.
3. Have students practice the conversation with a partner.
4. Ask students to look at the highlighted words in the conversation. Ask students what these words have in common.

■ GRAMMAR CHART

Will: *Affirmative and Negative Statements*

Go over the chart with the students. Go over the Notes. As you review both of these, refer to the examples from the reading to reinforce the rules.

PART ONE | *Will*: Affirmative and Negative Statements

■ GRAMMAR IN CONTENT

A Read and listen.

TR64

"Pills" of the Future

Doctor:	I'm writing you a prescription for a new medicine. Take these pills twice every day.
Patient:	More pills? Fine. **I'll take** them twice a day. But I hate swallowing all of these pills.
Doctor:	One day there **won't be** any more pills or capsules to swallow.
Patient:	What do you mean?
Doctor:	One day soon medicine **will come** in tiny computer microchips. Doctors **will put** the microchips under your skin. There **won't be** any pills to worry about.
Patient:	That **will be** great!

swallow: to take into the throat through the mouth

tiny: very small

microchip: the part of an electronic device that controls it

skin: the outer covering of a body

Will							
Affirmative				**Negative**			
Subject	*Will*	Base Verb		Subject	*Will*	*Not*	Base Verb
I You He /She / It We They	will	go.		I You He /She / It We They	will	not	go.

Notes:

- Use *will*:
  1. to make predictions about the future. Example: Scientists **will find** a cure for cancer.
  2. when the speaker decides to do something at the moment of speaking. Example: *I'm tired. I think* **I'll go** *to sleep.*
  3. for promises. Example: *I* **will be** *your friend forever.*
- Form the contraction with the subject pronoun and *will*: I will = I'll, You will = You'll.
- The contraction for *will not* is *won't*.

■ EXPANSION IDEA

Exercise A

1. Write the following questions on the board.

   Do you believe pills will come in computer chips one day? If yes, why? If no, why not?

   If they do, will you let the doctor put the chip under your skin?

2. Have students take out a piece of paper and write answers to these questions using complete sentences and *will, will not,* or *won't.*

3. When students are finished, have them read their answers aloud in small groups.

B Listen to each sentence. Decide whether each speaker uses *will* as a prediction, a sudden decision, or a promise.

	Prediction	Sudden Decision	Promise
1.		X	
2.	X		
3.			X
4.	X		
5.			X

C Complete the sentences with *will* or *won't* to give your opinions about life in the year 2100. **Answers will vary.**

In the year 2100 . . .

1. Most people _____ live to be over 100.

2. Medicine _____ come in computer chips.

3. There _____ be a cure for cancer.

4. People _____ choose the sex of their babies.

5. Robots _____ replace doctors.

6. Brain transplants _____ be possible.

D Correct the mistakes. There are four more mistakes.

> will
> My daughter is sick. I think I ʌ take her to the doctor tomorrow. Her doctor will
> give ~~s~~ her a prescription. I'll take the prescription to the pharmacy. It won't ⊘~~not~~
> take long to get the medicine. I think my daughter will ⊘~~to~~ feel better after
> she takes the medicine. I'll ⊘~~am~~ feel better when she feels better.

Part One | *Will*: Affirmative and Negative Statements   **203**

■ **EXERCISE B** *Track 65*

1. Go over the directions and the three choices: *prediction, sudden decision,* or *promise.* Make sure students understand the difference in meanings.

2. Play the recording once and have students complete the chart.

3. Have students share their answers with a partner to see if they came to the same conclusions.

4. Play the recording again for students to hear whether they were right.

5. Go over the answers as a class.

■ **EXERCISE C**

Have students complete the sentences with their own ideas and then share their answers with students around them.

■ **EXERCISE D**

1. Have students correct the paragraph with a partner.

2. Ask for volunteers to write the corrected sentences on the board.

■ **EXPANSION IDEA**

Exercise B

Play the recording from Exercise B or read it aloud as dictation. (See sentences below.)

1. *I don't feel very well. I think I will go to the doctor.*
2. *In 100 years, there will be over 12 billion people in the world.*
3. *I will always love you.*
4. *I think you will get married and have many children.*

5. *Thanks for paying for college, Mom. I will study hard and get good grades.*

Dictation suggestions:

1. Play each sentence once and pause the audio long enough for students to write. Play each sentence again if necessary.

2. Have students check their answers with a partner.

3. Play the recording all the way through or read each sentence one more time for students to check their work.

4. Call on students to write the sentences on the board.

5. Ask for students to come up and correct any mistakes they find.

Lesson 28   **203**

■ EXERCISE E

1. Go over the directions, the phrases, and the example.
2. Have students complete the conversation and then practice it with a partner.
3. Call on students to read parts of the conversation aloud for the class.

■ COMMUNICATE

The Communicate section allows students to practice the target grammar in more communicative, less-controlled ways through speaking and writing activities.

■ EXERCISE F

1. Go over the situations in the book.
2. Model the activity with an example promise for each situation.

For example:
1. *I will go to class every day next semester.*
2. *I will go to work early and stay late to help out.*
3. *I will eat five servings of fruits and vegetables every day.*

■ EXERCISE G

1. Refer students to the predictions they wrote for Exercise C on page 203.
2. Have students make some additional predictions to share with the class.

E Write a response to each sentence with *will* or *won't* and one of the phrases from the box. Use contractions.

take them when I wake up	go to work today
~~take it to the pharmacy now~~	make an appointment with the receptionist
forget	take them with breakfast

Doctor: Here's your prescription.

Patient: Thanks. *I'll take it to the pharmacy now* .

Doctor: Take the pills in the morning.

Patient: Okay. I _____ **will take them when I wake up** .

Doctor: Take them with some food.

Patient: Okay. I _____ **will take them with breakfast** .

Doctor: You need to rest today.

Patient: Oh, really? Okay. I _____ **won't go to work today** .

Doctor: I'd like to see you again next week.

Patient: Sure. I _____ **will make an appointment with the receptionist** .

Doctor: Don't forget!

Patient: Don't worry. I _____ **won't forget** .

■ COMMUNICATE

F WRITE Choose one of the following situations. Write a list of promises with *will*. Use a dictionary if necessary.

1. You are a student. You failed your classes this year. Your parents are upset. Write a list for your parents of all the things you promise to do better next semester.
2. You are an employee. You have not been doing a good job. You are afraid of being fired. You promise your supervisor that you will do a better job from now on. Make a list of ways you will improve as a worker.
3. You have not been feeling well. You went to the doctor. The doctor told you that you are too heavy. You promise yourself that you will lose weight and improve your health. Make a list of ways you will improve your health.

G WRITE Write five predictions about the future of medicine. Read the predictions to your class. Do your classmates agree with your predictions?

■ EXPANSION IDEAS

Exercise F

1. Ask students to write a list of promises for one of the situations that they didn't choose the first time.

Exercise G

1. Have students do Internet research about their predictions to see whether there is already research showing that their predictions might become reality.

■ GRAMMAR IN CONTENT

TR66

A Read and listen.

Doctors' Exams in the Future

Interviewer: **Will** examinations **be** very different in the future?

Scientist: Yes, they **will.**

Interviewer: **How will** they **be** different?

Scientist: Well, one day doctors will examine patients with a small piece of equipment called a "scanner."

Interviewer: **What will** it **look like?**

Scientist: It will look like a television remote control.

Interviewer: **How will** it **work?**

Scientist: The doctor will hold it over your body and it will find any health problems you have.

Will: Yes / No Questions				Affirmative			Negative		
Will: Short Answers									
Will	Subject	Base Verb		*Yes*	Subject	*Will*	*No*	Subject	*Won't*
Will	I you he she it we they	go?		Yes,	you I he she it we they	will.	No,	you I he she it we they	won't.

Will: *Wh-* Questions				
Wh- Word	*Will*	Subject	Base Verb	
Who What Where When Why How	will	I you he she we they	visit? do? go? arrive? stay? travel?	

Note:

When "who" or "what" is the subject of an information question, don't use a subject pronoun after *will*. Example: *Who will pay?*

Will: **Questions**

Part 2 introduces students to questions using *will.*

■ GRAMMAR IN CONTENT

This section exposes students to a theme-based reading that includes examples of the target structure. Students can refer to the grammar chart(s) to complete the controlled practice activities.

■ EXERCISE A *Track 66*

1. Have students look at the picture and ask them what they think it is.
2. Play the audio and have students follow along in their books.
3. Ask students what the item in the picture is and how it will work.
4. Have students practice the conversation with a partner.

■ GRAMMAR CHART

Will: *Questions*

Go over the chart with the students. Go over the Notes. As you review both of these, refer to the examples from the reading to reinforce the rules.

■ EXPANSION IDEA

Grammar Chart

1. Have students use the forms they learned in the *will: wh-* questions chart to write questions. Write this formula on the board:

wh- word + will + subject+ base verb?

2. Have students write ten questions using this formula and the chart.

3. Have students practice asking a partner these questions. (In most cases, the partner will have to make up an answer.)

EXERCISE B

Have students answer the questions and then practice the questions and answers with a partner.

EXERCISE C

1. Go over the directions and the information in the chart with students, making sure they understand all the ideas.
2. Have students write questions and answers based on the information presented in the chart.
3. Have students practice the questions and answers with a partner.
4. Ask for volunteers to write the questions and answers on the board.

B Look at the dialogue "Doctors' Exams in the Future." Answer the questions with short answers.

1. Will doctor's visits be different in the future? _____ Yes, they will.
2. Will doctors examine patients with remote controls? _____ **Yes, they will.**
3. Will doctors examine patients with scanners? _____ **Yes, they will.**
4. Where will the doctor hold the scanner? **The doctor will hold it over your body.**
5. What will the scanner find? **It will find any health problems.**

C A drug company is making a new super drug called Fixall. Look at the information about Fixall in the chart. Then write questions and short answers with *will* about the information.

FIX IT ALL WITH FIXALL.

	YES	NO
Help ease headaches	✓	
Help ease back pain	✓	
Help cure colds	✓	
Make you tired		✓
Make you thirsty		✓
Work quickly	✓	

FIXALL

1. help headaches _____ Will it help headaches _____ ?
   _____ Yes, it will _____ .

2. help back pain _____ **Will it help back pain** _____ ?
   _____ **Yes, it will** _____ .

3. help cure colds _____ **Will it help cure colds** _____ ?
   _____ **Yes, it will** _____ .

4. make you tired _____ **Will it make you tired** _____ ?
   _____ **No, it won't** _____ .

5. make you thirsty _____ **Will it make you thirsty** _____ ?
   _____ **No, it won't** _____ .

6. work quickly _____ **Will it work quickly** _____ ?
   _____ **Yes, it will** _____ .

EXPANSION IDEA

Exercise C

1. Have students work in small groups to create a new drug like the one in the exercise.
2. Have students make a chart like the one in Exercise C but with different information. (Some of the same information is OK.)
3. Post students' charts around the classroom.
4. Assign each group to look at a different group's chart. Have students ask and answer questions about the chart like the ones in Exercise C.

D Complete the dialogue. Put the words in the right order to form questions and answers.

Scientist: be / robots / will / important in the future of medicine (.)

1. _____ Robots will be important in the future of medicine _____.

Interviewer: we see them / will / where (?)

2. _____ **Where will we see them** _____?

Scientist: will / see them in operating rooms / we (.)

3. _____ **We will see them in operating rooms** _____.

Interviewer: what / they do there / will (?)

4. _____ **What will they do there** _____?

Scientist: they / surgery / do / will (.)

5. _____ **They will do surgery** _____.

Interviewer: will / be / in the operating room too / doctors (?)

6. _____ **Will doctors be in the operating room too** _____?

Scientist: will / they / yes (.)

7. _____ **Yes, they will** _____.

Interviewer: the doctors do / will / what (?)

8. _____ **What will the doctors do** _____?

Scientist: they / supervise the robots / will (.)

9. _____ **They will supervise the robots** _____.

■ **COMMUNICATE**

E **PAIR WORK** What do you think the world will be like ten years from now? Ask your partner *yes/no* questions with *will* and the words provided. Then ask more questions of your own. Take turns asking and answering questions.

scientists / find a cure for cancer	people / travel to the moon
brain transplants / be possible	medicine / be in microchips
most people / work from home	a woman / be president of the United States

■ **EXERCISE D**

1. Go over the first example with students and make sure they understand what to do.
2. Have them work with a partner to complete the dialogue.
3. Ask for volunteers to perform the dialogue for the class.

■ **COMMUNICATE**

The Communicate section allows students to practice the target grammar in more communicative, less-controlled ways through speaking and writing activities.

■ **EXERCISE E**

Go over the directions and get students started by forming a few of the questions as a class.

For example: *Do you think scientists will find a cure for cancer?*

■ **EXPANSION IDEA**

Exercise E

1. Give each student a note card and ask them to write a question about the future, ten years from now. Tell students to write about something different from the ideas listed in Exercise E.

For example: *In ten years, will people still listen to music CDs?*

2. Have students walk around the room and ask at least ten classmates their questions. Direct students to take notes on whether people say *yes* or *no*.
3. Have students report their findings to the class.

For example: *Eight students said people will listen to music CDs in ten years. Two students said people won't listen to music CDs in ten years.*

1. Go over the directions and get students started by forming a few of the questions as a class. For example:

Will the new drug help people who have asthma?

Connection

Putting It Together

The purpose of this section of the lesson is to connect and extend students' understanding of the grammar, vocabulary, and content from this lesson.

■ GRAMMAR AND VOCABULARY

Go over the examples in the book and model this activity for students, making sure they understand what they are supposed to do.

■ PROJECT

1. Go through each step with the students, making sure they understand what they are supposed to do.
2. Consider having students bring in or create a model or mock-up of their product to use as a visual aid during their presentation.

■ INTERNET

1. Have students work in pairs and then report their findings to the class.
2. You might want to search for and suggest some Web sites with a reading level accessible to your students.

■ VOCABULARY JOURNAL

Refer to the Pre-lesson (page 6) for an explanation of the vocabulary journal.

F Imagine you are a journalist interviewing the president of a drug company. The company will introduce an important new drug next year. You are going to write an article about the drug. Make a list of *wh-* questions with *will* to ask the drug company president. **Answers will vary.**

1. *What will this drug do?*   6. _____

2. _____   7. _____

3. _____   8. _____

4. _____   9. _____

5. _____   10. _____

Connection   Putting It Together

PAIR WORK Work with a partner. Imagine that your partner is from the year 3000. Ask your partner questions about the year 3000. Some topics you might want to ask about are medicine, work, transportation, food, and clothes. Use the grammar and vocabulary from this lesson.

Will food be different in the year 3000?

How will it be different?

Yes, it will.

Food will come in capsules. People will eat a whole meal in one little capsule!

PROJECT Create a new medicine or invention.

1. Work with a group. With your group, decide on the medicine or invention you want to create. Make a list of the things this product will and won't do.
2. Think of a name for your product.
3. Present your product to your class. After your group's presentation, let your classmates ask you questions about your product.

INTERNET Go online. Look for more information about the future of medicine. Use the keyword phrase "future of medicine." Share what you learned with your class.

VOCABULARY JOURNAL Write sentences for new vocabulary you learned in this lesson.

Example: *My doctor gave me a prescription for new medicine.*

208   LESSON 28 | Medicine: Today and Tomorrow

■ EXPANSION IDEAS

Exercise F

1. Have students write a dialogue of an interview with the president of a drug company using the questions they wrote in Exercise F.

Pair Work

1. Have students work with a partner to create a poster of what they think life will be like in the year 3000.

PART 1
Comparative Form of Adjectives:
-er and *More*

PART 2
As . . . As/Not As . . . As

Lesson 29

Engineering:
Energy Sources

■ CONTENT VOCABULARY

Look at the pictures. Do you know the words?

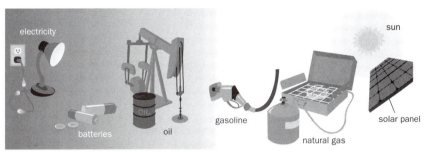

energy

Write the new words in your vocabulary journal.

■ THINK ABOUT IT

Discuss these questions with a partner.   Answers will vary.

What kind of energy source do you use to:

- heat or cool your home?
- cook your meals?
- listen to music?
- do your laundry?

Overview

Elicit students' prior knowledge. Ask: *What do you think we will learn about in this lesson?*

■ CONTENT VOCABULARY

1. Direct students' attention to the first set of pictures and ask what all of them have in common. (They are all related to energy.)
2. Go over the bottom row of pictures and help students define the vocabulary they aren't familiar with for their vocabulary journals.

■ THINK ABOUT IT

Have students do this activity with a partner and then share their answers with a pair of students sitting next to them.

■ CONTENT NOTES

Engineering

The topic for this lesson is Engineering: Energy Sources. Engineering is defined as the practical application of science to commerce or industry. There are numerous fields of engineering, including aeronautical, architectural, automotive, chemical, civil, communications technology, and computer technology. Branches of engineering dealing with energy include:

1. *Electrical engineering,* which is the branch of engineering that studies the uses of electricity and deals with the design of equipment for power generation and distribution, machine control, and communications.
2. *Industrial engineering,* which concentrates on the creation and management of systems that integrate people, materials, and energy in productive ways.
3. *Nuclear engineering,* which focuses on the design and construction of nuclear reactors.

PART ONE

Comparative Form of Adjectives: -er and *More*

Part 1 introduces students to the comparative form of adjectives with -er and *more*.

■ GRAMMAR IN CONTENT

This section exposes students to a theme-based reading that includes examples of the target structure. Students can refer to the grammar chart(s) to complete the controlled practice activities.

■ EXERCISE A Track 67

1. Ask students to look at the pictures and compare them. Ask: *How are they similar? How are they different?*
2. Play the audio and have students follow along.
3. Write two headings on the board: Electric Cars and Gasoline Cars. Have students brainstorm what they know about each type of car while you note their ideas on the board.

■ GRAMMAR CHART
Comparative Form of Adjectives: -er and More

1. Go over the first chart with the students.
2. Go over the Notes. As you go through each note, use the example for each case to make a complete sentence, following the pattern in the first chart, for example, *My mother is older than my father.*
3. Go over the second chart and the Note.
4. Have students look for and underline examples in the reading with –er and with *more*.

■ GRAMMAR IN CONTENT

 A Read and listen.

TR67

Making Better Automobiles

Automobile engineers are always working on ways to make **better** cars. At the moment, many engineers are working to create electric cars. Why? Traditional cars run on gasoline. The gases cars burn are very bad for the environment. Electricity is much **cleaner than** gasoline. Electric cars are also **quieter**.

So why isn't everybody driving an electric car? Gasoline is a **more efficient** energy source. Cars can run much **longer** on a tank of gasoline **than** on a fully charged battery. To solve this problem, automobile engineers have created hybrid cars. These cars run on both gasoline and electricity. Hybrid cars are still very new, but they are becoming **more popular** each year.

environment: the air, land, and water that people, plants, and things live in

efficient: productive, economical

source: beginning

charge: to load or fill

Comparative Adjectives with -er

Subject	Be	Comparative Adjective	Than	
An electric car	is	cleaner	than	a gasoline car.

Notes:
- For most one-syllable adjectives, add -er to form the comparative: *old / older.*
- For one- or two-syllable adjectives that end in y, change the y to i and add -er: *busy / busier.*
- For one-syllable adjectives that end in a single vowel + a single consonant, double the final consonant, then add -er: *big / bigger.*
- Some adjectives have irregular comparative forms. Examples: *good / better   bad / worse   far / farther*

Comparative Adjectives with *More*

Subject	Be	Comparative Adjective	Than	
Electric cars	are	more expensive	than	gasoline cars.

Note:
For adjectives with two syllables or more, place *more* in front of the adjective to form the comparative.

210 LESSON 29 | Engineering: Energy Sources

■ EXPANSION IDEA

Exercise A

1. In small groups, have students discuss which type of car they would rather drive and why.
2. Divide the class into two groups: those who want to drive an electric car and those who want to drive a gasoline car.
3. Help students participate in an informal debate about why one type of car is better than the other.

B Complete the sentences with the comparative form of the adjectives in parentheses.

1. Electric cars are (clean) _cleaner than_ gasoline cars.
2. Electric cars are (quiet) **quieter than** gasoline cars.
3. Gasoline cars are (loud) **louder than** electric cars.
4. Electric cars are (easy) **easier** to take care of **than** gasoline cars.
5. Electric cars are (expensive) **more expensive than** gasoline cars.
6. Hybrid cars are (practical) **more practical than** electric cars.

C Write comparative sentences about the cars and people in the picture. Use the words provided.

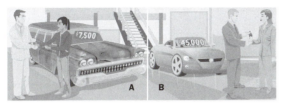

1. car A / car B / old _Car A is older than car B._
2. car A / car B / new **Car A is newer than car B.**
3. car A / car B / cheap **Car A is cheaper than car B.**
4. car A / car B / expensive **Car A is more expensive than car B.**
5. car A / car B / small **Car A is smaller than car B.**
6. car A / car B / large **Car A is larger than car B.**
7. woman A / woman B / young **Woman A is younger than woman B.**
8. woman A / woman B / old **Woman A is older than woman B.**
9. woman A / woman B / tall **Woman A isn't taller than woman B.**
10. woman A / woman B / short **Woman A is shorter than woman B.**

■ COMMUNICATE

D **PAIR WORK** Take turns creating comparative sentences about each pair of things below. The person who makes the most sentences wins.

| dogs / cats | bicycles / cars | gasoline / electricity | radio / television |

■ **EXPANSION IDEA**

Exercise C

1. Have students work with a partner to compare two similar items in the classroom. (You may want to talk about what sorts of things in the classroom they might decide to compare.)

2. Have students talk about the items first and then write six comparative sentences.

■ **EXERCISE B**

1. Have students complete the exercise by themselves after you go over the directions and the example with them.
2. When students are finished, call on volunteers to read their sentences aloud.

■ **EXERCISE C**

1. Look at both pictures with the students and ask them what is happening.
2. Have students complete the exercise by themselves after you go over the directions and the example with them.
3. When students are finished, ask for volunteers to write their comparative sentences on the board.

■ **COMMUNICATE**

The Communicate section allows students to practice the target grammar in more communicative, less-controlled ways through speaking and writing activities.

■ **EXERCISE D**

1. In pairs, have students take turns saying comparative sentences about each pair of things in the exercise.
2. Ask students to keep making sentences until they can't think of anything more to say about the pair of things.
3. The partner who says the last sentence wins that round. Then they go on to the next pair of things.
4. When students are finished, ask for volunteers to share some of the sentences they came up with.

■ EXERCISE E

1. Go over the model paragraph with students so they understand what to do.

2. When students are finished, ask for volunteers to read their paragraphs to the class.

PART TWO

As . . . As/Not As . . . As

Part 2 introduces students to sentences with *as . . . as* and *not as . . . as.*

■ GRAMMAR IN CONTENT

This section exposes students to a theme-based reading that includes examples of the target structure. Students can refer to the grammar chart(s) to complete the controlled practice activities.

■ EXERCISE A *Track 68*

1. Ask students who the person in the picture is and what he is doing.

2. Have students listen to the recording and follow along in their books.

3. Ask students what the differences are between solar panels and natural gas and oil.

■ GRAMMAR CHART

As . . . As/Not As . . . As

Go over the chart and the Notes with the students. As you go through the chart and the Notes, refer to the reading for examples.

E **WRITE** Write a paragraph comparing yourself to someone you know well, such as a parent, a brother or sister, or a friend. Share your paragraph with the class.

> **My Brother and I**
>
> Miguel is my brother. People are often surprised that we are brothers. We are very different. Miguel is much older than I am. I'm 21. He's 35. My hair is blond. His hair is brown. I'm taller than he is. Our personalities are different too. He's friendlier than I am. I am quieter than he is. But I think I am funnier than Miguel.

PART TWO	As . . . As/Not As . . . As

■ GRAMMAR IN CONTENT

A Read and listen.

TR68

A Better Way to Heat Homes

How do you heat your home? You probably use natural gas or oil. I'd like to change that. I'm an electrical engineer. I design solar panels. Solar panels change the sun's energy into heat.

Solar panels are **as effective as** natural gas and oil. But they are **not as common as** natural gas and oil yet, because they aren't **as cheap as** natural gas or oil. But natural gas and oil aren't **as safe as** solar power or **as clean as** solar power. The world needs someone to create a cheaper solar panel. That's my job.

As . . . As/Not As . . . As

Subject	Be	(Not) As	Adjective	As	
My house	is	(not) as	big	as	your house.
Jack's car	is		old		Alex's car.

Notes:
- Use as . . . as to say that two people or things are the same in some way.
- Use not as . . . as to say that two people or things are not the same in some way.

212 LESSON 29 | Engineering: Energy Sources

■ EXPANSION IDEA

Exercise D and Grammar Chart

1. Have students do Exercise D from page 211 again, but this time using the new grammar they just learned in Part 2 on this page.

B Complete each sentence with *as . . . as* or *not as . . . as* and one of the adjectives in the box.

| expensive | crowded | dirty | tall | difficult | ~~heavy~~ |

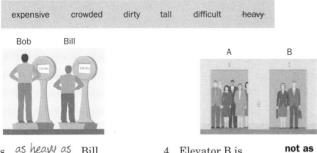

1. Bob is _as heavy as_ Bill.

4. Elevator B is ___**not as**___ ___**crowded**___ as elevator A.

2. Bill is ___**not as**___ ___**tall as**___ Bob.

5. The ring is ___**as expensive**___ ___**as**___ the necklace.

A | B
$2 + 2 = 4$ | $f(x) = \dfrac{20x}{x^2 + 12}$

3. Equation A is ___**not as**___ ___**difficult as**___ equation B.

6. The pants are ___**not as**___ ___**dirty as**___ the T-shirt.

■ COMMUNICATE

C **PAIR WORK** Talk with your partner and find at least three things that you have in common. Take notes on your conversation. Then tell the class what you have in common, using *as . . . as*.

> Marcia and I have a lot in common. She is as tall as I am. Her family is as large as my family. And she is as friendly as I am!

■ EXERCISE B

1. Have students do this exercise with a partner and make sure they agree on the correct answer before they write it in their books.
2. Go over the answers as a class.

■ COMMUNICATE

The Communicate section allows students to practice the target grammar in more communicative, less-controlled ways through speaking and writing activities.

■ EXERCISE C

1. Go over the example in the book.
2. Pair students up with a partner they don't usually work with so they can learn something new about someone in the class.
3. Have both partners participate in sharing with the class things they have in common.

■ EXPANSION IDEA

Exercise C

1. Have students use the information they learned about their partners to write a short paragraph, using comparatives with *–er*, *more*, and *as . . . as/not as . . . as*.

2. Have students share their paragraphs with the people they wrote about.

EXERCISE D

1. As a class, brainstorm a list of cities that students might compare. Write all the ideas on the board.
2. Explain that students will choose any two cities and write a paragraph like the model in their books.
3. Go over the example with students to help them get started.

Putting It Together

The purpose of this section of the lesson is to connect and extend students' understanding of the grammar, vocabulary, and content from this lesson.

■ GRAMMAR AND VOCABULARY

Bring in newspapers or magazines for students to work with.

■ PROJECT

1. Go through each step with the students, making sure they understand what they are supposed to do.
2. For additional suggestions on doing projects, see the Teacher's Notes on pages xvi–xviii.

■ INTERNET

1. Have students work alone or with a partner.
2. Have students share what they learned about hybrid cars.

■ VOCABULARY JOURNAL

Refer to the Pre-lesson (page 6) for an explanation of the vocabulary journal.

 **D WRITE** Write a paragraph comparing two cities. Use *as . . . as* and *not as . . . as.*

> #### Comparing Puno and New York City
> I am from Puno. Puno is a small city in Peru. I live in New York now. Puno is very different from New York. It isn't as big as New York. It isn't as crowded as New York. But there are some things that are similar. The people are as friendly in New York as they are in Puno. The food is as good in Puno as it is in New York, too.

Connection   Putting It Together

GRAMMAR AND VOCABULARY Work with a partner. Find advertisements for two cars in a magazine or newspaper. Look closely at the pictures. Read the advertisements carefully. Discuss and compare the cars. Use the grammar and vocabulary from this lesson.

PROJECT Design a new car.

1. Work with a group.
2. Imagine you are a group of engineers creating a new car. Decide:
   - What energy source will it run on?
   - What will it look like?
   - How fast will it go?
   - How much will it cost?
   - What special features will it have?
3. Present your car to the class. Explain how your car is similar to most cars on the road now. Explain how it is different. Give your classmates a chance to ask questions.

 INTERNET Go online. Look for more information about cars that run both on gas and electricity. Use the keyword phrase "hybrid cars." Share what you learned with your classmates.

VOCABULARY JOURNAL Write sentences for new vocabulary you learned in this lesson.

Example: *I fill my car with gasoline each week.*

■ EXPANSION IDEA

Internet

1. Have students work in small groups to make a poster about hybrid cars that includes all the information they learned on the Internet.

PART 1
Past Review: The Simple Past Tense of *Be*, the Simple Past Tense

PART 2
Present Review: The Present Tense of *Be*, the Simple Present Tense, the Present Progressive Tense

PART 3
Be Going To, Will

Lesson (30)

Computer Science: The Past, Present, and Future of Computers

■ CONTENT VOCABULARY

Look at the pictures. Do you know the words?

Personal Digital Assistant (PDA)

download

MP3 player

online

word processor

spreadsheet

database

Write the new words in your vocabulary journal.

■ THINK ABOUT IT

Discuss these questions with a partner. **Answers will vary.**

1. What similar inventions came before the computer?
2. How do people use computers?
3. How will people use computers in the future?

215

Overview

Elicit students' prior knowledge. Ask: *What do you think we will learn about in this lesson?*

■ CONTENT VOCABULARY

1. Direct students' attention to the pictures and ask them what all of the pictures have in common.
2. Help students define the vocabulary they aren't familiar with for their vocabulary journals.
3. Have students work in small groups to make a list of other computer technology items that are not depicted on page 215. (cell phone, fax machine, printer, etc.)

■ THINK ABOUT IT

1. Have students do this activity with a partner and then share their answers with a pair sitting next to them.
2. Discuss students' ideas as a class.

■ CONTENT NOTES

Computer Science

The topic for this lesson is Computer Science: The Past, Present, and Future of Computers.

The following topics will be covered in this lesson:

abacus—counting device
ENIAC—the first computer

Altair 8000—the first home computer
laptop—small portable computer
PDA—personal digital assistant
MP3 player—portable music player

As a pre-activity to the lesson, discuss with students what they already know about the above items.

PART ONE

Past Review: The Simple Past Tense of *Be*, the Simple Past Tense

Part 1 reviews the simple past tense of *be*, and the simple past tense.

■ GRAMMAR IN CONTENT

This section exposes students to a theme-based reading that includes examples of the target structure. Students can refer to the grammar chart(s) to complete the controlled practice activities.

■ EXERCISE A *Track 69*

1. Ask students to look at the pictures and ask them what they know about the abacus or the ENIAC.
2. Play the audio and have students follow along in their books.
3. Have students circle all of the past tense verbs in the reading (there are 13). Ask them how many of those verbs are a form of *be* (there are 5).

   NOTE: The above activity is similar to what students will do for Exercise B. You may decide to skip it here and do it after you explain the grammar.

■ GRAMMAR CHART

The Simple Past Tense of Be, *the Simple Past Tense*

1. Go over the chart illustrating the simple past tense of *be*. As you review the first three notes for the chart, refer to the chart for examples.
2. Go over the chart and the Notes illustrating the simple past tense, refer to the reading for additional examples.

■ GRAMMAR IN CONTENT

A Read and listen.

TR69

abacus

ENIAC

Long Before Laptops

It **took** thousands of years for people to create the computer. The first step (happened) about 5,000 years ago. Around this time, the Chinese (invented) the abacus. Before the abacus, people (counted) on their fingers or in their heads. The abacus **was** an important new tool. It (helped) people count much faster.

Thousands of years and many inventions later, an American team **built** the first real computer. The year **was** 1942. The team (called) their computer ENIAC. ENIAC **was** very large. It **was** 8 feet high and 78 feet long and (weighed) 27 tons. But this computer **was** less powerful than one modern home computer.

The Simple Past Tense of *Be*	
Form	**Example**
Affirmative	I **was** in class yesterday.
Negative	He **was not** sick yesterday.
Yes/No Questions	**Were** you in the computer lab yesterday?
Wh- Questions	Where **were** the students yesterday?

Notes:
- Use the simple past tense of *be* to talk about people, places, and things in the past.
- Use *was* with the subjects *I, he, she,* and *it.*
- Use *were* with the subjects *you, they,* and *we.*
- See Lessons 16, 17, and 20 for more information on the simple past of *be.*

The Simple Past Tense	
Form	**Example**
Affirmative	I **listened** to my instructor yesterday.
Negative	He **did not feel** well yesterday.
Yes/No Questions	**Did** you **work** in the computer lab yesterday?
Wh- Questions	Where **did** the students go yesterday?

Notes:
- Use the simple past tense to talk about actions that happened in the past.
- Add *-d* or *-ed* to regular past tense verbs in affirmative statements.
- Irregular verbs do not take the *-d/-ed* ending in the past tense. See appendix 4 for irregular verb forms.
- See Lessons 18, 19, and 20 for more information on the simple past tense.

216 LESSON 30 | Computer Science: The Past, Present, and Future of Computers

---

■ EXPANSION IDEA

Exercise A

1. Have small groups of students do Internet research about the abacus or the ENIAC.

2. Ask students to report what they learn to the class.

B Look at the reading "Long Before Laptops." Circle all the past tense *be* verbs. Underline all the simple past tense verbs.

C Circle the correct answers.

The Birth of the Personal Computer

A company called MITS (was created / (created)) the first home computer. The name of the
(1)
computer ((was) / were) Altair 8000. This computer ((was) / were) very different from modern computers.
(2)   (3)
People (was not / (did not)) buy the computer in stores. They (order / (ordered)) it from the company. It
(4)   (5)
(arrives / (arrived)) in the mail. It (camed / (came)) in pieces. People (builded / (built)) the computer from
(6)   (7)   (8)
these pieces. The computer (was not / (did not)) do many things.
(9)

In 1977, Apple (introduces / (introduced)) a small, useful personal computer. People (buys / (bought))
(10)   (11)
this computer in stores. During the 1980s computers (becomed / (became)) cheaper. Millions of people
(12)
(use / (used)) computers at home. Suddenly, computers (was / (were)) everywhere.
(13)   (14)

D Read "The Birth of the Personal Computer" in exercise C. Complete each question with *Was, Were,* or *Did.* Then answer each question with a short answer.

1. __Did__ Microsoft create the personal computer?

2. _____**Yes, it did**_____.

3. __Was__ the Altair 8000 like modern computers?

4. _____**No, it wasn't.**_____.

5. __Were__ computers popular in the 1980s?

6. _____**Yes, they were**_____.

■ COMMUNICATE

E **WRITE** Write a paragraph or two about the last time you used a computer.

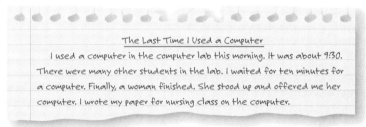

The Last Time I Used a Computer
I used a computer in the computer lab this morning. It was about 9:30.
There were many other students in the lab. I waited for ten minutes for
a computer. Finally, a woman finished. She stood up and offered me her
computer. I wrote my paper for nursing class on the computer.

Have students complete the exercise by themselves and then share their answers with a partner.

■ EXERCISE C

1. Have students complete the exercise by themselves and then share their answers with a partner.
2. Go over the answers as a class. As you go over each answer, ask students why the incorrect answer doesn't work in the sentence.

■ EXERCISE D

1. When students are finished, ask for volunteers to write the questions and answers on the board.
2. Have students practice saying the questions and answers with a partner.

■ COMMUNICATE

The Communicate section allows students to practice the target grammar in more communicative, less-controlled ways through speaking and writing activities.

■ EXERCISE E

1. Go over the model paragraph with students so they understand what to do.
2. When students are finished, ask for volunteers to read their paragraphs to the class.

■ EXPANSION IDEA

Exercise C

1. To review the comparative form of adjectives that students learned in the previous lesson, have them compare the Altair 8000 to the Apple computer invented in 1977. They can do this aloud with a partner or in writing.

Present Review: The Present Tense of *Be,* the Simple Present Tense, the Present Progressive Tense

Part 2 is a review of the present tense of *be,* the simple present tense, and the present progressive tense.

■ GRAMMAR IN CONTENT

This section exposes students to a theme-based reading that includes examples of the target structure. Students can refer to the grammar chart(s) to complete the controlled practice activities.

■ EXERCISE A *Track 70*

1. Ask students who the person in the picture is and what he is doing. Take a quick poll and see how many students have a laptop. Ask how many use the Internet on their laptops.
2. Have students listen to the recording and follow along in their books.
3. Ask students whether they use the Internet and what they use it for.

■ GRAMMAR CHARTS

The Simple Present Tense of Be, the Simple Present Tense, the Present Progressive Tense

Go over the chart with the students. Go over the Notes. As you go through the chart, refer to the reading for examples.

| PART TWO | Present Review: The Present Tense of *Be,* the Simple Present Tense, the Present Progressive Tense |

■ GRAMMAR IN CONTENT

A Read and listen.

TR70

modern: current, not old-fashioned

chat: to talk online

Computers in Modern Life

Computers (are) smaller, cheaper, and lighter than ever. People **bring** laptops and PDAs everywhere. They **use** word processors, spreadsheets, and databases in places like trains, airplanes, and cafés. The Internet (is) a big part of modern life. People **use** it to chat with friends, pay bills, order groceries, and buy everything from books to cars online. About 75 percent of Americans **use** the Internet, and the average American **spends** about three hours a day online.* Millions of people (are using) the Internet right now!

*Brad Stone, "Hi-Tech's New Day," Newsweek, April 11, 2005, p. 62

The Simple Present Tense of *Be*

Form	Example
Affirmative	I am in class.
Negative	He is not sick.
Yes/No Questions	Are you in the computer lab now?
Wh- Questions	Where are the students?

Notes:
- Use *be* to talk about people, places, and things in the present.
- Use *am* with the subject *I.* Use *is* with the subjects *he, she,* or *it.* Use *are* with the subjects *you, we,* and *they.*
- See Lessons 1, 2, and 9 for more information on the simple present tense of *be.*

The Simple Present Tense

Form	Example
Affirmative	I always **listen** to my instructor.
Negative	He **does not feel** well today.
Yes/No Questions	Do you **work** at the computer lab?
Wh- Questions	Where do you **go** for lunch?

Notes:
- Use the simple present tense for actions in the present.
- With the subjects *he, she,* and *it* in affirmative statements, add -s to most verbs.
- See Lessons 6, 7, 8, 9, and 13 for more information on the simple present tense.

The Present Progressive Tense

Form	Example
Affirmative	I am **listening** to my instructor right now.
Negative	He **was not feeling** well yesterday.
Yes/No Questions	Are you **working** at the computer lab now?
Wh- Questions	Where are the students **going** now?

Notes:
- Use the present progressive tense to talk about actions happening right now.
- To form the present progressive, add -ing to most verbs.
- See Lessons 11, 12, and 13 for more information on the present progressive tense.

218 LESSON 30 | Computer Science: The Past, Present, and Future of Computers

---

■ EXPANSION IDEA

Exercise A

1. To review the past tense, have students imagine that it is now the future and ask them to rewrite the paragraph in Exercise C, changing all the verbs to past tense.

B Look at the reading "Computers in Modern Life." (Circle) all the present tense of *be* verbs. <u>Underline</u> all the simple present tense verbs. Put a box around all the present progressive verb forms.

C Fill in the blanks with the correct tense and form of the verbs in parentheses.

Carlos: What <u>are</u> you <u>doing</u> ?
(1. do)

John: I <u>'m shopping</u> for a computer online.
(2. shop)

Carlos: But you <u>have</u> a computer already.
(3. have)

John: I know. But I <u>don't like</u> this computer. It <u>is</u> old and slow.
(4. not / like)(5. be)

Carlos: <u>Do</u> you <u>want</u> a laptop?
(6. want)

John: No. I <u>'m looking for</u> a PDA.
(7. look for)

Carlos: Why <u>do</u> you <u>want</u> a PDA?
(8. want)

John: I <u>need</u> a computer for home and school. PDAs <u>are</u> perfect! They
(9. need)(10. be)
<u>are</u> small and light.
(11. be)

Carlos: <u>Are</u> they expensive?
(12. be)

John: Yes, they <u>are</u>.
(13. be)

Carlos: Now what <u>are</u> you <u>doing</u> ?
(14. do)

John: I <u>'m going</u> onto my bank's Web site.
(15. go)

Carlos: Why?

John: I <u>'m checking</u> my balance. Uh-oh.
(16. check)

Carlos: What?

John: I <u>don't have</u> a lot of money in my account. Maybe this old
(17. not / have)
computer <u>is not</u> so bad after all.
(18. not / be)

D Find and correct the mistakes. (Hint: There are five more mistakes.)

becomingdo
Personal Digital Assistants are ~~become~~ very popular now. They ^not have a keyboard
don't
or a mouse. Most PDAs ~~doesn't~~ have word processors, spreadsheets, or databases. But
have
PDAs ~~has~~ a datebook, a clock, a calculator, and a notebook. You can even go on the

Internet with some PDAs. People sends and receives e-mails with these PDAs.

EXERCISE B

1. Have students do this exercise with a partner and make sure they agree on the correct answer before they write it in their books.
2. Go over the answers as a class.

EXERCISE C

1. Have students do this exercise on their own and then practice the completed conversation with a partner.
2. Go over the answers as a class.

EXERCISE D

1. Once students have found all the mistakes, go over the answers as a class.
2. Ask students why each mistake wasn't correct.

■ EXPANSION IDEA

Exercise C

1. Have students work with a partner to rewrite the conversation about something they might purchase online.

2. Ask for volunteers to perform their conversations for the class.

■ COMMUNICATE

The Communicate section allows students to practice the target grammar in more communicative, less-controlled ways through speaking and writing activities.

■ EXERCISE E

Model this activity with a few students in the class. Tell them about something you use and have them ask you questions about it.

PART THREE

Be Going To, Will

Part 3 is a review of sentences with *be going to* and *will*.

■ GRAMMAR IN CONTENT

This section exposes students to a theme-based reading that includes examples of the target structure. Students can refer to the grammar chart(s) to complete the controlled practice activities.

■ EXERCISE A *Track 71*

1. Ask students what they think the person in the picture is wearing.
2. Have students listen to the recording and follow along in their books.
3. At the end of the reading the engineer says the future of computers is "already beginning to happen." Ask students when they think the ideas in the reading with be a reality.

■ GRAMMAR CHARTS

The Future with Be Going To; The Future with Will

Go over the charts and the Notes with the students. As you review the Notes, refer to the charts and the reading for examples.

■ COMMUNICATE

E **PAIR WORK** Tell your partner about a computer, PDA, cell phone, MP3 player, or other electronic device you use. Describe it to your partner. Tell him or her how you use it and what you do with it. Answer any questions your partner has about it. Take turns.

PART THREE	*Be Going To, Will*

■ GRAMMAR IN CONTENT

A **Read and listen.**

TR71

The Future of Computers

Reporter: How **will** our computers **be** different in the future?

Engineer: Computers **are going to get** smaller and smaller. Soon most people **will wear** them. You **will see** the screen on a pair of glasses. You **won't need** a keyboard or a mouse. Computers **will understand** your thoughts and will follow your instructions.

Reporter: When **is** this **going to happen?**

Engineer: It's already beginning to happen!

The Future with *Be Going To*	
Form	**Example**
Affirmative	It is going to rain soon.
Negative	She is not going to graduate next year.
Yes/No Questions	Are you going to use this computer?
Wh- Questions	What are you going to do tomorrow?

Notes:
- Use *be going to* to talk about plans for the future.
- Make predictions about the future based on current evidence with *be going to*.
- See Lesson 27 for more information about *be going to*.

The Future with *Will*	
Form	**Example**
Affirmative	Computers **will understand** voices in the future.
Negative	I will not be late for class.
Yes/No Questions	Will he buy a PDA?
Wh- Questions	What will computers **look** like in the future?

Notes:
- Use *will* to make predictions about the future.
- Use *will* when the speaker decides to do something at the moment of speaking.
- Use *will* for promises.
- See Lesson 28 for more information on the future with *will*.

220 LESSON 30 | Computer Science: The Past, Present, and Future of Computers

---

■ EXPANSION IDEA

Grammar Charts

1. Write the following questions on the board:

What are you going to do after class?
What are you going to do tomorrow?
What will cars be like in the future?
What will you be like in the future?

2. Have students form small groups and then take turns, in a circle, answering each of the questions.

B What is each person saying? Choose the correct sentence.

1. a. I'm going to help you.
   (b.) I'll help you.

3. (a.) I'm going to fall asleep.
   b. I'll fall asleep.

2. a. I'm going to see you later.
   (b.) I'll see you later.

4. (a.) We're going to get married next year.
   b. We will get married next year.

C (Circle) the correct answers. In some cases both choices are correct.

Teenager: What ((are you going to do)/(will you do)) today, Mom?
                    (1)

Mother: I ((\'m going to go)/(\'ll go)) to the mall.
                (2)

Teenager: What ((are you going to buy)/(will you buy))?
                    (3)

Mother: I (\'m going to tell /(\'ll tell)) you later.
                (4)

Teenager: Come on. Tell me now.

Mother: Oh, OK. I ((\'m going to buy)/\'ll buy) a laptop.
                (5)

Teenager: That's great!

Mother: I want you to do your schoolwork on it.

Teenager: Sure. But I ((\'m going to use)/(\'ll use)) it for a few other things too.
                    (6)

Mother: Like what?

Teenager: I ((\'m going to play)/(\'ll play)) computer games.
                    (7)
            I ((\'m going to e-mail)/(\'ll e-mail)) my friends.
                (8)
            I ((\'m going to download)/(\'ll download)) music onto my MP3 player.
                (9)
            This ((is going to be)/(will be)) great!
                 (10)

Mother: This laptop is for the whole family.

Teenager: Sure. Don't worry. I (\'m going to /(\'ll let)) you use it.
                              (11)

Mother: Gee, thanks.

■ **EXERCISE B**

1. Go over the pictures as a class and ask students to tell you what is happening in each one.
2. Let students choose answers and then go over the answers as a class. Ask students to explain why they chose the answers they did, and make sure everyone understands what the correct answers were, and why.

■ **EXERCISE C**

1. Have students do this exercise with a partner, deciding on the correct answers before circling them in their books.
2. Go over the answers as a class, discussing why it is sometimes possible for two different answers to be correct.

■ **EXPANSION IDEA**

Exercise C

1. Go over the pronunciation and intonation of the correct answers in Exercise C.

2. Have students work with partners to act out the situation and practice the conversation.

■ COMMUNICATE

The Communicate section allows students to practice the target grammar in more communicative, less-controlled ways through speaking and writing activities.

■ EXERCISE D

1. Explain the "rules" to students.
2. Discuss some possible ideas that students might include in their paragraphs.
3. Give students a time limit for this writing so that students won't write for too long.

Connection

Putting It Together

The purpose of this section of the lesson is to connect and extend students' understanding of the grammar, vocabulary, and content from this lesson.

■ GRAMMAR AND VOCABULARY

Go over the examples in the book to help students get started on this activity.

■ PROJECT

1. Go through each step with the students, making sure they understand what they are supposed to do.
2. For additional suggestions on doing projects, see the Teacher's Notes on pages xvi–xviii.

■ INTERNET

1. Have students work with their project group to do their Internet research.
2. Encourage students to share what they learned.

■ VOCABULARY JOURNAL

Refer to the Pre-lesson (page 6) for an explanation of the vocabulary journal.

D **WRITE** Imagine you are entering a contest to win a new computer. Each contestant must write a paragraph explaining why he or she wants the computer. The person with the best paragraph wins. Write your paragraph. Be sure to use *be going to* and *will* in your paragraph. After each person in your class is finished, read your paragraphs out loud. Decide who should win the computer.

Connection   Putting It Together

GRAMMAR AND VOCABULARY Work with a partner. Take turns asking and answering questions about the past, present, and future of computers. Use information you learned in this lesson, as well as other information you know about computers. Use the grammar and vocabulary from this lesson.

> What company introduced the first personal computer?   Apple.
> What kind of computer fits in a person's hand?   A PDA.

PROJECT Give a presentation about the past, present, and future of the topic of your choice.

1. Work with a group.
2. Choose one of the following topics, or think of a topic of your own.
   - the United States
   - another country
   - movies
   - television
   - equipment for playing music
   - telephones
3. Brainstorm what you know about the past and present of your topic with your group. Work together to make predictions about the future of your topic.
4. Organize the information your group brainstormed. First put together all of the information about the past, then all of the information about the present, and finally, put together all of the predictions your group made about the future.
5. Give a presentation about your topic to the class.

 INTERNET Look on the Internet for more information about the topic you focused on for your project. Try to find out at least one more fact about the history of your topic, one more fact about the present of your topic, and one more prediction about its future. Use "the history of (your topic)," "facts about (your topic)," and "the future of (your topic)" as keyword phrases.

VOCABULARY JOURNAL Write example sentences in your vocabulary journal. Use the vocabulary and grammar from this lesson.

Example: *I don't have an MP3 player. I listen to music on a CD player.*

222 LESSON 30 | Computer Science: The Past, Present, and Future of Computers

■ EXPANSION IDEA

Exercise D

1. In groups, have students come up with their own contest like the one in Exercise D.
2. Ask students to write directions similar to those in Exercise D.
3. Have students present their contests to the class and have the class vote on which would make the best contest.

A Complete the sentences with *have to*, *don't have to*, or *mustn't*.

Ivan: How is the trial going?

Linda: It is very interesting. I ____have to____ listen carefully all of the
(1)

time. So I'm a little tired. But we finally made a decision. I'm glad I

____don't have to____ be here tomorrow. Oh! The jury is going into the
(2)

courtroom. I ____have to____ go now.
(3)

Ivan: OK. I can pick you up after the trial.

Linda: That's very nice, but you ____don't have to____.
(4)

Ivan: It's no problem. I ____have to____ go downtown anyway.
(5)

Linda: Great! But remember—you ____mustn't____ park in front of the
(6)

courthouse.

B Choose the correct answers to complete the questions and answers.

1. **Tom:** Are you _____ back to China after graduation?
   a. go to go   (b.) going to go   c. go to going

2. **Ming:** No, I'm not. I _____ stay here.
   a. am go to   b. am go   (c.) am going to

3. **Tom:** _____ are you going to do?
   a. Where   (b.) What   c. When

4. **Ming:** I _____ my own restaurant.
   a. open   b. am open   (c.) am going to open

5. **Tom:** What kind of restaurant _____ open?
   a. you going to   (b.) are you going to   c. you are going to

6. **Ming:** I _____ a traditional Chinese Dim Sum restaurant here.
   (a.) 'm going to open   b. 'm open   c. 'm to open

Review 26–30

Lessons 26–30

The purpose of this lesson is help
students review the concepts they
have learned in the last five lessons.
Encourage them to go back to the
lessons and review the grammar
charts to help them complete the
review exercises.

■ EXERCISE A

1. Have students do this activity by
   themselves and then share their
   answers with a partner.
2. Go over the answers as a class
   by asking students to read the
   conversation aloud.

■ EXERCISE B

1. Have students do this activity by
   themselves and then share their
   answers with a partner.
2. Go over the answers as a class
   by asking students to read the
   conversation aloud.

■ EXPANSION IDEA

Exercises A and B

1. Have students and partners choose
   one of the conversations and
   memorize it. Have the pairs perform it
   for the class.

EXERCISE C

1. Have students do this activity by themselves and then share their answers with a partner.
2. Go over the answers as a class by asking students to read the conversation aloud.

EXERCISE D

1. Have students work with a partner to write the correct answers.
2. Have students practice the conversation.

EXERCISE E

1. Have students do this activity by themselves and then share their answers with a partner.
2. Go over the answers as a class by asking students to read the conversation aloud.

C (Circle) the correct answers.

Doris: Bill! Bill! Why are you carrying that TV? You (are /(will)) hurt your back
₍₁₎ again. Wait. I ('m /('ll)) help you.
₍₂₎

Bill: Don't worry, Doris. I'm fine. I (willn't /(won't)) hurt my back. Oow! I hurt
₍₃₎ my back.

Doris: (You will /(Will you)) listen to me? (Are /(Will)) you go to the doctor?
₍₄₎   ₍₅₎

Bill: (Who /(What)) will the doctor do for me?
₍₆₎

Doris: He ((ll take) / 'll takes) an X-ray and find the problem.
₍₇₎

Bill: Oh. OK, OK. (I am will /(I will)) make an appointment tomorrow.
₍₈₎

D Complete the dialogue with the correct form of comparison.

Salesperson: Don't look at that old car. This sports car is much (good) **better** .
₍₁₎

Customer: Yes, but it's also much (expensive) **more expensive**
₍₂₎

Salesperson: But the sports car is (exciting) **more exciting** . The sports car goes
₍₃₎
(fast) **faster than** that car.
₍₄₎

Customer: I don't mind. The old car goes (fast) **as fast as** I need it to go.
₍₅₎

Salesperson: But the sports car is (pretty) **prettier** .
₍₆₎

Customer: Yes, but this old car looks (comfortable) **more comfortable than** the
₍₇₎
sports car.

Salesperson: I think you're making a mistake! I would choose the sports car.

Customer: Well, I guess I'm (rich) **not as rich as** you. I'll take the used car.
₍₈₎

E Choose the correct answers to complete the questions and answers.

Wife: What _____ you doing?
₍₁₎
(A) are   B) do

Husband: I _____ at our bank statement online. It doesn't look right.
₍₂₎
A) am look   (B) am looking

Wife: Why?

Husband: I _____ see much money in the account.
    (3)
    A) am not   Ⓑ don't

Wife: There isn't much money in it right now.

Husband: But we _____ a big check into the account a few weeks ago.
    (4)
    A) is put   Ⓑ put

Wife: We _____ that money.
    (5)
    A) spended   Ⓑ spent

Husband: What _____ about?
    (6)
    A) do you talk   Ⓑ are you talking

Wife: We _____ our rent and our credit card bill last week.
    (7)
    A) did pay   Ⓑ paid

Husband: _____ a big credit card bill?
    (8)
    Ⓐ Did we have   B) Did we had

Wife: Yes, we _____ the new computer last month.
    (9)
    A) were bought   Ⓑ bought

Husband: Oh, that's right.

Wife: Why _____ the computer?
    (10)
    A) are you shut off   Ⓑ are you shutting off

Husband: I don't want to look at our bank account anymore!

LEARNER LOG Check (✔) *Yes* or *I Need More Practice.*

Lesson	I Can Use . . .	Yes	I Need More Practice
26	*Must/Must Not* and *Have To/Don't Have To*		
27	Affirmative and Negative Statements and Questions with *Be Going To*		
28	*Will*: Affirmative, Negative Statements and Questions		
29	The Comparative Form of Adjectives: *-Er* and *More, As . . . As,* and *Not As . . . As*		
30	Past, Present, and Future Tense Review		

■ **LEARNER LOG**

1. Help students understand how to complete the Learner Log by going over it with them and offering examples of the grammar structures.

2. If students checked "I Need More Practice" for any of the structures, suggest that they review those lessons. If possible, meet with students individually to discuss their Learner Logs and make suggestions for ways to get more practice with the structures.

■ **EXPANSION IDEA**

Learner Log

1. Have students form groups and generate a list of ideas for what they can do if they checked the "I Need More Practice" column in the Learner Log. Have each group share its best ideas with the class.

2. Since this is the last lesson in the book, consider conducting a class discussion about which lessons have been the most helpful and which structures students need to continue working on.

APPENDIX 1 | Activities for Student B

LESSON 5, PART 2, EXERCISE F (p. 39)
Student B looks at the picture on this page. Student A looks at the picture on page 39. Find the differences. Ask and answer *is there/are there* questions.

LESSON 5, GRAMMAR AND VOCABULARY (p. 40)
Work with a partner. Partner B looks at the picture on this page. Partner A looks at the picture on page 40. Ask and answer questions to find out how your partner's picture is different from yours. How many differences can you find? Make notes on the differences. Use the grammar and vocabulary from this lesson.

LESSON 11, PART 3, EXERCISE D (p. 91)
Student B looks at the picture on this page. Student A looks at the picture on page 91. Talk about your pictures. Find the differences. Use the present progressive.

LESSON 19, PART 2, EXERCISE C (p. 145)
One partner looks at Text B. The other looks at Text A on page 145. Take turns asking each other past tense *wh-* questions to find the missing information.

Text B: Crimes of the Century

The Great Train Robbery happened in Oxford, England.

The robbery happened on _____ (When?). 15 people
(1)
robbed the train. They took _____ (What?).
(2)
They took 2.6 million pounds. They hurt _____
(3)
(How many people?). They hurt _____ (Who?).
(4)
They hit him over the head with an iron bar. The police found

_____ (What?). The police caught 14 of the robbers.
(5)

LESSON 27, PART 2, EXERCISE C (p. 198)
It is now a week before the opening of Elisa's restaurant. Student B looks at the calendar and statements below. Student A looks at the calendar and statements on page 198. Take turns asking each other *wh-* questions with *going to* to find the missing information in your statements.

Student B Questions

1. On Tuesday she is going to hire _____. (Who?)

2. On Thursday she is going to put an advertisement in _____. (Where?)

3. On Saturday she is going to _____. (What?)

APPENDIX 2   **Glossary**

- **Adjective** An adjective describes a noun. Example: *That's a **small** desk.*
- **Adverb** An adverb describes the verb of a sentence or an adjective. Examples: *He is **very** smart. I run **quickly**.*
- **Adverb of Frequency** An adverb of frequency tells how often an action happens. Example: *I **always** go to the library after class.*
- **Affirmative** An affirmative means *yes*.
- **Apostrophe (')** See Appendix 6.
- **Article** An article (*a, an,* and *the*) comes before a noun. Example: *I have **a** book and **an** eraser.*

- **Base Form** The base form of a verb has no tense. It has no ending (*-s* or *-ed*). Examples: *be, go, eat, take, write*
- **Capitalization** See Appendix 5.
- **Comma (,)** See Appendix 6.
- **Comparative Form** A comparative form of an adjective or adverb is used to compare two things. Example: *I am **taller** than you.*
- **Consonant** The following letters are consonants: *b, c, d, f, g, h, j, k, l, m, n, p, q, r, s, t, v, w, x, y, z.*
- **Contraction** A contraction is made up of two words put together with an apostrophe. Example: ***She's** my friend.* (She is = she's)
- **Count Noun** Count nouns are nouns that we can count. They have a singular and a plural form. Examples: *book – books, nurse – nurses*
- **Frequency Expressions** Frequency expressions answer *How often* questions. Examples: *once a week, three times a week, every day*
- **Imperative** An imperative sentence gives a command or instructions. An imperative sentence usually omits the word *you*. Example: ***Open** the door.*
- **Irregular Verbs** See Appendix 4.
- **Modal** Some examples of modal verbs are *can, could, should, will, would, must.*
- **Negative** Means *no.*
- **Noncount Noun** A noncount noun is a noun that we don't count. It has no plural form. Examples: *water, money, rice*
- **Noun** A noun is a word for a person, a place, or a thing. Nouns can be singular (only one) or plural (more than one).
- **Object** The object of the sentence follows the verb. It receives the action of the verb. Example: *Kat wrote a **paragraph.***
- **Object Pronoun** Use object pronouns (*me, you, him, her, it, us, them*) after the verb or preposition. Example: *Kat wore **it.***
- **Period (.)** See Appendix 6.
- **Plural** Plural means more than one. A plural noun usually ends with *-s* or *-es*. Examples: *The book**s** are heavy. The bus**es** are not running.*
- **Preposition** A preposition is a short, connecting word. Examples: *about, above, across, after, around, as, at, away, before, behind, below, by, down, for, from, in, into, like, of, on, out, over, to, under, up, with*
- **Punctuation (. , ' ?)** Punctuation marks are used to make writing clear (for example: periods, commas, apostrophes, question marks). See Appendix 6.
- **Question Mark (?)** See Appendix 6.
- **Regular Verb** A regular verb forms its past tense with *-d* or *-ed*. Example: *He **lived** in Mexico.*
- **Sentence** A sentence is a group of words that contains a subject and a verb and expresses a complete thought.
- **Singular** Means one.
- **Subject** The subject of the sentence tells who or what the sentence is about. Example: *The **water** does not taste good.*

- **Subject Pronoun** Use subject pronouns (*I, you, he, she, it, we, they*) in place of a subject noun. Example: *They (= the books) are on the desk.*

- **Tense** A verb has tense. Tense shows when the action of the sentence happened.

    Simple Present: *She occasionally **reads** before bed.*

    Present Progressive: *He **is thinking** about it now.*

    Simple Past: *I **talked** to him yesterday.*

- **Verb** Verbs are words of action or state. Example: *I **go** to work every day. Joe **stays** at home.*

- **Wh- Questions** *Wh-* questions (beginning with *what, when, where, why, who, how*) ask for information. Example: ***Where** is your homework?*

- **Yes/No Questions** *Yes/No* questions ask for a *yes* or *no* answer. Example: *Is she from Mexico? **Yes,** she is.*

APPENDIX 3	Spelling Rules

Spelling of Regular Plural Nouns

Base Form	Plural Form	Rule
book teacher	books teachers	For most plural nouns: Add -*s*
bus box	buses boxes	If the noun ends in *s, z, x, ch, sh:* Add -*es*
dictionary library	dictionaries libraries	If the noun ends in a consonant + *y:* Change *y* to *i* and add -*es*
shelf knife	shelves knives	For some nouns that end in *f* or *fe:* Change the *f* or *fe* to -*ves*
photo tomato	photos tomatoes	If the noun ends with a consonant + *o*, some words take -*s* and others take -*es*.

Simple Present Spelling of Third-Person -*s* Form

Base Form	Spelling with *He, She,* or *It*	Rule
see	sees	Most verbs: Add -*s*
teach	teaches	Verbs that end in *sh, ch, x, z,* or *ss:* Add -*es*
study	studies	Verbs that end in consonant + *y:* Change *y* to *i* and add -*es*

Spelling of Verbs in the *-ing* Form

Base Form	*-ing* Form	Rules:
work eat	work**ing** eat**ing**	For most verbs: Add *-ing*.
live write	liv**ing** writ**ing**	For verbs that end in a consonant + *e*: Drop the *e* and add *-ing*. Do not double the consonant. Wrong: ~~writting~~
sit plan	sit**ting** plan**ning**	For one-syllable verbs that end in *one* vowel + one consonant: Double the consonant and add *-ing*.
say sleep listen think	say**ing** sleep**ing** listen**ing** think**ing**	Do not double the last consonant before *-ing* when the verb: • ends in *w, x,* or *y.* • ends in two vowels and then one consonant. • has more than one syllable (when the stress is on the first syllable). • ends in two or more consonants.

Spelling of Past Tense of Regular Verbs

Base Form	Past Form	Rule
work walk	work**ed** walk**ed**	For most verbs: Add *-ed*.
live dance	live**d** dance**d**	For verbs that end in an *e*: Add *-d* only.
study cry	stud**ied** cr**ied**	For verbs that end in a consonant + *y*: Change *y* to *i* and add *-ed*.
play enjoy	play**ed** enjoy**ed**	For verbs that end in a vowel + *y*: Add *-ed*.
drop hug	drop**ped** hug**ged**	For one-syllable verbs that end in a consonant + vowel + consonant: Double the final consonant and add *-ed*.
show relax	show**ed** relax**ed**	For verbs that end in *w* or *x*: Do not double the consonant. Just add *-ed*.
happen open	happen**ed** open**ed**	For two-syllable verbs that end in a consonant + vowel + consonant: If the first syllable is stressed, add *-ed*. Do not double the consonant.
prefer admit	prefer**red** admit**ted**	For two-syllable verbs that end in a consonant + vowel + consonant: If the second syllable is stressed, double the final consonant and add *-ed*.

Common Irregular Past Tense Verbs

Base Form	Simple Past Form	Base Form	Simple Past Form
be	was/were	let	let
become	became	make	made
begin	began	meet	met
break	broke	pay	paid
bring	brought	put	put
build	built	read	read
buy	bought	run	ran
catch	caught	say	said
choose	chose	see	saw
come	came	sell	sold
cost	cost	send	sent
cut	cut	shut	shut
do	did	sing	sang
drink	drank	sit	sat
drive	drove	sleep	slept
eat	ate	speak	spoke
fall	fell	spend	spent
find	found	steal	stole
fly	flew	swim	swam
forget	forgot	take	took
get	got	teach	taught
give	gave	tell	told
go	went	think	thought
have	had	understand	understood
hear	heard	wake	woke
hit	hit	wear	wore
know	knew	win	won
lead	led	write	wrote
leave	left		

Capitalize:

- the first word in a sentence. Example: *The college is closed today.*
- names and titles. Examples: *Manuel, Mrs. Jones, the President*
- geographic names. Examples: *Brazil, Paris, Federal Street, the Atlantic Ocean*
- names of organizations and businesses. Examples: *Boston University, United Nations, Thomson Heinle*
- days of the week, months, and holidays. Examples: *Monday, July, Christmas*
- nationalities, languages, religions, and ethnic groups. Examples: *Russians, English, Islam, Hispanics*
- book and movie titles. Examples: *Grammar Connection, Gone with the Wind*

- Use an **apostrophe (')**:
  1. to show possession. Example: *That is Ivan's pen.*
  2. for contractions. Example: *I didn't (= did not) go to class yesterday.*
- Use a **comma (,)**:
  1. in a list of two or more things. Example: *I have class on Monday, Wednesday, and Friday.*
  2. in answers with *yes* or *no.* Examples: *Yes, I do. No, I don't feel well.*
  3. in statements or questions with *and, but,* or *so.* Examples: *My sister is a student, and she is studying engineering. Kobe is good at math, but Simone is good at art.*
- Use a **period (.)**:
  1. at the end of a sentence. Example: *Francis goes to Hedden Community College.*
  2. after many common abbreviations. Examples: *Mr., Mrs., Dr., Ave.*
- Use a **question mark (?)** at the end of a question. Example: *Do you study math?*

Cardinal Numbers

1	one
2	two
3	three
4	four
5	five
6	six
7	seven
8	eight
9	nine
10	ten
11	eleven
12	twelve
13	thirteen
14	fourteen
15	fifteen
16	sixteen
17	seventeen
18	eighteen
19	nineteen
20	twenty
21	twenty-one
30	thirty
40	forty
50	fifty
60	sixty
70	seventy
80	eighty
90	ninety
100	one hundred
1,000	one thousand
10,000	ten thousand
100,000	one hundred thousand
1,000,000	one million

Ordinal Numbers

first	1st
second	2nd
third	3rd
fourth	4th
fifth	5th
sixth	6th
seventh	7th
eighth	8th
ninth	9th
tenth	10th
eleventh	11th
twelfth	12th
thirteenth	13th
fourteenth	14th
fifteenth	15th
sixteenth	16th
seventeenth	17th
eighteenth	18th
nineteenth	19th
twentieth	20th
twenty-first	21st

Days of the Week

Sunday
Monday
Tuesday
Wednesday
Thursday
Friday
Saturday

Seasons

winter
spring
summer
fall

Months of the Year

January
February
March
April
May
June
July
August
September
October
November
December

Write the Date

April 5, 2004 = 4/5/04

Temperature Chart

Degrees Celsius (°C) and Degrees Fahrenheit (°F)

100°C	212°F
30°C	86°F
25°C	77°F
20°C	68°F
15°C	59°F
10°C	50°F
5°C	41°F
0°C	32°F
−5°C	23°F

Weights and Measures

Weight:
1 pound (lb.) = 453.6 grams (g)
16 ounces (oz.) = 1 pound (lb.)
1 pound (lb.) = .45 kilograms (kg)

Liquid or Volume:
1 cup (c.) = .24 liter (l)
2 cups (c.) = 1 pint (pt.)
2 pints = 1 quart (qt.)
4 quarts = 1 gallon (gal.)
1 gallon (gal.) = 3.78 liters (l)

Length:
1 inch (in. or ")= 2.54 centimeters (cm)
1 foot (ft. or ') = .3048 meters (m)
12 inches (12") = 1 foot (1')
1 yard (yd.) = 3 feet (3') or 0.9144 meters (m)
1 mile (mi.) = 1,609.34 meters (m) or 1.609 kilometers (km)

Time:
60 seconds = 1 minute
60 minutes = 1 hour
24 hours = 1 day
28–31 days = 1 month
12 months = 1 year

Review: Lessons 1–5
(pages 41–42)

A.
1. 's / is
2. 's / is
3. 'm / am
4. 'm / am
5. 'm not / am not
6. 'm / am
7. is
8. isn't / is not

B.
1. c   4. b
2. a   5. d
3. e

C.
1. a
2. students
3. programs
4. libraries
5. students
6. countries
7. a
8. classes

D.
1. This is
2. These are
3. That is
4. This is
5. Those are

E.
1. There are
2. There are
3. There is
4. Is there
5. there is
6. there are
7. There are
8. Is there
9. there is

Review: Lessons 6–10
(pages 83–84)

A.
1. plays   5. do not
2. sings   6. does not
3. knows   7. listen
4. helps   8. helps

B.
1. goes   6. on
2. on   7. has
3. does   8. on
4. on   9. at
5. at

C.
1. What   5. don't
2. Where   6. Do
3. How   7. do
4. Do   8. Who

D.
1. do   5. Do
2. are   6. do
3. Are   7. are
4. are

E.
1. every day
2. twice a week
3. always
4. never
5. How often
6. rarely

Review: Lessons 11–15
(pages 119–120)

A.
1. am watching
2. is reading
3. is showing
4. are not / aren't talking
5. are listening
6. are not / aren't crying
7. are smiling

B.
1. going
2. Is
3. isn't
4. doing
5. No
6. is
7. working

C.
1. writing
2. thinking
3. are
4. cooking
5. is
6. Is
7. reads
8. reading
9. does
10. miss
11. Do

D.
1. João
2. João's
3. His
4. Her
5. Her
6. Their
7. grandparents
8. grandparents'
9. Nina's

E.
1. She
2. They
3. them
4. reads Jane stories / reads stories to Jane
5. him
6. him
7. He

8. her
9. They
10. tells a story to Jane /
    tells Jane a story
11. him

Review: Lessons 16–20
(pages 153–154)

A.
1. was   4. was
2. were   5. were not
3. was

B.
1. Where   6. Were
2. Who   7. weren't
3. Was   8. Where
4. was   9. Why
5. wasn't

C.
1. was
2. went
3. wrote
4. did not / didn't graduate
5. dropped
6. started
7. made

D.
1. Did he take
2. Yes, he did
3. What
4. Did the police catch
5. Yes, they did
6. When did they catch

E.
1. was   6. was
2. was   7. Did
3. did   8. did
4. ruled   9. How
5. was   10. Who

Review: Lessons 21–25
(pages 185–186)

A.
1. any   6. money
2. a   7. dollars
3. any   8. a
4. a   9. a
5. some

B.
1. a little
2. a few
3. many
4. many
5. a little
6. a few
7. How much
8. a few
9. a little

C.
2. Take a seat.
   Would you take a seat,
   please?
3. Open your book.
   Would you open your
   book, please?
4. Work with a partner.
   Would you work with a
   partner, please?
5. Turn off the equipment.
   Would you turn off the
   equipment, please?

D.
1. can
2. Can you
3. can
4. can
5. Can
6. can't

E.
1. Should I
2. Yes,
3. Should I wrap the gift?
4. should wrap

5. Should I shake
6. you should
7. Should
8. No,

Review: Lessons 26–30
(pages 223–225)

A.
1. have to
2. don't have to
3. have to
4. don't have to
5. have to
6. mustn't

B.
1. b   4. c
2. c   5. b
3. b   6. a

C.
1. will
2. 'll
3. won't
4. Will you
5. Will
6. What
7. 'll take
8. I will

D.
1. better
2. more expensive
3. more exciting
4. faster than
5. as fast as
6. prettier
7. more comfortable than
8. not as rich as

E.
1. a   6. b
2. b   7. b
3. b   8. a
4. b   9. b
5. b   10. b

Vocabulary Index

Words in blue are part of the Content Vocabulary section at the start of each Lesson.
Words in black are words glossed with the readings in each lesson.
Words in **bold** are words from the Academic Word List.

Credits

Illustrators

Precision Graphics: pp. 6, 10, 12–13, 15, 18–20, 22, 27 (right), 31–33, 35–36, 38, 43 (left), 51, 57, 66, 69, 78, 88, 99 (top right 3 illustrations), 101, 106, 109, 118, 124, 126, 132, 135, 137, 145, 149, 172, 174–175, 178, 182, 189, 196, 198–199, 206, 212, 213 (only item 3), 214, 215 (top middle illustration and right 3 illustrations), 217, 228

Richard Carbajal/illustrationOnLine.com: pp. 23, 30 (bottom 6 illustrations), 121, 127, 133, 167, 169, 171, 211

Amy Cartwright/illustrationOnLine.com: pp. 155–156, 159–160, 215 (bottom middle illustration), 221

Alan King/illustrationOnLine.com: pp. 161, 163, 165, 213 (all except item 3), 215 (left 2 illustrations)

Katie McCormick/illustrationOnLine.com: pp. 2, 7, 9, 27 (left), 28–29, 43 (right 4 illustrations), 45, 53, 56, 193–195

David Preiss/Munro Campagna.com: pp. 3, 5, 59, 89, 98, 99 (top left), 113, 117, 143, 177

Stacey Previn/Munro Campagna.com: pp. 21, 24, 26, 30 (top), 62, 92, 94–95, 107, 141

Scott Wakefield/Gwen Walters: pp. 4, 39–40, 75, 85, 87, 90–91, 147, 173, 187, 209, 227

Philip Williams/illustrationOnLine.com: pp. 179, 201

Photo Credits

Page 1: Left: © PhotoObjects.net; Left Center: © Alexander Benz/zefa/Corbis; Center: © Bryan Mullennix/Iconica/Getty; Right Center: © PhotoObjects.net; Right: © PhotoObjects.net **Page 2:** Top Left: © PhotoObjects.net; Top Center: © PhotoObjects.net; Top Right: © PhotoObjects.net; Bottom Left: © Royalty-Free/Corbis; Bottom Center: © Charles Gupton/Corbis; Bottom Right: © PhotoObjects.net **Page 8:** © Royalty-Free/Corbis **Page 10:** © Stephen Simpson/Stone/Getty **Page 13:** © Ed Honowitz/The Image Bank/Getty **Page 14:** © Kim Steele/Photodisc Green/Getty/RF **Page 22:** © PhotoObjects.net **Page 33:** © Charles Gupton/Corbis **Page 34:** © Chuck Pefley/Alamy **Page 37:** © Photos.com/RF **Page 44:** © Royalty-Free/Corbis **Page 49:** Top: © Royalty-Free/Corbis; Bottom: © Henrick Sorensen/Photonica/Getty **Page 54:** © Stewart Cohen/Stone/Getty **Page 55:** © Royalty-Free/Corbis **Page 58:** Left: © Karen Moskowitz/Stone+/Getty; Center: © Stockbyte/Getty/RF; Right: © Photos.com **Page 60:** © Getty Images **Page 63:** © Titus Lacoste/Taxi/Getty **Page 64:** © Photos.com **Page 67:** Top Left: © John Giustina/Iconica/Getty; Top Center: © Photos.com; Top Right Center: © Photos.com; Top Right: © PhotoObjects.net; Bottom Left: © Henry Horenstein/Photonica/Getty; Bottom Center: © PhotoObjects.net; Bottom Right: © PhotoObjects.net **Page 68:** Left: © AFP/Getty Images; Right: © Getty Images **Page 70:** © Anna Clopet/Corbis **Page 76:** © Rob Lewine/Corbis **Page 79:** © Photodisc Green/Getty/RF **Page 86:** © Gaetano Images Inc./Alamy **Page 93:** Top Left: © Royalty-Free/Corbis; Top Right: © Alexander Benz/zefa/Corbis; Bottom: © Photos.com **Page 96:** © Simon Marcus/Corbis **Page 100:** © Shoot/zefa/Corbis **Page 102:** © BananaStock/Alamy/RF **Page 104:** © image100/Alamy/RF **Page 108:** © Bubbles Photolibrary/Alamy **Page 110:** © Stockbyte Platinum/Alamy **Page 114:** © Popperfoto/Alamy **Page 115:** © Thomas Barwick/Photodisc Red/Getty/RF **Page 116:** © Content Mine International/Alamy **Page 122:** Left: © Bettman/Corbis; Left Center: © MinBuZu/Peter Arnold, Inc.; Center: © Bettmann/Corbis; Right Center: © Michael Ochs Archives/Corbis; Right: © Andy Warhol Foundation/Corbis **Page 123:** Left: © Bettmann/Corbis; Right: © Bettmann/Corbis **Page 128:** © 1996 Corbis; Original image courtesy of NASA/Corbis **Page 130:** © Bettman/Corbis **Page 134:** © Doug Norman/Alamy **Page 135:** Top: © Nigel Wright/Pool/Reuters/Corbis; Bottom: © Lawrence Manning/Corbis **Page 138:** © Colin McPherson/Corbis **Page 142:** © Seanna O'Sullivan/Corbis Sygma **Page 144:** © Kevin Flemming/Corbis **Page 145:** © Getty Images **Page 148:** © Jon Arnold Images/Alamy **Page 150:** © John T. Fowler/Alamy **Page 157:** Top Left: © Cephas Picture Library/Alamy; Top Right: © Nikreates/Alamy; Bottom Left: © PhotoObjects.net; Bottom Right: © Photos.com **Page 158:** © Royalty-Free/Corbis **Page 162:** © BananaStock/Alamy/RF **Page 164:** © Photos.com **Page 165:** © Photos.com **Page 168:** © Phototake Inc./Alamy **Page 169:** © Betsie Van der Meer/Stone/Getty **Page 170:** © Photos.com **Page 176:** © Phototake Inc./Alamy **Page 180:** Left: © JG Photography/Alamy/RF; Right: © JG Photography/Alamy/RF **Page 181:** First: © Photos.com; Second: © image100/Alamy/RF; Third: © Pacific Press Service/Alamy; Fourth: © image100/Alamy/RF; Fifth: © Photos.com; Sixth: © PhotoAlto/Alamy/RF **Page 182:** © BananaStock/Alamy/RF **Page 188:** © Comstock Images/Alamy **Page 190:** © Dennis Macdonald/Index Stock Imagery **Page 197:** © Jon Riley/Stone/Getty **Page 202:** © Ryan McVay/Photodisc Green/Getty/RF **Page 205:** © Photodisc Blue/Getty/RF **Page 210:** Top: © Spencer Grant/Photo Researchers, Inc.; Bottom: © Martin Bond/Photo Researchers, Inc. **Page 212:** © Steven Puetzer/Photonica/Getty **Page 216:** Top: © PhotoObjects.net; Bottom: © Jerry Cooke/Corbis **Page 218:** © Tom & Dee Ann McCarthy/Corbis **Page 220:** © Forestier Yves/Corbis Sygma

PRE-UNIT

Part 1: Parts of Speech

A.

1. books	**3.** students	**5.** computers
2. window	**4.** door	**6.** chair

B.

1. a teacher	**3.** a school	**5.** a mother
2. a book	**4.** a desk	**6.** a house

C.

1. he	**3.** they	**5.** they
2. it	**4.** she	**6.** it

D.

1. it	**5.** they	**9.** it
2. he	**6.** we	**10.** she
3. she	**7.** it	**11.** they
4. he	**8.** they	**12.** it

E.

1. walk	**3.** write	**5.** read
2. study	**4.** talk	**6.** love

F. Answers will vary.

G.

1. blue	**3.** new	**5.** nice
2. large	**4.** heavy	**6.** difficult

H.

1. c	**4.** b
2. a	**5.** e
3. d	

I. Answers will vary

Part 2: Classroom Instructions

A.

1. b	**3.** d
2. a	**4.** c

B.

a clock, a teacher, a backpack

C.

read, eat, talk

D.

1. a noun	**3.** an adjective
2. a verb	**4.** a pronoun

E.
1. "An instructor" is a ~~verb~~ noun.
2. "Eat" is a ~~noun~~ verb.
3. "It" is an ~~adjective~~ pronoun.
4. "Happy" is a ~~pronoun~~ adjective.

LESSON 1

The Present Tense of *Be:* Affirmative Statements; *Be* + Adjective; Negative Statements

Part One

Exercise A
Page 1

1. am	**5.** are
2. is	**6.** is
3. are	**7.** is
4. is	**8.** are

Exercise B
Page 1

1. **I am in class**
2. He is from Haiti.
3. We are happy today.
4. Andrea is 36.
5. You are nice.
6. They are computer science students.
7. It is a great class.
8. It is late.
9. Bruno is from Brazil.

Exercise C
Page 2

1. **She's a nice teacher.**
2. I'm a chemistry teacher.
3. We're from Pakistan.
4. They're nice students.
5. You're nervous.
6. It's my first day at college.

Part Two

Exercise A
Page 2

1. am not	**6.** am
2. is	**7.** is not
3. am	**8.** are not
4. am	**9.** is not
5. am not	**10.** are

Exercise B
Page 3

1. **He's not a chemistry teacher.**
2. I'm not a student.
3. We're not from Korea.
4. They're not art students.
5. You're not happy.

6. It's not 12:00.
7. She's not a nervous student.
8. You're not in English 205.
9. He's not Professor David.

Putting It Together: Grammar

Exercise A
Page 3
Answers will vary.

Exercise B
Page 3
1. **I am from Ecuador.**
2. She's not 28.
3. They're nervous.
4. Today is my first day at college.
5. C
6. Julia Marks is nice. She's a chemistry teacher.
7. C
8. It's not 3:45.
9. I am not happy.
10. They are not from Brazil.
11. C
12. We're not in class.
13. C
14. Tomorrow is my birthday.

Putting It Together: Vocabulary

Page 5
1. **student**
2. instructor
3. nervous
4. confused
5. late
6. excited
7. class

LESSON 2

Yes/No Questions and Short Answers
The Present Tense of *Be: Wh-* Questions

Part One

Exercise A
Page 6
1. **Is this the English Department?**
2. Are you my instructor?
3. Is her birthday today?
4. Is she 25 years old?
5. Is this my social security number?
6. Is this the registration form?
7. Is his e-mail address arios@realnet.com?
8. Is Yon Lu's date of birth 3/5/87?
9. Is your favorite color blue?

Exercise B
Page 7
1. **Yes, it is.**
2. Yes, she is.
3. No, he is not.
4. No, she is not.
5. Yes, she is.
6. No, she is not.

Exercise C
Page 7
Answers will vary.

Exercise D
Page 7
1. **Is** / is not
2. Is / it is
3. Are you / I am

Part Two

Exercise A
Page 8
1. **What**
2. Who
3. When
4. Where
5. What

Exercise B
Page 8
Ms. Adiya: **What is your name?**
Carlos: Carlos Beltran. Who is the English instructor?
Ms. Adiya: Your English instructor is Kate Banning.
Carlos: When is English class?
Ms. Adiya: English class is at 2:15.
Carlos: Where is English class?
Ms. Adiya: It's in room 311.
Carlos: What is the instructor's e-mail address?
Ms. Adiya: It's kbanning@yourcollege.edu.
Carlos: Where is her office?
Ms. Adiya: Her office is in the ESL center.
Carlos: Thanks for your help!

Exercise C
Page 9
1. **What's her name? / Debbie Towne.**
2. When was she born? / 3/22/72
3. What is her social security number? / 057-xx-3242
4. What is her telephone number? / (617) 814-5555
5. Where does she live? / Austin, TX
6. What road does she live on? / Bondi Lane
7. What is her e-mail address? / dtowne@realnet.com
8. When is class? / 2:15 – 3:15
9. What class is it? / English 1
10. Who is her instructor? / Harry Chin

Putting It Together: Grammar

Exercise A
Page 10

Lorenzo: Hi, I'm Lorenzo. **What's your name?**

Maya: My Name is Maya. <u>Are you new here?</u>

Lorenzo: Yes, it's my first day.

Maya: <u>Are you</u> excited?

Lorenzo: Yes, and I'm nervous, too.
<u>Are you a</u> chemistry student?

Maya: No, I'm a computer science student.

Lorenzo: <u>Who is your instructor?</u>

Maya: Mr. Lenox.

Lorenzo: Is he nice?

Maya: Yes, <u>he is.</u>

Lorenzo: <u>Where is computer science class?</u>

Maya: It's in room 304.

Lorenzo: Is it in the science building?

Maya: No, <u>it is not.</u> It's in the computer building.

Lorenzo: <u>When is your class?</u>

Maya: My computer class is at 9:45.

Lorenzo: <u>Who is</u> your English instructor?

Maya: Kate Banning.

Lorenzo: She's my instructor, too!

Exercise B
Page 11

Administrator: What's your first name?

Lorenzo: Lorenzo.

Administrator: Ok. **Is** your last name Chavo?

Lorenzo: No, <u>it is not.</u> <u>It is</u> Chavez.

Administrator: <u>Where are you from?</u>

Lorenzo: Chile.

Administrator: <u>What is your address?</u>

Lorenzo: My address is 55 First Street, Newton. My phone number is (555) 877-6090.

Administrator: <u>What is your date of birth?</u>

Lorenzo: December 7, 1983.

Administrator: That's it! You're a student now, Mr. Chavez!

Putting It Together: Vocabulary

Page 12

1. **name**
2. date
3. sex
4. telephone
5. address
6. e-mail

Singular and Plural Nouns
Spelling and Pronunciation of Regular Plural Nouns

Part One

Exercise A
Page 13

1. **an**	7. a
2. a	8. an
3. an	9. a
4. a	10. a
5. a	11. a
6. a	12. a

Exercise B
Page 13

1. S	9. S
2. P	10. P
3. P	11. P
4. S	12. P
5. P	13. S
6. S	14. S
7. P	15. P
8. S	16. S

Exercise C
Page 14

1. **It's a college.**
2. She's a teacher.
3. I'm a student.
4. C
5. Fifty-five South Street is an address.
6. It's a registration form.
7. C
8. They're great pens.
9. Is it a whiteboard?

Part Two

Exercise A
Page 14

1. **addresses**	12. instructors
2. pantries	13. colleges
3. bakeries	14. births
4. spies	15. cakes
5. loaves	16. clocks
6. watches	17. heroes
7. babies	18. potatoes
8. desks	19. names
9. thieves	20. notebooks
10. volcanoes	21. windows
11. elves	

Exercise C
Page 15

/s/ as in "books"	/z/ as in "teachers"	/əz/ as in "classes"
desks	pantries	addresses
notebooks	bakeries	watches
births	spies	colleges
clocks	loaves	
cakes	babies	
	thieves	
	elves	
	heroes	
	potatoes	
	windows	
	volcanoes	
	instructors	
	names	

Putting It Together: Grammar

Exercise A
Page 15

1. **Is it a knife?**
2. Is it a leaf?
3. Is it an elevator?
4. Is it a dictionary?
5. Is it a college?
6. Is it a dish?
7. Is it a box?
8. Is it a tomato?
9. Is it a shelf?
10. Is it an e-mail address?
11. Is it a city?
12. Is it an umbrella?

Exercise B
Page 16

1. **They're books.**
2. iMac is a computer.
3. It's a leaf.
4. C
5. It's an apple.
6. Morocco and India are countries.
7. Yale and Columbia are universities.
8. C
9. They're potatoes.
10. It's a library.

Exercise C
Page 16

1. *Lily:* Here are the form<u>s</u>.
Tan: Are they <u>x</u> registration form<u>s</u>?
Lily: Yes, they are.
2. *Sandra:* I'm confused. Is this <u>a</u> telephone number <u>x</u>?
Mr. Stockton: No, it isn't. It's <u>a</u> social security number <u>x</u>.
Sandra: Oh, OK. Thank you.
3. *Ali:* Who is your biology teacher <u>x</u>?
Yasmin: Mrs. Garcia.
Ali: She's <u>a</u> nice teacher <u>x</u>.

4. *Leo:* Are you <u>an</u> art student <u>x</u>?
Andrea: Yes, I am.
5. *Lorenzo:* The form<u>s</u> are confusing.
Maya: Yes, they are. They're <u>x</u> new form<u>s</u>.
6. *Fernanda:* Are they class<u>es</u>?
Simon: No, they're not. They're <u>x</u> offic<u>es</u>.

Putting It Together: Vocabulary
Page 17

1. textbook
2. whiteboard
3. highlighter
4. pen
5. pencil
6. eraser
7. window
8. table
9. door
10. chair
11. clock
12. notebook
13. what is it?

LESSON 4

This, That, These, Those
Prepositions of Location

Part One
Exercise A
Page 18

1. **This is**
2. Those are
3. That is
4. Those are
5. This is
6. That is
7. This is
8. These are

Exercise B
Page 18

1. **This registration form is confusing**
2. Those are new dormitories.
3. This highlighter is helpful.
4. This is a confusing parking lot.
5. That teacher is nice.
6. This is an interesting English class.
7. That student is nervous.
8. This is an excellent library.
9. Those students are quiet.
10. Those classes are difficult.

Exercise C
Page 19

1. **this**
2. This
3. these?
4. that
5. this
6. this; this

Part Two
Exercise A
Page 20

1. on
2. in
3. in front of
4. between

5. inext to
6. across from
7. on

8. near
9. next to
10. on

Exercise B
Page 20

1. in
2. in
3. near

4. across from
5. in front of

Putting It Together: Grammar

Exercise A
Page 21

Carlos: <u>This</u> campus is so confusing.

Shigero: Don't worry. I can help you.

Carlos: Wow! What's <u>that</u> over there?

Shigero: It's the library.

Carlos: And what are <u>those</u>, near the library?

Shigero: <u>They're</u> dormitories.

Carlos: OK. Where's the cafeteria?

Shigero: It's beside the dormitories. It's right <u>next to</u> them.

Carlos: That's helpful. Oh, where are we now?

Shigero: <u>These</u> are the classrooms. They're <u>in</u> this building.

Carlos: Where is the parking lot?

Shigero: It's *across from* this building. Can you see it over there?

Carlos: Yes, I can see it now. What's this?

Shigero: <u>It's</u> a map of the campus. My e-mail and telephone
    number are <u>on</u> the map.

Carlos: Great! Thanks.

Exercise B
Page 22
Answers will vary.

Putting It Together: Vocabulary

Page 22

ACROSS	DOWN
4. library	1. lab
5. stadium	2. classroom
6. lot	3. map
8. dormitories	7. statue
9. campus	9. cafeteria
10. bookstore	

LESSON 5

There is/There are
Is there/Are there Questions and Short Answers

Part One

Exercise A
Page 24

1. **There is**
2. There is

3. There are
4. There are

5. There is
6. There are
7. There is

8. There is
9. There are
10. There are

Exercise B
Page 24

1. **There's a cafeteria at the college.**
2. There are new dormitories on the campus.
3. There are 35 programs for undergraduates.
4. There's a teacher for every 15 students.
5. There are 80 rooms in my dorm.
6. There's a bookstore on every campus.
7. There are 500,000 books in the library.
8. There are some students from Oceania.

Exercise C
Page 25
Answers will vary.

Part Two

Exercise A
Page 25

1. **Is there; Yes, there is. / No, there isn't.**
2. Are there; Answers will vary.
3. Are there
4. Are there
5. Is there
6. Are there
7. Is there
8. Are there
9. Is there
10. Is there

Exercise B
Page 26

1. **Is there a whiteboard?; Yes, there is./No, there isn't.**
2. Are there tables for students?; Answers subject to vary.
3. Are there desks for students?
4. Is there a desk for the teacher?
5. Are there books?
6. Are there windows?
7. Are there computers for students?
8. Is there a computer for the teacher?
9. Is there an elevator near the classroom?
10. Are there posters?
11. Is there a clock?
12. Are there computers?

Putting It Together: Grammar

Exercise A
Page 27

1. **Are there; Yes, there are.**
2. Is there; Yes, there is.

3. Is there; No, there is not.
4. Are there; No, there are not.
5. Is there; Yes, there is.
6. Are there; Yes, there are two.
7. Are there; No, there are not.

Exercise B
Page 28
Answers will vary.

Putting It Together: Vocabulary
Page 28

1. art
2. biology
3. business
4. chemistry
5. communication
6. engineering
7. history
8. mathematics
9. nursing
10. physical education
11. computer science
12. criminal justice
13. psychology
14. sociology
15. This is the right program for me.

Connection
Content Writing

I. Identifying the Topic Sentence

Exercises A & B
Page 29

✔There are 25 dormitories.
✔There are many parking lots.
✔There are 20,000 students.
___Mr. Jones teaches ESL.
✔There is a library with 700,000 books.
___*My university is very big.*
___The café is near the bookstore.
___The statue is in Hilton Hall.
___Many students drive to school.
✔There are many buildings on campus.

Exercise C
Page 29

    My university is very big. There are 20,000 students. There are 25 dormitories. There are many parking lots. There is a library with 700,000 books. There are many buildings on campus.

Exercise D
Page 30
Answers will vary.

II. Writing a Paragraph

Exercise E
Page 30
Answers will vary.

Exercise G
Page 31
Answers will vary.

Exercise H
Page 31
Answers will vary.

Exercise I
Page 31
Answers will vary.

LESSON 6

The Simple Present Tense: Affirmative Statements;
Spelling and Pronunciation Third Person –s Form;
The Simple Present Tense: Negative Statements

Part One
Exercise A
Page 32

1. hears	6. sends
2. smell	7. makes
3. wee	8. leave
4. weighs	9. wash
5. take	10. brings

Exercise B
Page 32

1. **smells**
2. see
3. hear
4. leaves
5. tastes

Exercise C
Page 33
Answers will vary.

Part Two
Exericse A
Page 33

1. **worries**	9. uses
2. enjoys	10. gets
3. catches	11. passes
4. understands	12. accepts
5. plans	13. flies
6. runs	14. watches
7. thinks	15. sits
8. tells	

Exercise B
Column 1 (/s/ as in "eats")

thinks

gets

accepts

sits

Column 2 (/z/as in "lives")

worries

enjoys

understands

plans

tells

runs

flies

Column 2 (/az/ as in "teaches")

catches

uses

passes

watches

Exercise C
Page 34

1. **studies**
2. cleans
3. tries
4. brushes
5. teaches
6. lives
7. eats
8. speaks
9. weighs
10. worries

Part Three

Exercise A
Page 34

1. **It doesn't taste good.**
2. It doesn't smell strange.
3. I don't hear the phone.
4. Sometimes she doesn't see her sister in the cafeteria.
5. He doesn't weigh 180 lbs.
6. They don't enjoy class.
7. My brother and I don't think alike.
8. I don't understand modern art.
9. My father doesn't make breakfast every morning.
10. We don't live in Turkey.
11. She doesn't watch TV at home.
12. I don't like science.

Exercise B
Page 35

Answers will vary.

Exercise C
Page 35

Answers will vary.

Putting It Together

Exercise A
Page 36

1. **c.**
2. f.
3. g.
4. h.
5. d.
6. e.
7. a.
8. b.

Exercise B
Page 36

1. **They're**; don't; need
2. smell; like; You're
3. There; see; She's; like/enjoy

Exercise C
Page 37

1. **He smells the coffee.**
2. C
3. I don't weigh 125 pounds.
4. The teacher writes on the board.
5. He doesn't work at the college.
6. We don't think alike.
7. C

Vocabulary

Page 37

ACROSS	DOWN
1. nose	2. skin
3. tongue	4. ear
5. brain	6. nerves
7. eyes	

LESSON 7

Irregular Verbs: *Have, Go, Do*
Prepositions of Time: *In, On, At*

Part One

Exercise A
Page 38

1. **has**
2. has
3. has
4. has
5. does
6. has
7. goes
8. has
9. has
10. does
11. has
12. goes
13. goes

Exercise B
Page 38

have; go; go; goes; have; have; have; has; does

Exercise C
Page 39

1. **I don't have an interesting job.**
2. She doesn't go to work by train.

3. My brother doesn't do his homework.
4. Rula doesn't have an English class in the morning.
5. We don't go to class together.
6. They don't do the math problems on the board in class.
7. I don't go to the computer lab in the library.
8. Paolo doesn't have a computer.

Part Two
Exericise A
Page 39

1. in	7. on
2. at	8. in
3. at	9. in
4. in	10. at
5. on	11. on
6. at	12. at

Exercise B
Page 40
Answers will vary.

Putting It Together
Exercise A
Page 41

1. **He walks to work in the morning.**
2. Andrea doesn't have a job.
3. Sam does his homework in class.
4. My birthday is on July 31.
5. C
6. C
7. He doesn't have a desk in class.
8. We don't go to school in August.
9. They get up at 7:00 in the morning.
10. The students don't have an appointment.
11. C
12. The class finishes in 2006.

Exercise B
Page 41
Answers will vary.

LESSON 8

The Simple Present Tense: *Yes/No* Questions
and Short Answers
Simple Present *Wh-* Questions

Part One
Exercise A
Page 43

1. **Do you like game shows?**
2. Do your children like cartoons?
3. Do you watch the news at 11:00?
4. Do Americans watch too much TV?

5. Does your brother watch TV on the Internet?
6. Do students like to watch TV while they study?
7. Do they watch TV on the weekend?
8. Do you have cable TV?

Exercise B
Page 44
Answers will vary.

Part Two
Exercise A
Page 44

1. **Where do you**	4. How do you
2. What do you	5. Where do you
3. When do you	6. Why do you

Exercise B
Page 45
Answers will vary.

Putting It Together.
Exercise A
Page 45

How do you; watch; Do you watch; I don't; I do; watch TV; watches; Does she; she does; What does she

Exercise B
Page 46

1. **When do you have English class?**
2. Where do you do your homework?
3. Do you like nature programs on TV?
4. What do you eat for lunch?
5. Who does he study with?/ With whom does he study?
6. Do you like to drive to work?
7. Do you use the remote control?
8. What does the nurse do?
9. Where do you go?
10. What color is the cat?
11. Where is the bank?
12. Do you like to eat pasta?

Vocabulary
Page 47

ACROSS	DOWN
4. game show	1. outside
5 remote control	2. sitcoms
6. news	3. cartoons

LESSON 9

The Present Tense of *Be* vs. the Simple Present Tense: Statements; *Yes/No* Questions and Short Answers; *Wh-* Questions

Part One

Exercise A
Page 48

1. works
2. is
3. are
4. is
5. studies
6. goes
7. is
8. stays
9. takes
10. gives
11. is

Exercise B
Page 48

1. **I go to class on Monday and Wednesday.**
2. He doesn't have a job.
3. Ms. Chavez is my English instructor.
4. He isn't a teacher.
5. He works every day.
6. I don't study animals.
7. Mr. Donner teaches biology.
8. C

Exercise C
Page 49

1. **am**
2. studies
3. doesn't go
4. take
5. don't enjoy
6. use
7. is
8. are
9. don't like

Part Two

Exercise A
Page 49

1. **Do; do**
2. Is; isn't
3. Do; don't
4. Do; do
5. Are; am not
6. Is; is
7. Do; do
8. Are; am
9. Does; doesn't
10. Does; does
11. Are; are
12. Do; don't

Exercise B
Page 50

1. **Do you work with laboratory animals?**
2. Do you and your brother think alike?
3. Are you nervous?
4. Does she wash the dishes?
5. Are you excited about class?
6. Do they like to watch reality shows?

Part Three

Exercise A
Page 50

1. g
2. d
3. a
4. b
5. f
6. h
7. e
8. c

Exercise B
Page 51

1. **When do your children watch TV?**
2. Where do your parents live?
3. What is his name?
4. What does she teach?
5. What is your phone number?
6. When is your birthday?
7. Where are you?
8. What does she have?
9. What do you watch?
10. How old is your sister?
11. What is her favorite class?
12. When does the class start?

Putting It Together

Exercise A
Page 52

1. How are you?
2. Where do
3. work
4. What do
5. Do you
6. I do
7. Do you
8. When do you
9. I get up
10. Do you
11. I'm
12. I do

Exercise B
Page 52

Answers will vary.

Vocabulary
Page 53

1. **chimpanzee**
2. dolphin
3. elephant
4. fruits
5. insects
6. leaves
7. mice
8. nest
9. nuts

LESSON 10

Adverbs of Frequency Questions with *How Often* Frequency Expressions

Part One

Exercise A
Page 54

1. **I usually exercise in the morning.**

2. My friends never exercise.

3. I rarely get headaches.

4. I often go out with friends on the weekend.

5. I sometimes go to sleep at 1:00 A.M.

6. My sister always calls me.

7. I never forget to eat breakfast.

8. Jason always plays football.

9. My mom rarely gets mad.

Exercise B
Page 55

1. **I always drive to work.**

2. New students sometimes get confused.

3. My instructor is never late.

4. Class is rarely exciting.

5. They often ask you for your social security number.

6. I always look at the clock.

7. Katerina never has her textbook.

8. We usually eat in the cafeteria.

Exercise C
Page 55

Answers will vary.

Part Two

Exercise A

1. **How often does he go to the laundromat?**

2. How often does he go to the doctor?

3. How often do you eat out?

4. How often do they go to the movies?

5. How often do you go on vacation?

6. How often do you visit your grandmother?

Exercise B
Page 56

Answers will vary.

Putting It Together

Answers will vary.

Vocabulary

Page 58

Worried

In a rush

Headache

Stomachache

Relax

Exercise

Sleep

Go out with friends

1. d		4. t	
2. o		5. s	
3. n		6. t	

7. r

8. e

9. s

10. s

11. o

12. u

13. t

LESSON 11

The Present Progressive Tense: Affirmative;
Spelling Verbs in the *–ing* Form;
The Present Progressive Tense: Negative

Part One

Exercise A
Page 62

1. 'm looking

2. 're thinking

3. are experimenting

4. 's listening

5. 's measuring

6. 'm reading

7. 's erasing

8. 're driving

9. 's taking

10. 'm watching

Exercise B
Page 62

is helping; is writing; is talking; are taking; is cleaning; is reading; are listening; am watching

Part Two

Exercise A
Page 63

1. **shopping**

2. staying

3. dropping

4. giving

5. keeping

6. tasting

7. clicking

8. taking

9. swimming

Exercise B
Page 63

1. **I'm shopping**

2. 's parking

3. 're swimming

4. 'm studying

5. 'm taking

6. 's dropping

7. 's making

8. 's sleeping

Part Three

Exercise A
Page 64

1. **Carla isn't swimming. Carla is shopping.**

2. Carla's mother isn't parking the car. Carla's mother is shopping.

3. Carla's brother isn't dropping off a video. Carla's brother is swimming.
4. Carla's father isn't watching TV. Carla's father is parking the car.
5. Fatima isn't meeting a friend at the library. Fatima is studying at the library.
6. Fatima's husband isn't listening to the radio. Fatima's husband is making dinner.
7. Fatima's daughter isn't cooking dinner. Fatima's daughter is sleeping.
8. Fatima's sister isn't watching a video. Fatima's sister is dropping the video off at the store.

Exercise B
Page 64
Answers will vary.

Putting It Together
Exercise A
Page 65
1. **My instructor is walking to class.**
2. I'm writing on the board.
3. She's eating the sandwich.
4. He's not sitting in the chair.
5. C
6. My family is eating dinner now.
7. The teacher is giving the homework assignment.
8. The baby is sleeping now.
9. C
10. I'm not living in an apartment.

Exercise B
Page 65
1. **I'm doing my homework/ I'm not doing my homework.**
2. My friends are listening to music/My friends aren't listening to music.
3. His neighbor is washing the car/His neighbor isn't washing the car.
4. My mother is reading a book/My mother isn't reading a book.
5. Your sister is checking her e-mail/Your sister isn't checking her e-mail.
6. You are checking your e-mail/You aren't checking your e-mail.
7. The teacher is talking about grammar/The teacher isn't talking about grammar.
8. My classmates are listening to the teacher/My classmates aren't listening to the teacher.
9. They are writing on the board/They aren't writing on the board.

Vocabulary
Page 66

ACROSS	DOWN
2. look	1. experiment
3. measure	2. listen
4. think	4. touch

LESSON 12
The Present Progressive Tense: *Yes/No* Questions and Short Answers; The Present Progressive Tense: *Wh-* Questions

Part One
Exericse A
Page 67
1. **Are you using a new mouse?**
2. Is Elena bringing her laptop on vacation?
3. Is the printer working?
4. Are they looking at the computer screen now?
5. Is she cleaning the keyboard?
6. Are you writing an e-mail to your mother?
7. Are you searching the Internet for good restaurants?
8. Is the school buying desktop computers?

Exercise B
Page 68

1. **Yes, I am.**	4. Yes, he is.
2. No, I'm not.	5. No, they aren't.
3. Yes, I am.	

Part Two
Exercise A
Page 68

1. **line to d**	4. line to e
2. line to b	5. line to c
3. line to a	

Exercise B
Page 68
1. **is coming to class now?**
2. are you writing a letter to your friend?
3. are they going?
4. classes are you taking?
5. is Keiko feeling?
6. are you doing?
7. is Dan going home?

Putting It Together
Exercise A
Page 69
1. **Are you buying a new computer?**   **Yes, I am/No, I'm not.**
2. Are they looking at the monitor?   Yes, they are/ No, they aren't.

3. Are you using a laptop computer? Yes, I am/No, I'm not.
4. Is the printer working? Yes, it is/No, it isn't.
5. Is she writing an e-mail? Yes, she is/No, she isn't.

Exercise B
Page 69
Answers will vary.

Exercise C
Page 69
What; studying; How; doing; I'm watching; Why; Who; are you watching?

Vocabulary
Page 71

ACROSS	DOWN
2. printer	**1.** desktop computer
3. laptop	**4.** Internet
5. monitor	
6. mouse	
7. keyboard	
8. screen	

LESSON 13

The Simple Present Tense vs. the Present Progressive Tense: Statements; *Yes/No* Questions; *Wh-* Questions

Part One
Exercise A
Page 72

1. take	**8.** get
2. go	**9.** am writing
3. study	**10.** am doing
4. have	**11.** is sitting
5. work	**12.** is reading
6. get	**13.** are drinking
7. take	

Exercise B
Page 72
1. **He's not working right now.**
2. I don't worry about the weather.
3. I understand you.
4. C
5. I'm telling a story to the children.
6. They don't like the restaurant.
7. She's not thinking about her problems.
8. They always get up at 6:00 A.M.
9. He isn't watching TV right now.
10. C
11. She writes a poem every day.
12. C

Part Two
Exercise A
Page 73
1. **Are you thinking about class?**
2. Does he go to class every day?
3. Do you like Professor Harris?
4. Are you watching TV right now?
5. Do they watch reality shows?
6. Are you talking on the phone now?
7. Do they live in the dormitories?
8. Are you using the dictionary?
9. Are you writing in your journals?
10. Does he have a social security number?
11. Does she feel excited?
12. Are you turning off the light now?
13. Do you like cats?
14. Are you driving to New York?

Exercise B
Page 74
1. **I'm wearing jeans.**
2. he isn't going to the hospital.
3. she teaches at the university.
4. they aren't thinking about money.
5. I have a journal.
6. we aren't going to eat now.
7. I like my classes.
8. he doesn't feel nervous.
9. they're parking the car.
10. I don't smell the coffee.

Part Three
Exercise A
Page 74
Answers will vary.

Exercise B
Page 75
Answers will vary.

Putting It Together
Exercise A
Page 75

1. what are you	**7.** Do you
2. am doing	**8.** What is
3. What are you	**9.** He's
4. Are you	**10.** Is he working
5. Are you	**11.** does
6. I am	

Exercise B
Page 76
1. **Where do you work?**
2. I'm going home now.

3. She's not helping me.
4. C
5. They're not going to class.
6. What do you watch on TV?
7. Is he going to class?
8. Yes, I am.
9. No, she doesn't.

LESSON 14

Possessive Nouns; Possessive Adjectives

Part One
Exercise A
Page 78

1. **teacher's**
2. friend's
3. Carlos'
4. cat's
5. father's
6. family's
7. Martha's
8. parent's
9. men's
10. sister's
11. singer's
12. uncle's
13. Tara's

Exercise B
Page 79

1. **husband's**
2. daughter's
3. son's
4. sister's
5. brother-in-law
6. Julia's/Margo's
7. Julia's/James'
8. Jim's
9. Julia's uncle

Part Two
Exercise A
Page 80

1. **b**
2. a
3. b
4. a
5. a
6. b
7. a
8. a
9. b
10. b

Exercise B
Page 80

1. **My**
2. Her
3. Their
4. His
5. Our
6. Your
7. My
8. Our
9. His
10. Your
11. Her
12. His

Exercise C
Page 81

1. I
2. I
3. I
4. My
5. They
6. My
7. They
8. My
9. They
10. My
11. He
12. His
13. Her
14. He
15. His

Putting It Together
Exercise A
Page 81

1. **Paul's hat is on the chair.**
2. Her class is in room 151.
3. Our parents live in Costa Rica.
4. Abdul's desk is near the window.
5. Their laptop doesn't work.
6. My friend's apartment is in the city.
7. My sister's husband is from Turkey.
8. Their car isn't from Japan.

Exercise B
Page 82

I; I; My; 's; She; My; My; 's; He; He; My; I; My ; 's; He; He; His; They; Her; My; 's; She; She

Vocabulary
Page 83

ACROSS	DOWN
2. sister	1. grandmother
5. daughter	3. grandfather
6. son	4. mother
8. uncle	7. nephew
9. father	
10. aunt	
11. niece	

LESSON 15

Object Pronouns;
Indirect Objects

Part One
Exercise A
Page 84

1. **She calls my mother every day.**
2. The students bring them to class.
3. The instructor always writes it on the board.
4. She writes her e-mail address in her book.
5. She also writes it in her notebooks.
6. The administrator asks them their social security numbers.

Exercise B
Page 84

1. **him**	5. it
2. it	6. It
3. They	7. It
4. them	

Part Two
Exercise A

1. **She is giving the <u>thermometer</u> to the patient.**
2. He is reading <u>the poem</u> to me.
3. I am drawing the students <u>a circle</u> on the board.
4. She is telling us <u>her thoughts.</u>
5. The landlord is giving me <u>the phone bill.</u>
6. She is ordering me <u>a book</u> online.

Exercise B
Page 85

See Exercise A

Exercise C

1. **She's playing me the song.**
2. My father is writing me an e-mail right now.
3. Jack is developing us a Web site.
4. My daughter is making you a birthday cake.
5. The instructor is telling us a story.
6. My grandparents are leaving my brother and me money.

Putting it Together
Exercise A
Page 86

1. **He likes to tell them jokes every day.**
2. There are a lot of actors in this play.
3. My brother and I are talking on the phone.
4. C
5. Maria likes Felipe, but he doesn't like her.
6. They're really nice students.
7. Your notebook is in the classroom.
8. C
9. I am sending you an e-mail.
10. You're buying lunch today.
11. The teacher is talking to my partner and me.
12. Jazz is my favorite kind of music. I like it a lot.

Exercise B
Page 86

1. **them**	6. it
2. They	7. they
3. me	8. we
4. I	9. them
5. we	

Vocabulary
Page 87

Author
Characters
Stage
~~Action~~ ACTOR
Costume
Audience

1. t	
2. o	
3. e	
4. o	
5. r	
6. n	
7. o	
8. t	
9. t	
10. e	

LESSON 16

The Past Tense of *Be:* Affirmative Statements;
The Past Tense of *Be:* Negative Statements

Part One
Exercise A
Page 91

1. **were**	6. was
2. was	7. wa s
3. was	8. was
4. was	9. were
5. were	

Exercise B
Page 91

1. **were**	6. was
2. was	7. were
3. were	8. was
4. was	9. was
5. were	10. were

Exercise C
Page 19

1. **were**	4. was
2. was	5. were
3. was	6. was

Part Two
Exercise A
Page 92

Answers will vary.

Exercise B
Page 93

Answers will vary.

Putting It Together

Exercise A
Page 93

1. **weren't**
2. was
3. were
4. weren't
5. wasn't
6. were
7. weren't
8. were
9. was
10. were
11. was

Exercise B

1. **weren't**; was
2. weren't; was
3. weren't; was
4. weren't; was

LESSON 17

The Past Tense of *Be: Yes/No* Questions;
The Past Tense of *Be: Wh-* Questions

Part One

Exercise A
Page 95

1. **Was Gabriel Garcia Marquez a Nobel Prize winner?**
   Yes, he was.
2. Was your teacher late today?
   Yes, he/she was.
   No, he/she wasn't.
3. Were Marie Curie and Louis Pasteur scientists?
   Yes, they were.
4. Were you tired yesterday?
   Yes, I was.
   No, I wasn't.
5. ~~Are~~ Were your grandparents from the U.S.?
   Yes, they ~~are~~ were.
   No, they ~~aren't~~ weren't.
6. Was Thomas Jefferson a U.S. president?
   Yes, he was.
7. Was Helen Keller an astronaut?
   No, she wasn't.
8. Were the Beatles a rock group?
   Yes, they were.
9. Were you at the movies last night?
   Yes, I was.
   No, I wasn't.

Part Two

Exercise A
Page 96

1. **Who was Albert Einstein?**
   He was a great scientist.
2. When was the American Revolution?
   It was from 1775 to 1781.
3. Where were Franklin and Eleanor Roosevelt born?
   They were born in New York.
4. Why was Anne Sullivan famous?
   She was Helen Keller's teacher.
5. Who was Babe Ruth?
   He was a famous baseball player.

Exercise B
Page 96

1. **When was English class today?**   **It was at 10:00 a.m.**
2. Where were your parents born?   Answers will vary.
3. Who was your favorite teacher in   Answers will vary.
   elementary school?
4. What was your favorite movie last year? Answers will vary.
5. When were you on vacation last year?   Answers will vary.

Putting It Together

Exercise A
Page 97

1. **Who**; she was
2. I was
3. she wasn't
4. Were you; I was
5. When was; was
6. were you; was

Exercise B
Page 97

1. What was your favorite subject in high school?/What were your favorite subjects in high school?
2. Were you at home last night?
3. C
4. Yes, you were.
5. Why was he famous?
6. C
7. Who were you with at the movies?
8. Yes, you were.
9. Where were you yesterday?

Vocabulary
Page 98

ACROSS	DOWN
2. astronaut	1. painter
4. writer	3. scientist
6. first lady	5. president
7. explorer	6. fashion designer

LESSON 18

The Simple Past Tense of Regular Verbs: Affirmative and Negative; Spelling and Pronunciation of the Simple Past Tense of Regular Verbs; The Simple Past Tense of Irregular Verbs

Part One

Exercise A
Page 99

founded; started; created; distributed; loved; received; produced; purchased

Exercise B
Page 99

1. don't manufacture
2. didn't complain
3. didn't graduate
4. didn't sign
5. didn't arrive
6. didn't travel
7. didn't talk
8. didn't create
9. didn't study
10. didn't dance

Part Two

Exercise A
Page 100

1. **applauded**
2. bowed
3. called
4. clapped
5. closed
6. faxed
7. fried
8. hugged
9. permitted
10. shopped
11. traveled
12. worried
13. zipped
14. regretted
15. invited

Exercise B
Page 100

Column 1 (/t/ as in "cooked")

clapped
shopped
zipped

Column 2 (/d/ as in "lived")

bowed
called
closed
faxed
fried
hugged
traveled
worried

Column 3 (/id/ as in "wanted")

applauded
permitted
regretted
invited

Part Three

Exercise A
Page 101

1. **paid**
2. left
3. took
4. saw
5. got
6. did

Exercise B
Page 101

Answers will vary.

Putting It Together

Exercise A
Page 101

1. **had**
2. didn't do
3. walked
4. bought
5. was
6. saw

Exercise B
Page 101

1. **I didn't watch the news on TV last night.**
2. He took a break after class.
3. The baby cried all night.
4. The nurse dropped the thermometer.
5. C
6. C
7. They stayed inside all day.
8. I didn't have a headache.
9. She wrote in her diary every day.
10. C
11. The girl looked pretty yesterday.
12. C
13. I made tea last night.

Vocabulary

Page 103

1. manufactures
2. manager
3. employee
4. buys
5. sells
6. pay
7. millionare

LESSON 19

The Simple Past Tense: *Yes/No* Questions and Short Answers; The Simple Past Tense: *Wh-* Questions

Part One

Exercise A
Page 104

Answers will vary.

Exercise B
Page 104

1. **Did the police officer arrest the criminal? Yes, he did.**
2. Did the police officer use handcuffs?   Yes, he did.
3. Did the criminal vandalize the apartment?   No, he/she didn't.
4. Did the police take fingerprints?   Yes, they did.
5. Did she watch the evening news?   No, she didn't.
6. Did they talk about the criminal?   Yes, they did.
7. Did the criminal go to jail?   Yes, he/she did.
8. Did he read about it in the newspaper?   No, he didn't.

Part Two
Exercise A
Page 105

1. Why did you; Where did you; How did you; What did you; When did you
2. Who did you; Why did you; What did he
3. What; How did; What did you; did you talk

Exercise B
Page 106
Answers will vary.

Putting It Together
Exercise A
Page 106
Did you; I did; What; Who; Did; they did; What did; Did they; they did

Exercise B
Page 107

1. **Did he steal the statue?**
2. Why did he vandalize the car?
3. What happened in the park yesterday?
4. C
5. Why did he have a gun?
6. C
7. Why did she give him the money?
8. C
9. Yes, I did.
10. Did you see the crime?

Vocabulary
Page 108

1. **criminal**
2. steal
3. vandalize
4. arrest
5. handcuffs
6. jail
7. fingerprints

The Past Tense of *Be* and the Simple Past Tense: Statements; The Past Tense of *Be* and the Simple Past Tense: Questions

Part One
Exercise A
Page 109

1. lived; were; developed; invented; created; used; wrote; were; built
2. thought; were; were; were; sacrificed; played; died

Exercise B
Page 109

1. **didn't go to Spain**
2. didn't travel
3. didn't see
4. didn't use
5. didn't like
6. didn't stay
7. didn't take a tour of

Part Two
Exercise A
Page 110

Where is; Who; Did; What; Who discovered; When did; Where is; He is

Exercise B
Page 110

1. **When were you in Guatemala?**
2. Were you there for two weeks?
3. Where did you visit?
4. What did you see?
5. Who did you go with?
6. Did your children go with you?
7. Did they like it?

Putting It Together
Exercise A
Page 111

Were you; Where; were; did; did; saw; it was; What did you do; Where; stayed

Exercise B
Page 112

1. **Where was he?**
2. Why did he go?
3. C
4. They visited the pyramids last year.
5. We traveled to Guatemala.
6. C
7. Who did you go with?

8. Why did you go to Mexico last year?

9. C

LESSON 21

Count and Noncount Nouns: *A/An, Some, Any*

Part One
Exercise A
Page 117

1. noncount	11. noncount
2. noncount	12. noncount
3. noncount	13. count
4. count	14. count
5. noncount	15. noncount
6. count	16. count
7. noncount	17. noncount
8. count	18. noncount
9. noncount	19. noncount
10. count	20. count

Exercise B
Page 117

See Exercise A

Exercise C
Page 118

bread; meat; potato chips; cookies; a salad; lettuce; tomatoes; bananas; milk; water

Part Two
Exercise A
Page 118

1. an	6. a
2. some	7. a
3. a	8. some
4. some	9. some
5. any	10. some

Exercise B
Page 119

1. Do you have any money?

2. Are there any ads for jobs in the newspaper today?

3. Are you wearing any jewelry?

4. Do you have some bleach?

5. Do you need some help?

6. Do you have an apple and a sandwich?

7. Is there any coffee in the kitchen?

Exercise C
Page 119

Answers will vary.

Putting It Together
Exercise A
Page 120

1. any; a; a; any

2. a; a; any

3. some; a; any

4. any; a; an

Exercise B
Page 120

1. I don't have any lipstick.

2. C

3. Is there food in the refrigerator?

4. Do you like milk?

5. She needs information about the classes.

6. C

7. I ate an apple today.

8. Do you have any spare time to help?

9. My husband bought me some jewelry for my birthday.

10. I found an earring on the floor.

Vocabulary
Page 122

1. consumer	5. billboards
2. clothes	6. advertisements
3. food	7. money
4. furniture	8. products

LESSON 22

Quantity Expressions: *How Many/How Much*

Part One
Exercise A
Page 123

1. many	7. many
2. much	8. much
3. many	9. many
4. much	10. much
5. many	11. much
6. much	12. much

Exercise B
Page 123

1. a few	7. a little
2. a little	8. a little
3. a few	9. a few
4. a little	10. a little
5. a few	11. a little
6. a little	12. a little

Part Two

Exercise A
Page 124

1. **How many**		7.	How many
2. How much		8.	How much
3. How many		9.	How much
4. How much		10.	How many
5. How many		11.	How much
6. How much		12.	How much

Exercise B
Page 125

1. **How many elephants are there at the nature preserve?**
2. How much traffic is there in Rome?
3. How many tourists visit New York City every year?
4. How many travel agents are there online?
5. How much makeup do you wear?
6. How many bookstores are there near the university?
7. How much food did your mother buy this week?

Exercise C
Page 125

1. **There are no restaurants in my neighborhood.**
   There aren't any restaurants in my neighborhood.
2. There are some parks in the city.
   There aren't any parks in the city.
3. There's a little traffic near my house.
   There's not much traffic near my house.
4. There are a few students from Ecuador in class.
   There aren't a lot of students from Ecuador in class.
5. There's no information on my country in our library.
   There isn't any information on my country in our library.
6. There's some milk in the refrigerator.
   There's not much milk in the refrigerator.

Putting It Together

Exercise A
Page 126

1. **how much**; some/a little; some; a lot of/a few/some
2. no; a lot of; a lot of/ a few; How many
3. no; a lot of; any/a lot of

Exercise B
Page 127

1. C
2. C
3. I ate some pizza for lunch.
4. C
5. I didn't give them any advice.
6. There aren't any museums in my town/ There are no museums in my town.
7. She wears a lot of makeup.
8. How many students were in class today?

9. I bought a few postcards.
10. C

Vocabulary
Page 128

ACROSS	DOWN
1. museum	2. souvenirs
4. tourist	3. postcards
5. travel agent	8. crime
6. park	
7. traffic	

LESSON 23

Can: Affirmative and Negative; Can: *Yes/No* Questions and Short Answers

Part One

Exercise A
Page 129

Answers will vary.

Exercise B
Page 130

1. can't		6.	can't
2. can do		7.	can
3. can't		8.	can't
4. can't		9.	can
5. can		10.	can

Part Two

Exercise A
Page 130

1. **Can you rollerskate?** — **Yes, I can./No, I can't.**
2. Can your father speak English? — Yes, he can./No, he can't.
3. Can your sister play soccer? — Yes, she can./No, she can't.
4. Can you run a marathon? — Yes, I can./No, I can't.
5. Can you sail a boat? — Yes, I can./No, I can't.
6. Can your mother use a computer? — Yes, she can./No, she can't.
7. Can your brother ride a motorcycle? — Yes, he can./No, he can't.
8. Can you take care of a baby? — Yes, I can./No, I can't.
9. Can you read a book in one day? — Yes, I can./No, I can't.
10. Can you ride a horse? — Yes, I can./No, I can't.

Putting It Together

Exercise A
Page 131

Answers will vary.

Exercise B
Page 132

1. D	6. A
2. G	7. E
3. F	8. I
4. B	9. H
5. C	10. J

Vocabulary
Page 133

Knee
Bend
Pain
Hurt
Cane
Physical therapist
Cast
Crunches
Injury
Leg
Bone
Break

1. o	8. t
2. u	9. h
3. c	10. u
4. h	11. r
5. t	12. t
6. h	13. s
7. a	

LESSON 24

Imperatives; Polite Requests with *Could You/Would You*

Part One
Exercise A
Page 134

1. G	7. K
2. I	8. L
3. J	9. B
4. H	10. E
5. C	11. A
6. D	12. F

Exercise B
Page 135

1. Clean	7. Don't get
2. Be quiet	8. Don't
3. Turn off	9. Write
4. Wash	10. Send
5. Wear	11. Don't drive
6. Don't be	12. Don't talk

Part Two
Exercise A
Page 135

1. **Could you close the door?/Would you close the door?**
2. Could you give me your telephone number?/Would you give me your telephone number?
3. Could you clean the whiteboard?/Would you clean the whiteboard?
4. Could you speak a little louder?/Would you speak a little louder?
5. Could you call the nurse?/Would you call the nurse?
6. Could you turn off the TV?/Would you turn off the TV?
7. Could you find the remote control?/Would you find the remote control?
8. Could you play outside?/Would you play outside?
9. Could you look at the board?/Would you look at the board?
10. Could you turn on the computer?/Would you turn on the computer?
11. Could you lend me your pen?/Would you lend me your pen?
12. Could you tell the children a story?/Would you tell the children a story?

Exercise B
Page 136

1. F	5. E
2. G	6. A
3. H	7. B
4. C	8. D

Putting It Together
Exercise A
Page 136

Answers will vary.

Exercise B
Page 137

Answers will vary.

Vocabulary
Page 138

Laboratory
Lab technician
Microscope
Slide
Rubber gloves
Safety glasses
Test tubes
Chemicals
Bunsen burner
Flame
Experiment
Equipment

1. t	12. l
2. h	13. a
3. e	14. b
4. o	15. o
5. r	16. r
6. l	17. a
7. d	18. t
8. i	19. o
9. s	20. r
10. m	21. y
11. y	

LESSON 25

Should/Should Not; Should: Yes/No Questions
and Short Answers

Part One

Exercise A
Page 139

1. **You should reply to invitations promptly.**
2. You should take a gift.
3. You should offer to help clean up.
4. You should make introductions.
5. You should talk to everyone.
6. You should thank your guests for coming.
7. You should shake hands firmly.
8. You should not use a first name until invited to do so.
9. You should pay for lunch or dinner if you are the host.
10. You should not put your elbows on the table.
11. You should not play with your hair or jewelry.
12. You should place the napkin on your lap.
13. You should not use a toothpick at the table.

Exercise B
Page 140

1. **You should go to the doctor.**
2. He should get a license.
3. They should bring flowers.
4. You should fill out an application.
5. You should not use a cell phone at the table.

Part Two

Exercise A
Page 140

Should I; You should; Should I; you should; Should I; you should; shouldn't; Should I; you shouldn't; should

Exercise B
Page 140

1. **Should I bow to the manager from Japan?**
2. Should I kiss Ms. Smith at the meeting?
3. Should I send a thank-you note by e-mail?
4. Should I help clean after the party?
5. Should I call her now?
6. Should I bring the host of the party a gift?
7. Should I arrive late?

Putting It Together

Exercise A
Page 141

Answers will vary.

Exercise B
Page 141

Answers will vary.

Vocabulary

Page 142

1. **point**	5. kiss
2. thumb	6. yawn
3. shake	7. polite
4. bow	8. rude

LESSON 26

Must/Must Not; Have to/Don't Have To

Part One

Exercise A
Page 146

1. **You must not bring alcoholic beverages.**
2. You must not litter in the park.
3. You must keep dogs on a leash.
4. You must not hunt in the park.
5. You must not swim in the park.
6. You must not ride horses in the park.
7. You must not cut or remove timber.
8. You must not remove plants.
9. You must register bicycles in the office.
10. You must keep boats and canoes in the boathouse.

Exercise B
Page 146

1. **must**	7. must
2. must not	8. must
3. must	9. must
4. must not	10. must
5. must	11. must not
6. must not	

Part Two

Exercise A
Page 147

Answers will vary.

Exercise B
Page 147

Answers will vary.

Putting It Together

Exercise A
Page 148

1. **doesn't have to**
2. must not
3. must not
4. don't have to
5. don't have to
6. must not
7. must not
8. don't have to
9. must not
10. must not

Exercise B
Page 149

1. **b.**
2. c.
3. b.
4. a.
5. c.
6. a.
7. b.
8. b.

Vocabulary
Page 150

ACROSS

1. jury
3. lawyers
5. court room
6. judge

DOWN

1. jurors
2. reporter
4. witnesses

LESSON 27

Be Going to: Affirmative and Negative Statements; *Be Going to:* Questions

Part One

Exercise A
Page 151

1. **We are not going to eat at home.**
2. He is going to drink coffee.
3. I am not going to order pasta.
4. My husband is going to order a salad.
5. We are going to see a movie after dinner.
6. I am going to do yoga tomorrow.
7. Jan is going to take a trip next month.
8. She is not going to fly to Florida.
9. She is going to drive.
10. It's going to be fun.

Exercise B
Page 151

1. **I'm going to do homework tonight.**
2. We're going to travel to Europe.
3. I'm going to write a letter.
4. They're going to love the new sitcom.
5. She's going to teach a biology class.
6. He's going to join a gym.
7. They're going to open a new restaurant.
8. He's going to begin elementary school.
9. I'm going to buy a new computer.
10. I'm going to start a journal.
11. They're going to get divorced.
12. She's going to have a baby.
13. We're going to meet the president.

Part Two

Exercise A
Page 152

1. **Is she going to start school?**   Yes, she is.
2. Are we going to walk to the restaurant?   No, we aren't.
3. Are they going to work late?   Yes, they are.
4. Are you going to do the laundry?   No, I'm not.
5. Is he going to take a walk?   No, he's not.

Exercise B
Page 152

1. **What are you going to do this weekend?**
2. Who are you going to go out with?
3. What are you going to do?
4. What are you going to order?
5. When are you going to meet?
6. Why are you going to eat there?

Putting It Together

Exercise A
Page 152

Answers will vary.

Exercise B
Page 153

1. **I'm going to take a shower now.**
2. We're going to study this weekend.
3. He's going to look for a job next month.
4. She's going to work tonight.
5. Is he going to drive to class tonight?
6. C
7. What are you going to do this weekend?
8. Who are we going to visit tomorrow?

LESSON 28

Will: Affirmative and Negative Statements;
Will: Questions

Part One
Exercise A
Page 156

1. **prediction**
2. sudden decision
3. promise
4. prediction
5. prediction
6. sudden decision
7. prediction
8. promise

Exercise B
Page 156

Answers will vary.

Part Two
Exercise A
Page 157

1. **Will we travel by spaceship in the future?**   **Yes, we will.**
2. Will we live in outer space?   Yes, we will.
3. Will we go to school?   No, we won't.
4. Will we have to eat and sleep?   No, we won't.
5. Will we have babies?   Yes, we will.
6. Will we use robots?   Yes, we will.
7. Will we get sick?   No, we won't.
8. Will we use money?   No, we won't.

Exercise B
Page 158

1. **What will you eat for lunch tomorrow?**   Answers will vary.
2. Where will you go next weekend?   Answers will vary.
3. Who will you call next week?   Answers will vary.
4. When will you go on vacation this year?   Answers will vary.
5. How will you feel in three months?   Answers will vary.

Putting It Together
Exercise A
Page 158

what; Are you going to/will you; are you going to/will you; 'm going to; aren't you going to; will you work; won't; I will; When will you/when are you going to; I'm going to go back; are you going to

Exercise B
Page 159

Answers will vary.

Vocabulary
Page 159

Capsule
Pill
Medicine
Robot
Examination
Pharmacist
Prescription
Surgeon
Transplant

1. t
2. h
3. e
4. u
5. t
6. u
7. r
8. e
9. b
10. e
11. g
12. i
13. n
14. s
15. n
16. o

LESSON 29

The Comparitive Form of Adjectives: *-er* and *More*;
As . . . As/Not As . . . As

Part One
Exercise A
Page 160

1. **cleaner than**
2. more common than
3. more expensive than
4. newer than
5. dirtier than
6. more efficient than
7. heavier than
8. slower than
9. worse than
10. safer than

Exercise B
Page 161

1. **Earth is smaller than the moon.**
2. Car crashes are more common than airplane crashes.
3. Air is heavier than water.
4. Television is younger than radio.
5. Light is faster than sound.

Exercise C
Page 161

1. **State University is older than Westville College.**
2. State University is larger than Westville College.
3. Westville College is younger than State University.
4. Westville College is more expensive than State University.
5. Westville College is safer than State University.

Part Two

Exercise A
Page 161

1. **Sarah isn't as friendly as Lily.**
2. I'm not as short as you.
3. The old chair is as comfortable as the new chair.
4. Wind power is as effective as solar power.
5. Jazz isn't as popular as pop music.
6. The math test wasn't as difficult as the physics test.
7. My brother isn't as heavy as my father.
8. Math isn't as interesting as science.

Exercise B
Page 162
Answers will vary.

Putting It Together

Exercise A
Page 162

1. **My brother is bigger than I am.**
2. Finny's department store is not as crowded as Blake's shopping center on the weekends.
3. My English is worse than your English.
4. In Maine a car is more practical than a motorcycle.
5. C
6. A train ticket is more expensive than a plane ticket.
7. Bill Gates is richer than the Queen of England.
8. Greek civilization is older than Mayan civilization.

Exercise B
Page 163
Answers will vary.

Vocabulary

Page 164

ACROSS
2. **gas**
5. expensive
8. electricity
9. battery

DOWN
1. quiet
3. SUV
4. oil
6. energy
7. clean

LESSON 30

Past Review: The Simple Past Tense of *Be,*
the Simple Past Tense; Present Review; the Present
Tense of *Be,* the Simple Present Tense; the
Present Progressive Tense; *Be Going to, Will*

Part One

Exercise A
Page 165

bought; gave; didn't work; crashed; bought; looked; didn't want; wanted; was; chose; filled; clicked; sent

Exercise B
Page 165

Were; I wasn't; Were; I was; It was; What was; There was; Was it; it was; Were there; there weren't

Exercise C
Page 166

go; saw; got; had; wrote; used

Part Two

Exercise A
Page 166
Answers will vary.

Exercise B
Page 166

1. **She goes to the computer lab every day.**
2. He is at the museum now.
3. We are walking to the park now.
4. I go to the computer lab two times a day.
5. Do they talk about clothes every day?
6. I'm not nervous about English class.

Part Three

Exercise A
Page 167

1. **will**
2. will
3. are going to
4. is going to/will
5. will
6. will
7. is going to
8. are going to/will
9. will
10. will
11. am going to

Exercise B
Page 167
Answers will vary.

Putting it Together

Exercise A
Page 168

are; doing; 'm looking; are; going to take; I am; 'm going to get; Did; like; liked; were; liked; learned; Are; going to study; 'm not going to study; 'm going to take; are; going to do; 'll go; Are; going to go; 'm not going to go; want; go; 'm not; need

Vocabulary

Page 169

1. **PDA**
2. player
3. processor
4. database
5. spreadsheets
6. download
7. online

Part 1: Parts of Speech

A.
1. books
2. window
3. students
4. door
5. computers
6. chair

B.
1. a teacher
2. a book
3. a school
4. a desk
5. a mother
6. a house

C.
1. he
2. it
3. they
4. she
5. they
6. it

D.
1. it
2. he
3. she
4. he
5. they
6. we
7. it
8. they
9. it
10. she
11. they
12. it

E.
1. walk
2. study
3. write
4. talk
5. read
6. love

F. Answers will vary.

G.
1. blue
2. large
3. new
4. heavy
5. nice
6. difficult

H.
1. c
2. a
3. d
4. b
5. e

I. Answers will vary

Part 2: Classroom Instructions

A.
1. b
2. a
3. d
4. c

B.
a clock, a teacher, a backpack

C.
read, eat, talk

D.
1. a noun
2. a verb
3. an adjective
4. a pronoun

E.
1. "An instructor" is a ~~verb~~ noun.
2. "Eat" is a ~~noun~~ verb.
3. "It" is an ~~adjective~~ pronoun.
4. "Happy" is a ~~pronoun~~ adjective.

Track 4. Page 16, Lesson 2, Part 1, Exercise E.

Listen. Complete the conversation.

1. Instructor: Are you an art student?
   Herman: Yes, I am.
2. Akiko: Is she a biology student?
   Sofia: Yes, she is.
3. Ricardo: Are they professors?
   Toshi: Yes, they are.
4. Yang-sook: Is it 10.00?
   Instructor Jones: No, it isn't.

Track 7. Page 25, Lesson 3, Part 2, Exercise C.

Listen. Check the plural sound you hear at the end of each word.

1. exercises (pause) exercises
2. busses (pause) busses
3. days (pause) days
4. pages (pause) pages
5. students (pause) students
6. clocks (pause) clocks
7. pages (pause) pages
8. rooms (pause) rooms

Track 12. Page 48, Lesson 6, Part 2, Exercise C.

Listen. Check the –s sound you hear.
1. speaks…speaks
2. washes…washes
3. buys…buys
4. likes…likes
5. works…works
6. reads…reads
7. watches…watches
8. writes…writes
9. uses…uses
10. sees…sees

Track 13. Page 48, Lesson 6, Part 2, Exercise D.

Read each sentence aloud. Make sure you pronounce the third person –s in the verb correctly. Then listen to the sentences to check your pronunciation.

1. Every day Jana **hears** her alarm clock.
2. She **sees** the sun.

3. She **feels** the water in the shower.
4. She **smells** coffee. She **tastes** her breakfast.
5. The brain **takes in** the information.
6. The brain **weighs** only about three pounds.

Track 23. Page 80, Lesson 10, Part 2. Exercise D.

Listen to the woman talk about her schedule. Circle the correct answers.

1. I have a large family. I'm so tired and stressed. I do too much. I clean the house twice a week.
2. I do the laundry four times a week.
3. I cook dinner every day.
4. I take my kids to soccer practice three times a week.
5. I drink a cup of coffee about six times a day.
6. I have trouble sleeping every night. I wonder why?

Track 30. Page 103, Lesson 13, Part 2, Exercise C.

Listen to each question. Circle the correct answer.

1. Does Ella study English?
2. Is she studying in the library right now?
3. Are Sam and Carlo writing in their journals?
4. Do they draw in their journals?
5. Do I need a pen?

6. Am I using correct punctuation?

Track 41. Page 138, Lesson 18, Part 2, Exercise C.

Listen. Check the *-ed* ending you hear.

1. loved
2. started
3. washed
4. used
5. jumped
6. needed
7. helped
8. learned
9. waited
10. opened

Track 49. Page 159, Lesson 21, Part 2, Exercise C.

Listen and complete the sentences with a/an, some, or any.

Look at all of these dirty clothes!
I have <u>a</u> family, <u>a</u> job, and a busy house.
I don't have <u>any</u> spare time.
I need <u>some</u> help! I need <u>an</u> answer!